THE
KEATS
CIRCLE

LETTERS AND PAPERS
1816–1878

VOLUME I
NUMBERS 1–148

THE
KEATS
CIRCLE

LETTERS AND PAPERS
1816–1878

VOLUME I
NUMBERS 1–148

THE

KEATS

CIRCLE

LETTERS AND PAPERS
AND
MORE LETTERS AND POEMS
OF THE KEATS CIRCLE

Second Edition

EDITED BY
HYDER EDWARD ROLLINS

VOLUME I

HARVARD UNIVERSITY PRESS
CAMBRIDGE · MASSACHUSETTS
1965

THE PUBLICATION OF THESE VOLUMES HAS BEEN AIDED
BY A GRANT FROM THE CARL AND LILY PFORZHEIMER
FOUNDATION, INC.

DISTRIBUTED IN GREAT BRITAIN BY
OXFORD UNIVERSITY PRESS, LONDON

LIBRARY OF CONGRESS CATALOG CARD NUMBER 65-13632
PRINTED IN THE UNITED STATES OF AMERICA

PREFACE TO THE SECOND EDITION

When the two volumes of *The Keats Circle* appeared in 1948, it was immediately obvious that there had been far more new information available about Keats's life, and about the lives of those most closely connected with him, than had been generally suspected. Many scholars over the years had consulted separately the two largest collections of Keatsiana — The Crewe and The Lowell collections, but perhaps only a handful had used both of them very extensively. Meanwhile, when these two great collections were combined in the Houghton Library at Harvard, still more material was added (and has continued to be added). The size of the material was formidable; the allusions and references throughout much of it were puzzling, even to the trained historian of letters; and the handwriting in many cases (especially that of Benjamin Bailey) was discouraging to scholars not accustomed to working directly from manuscripts of the period. There was no doubt but that this rich assemblage of material would be widely used. But the probability was that (as in the use of any collection of unpublished material) particular details would be excerpted for special purposes, while other details that might serve as a qualification would be neglected — either because of a scholar's haste, or because of his eagerness to support or disprove a particular point, or because he was baffled by obscure allusions or intimidated by sheer bulk. Hence, even though the amount of new information was underestimated before *The Keats Circle* appeared, there was a widespread sense of relief when it was learned that Rollins, after carefully surveying the material, had decided to undertake the task of selecting and editing it. I myself remember vividly the discussions that took place at Harvard, where Keats (as Rollins was fond of demonstrating) had been a subject of intense interest for over a century. Naturally, in a place like Harvard, there was in the 1930's and early 1940's (as now) an extreme diversity of approach — to literature in general, to literary history, even to the study of a single author. But the agreement was unanimous that Rollins was the man to bring order out of this rich chaos and to present it objectively.

Hyder Rollins was indeed uniquely qualified for this task. And when he praised such earlier scholars as Francis James Child, Kittredge, or Lowes, or such colleagues as Douglas Bush, as exemplars of a Harvard tradition, or spoke of the range of such nineteenth-century critics as James Russell Lowell, he was indicating the standards he applied to himself and his students. To begin with, he was no specialist who had concentrated solely on Keats — or even Keats's period. Bacon was altogether right when, in *The Advancement of Learning*, he stated that the pioneer and creative work in any field is rarely done by those who continue their investigative work on the same "level" where they began, and who lack perspective (historical or otherwise) to see the subject for what it is. The work that compels our admiration, and that proves to be fertile for later thought, usually turns out to be that of the scholar or thinker who brings to bear, on a particular subject, what Santayana called a rich "internal fund" of general knowledge and *expertise*. Rollins was already an established scholar of both Elizabethan and nineteenth-century literature. In addition, he was sophisticated in the techniques of literary history. He had himself been teaching them, in one of the great graduate schools of the world, to several hundred advanced students over a period of twenty-five years — and in a wide variety of period and subject. Again, through daily research for over thirty-five years, he was familiar with the intelligent uses of a great research library. Finally (a further qualification especially necessary for this particular task) he was a patient — often clairvoyant — student of handwriting.

The result, when Rollins published the present work, was the greatest single body of new source material for the subject since Monckton Milnes's biography of Keats (1848), which had appeared exactly a century before *The Keats Circle*. Further material was added in the supplement published in 1955: *More Letters and Poems of the Keats Circle*.

Rollins' great edition of *The Letters of John Keats* (1958) was carried out in the wake of his work on *The Keats Circle*; and many of his colleagues and students, especially Professor J. C. Stillinger, were closely involved in helping him. They were all aware, when the first edition of *The Keats Circle* was sold out, that a second was deferred only until Rollins could complete his work on the *Letters*. Because of this, and because of his death at the time that the *Letters* were published, the present work has been out of print for several years. It is a pleasure not only to his friends and students but also to Keats scholars everywhere to know that a new edition is now possible. At the same time we have seized the opportunity to publish with it the supplement, *More Letters and Poems*, which has also recently gone out of print. Though this resulted in a somewhat bulkier volume, scholars were unanimous in asking that the supplement be included.

While working on the *Letters*, Rollins made many corrections in his personal copies of both works (now in the Houghton Library). Miss Marie Edel, who assisted him in so much of his work and who has just seen through the press a new edition of his *Tottel's Miscellany*, generously agreed to incorporate these changes (which came to about 160) together with other corrections and additions. We are gratified that we were able to do this while retaining the original pagination. Our concern with keeping the original page numbers was a recognition of the fact that *The Keats Circle*, like other publications of basic material, has become a standard work of reference.

W. J. BATE

Harvard University
September 1964

CONTENTS

VOLUME I

ILLUSTRATIONS

VOLUME I

ACKNOWLEDGMENTS

For permission to use letters or illustrations or both I owe thanks to Mr. William A. Jackson, of the Houghton Library; the officials of the Keats House, Hampstead, the National Portrait Gallery, London, and the Pierpont Morgan Library, New York; Miss Ludie J. Kinkead, Curator and Librarian of the Filson Club, Louisville, Kentucky; the literary executor of Oscar Wilde; Mr. James Pope-Hennessy, the official biographer of Lord Houghton, and the Marchioness of Crewe; Miss Gertrude M. Tuckwell and Mr. H. K. Hudson; Mr. Maurice Buxton Forman; Mr. James F. Clarke; Mr. Arthur A. Houghton, Jr.; Mr. Hesketh Pearson; and several descendants of George Keats, notably the late Mrs. Samuel A. Hartwell, of Cambridge. For answering queries of one sort or another I am indebted to Miss Carrie Hunt, of the Lexington, Kentucky, Public Library; Miss Lois Trice, of the University of Texas; my colleagues, Professors Douglas Bush, Howard M. Jones, and James B. Munn, and Mr. William H. McCarthy, Jr.; and my old students, Professors Bradford A. Booth and Roy Lamson, Jr., Mr. Marvin Perry, Jr., Father Edward Louis Surtz, Mr. Dick Taylor, Jr., Miss Mabel A. E. Steele, Curator of the Harvard Keats Collection, and Miss Marie Louise Edel. Furthermore, Mr. Munn, ably assisted by Mrs. Munn and by Mr. Richard Allison and Mr. Charles R. Staples, of Lexington, Kentucky, provided me with a good deal of new documentary information about the Keats family in America, while Miss Steele and Miss Edel were invaluable assistants in establishing and verifying the texts of the letters. Finally, I am greatly indebted to Phoebe deKay Donald, of the Harvard University Press, for compiling the Indexes. My obligations to scholars who have written on Keats will be too obvious to require specific comment.

INTRODUCTION

The letters and other documents—the so-called Crewe papers—collected mainly by Richard Monckton Milnes, first Baron Houghton, when he was writing the life (1848, 1867) and later editing the poems of John Keats were bought from his son, then the Marquess of Crewe, by Mr. Arthur A. Houghton, Jr., of New York, in 1939 and deposited, along with many other invaluable manuscripts and books, in the Harvard University Library two years later. Miss Amy Lowell's fine collection of Keatsiana had already been received there in 1927. The gifts of Miss Lowell and Mr. Houghton, with other books and manuscripts since added, form the notable Harvard Keats Collection, which is housed in special rooms in the new Houghton Library. It contains various presentation copies of Keats's books, numerous manuscripts of his poems, the proofsheets of *Lamia* with his alterations, sixty-six letters in his holograph, and too many other treasures to mention. In it also are letters and papers written by friends, relatives, admirers, and students of Keats from around 1806 down to the present day.

Because Keats's own letters have been printed by Mr. M. Buxton Forman and his poems adequately edited by Professor H. W. Garrod, for the scholar as well as the general reader the material set forth in the present volumes is now about the most interesting part of the Houghton Library collection. It is an important source of information about the life and work of the poet and his family and friends, about Milnes and his biography, and about the group of editors and writers who made the

London Magazine famous. No catalog, not even a list, of these manuscripts has been published, but because they are greatly in demand by students it has seemed wise to the authorities of the Harvard University Library to make them available in print for reading and study.

While the editorial work was progressing, the Pierpont Morgan Library, of New York, kindly deposited for several months in the Houghton Library its celebrated scrapbook of Keatsiana—letters, poems, notes—compiled by Richard Woodhouse. This "Morgan MS.," as I call it, is intimately connected with other volumes of Woodhouse's transcripts now at Harvard. Its contents are well-known to students of Keats, but with the gracious permission of the Morgan Library most of them are here printed, and they add greatly to the value of this "sourcebook." Students of Keats and romantic poetry would be happier and better informed if other libraries, notably the library of the Keats House, Hampstead, would follow the examples of the Houghton and Morgan libraries by making more of their Keats circle manuscripts accessible in print.

The "Crewe papers" were consulted by Sir Sidney Colvin for his biography of Keats and by Professor Garrod for his edition of the poems. Most other students have had access to them at second hand, as by reproducing Colvin's extracts or summaries. Miss Lowell's collection, in turn, was inaccessible to British scholars, who ordinarily, too, in the case of the Morgan MS. have necessarily relied on inaccurate transcripts.

A rapid count shows that of the three hundred fifty-two separate documents included in the present edition about fifty have hitherto been printed entire, though usually with considerable inexactness, in miscellaneous books, magazines, or newspapers. Frequently the printing has taken the shape of sentences or paragraphs scattered over widely separated pages of some book or other, so that the reader gets no unified impression of the letter and, indeed, seldom knows whether it is or is not given in its entirety. More unsatisfactory still are the excerpts or summaries printed here and there. Even the famous shipboard letters of Severn have never before been reproduced literally, and to read the highly incomplete version given in one Keats biography of the letter Severn wrote on the first two days of November, 1820 (No. 77), one must chase it, after many digressions and interruptions, through a dozen pages. The almost equally famous "Abbey Memoir" (No. 140) could up to now be read only by tracing it through the first one hundred thirty pages of a certain biographical-critical work. The mere inconvenience of hunting down such letters as have heretofore been printed warrants their inclusion in a single reference work; and to see them as complete units with texts as literal as possible should be a gratifying experience for readers and students alike. Except to the few students who *have* seen the originals, the texts here given will throw new and vivid light on Keats himself and on such persons as Haslam, Bailey, and Reynolds, Brown and Milnes, Hessey, Taylor, and others of his circle. That their value has seldom been diminished, almost never exhausted, by the investigations of those few will become obvious to anyone who compares what they have said with the actual letters, for example, of Miss Woodhouse (No. 49), Caroline Mathew (No. 214), Charles Brown, Jr. (I, liv-lxii), Henry Stephens (No. 221), Bailey (No. 253), Reynolds (No. 231), or Mrs. Procter (No. 192), or with Brown's List of Keats's Books (No. 122).

The letter writers picture Keats as man and poet with unforgettable vividness, and also provide a large part of the material available for their own biographies. "What fools we mortals are," George Keats wrote in 1829 (No. 147), "how we are straining for ever so small a niche in the temple of Fame." Though on the whole Keats's friends were men of importance or interest in their own right, yet all have achieved fame of a sort because of their association with him. "I could not live without the love of my friends," Keats once confessed to Reynolds. He had no real worry on that score, for what comes out most emphatically in the letters is his own lovable character and the complete devotion of their writers. On the day he sailed for Italy Fanny Brawne wrote to his sister: "I cannot tell you how much every one have exerted themselves for him, nor how much he is liked. . . . I am certain he has some spell that attaches them to him, or else he has fortunately met with a set of friends that I did not believe could be found in the world." [1] The spell was his beauty, his courage, his endearing and affectionate personality, his genius. Even as a schoolboy, says Edward Holmes (No. 198), "the generosity & daring of his character" and his "extraordinary beauty of person & expression . . . captivated the boys, and no one was ever more popular." "Love" is the somewhat unconventional word the Keats circle use in referring to him. Thus in his old age Bailey (No. 251) declared that Keats was "the most *loveable* creature . . . I think I ever knew as a man." Reynolds (No. 204) considered him "the sincerest Friend,—the most loveable associate" he had ever known. Brown remarked, "The highest praise that mortal can have belonged to Keats: no one ever saw him without loving him, no one could know him and treat him unkindly." [2] "If I know what it is to love," Haslam told Severn, "I truly love John Keats." [3] Charles Cowden Clarke (No. 187) had "never heard a schoolfellow, or a friend in after life speak lukewarmly of him: whatever may be the feeling of respect for his memory with posterity, . . . it will be cherished by all his early friends; for all loved him."

It is remarkable, furthermore, how these men recog-

[1] Edgcumbe, p. 4.
[2] Sharp, p. 98.
[3] The same, p. 73.

nized his genius, and how completely unspoiled (despite his occasional outbursts of "rodomontade") he was by their praise. If a few of the reviewers dismissed him as a worthless Cockney versifier, no man or woman who really knew him had the slightest doubt that he would become a rival of Milton and Shakespeare. In October, 1818, Bailey, who worshiped Milton and Wordsworth, called him "a great poet," just as earlier in an Oxford newspaper he had spoken of the *Poems* (1817) as "the richest promise I ever saw of an etherial imagination maintained by vast intellectual powers" and of *Endymion* as containing "the germs of immortality." Severn considered him "the most noble-feeling and brightest genius to be found in existence." Reynolds, Brown, Woodhouse, Haydon, Taylor, Hessey, and everyone else but the tradesman Abbey were likewise sure that he was destined to be immortal. Few poets have ever been blessed with so many steadfast friends, and almost no other poet seems to present-day readers—more than a century and a quarter after his death—so human and lovable.

After Keats left England his circle waited for Severn's letters with intense anxiety—and a single letter from Rome to London, or vice versa, cost one shilling sixpence. Upon arrival in London, the letters were widely circulated. Brown, for example, would forward a message from Severn to Taylor and Hessey, who then would send it to Woodhouse, Haslam, and Holmes, ultimately returning it for Brown to show to Thomas Richards. Sometimes a transcript by Hessey or Woodhouse was making the rounds along with the original. Fanny Brawne copied passages or whole letters from Severn's communications to Haslam and dispatched them to Fanny Keats. Dr. Clark's notes to a friend in London were in the same fashion passed from hand to hand.

Hence, arranged as it is chronologically, the ensuing correspondence—although but a part of that still in existence—tells a fascinating and poignant story of the poet during his lifetime, and an almost equally fascinating story of the growth of his posthumous fame and of the fortunes and misfortunes of his friends and relations. What Keats could have become if he had had only one further year, not to mention three or four years, of health and literary composition is an absorbing, if useless, topic for speculation. What happened to many of his circle—Reynolds and his drunkenness, Rice and his incurable disease, Haydon and his suicide, Brown and his thwarted hopes in New Zealand, Caroline Mathew and her religious mania, G. F. Mathew and his struggles to support a family of thirteen, George Keats and his fortune's vanishing just as he died—is a melancholy illustration of what added years all too often do bring.

Some twenty years after Keats's death, what remained of the circle (Woodhouse, George Keats, Rice, and Brown were dead) was revivified as Milnes took over the task of writing the biography, and letters giving advice and help flew back and forth. The raw material of Milnes's book, and of much of Colvin's, Miss Lowell's, Miss Hewlett's, Miss Askwith's, and biographers yet to come, is to be found in these two volumes, which also show in process of formation a new "Keats circle" that grows in circumference as the years pass by. Mere limitations of space dictated ending the letters in 1878. The Harvard Keats Collection has far more letters written after than before that year; and possibly this edition may some day be expanded to further volumes in which the correspondence of F. Holland Day, Charles Eliot Norton, and others about the Anne Whitney bust in Hampstead church, of Day and the Llanos family, of Miss Lowell and others will be reproduced.

THE PLAN OF THIS EDITION

The Texts. The printed texts attempt to reproduce exactly the spellings, capitalization, and punctuation of the manuscripts, with a few slight exceptions designed to make the latter readable and the typography unobtrusive. The Keats circle, like writers today, were often hasty and careless in forming letters and punctuation marks and in distinguishing between capital and small letters, so that numerous arbitrary decisions have been forced upon the editor. The handwriting, unbelievably bad, of some of them was castigated by the poet himself. On March 4, 1820, he told Dilke: "You must improve in your penmanship; your writing is like the speaking of a child of three years old, very understandable to its father but to no one else. The worst is it looks well—no that is not the worst—the worst is, it is worse than Bailey's. Bailey's looks illegible and may perchance be read; your's looks very legible and may perchance not be read." "If the only copies of the greek and Latin Authors had been made by you, Bailey and Haydon," he concluded, "they were as good as lost."

Rapid writers seldom form all letters with exactness, but the "Kaligraphy" of Bailey, described by himself too moderately as "my vile hand," demands flashes of intuition (which do not always come) rather than a careful scrutiny of each pen-stroke. As a mere example, one of his words can be deciphered as possibly "during," "through," or "strong"; another, as "talent" or "interest"; a third, as "rarely" or "scarcely." Again, one transcriber of his letter No. 112 reads what is surely "of that 'insatiable archer' . . . of unfeeling satire" as "of that 'insatiable ardor' . . . of awful satire," another as "of that 'insatiable ardor' . . . of awfully [ ]." Severn, too, is at times illegible. He himself would have blamed seasickness (No. 67), or the disinfectants used by Italian immigration officials (No. 76), or (No. 194) the "painfull circumstances" under which at Rome he wrote "always spontaneously" for "any striking error" or undecipherable word. But bad as he sometimes is, bad as Bailey and Dilke always are, Lord Houghton is perhaps the most unreadable of

xvii

the group. In many cases, then, all that can be done is to let the context aid the eye (and the electric magnifying glass and the intuition!) of the copyist—and to hope for the best.

The many unorthodox spellings in the manuscripts will not often cause any difficulty, and in most cases have been retained without comment. But occasionally, where a possibility of confusion exists, spellings are modernized by letters inserted in square brackets ([ ]). Such brackets, too, enclose all other editorial insertions, like words necessary for the sense and absent because of mere oversight. Where square brackets occur in the manuscripts themselves, they are retained with an explanatory note. Often a mere flourish at the end of a word stands for a period or for some letter like *s* or *r*, and it is impossible, for example, to tell whether the writer meant "M^r" or "Mr" or "Mr." In this particular case the form "M^r" is printed, and all dashes and dots are omitted. Often only individual judgment—which is likely to alter at each examination—can decide whether a mark of punctuation is meant for a comma, a period, or sometimes a dash, and in most cases it is printed as a period.

Where a reading is doubtful, it is followed by a question mark within square brackets or else is commented on in a note. In the very few places where a word could not be read at all, a statement to that effect is printed within brackets as "[*word illegible*]" or it is given as "[. . .]" with a note of explanation. Curly braces ({}) enclose editorial insertions to fill lacunae caused by tears, holes, frayed edges, and the like. Where they enclose three dots ({. . .}) they mark a gap, the extent of which is indicated in a footnote, and which the editor was unable or unwilling to supply conjecturally.

Canceled letters or words are ignored in the frequent instances where they result merely from the writers' correction of inadvertent misspellings, repetitions, and so on. Every letter writer indulges in such changes, and nothing would be gained, except an ugly page, by recording them all. But whenever the canceled readings appear (especially as in the letters of Wood-house and Taylor) to have any interest or significance, they are, if decipherable, printed within shaped brackets ($<$ $>$) or else recorded in footnotes. Three asterisks (* * *) at the beginning or end of a document warn that part of it is missing. *I* ($=j$) and *u* ($=v$) have been modernized everywhere to *j* and *v;* flourishes, lines, or braces attached to addresses, signatures, or dates (as well as some aimless dashes at the ends of certain lines) have been ignored; and postscripts, no matter where written, are printed at the end of the letters.

Headnotes. If a letter has an address and postmarks, they are included in the headnotes, which also, except in a few special cases, indicate whether each document has been printed wholly or in part. I have not listed all the printed or quoted texts, for one reason because it is often impossible to tell whether they follow the originals or, say, Colvin's or Miss Lowell's transcripts.

Footnotes. The footnotes make no effort to enumerate all the misreadings of other transcribers, since two people will rarely transcribe a letter exactly alike in all details, and since I have doubtless (I hope not often) made errors of my own. But it may be assumed that in each instance I have collated with the originals the printed texts mentioned in the headnotes, even when variations are not given, and that when another printed text reads "grouching" or "proper" and my text reads "growling" and "presses," I have examined and rejected the earlier reading. Similarly I have not felt it necessary to correct all misstatements of fact made by the letter writers, even those dealing strictly with Keats's life, or to annotate elaborately throughout. On the other hand, I have (as in the notes to Nos. 2, 5, 49, 107, 116. 130, 150, 248, 253, 323, 341) presented many details that clear up disputed points in Keats's and his friends' biographies and bibliographies.

Biographical Sketches. The Biographical Sketches were written for the convenience and assistance of readers, and make no special claims to originality. Nevertheless, they trace more fully than has been customary the post-1821 lives of the individuals concerned, show the parts they played in the composition of Lord Houghton's biography, and, in conjunction with the notes, do add a considerable number of new facts, particularly to the biographies of Brown, De Wint and Hilton, Haslam, Hessey, George Keats, James Rice, John and Georgiana Keats Jeffrey, and Reynolds. Each sketch is a unit in itself, a fact that has necessitated some slight repetition of details.

Cross-references. To save space and to avoid cluttering the pages with "see below" and "see above," all cross-references, except when the documents are referred to by their numbers, are given in the form "See I, 198" and "See II, 123," which means volume I, volume II, and the appropriate pages.

October 1, 1947

H.E.R.

LIST OF LETTERS AND PAPERS

No.	Date	Writer	Recipient
50	May 25, January 6, 1821	George Keats	Fanny Keats
51	June (?)	Richard Woodhouse	John Taylor
52	June 18	George Keats	John Keats
53	June (?)	Richard Woodhouse: Draft of the "Advertisement" to *Lamia*	
54	June 30 (?)	Richard Woodhouse	John Taylor
55	July 4	J. H. Reynolds	John Taylor
56	July 12 (?)	Joseph Severn	William Haslam
57	July 27	Percy Bysshe Shelley	John Keats
58	July 27	Benjamin Bailey	John Taylor
59	July (?)	Richard Woodhouse: Criticism of a Sonnet by Keats	
60	August 17	John Aitken	John Keats
61	August 31	John Taylor	J. A. Hessey
62	September 11	John Taylor	John Keats
63	September 13	William Haslam	John Taylor
64	September 13	John Taylor	William Haslam
65	September 16	John Keats: Assignment of Copyright	
66	September 16	Richard Woodhouse	John Keats
67	September 19	Joseph Severn	William Haslam
68	September 19	Taylor and Hessey	—— Brown
69	September 21	Joseph Severn	William Haslam
70	September 21	J. H. Reynolds	John Taylor
71	September 23	William Haslam	Taylor and Hessey
72	September 30	Charles Brown	William Haslam
73	October 5	Charles Brown	John Taylor
74	October 6	J. A. Hessey	John Taylor
75	October 6, 21	J. A. Hessey	William Haslam
76	October 22	Joseph Severn	William Haslam
77	November 1, 2	Joseph Severn	William Haslam
78	November 8	George Keats	John Keats
79	November 23	J. A. Hessey	William Haslam
80	November 27	Dr. James Clark	?

No.	Date	Writer	Recipient
114	April 18	Richard Abbey	John Taylor
115	April 28	Benjamin Bailey	John Taylor
116	May 5	Joseph Severn	William Haslam
117	May 5	J. A. Hessey	William Haslam
118	May 8	Benjamin Bailey	John Taylor
119	May 8	Benjamin Bailey: Notes on His Conversation with Lockhart	
120	May 16	Joseph Severn	John Taylor
121	July 12	Joseph Severn	William Haslam
122	July (?)	Charles Brown: List of Keats's Books	
123	July 24	Charles Brown	J. A. Hessey
124	August 7	J. A. Hessey	William Haslam
125	August 12	Charles Brown	John Taylor
126	August 18	J. A. Hessey	William Haslam
127	?	Charlotte (?) Reynolds	Richard Woodhouse

1822

No.	Date	Writer	Recipient
128	January 5	Joseph Severn	John Taylor
129	February 15	Frederick Salmon	Richard Woodhouse

1823

No.	Date	Writer	Recipient
130	June 1	Joseph Severn	William Haslam
131	August 21	Richard Woodhouse: Notes on Keats's Life	
132	December 29	Charles Cowden Clarke	Richard Woodhouse

1824

No.	Date	Writer	Recipient
133	April 10	George Keats	C. W. Dilke
134	May 10	Benjamin Bailey	John Taylor

No.	Date	Writer	Recipient
		1825 (?)	
135	?	J. H. Reynolds	J. A. Hessey
136	April 20	George Keats	C. W. Dilke
		1826	
137	February 16	William Howitt	William Hone
138	May 31	Fanny Keats Llanos and Valentin Llanos	George Keats
139	October 18	George Keats	C. W. Dilke
		1827	
140	April 20, 23	John Taylor	Richard Woodhouse
		1828	
141	March 25	George Keats	C. W. Dilke
142	April 16, May 12	George Keats	C. W. Dilke
143	July 12	George Keats	C. W. Dilke
144	August 17	Charles G. Wylie	John Taylor
		1829	
145	March 19	George Keats	Mrs. C. W. Dilke
146	November 14	George Keats	C. W. Dilke
		1830	
147	May 7	George Keats	C. W. Dilke
148	November 22	George Keats	C. W. Dilke
		1832	
149	May 11	George Keats	C. W. Dilke
		1833	
150	February 12	C. W. Dilke	George Keats
151	November 24, December 14	George Keats	C. W. Dilke

LIST OF LETTERS AND PAPERS

No.	Date	Writer	Recipient
		1836	
152	January 2, 11	J. W. Dalby	George James De Wilde
153	March 14, October 8	George Keats	C. W. Dilke
154	December 21	Charles Brown	Leigh Hunt
		1837	
155	June 18	George Keats	L. J. Cist
		1838	
156	March 1	George Keats	C. W. Dilke
157	September	C. W. Dilke	George Keats
		1839	
158	August 10	George Keats	James Freeman Clarke
159	November 15	George Keats	Anna Barker
		1840	
160	October 18	Charles Brown	R. M. Milnes
161	October 25	Charles Brown	R. M. Milnes
162	November 25	George Keats	James Freeman Clarke
		1841	
163	January 17	George Keats	James Freeman Clarke
164	March 14	Charles Brown	R. M. Milnes
165	March 19	Charles Brown	R. M. Milnes
166	March 19	Charles Brown: Life of John Keats	
167	March (?)	Joseph Severn	John Taylor
168	March 29	Charles Brown	R. M. Milnes
169	April 9	Charles Brown	R. M. Milnes
170	April (?)	C. W. Dilke	Joseph Severn
171	July 4	George Keats	James Freeman Clarke

No.	Date	Writer	Recipient
		1842	
172	July 27	Joseph Severn	R. M. Milnes
		1844	
172a	March 8	John Jeffrey	W. L. Breckinridge
		1845	
173	January 27	Thomas Wade	R. M. Milnes
174	February 13	John Taylor	Edward Moxon
175	May 13	John Jeffrey	R. M. Milnes
176	May 26	Thomas Wade	R. M. Milnes
177	July 26	John Jeffrey	R. M. Milnes
178	September 8	John Jeffrey	R. M. Milnes
179	?	Georgiana Keats Jeffrey	Alexander Jeffrey
180	September 30	John Taylor and Edward Moxon: Agreement	
181	October 6	Joseph Severn	R. M. Milnes
182	October (?)	Joseph Severn: Biographical Notes on Keats	[R. M. Milnes]
183	October 31	James Freeman Clarke	R. M. Milnes
184	November 28	B. R. Haydon	Edward Moxon
185	November 29	B. R. Haydon	Edward Moxon (?)
186	November 30	B. R. Haydon	Edward Moxon
		1846	
187	March 16	Charles Cowden Clarke: Biographical Notes on Keats	[R. M. Milnes]
188	March 17	Charles Cowden Clarke	R. M. Milnes
189	March 17	Charles Cowden Clarke	R. M. Milnes

LIST OF LETTERS AND PAPERS

No.	Date	Writer	Recipient
		1818	
317	August 29	J. A. Hessey	John Taylor
		1822	
318	October 7	J. A. Hessey	John Taylor
319	November 5	J. A. Hessey	John Taylor
		1823	
320	January 15	J. A. Hessey	John Taylor
321	January	J. H. Reynolds	J. A. Hessey
322	January	J. H. Reynolds	J. A. Hessey
323	January (?)	J. H. Reynolds	John Taylor
324	January 21, 22	J. A. Hessey	John Taylor
325	March 14	J. A. Hessey	John Taylor
326	March 17	J. A. Hessey	John Taylor
327	March 18	J. A. Hessey	John Taylor
328	March 21	J. A. Hessey	John Taylor
329	March 21	J. A. Hessey	John Taylor
330	About March 25	J. A. Hessey	John Taylor
331	March 26	J. A. Hessey	John Taylor
332	March 27	J. A. Hessey	John Taylor
333	April 2	J. A. Hessey	John Taylor
334	July 1	J. A. Hessey	John Taylor
335	August 15	J. H. Reynolds	John Taylor
336	September 3	J. A. Hessey	John Taylor
337	September 23	J. A. Hessey	John Taylor
338	October 20	J. A. Hessey	John Taylor
		1824	
339	April 2	Benjamin Bailey	John Taylor
340	June 9	Benjamin Bailey	John Taylor
341	June 11	John Taylor	J. H. Reynolds
342	June 14	Benjamin Bailey	John Taylor
343	June (?)	J. H. Reynolds	J. A. Hessey

ABBREVIATED NAMES AND TITLES

Adami. Marie Adami, *Fanny Keats*. London, 1937.

Aldine. *The Poetical Works of John Keats. Chronologically Arranged and Edited, With a Memoir,* by Lord Houghton (Aldine Edition of the British Poets). London, 1876.

Askwith. Betty Askwith, *Keats*. London, 1941.

Blunden. Edmund Blunden, *Keats's Publisher: A Memoir of John Taylor (1781–1864)*. London, 1936.

Bodurtha. *Life of John Keats by Charles Armitage Brown,* ed. Dorothy Hyde Bodurtha and Willard Bissell Pope. Oxford University Press, 1937.

Colvin. Sir Sidney Colvin, *John Keats, His Life and Poetry, His Friends, Critics and After-Fame,* 3d ed. London, 1920.

DNB. *Dictionary of National Biography.*

Edgcumbe. *Letters of Fanny Brawne to Fanny Keats 1820–1824,* ed. Fred Edgcumbe. New York, 1937.

Finney. Claude Lee Finney, *The Evolution of Keats's Poetry,* 2 vols. Harvard University Press, 1936.

Forman. *The Poetical Works and Other Writings of John Keats,* ed. Harry Buxton Forman, 4 vols. London, 1883.

M. B. Forman, *Some Letters. Some Letters & Miscellanea of Charles Brown the Friend of John Keats & Thomas Richards,* ed. Maurice Buxton Forman. Oxford University Press, 1937.

Garrod. *The Poetical Works of John Keats,* ed. H. W. Garrod. Oxford, 1939.

Hewlett. Dorothy Hewlett, *Adonais, A Life of John Keats*. London, 1937.

Hampstead Keats. *The Poetical Works and Other Writings of John Keats,* ed. Harry Buxton Forman, revised by Maurice Buxton Forman (Hampstead Edition), 8 vols. New York, 1938, 1939.

JEGP. *Journal of English and Germanic Philology.*

Keats' Reputation. Hyder Edward Rollins, *Keats' Reputation in America to 1848*. Harvard University Press, 1946.

Letters. *The Letters of John Keats,* ed. Maurice Buxton Forman, 2d ed., revised. New York, 1935.

ABBREVIATIONS

Lowell. Amy Lowell, *John Keats*, 2 vols. Boston and New York, 1925.

Marsh. George L. Marsh, *John Hamilton Reynolds, Poetry and Prose*. London, 1928.

Milnes. Richard Monckton Milnes, *Life, Letters, and Literary Remains, of John Keats*, 2 vols. London, 1848. (The revised ed., *The Life and Letters of John Keats* [London, 1867], is cited as "Milnes, 1867.")

Morgan MS. Richard Woodhouse's "Scrapbook," Pierpont Morgan Library (see the Introduction, I, x).

NED. A New English Dictionary Founded on Historical Principles, 12 vols. Oxford, 1888–1928.

NQ. Notes and Queries.

Papers. Sir Charles W. Dilke, *The Papers of a Critic*, 2 vols. London, 1875.

Penrose. *The Autobiography and Memoirs of Benjamin Robert Haydon*, ed. Alexander P. D. Penrose. London, 1927.

PMLA. Publications of the Modern Language Association of America.

Pope. Willard Bissell Pope, "Studies in the Keats Circle." Unpublished Harvard University Thesis, 1932.

Reid. T. Wemyss Reid, *The Life, Letters, and Friendships of Richard Monckton Milnes, First Lord Houghton*, 2 vols., 2d ed. London, 1890.

Sharp. William Sharp, *The Life and Letters of Joseph Severn*. London, 1892.

TLS. The [London] *Times Literary Supplement.*

Williamson. G. C. Williamson, *The Keats Letters, Papers, and Other Relics Forming the Dilke Bequest in the Hampstead Public Library*. London, 1914.

BIOGRAPHICAL SKETCHES OF CERTAIN CORRESPONDENTS AND OTHER PERSONS FREQUENTLY MENTIONED

RICHARD ABBEY

After the death of Keats's mother in 1810, his grandmother, Mrs. John Jennings, aged seventy-four, found herself responsible for four children ranging from about seven to fifteen years of age. Very wisely in July "she executed a deed by which the four children and the greater part of the money left to her by her husband were placed in the charge of two trustees, and to them, though there was no outward change in the arrangements of her household, she virtually relinquished the greater part of her responsibilities from that moment." [1] The trustees were John Nowland Sandell, merchant, Broad Street Buildings, and Richard Abbey, an old friend whom Mrs. Jennings had known in Colne. Sandell apparently took almost no part in the trusteeship, and, so Dilke writes, "was obliged to fly to Holland & there died." [2]

Abbey, Cock, and Company [3] were merchants and tea dealers at 4 Pancras Lane. Abbey with his wife and adopted daughter lived at that address or on Marsh Street, Walthamstow. In the Pancras Lane countinghouse George and Tom Keats

---

[1] Adami, p. 30. Her account of Abbey is the best yet written.

[2] See II, 175. Adami, p. 30, says he fled "after 1816" and died "the next year."

[3] So given in the *Post Office London Directory*, 1819, 1820, although the issue for 1814 has "Abbey and Cocks" and that for 1825 "Abbey and Cock."

worked for a while, but the latter quit because of illness, the former because of a quarrel with Abbey's junior partner. This partner, Hodgkinson, is a footnote in literary history, even though his first name is not recorded, because of the quarrel and of John's slurs. "That Hodgkinson," John wrote contemptuously in 1819, or "Hodgkinson, whose name I cannot bear to write." Hodgkinson was "more than polite" in September, but in July, 1820, Keats remarked of his "ill fortune," "I must own illness has not made such a Saint of me as to prevent my rejoicing at his reverse." [4] He recovered from the "reverse," and, according to Fanny Keats,[5] was in June, 1826, "prosperous."

When the Keats brothers went into lodgings of their own, Fanny of course remained under her guardian's control. After three years in a Walthamstow boarding school, she lived in one or the other of Abbey's homes until she came of age in 1824. That merchant impressed Taylor (No. 140) as a worthy, honest fellow—a "good natured looking Man with a great Piece of Benevolence standing out on the Top of his Forehead." To John and Fanny he was a tyrant with unreasonable and inexplicable ways. He tried to make John a hat maker and a tea broker, and did apprentice him to a surgeon. Fanny disliked him intensely. As a grown woman she called him "that consummate villain" and robber.[6] Mrs. Abbey was perhaps even more distasteful to John and Fanny and their friends. Fanny Brawne, who had heard only one side of the story, made strenuous and partially successful efforts to ingratiate herself with Mrs. Abbey, whom she found to be "much more in the motherly-nursey stile" than she had expected but "more disagreeable than usual" in the presence of Fanny's visitors.[7] Miss Abbey, to

[4] See *Letters*, pp. 348, 376, 406, 498.
[5] See I, 299f.
[6] See I, 297f.
[7] Edgcumbe, pp. 46, 60.

whom George several times sent his respects from America, remains a shadow.[8]

Probably the Abbeys were not actually unkind to Fanny. But they were convinced that there was bad blood in the family, they distrusted John's addiction to poetry, spoke contemptuously of his publications, and so far as possible kept him from visiting his sister. The result, painful for them both but happy for readers today, was the tender and beautiful letters from John to Fanny. The Abbeys were such successful obstructionists that John sailed to Italy without having seen his sister in months. But George liked the whole family. Often to Fanny he wrote of that "good" or "excellent" man Abbey, and he took comfort in the belief that Abbey, no less than Dilke, believed in his honesty.

Abbey kept a firm hand on the purse strings—a habit ordinarily praised in a guardian. He gave little pocket money to Fanny; he refused to lend John money in August, 1820, and even more tartly (though no doubt as "good business") in April, 1821 (No. 114), disclaimed any responsibility for repaying the donations Taylor had collected and sent to Rome; but in 1820 he was generous and helpful to George. His duties as guardian ended on June 3, 1824. Fanny, much alarmed over reports of his financial losses, found him unwilling (or unable) to settle and turn over her estate. The Court of Chancery, to which in 1823 George had applied for his share of his grandfather, John Jennings', 1805 bequests to the Keats family, also investigated Abbey's handling of Mrs. Jennings' trust fund, and apparently found nothing wrong.

In April, 1827, Taylor visited Abbey, probably at Woodhouse's urgency, and took notes (No. 140) of his gossip about Keats's family. Taylor accepted Abbey's remarks as shocking but true: "How strange it seems that such a Creature of the

[8] For Abbey's account of her see I, 306f.

Element as he should have sprung from such gross Realities!"
Up to the present time biographers have been inclined to discredit Abbey as spiteful and malicious, though much of what he
says is confirmed by Hunt, Haydon, and other witnesses. Future
biographers will no doubt pay more heed to Abbey, who, at any
rate, has already attained a sort of immortality.

BENJAMIN BAILEY [1]

Bailey was born in Cambridgeshire on June 5, 1791. As
early as 1814 he was a close friend of Rice and Reynolds, and
through Rice the two other young men became intimately associated with the three daughters, Mary, Sarah, and Thomasine,
of William Leigh, who lived at Salcombe Regis near Sidmouth.
During March, 1815, in a commonplace book of the Leighs'
they wrote numerous poems—nine by Rice and a "hundred-odd
by both Bailey and Reynolds." In another manuscript, called
"Poems by Two Friends" and given to Thomasine Leigh on
December 25, 1816, there are thirty-two poems by Bailey,
twenty-five by Reynolds.[2] Two months earlier, on October 19,
Bailey had matriculated at Oxford,[3] and had begun reading for
the Church.

Reynolds had told him about Keats, and in the spring of
1817 [4] he made the acquaintance of the young poet. On another
visit to London in the late summer Bailey "saw much of" him,
and invited him to Oxford. Throughout September Keats lived

---

[1] The best account yet written of Bailey, as of Haydon, Reynolds, and
Rice, is that in Pope's admirable, but unfortunately unpublished,
Harvard dissertation (1932). Of published accounts those given by Blun-
den and in *Letters* are the most complete.

[2] Pope, pp. 39f., 42f., 629-638. The commonplace books are now in the
Keats Museum, Hampstead.

[3] Joseph Foster, *Alumni Oxonienses*, I (1887), 47.

[4] See II, 267.

in Bailey's college quarters, where he composed the third book of *Endymion*. The two young fellows walked and boated together, visited Stratford-on-Avon, read and criticized Wordsworth, Chatterton, and Milton. Bailey parted from Keats with "much real regret & personal affection," and saw him only infrequently thereafter in London. They corresponded, however, and ten letters that Keats wrote to Bailey from October 8, 1817, to August 14, 1819, have been preserved. Bailey defended Keats in an Oxford newspaper (May, June, 1818), made valiant efforts to answer his assailants in some Edinburgh magazine, and had a memorable talk with Lockhart, whom he tried to influence in favor of the poet. Before August 29, 1818, he was given a curacy near Carlisle.

Though he had been an ardent suitor of Marianne Reynolds, early in 1819 Bailey became engaged to Hamilton Gleig, daughter of George Gleig, LL.D., F.R.S., Bishop of Brechin and Primus of the Scots Episcopal Church, and sister of G. R. Gleig, a member of the staff of *Blackwood's Edinburgh Magazine* [5] and afterwards Chaplain-General of the Forces. As a result, the Reynolds family quarreled with him, Rice "abandoned Bailey entirely," while Keats (February 18, 1819), uncertain whether his "very bad" conduct was caused by "want of delicacy and principle or want of Knowledge and polite experience," decided that "his so quickly taking to miss Gleig can have no excuse—except that of a Ploughmans who wants a wife." Later (August 14) he sent congratulations to Bailey on his marriage, using rather formal, awkward terms. Whether thereafter he retained the opinion he had expressed of Bailey in January, 1818—"he is one of the noblest men alive at the

[5] See Margaret O. W. Oliphant's *Annals of a Publishing House*, I (1897), 478f., 483-489. Charles MacFarlane, *Reminiscences* (ed. J. F. Tattersall [1917], pp. 180f.), reports that he seriously considered challenging Macaulay to a duel in 1841 because of insults in the latter's essay on "Warren Hastings."

xliii

present day"—may well be doubted. At any rate, their correspondence ended, though Bailey in subsequent letters to Taylor often mentioned Keats with admiration and affection. In exactly the same way he expressed himself to Milnes in 1848, saying that Keats was "the most *loveable* creature" he had known.

Bailey's life and character are described well enough in the verbose and almost undecipherable letters herein printed. He was a country parson at Dallington, Northamptonshire, in 1819, at Gayhurst and Stoke Goldington, near Olney, and Burton-on-Trent at unspecified dates, and apparently at Townfield, Scotland, in 1827.[6] Then for a time he lived in France.[7] During these years he wrote some bad verse and indifferent prose, but, in spite of (or possibly because of) his fine education, the list of his publications before and after 1831 as given by Blunden [8] contains nothing that the world has not willingly let die, unless it be his Malayan language translations and dictionary.

In 1831 the Bishop of London arranged for his migration to Ceylon as senior Colonial Chaplain.[9] "Almost immediately" [10] (March 31, 1832) after their landing at Colombo his wife died, and by October, 1848, of his various children only a son and a daughter, Mrs. Edward L. Mitford, both residents of Ceylon, remained alive. He was made archdeacon in February, 1846.[11]

Meanwhile Bailey had lost touch with the Keats circle except for occasional letters from Dilke. Hence when Milnes

[6] Lowell, I, 479, says "that he was, at one time, private chaplain to Lord Hawke, and, at another, rector of Minster, Kent."

[7] See II, 262.

[8] Page 212.

[9] See II, 262. His name ("Rev. —— Bailey") first appears in the *Royal Kalendar* for 1833.

[10] See II, 262.

[11] So M. B. Forman in *Letters*, p. xlvi, but his name as archdeacon first appears in the *Royal Kalendar* for 1848.

published his *Life* [12] he remarked, " 'Brothers' they were in affection and in thought—brothers also in destiny. Mr. Bailey died soon after Keats." This "exaggerated" comment resurrected Bailey. He wrote to Taylor and, voluminously, to Milnes, pointing out some of the latter's errors, making suggestions for improvements, giving new facts, and enclosing a letter from Keats. In subsequent publications Milnes acknowledged Bailey's help, and made considerable use of the material he had provided.

In 1852 Bailey returned to England, where he died on June 25, 1853.

FANNY BRAWNE

Mrs. Samuel Brawne, since 1810 a widow with three children—Fanny (Frances), Samuel, Margaret—rented Brown's half of Wentworth Place in the summer of 1818. She is now a shadowy figure, but she seems to have been liked and respected by all the poet's circle. Severn called her a "fine" and a "kind" lady; Keats, "a very nice woman," and to her he signed his one letter "affectionate[ly]." Shortly after her son died, she was burned to death at the door of her home, and was buried on December 1, 1829. Samuel and Margaret Brawne have little importance in Keats's biography, though he was fond of both, as casual references in the letters indicate. M. B. Forman has discovered that the former was born on July 26, 1804, and died at Wentworth Place in April, 1828, and that the latter was born on April 19, 1809, and married Chevalier Joao Antonio Pereira da Cunha,[1] son of the Marquis d'Inleamprepa, in France on November 30, 1833.

[12] I, 62.

[1] Sir Charles W. Dilke, *Papers*, I, 34, calls him "M. D'Acunha, the Brazilian Minister to France."

Fanny was born at Hampstead, August 9, 1800. Dilke asserted that Keats met her "for the first time at my house." "Brown," he went on, "let his house when he and Keats went to Scotland to Mrs. Brawne, a stranger to all of us. As the house adjoined mine in a large garden, we almost necessarily became acquainted. When Brown returned, the Brawnes took another house at the top of Downshire Hill; but we kept up our acquaintance and no doubt Keats, who was daily with me, met her soon after his return," [2] that is, perhaps in August or September, 1818.[3]

During the next few months Keats's time and energy were largely absorbed in nursing Tom, who died on December 1. But Fanny was always in his thoughts. She 'took possession' of him: "the very first week I knew you I wrote myself your vassal." [4] Such confessions were not made to others. Hence in writing to the George Keatses a fortnight after Tom's death he describes Fanny as "beautiful and elegant, graceful, silly, fashionable and strange we have a little tiff now and then—and she behaves a little better, or I must have sheered off." Sheering off was impossible. Just two days later he gave an elaborate account of her looks and manners, adding that "she is ignorant—monstrous in her behaviour flying out in all directions, calling people such names," in short a *"Minx . . .* no[t] from any innate vice but from a penchant she has for acting stylishly." [5] "An

[2] *Letters*, pp. 217f., n. "Carlino" Brown (and *DNB*) says that his father introduced Keats to Fanny. See I, lvi.

[3] Edgcumbe, p. xxi, says that Keats arrived at Hampstead on August 18; "calling immediately upon Mrs. Dilke . . . he was probably at once introduced to the Brawnes." Lowell, II, 126, thought the meeting was "not later than some time early in September," but her captious *TLS* reviewer (March 19, 1925, pp. 177f.) declared, "the probability is overwhelming that he did not have his first sight of her until after the death of his brother Tom."

[4] *Letters*, p. 362.

[5] The same, pp. 249, 254f.

attraction which begins by repulsion," Colvin [6] remarks, "is ever the most dangerous of all." However dangerous, it resulted in an informal engagement to the "minx," apparently on December 25, a day Fanny once called the happiest of her life.[7] The engagement was kept as secret as possible. Keats did not mention it to his American relatives. "Miss Brawne and I," he told them on February 14, "have every now and then a chat and a tiff." [8] The tiffs were often caused by Fanny's flirtations with Brown or Severn or by her natural desire for social activities. She was young and gay; Keats, a jealous, possessive, suspicious lover as well as a desperately sick man. The two were star-crossed from the beginning.

The Dilkes moved to Westminster in April, 1819, and the Brawnes were back at Wentworth Place at the latest by June.[9] Keats lived next door to them from about the middle of October till early May, 1820, and stayed in their home for a month in August-September. He saw Fanny for the last time on September 13. He never wrote to her again, nor could he bear to look at her letters, which at his request were placed, unopened, in his coffin. More than twelve years after his death, on June 15, 1833, Fanny married Louis Lindo (afterwards Lindon), who was twelve years her junior.[10] Lindon, who later became a wine merchant in London, is described by Lowell [11] as "a Spanish Jew," by Adami [12] as "a Jewish banker," and by Askwith [13]

[6] Page 329.

[7] *Letters*, p. xxx; Edgcumbe. p. 56.

[8] *Letters*, p. 297.

[9] The same, pp. 291, 352.

[10] According to his tombstone, he was aged sixty when he died in October, 1872. Mrs. Oswald Ellis, as quoted in the *Sphere* (p. 137), said, "Fanny Brawne was thirty-five before she accepted an offer of marriage from a man fifteen years her junior."

[11] II, 136.

[12] Page 137.

[13] Page 197.

as "of Portuguese extraction." His granddaughter, Mrs. Oswald Ellis, is quoted in the *Sphere*, May 16, 1925,[14] as saying, "Mr. Lindon chivalrously joined the British Legion in Spain for a time, and distinguished himself for courage in the fights with the Carlists," "After marriage, owing to delicate health, she mostly lived with him in Germany, with occasional visits to Boulogne and to London." Fanny Lindon had two sons, Herbert and Edmund, and a daughter Margaret. She died on December 4, 1865, by which time Keats was famous.

The lives of great men's sweethearts sooner or later become public property, and as the years went by Fanny had an unduly harsh fate. In December, 1829, Brown asked her for permission to include certain verses and prose passages referring to her in his proposed "Life and Remains" of Keats. "Your name," he said, "will still remain as secret to the world as before." Replying just about four weeks after her mother's terrible death, she made a remark that, taken out of its context, was extremely damaging: "I fear the kindest act would be to let him rest for ever in the obscurity to which unhappy circumstances have condemned him." [15] These words were given currency by Sir Charles Dilke, who in the memoir of his grandfather said: "When the first memoir was proposed, the woman he had loved had so little belief in his poetic reputation, that she wrote to Mr. Dilke, 'The kindest act would be to let him rest for ever in the obscurity to which circumstances have condemned him.' " [16] Even more damaging was the publication of the now famous love letters.

Thirty-seven of the thirty-nine letters from Keats to

[14] Page 190. Sir Charles Dilke, *Papers*, I, 34, likewise calls him "an officer in the English Legion."

[15] *Letters*, pp. lxi-lxiv.

[16] *Papers*, I, 11. He quotes them again in the *Athenaeum*, February 16, 1878, p. 218. Evidently his grandfather had copied them from the letter shown him by Brown.

Fanny were published for the first time by Forman in 1878 with a dedication to Severn. Hitherto she had been unknown to the public. Brown in 1836 [17] and Milnes in 1848 [18] and 1867 had kept her nameless, Sir Charles Dilke in 1875 had referred to her as "Miss ——" or "Miss B.," and the casual reference to "Miss Brawn" in Houghton's Aldine edition of Keats's poems (1876) may have aroused but did nothing to satisfy curiosity. The existence of the letters was, however, known to various people. At some unspecified date Sir Charles Dilke had bought them to stop publication but had surrendered them on the demand of Herbert Lindon.[19] Previously Sir Charles had shown them to Houghton, who considered them unfit for the press (No. 278), and to whom Lindon offered to sell them in December, 1876 (No. 292). When the offer was rejected, Forman came into the picture. Just how is not clear. In a prefatory "Note" he says that Mrs. Lindon herself "did not, towards the end of her life, regard their ultimate publication as unlikely; and it is by her family that they have been entrusted to the editor." Mrs. Ellis,[20] however, authorized the statement that "Margaret Lindon was obliged, owing to illness and some financial troubles, to part with the Keats letters for a hundred pounds."

Keats himself had considered, even if jocosely, the possibility that the letters would be printed. "Not intending," he told Fanny, "that there shall be any interruption to our correspondence (which at some future time I propose offering to [John] Murray) I write something." [21] Few important men and women can, unless they are incredibly naive, overlook such a possibility. None the less, the publication of the letters caused

[17] See II, 27, 71.
[18] As at II, 33, 74f. Milnes once (I, 243f.) referred to her as a woman who "has preserved his [Keats's] memory with a sacred honour."
[19] See II, 353n.
[20] In the *Sphere* article cited above.
[21] *Letters*, p. 482.

a sensation in Great Britain and America, most of it highly unfavorable to their recipient and editor (No. 297), and Miss Brawne's reputation suffered more than her lover's. But Lowell's opinion sounds more reasonable than that of critics around 1878: "Far from condemning the suggestion which induced her children, years after her death, to permit the publication of these same letters, we should esteem it the crowning act of a love that, with the contemplation of years, had become heroic." [22]

Meanwhile, Mrs. Lindon, still anonymously, had contributed a judicious and discriminating analysis of Keats to Thomas Medwin's life of Shelley (1847).[23] Even so, it was more or less fashionable after 1878 to characterize her as unworthy of the poet's adoration. Thus R. H. Stoddard presented her as a "cold, hard, haughty young woman," who cared nothing for her lover's poetry and made him ridiculous in life and after death.[24] Similarly an English reviewer [25] of Lowell asserted that Fanny "was probably in love with Keats as far as she was able," "she was a flirt and a coquette," "all Keats's friends . . . without exception deplored his having fallen in love" with Fanny, who "was in some part responsible" for his "swift and sudden death." Hence Colvin [26] can scarcely be blamed for deciding that "she did not half realize what manner of man he was, nor how high and privileged was the charge committed to her. She had no objection to the prospect of a long engagement, and despite her lover's remonstrances held herself free in the meantime to enjoy to the full the pleasures of her age and the admiration of other men." This characterization was influenced by what a cousin of

[22] II, 136.
[23] Ed. Forman (1913), pp. 294-297.
[24] *Appleton's Journal*, IV (1878), 382.
[25] *TLS*, March 19, 1925, p. 178.
[26] Page 330.

1

Fanny's is said to have told a reporter around 1889: [27] he stressed her vanity and desire for admiration, and twice insisted that she did not 'care for' Keats.

Even in 1818–1820 Fanny made a poor impression on the Keats circle. George, as she herself realized, "never liked me." [28] Brown thought she had "many faults," even though he enjoyed flirting with her then and, years later, called her the person who knew Keats best. "No greater honour can be paid to a woman," he added, "than to be beloved by such a man." [29] At a first meeting Severn formed a poor impression of her, and to him she "always seemed a cold and conventional mistress." [30] Dilke (or perhaps his wife) wrote: "It is quite a settled thing between Keats and Miss ——. God help them. It's a bad thing for them. The mother says she cannot prevent it, and that her only hope is that it will go off." [31] As an old man William Dilke (No. 279)

[27] Colvin refers incorrectly to the New York *Herald*, April 12, 1889, and Lowell and the rest merely quote him. The editor of the *Herald* (like the editors of the New York *World* and *Times*) informs me that his indexes show no reference at all to Fanny Brawne. No copy of the Paris edition of the *Herald*, April 12, 1889 (if Colvin referred to *it*), is available in America, England, or Paris. Against the cousin's testimony might be placed that of Rosa Perrins (*Literary World*, August 11, 1893, p. 109), who, objecting to a reviewer's dismissal of Fanny as "a commonplace girl," remarked: "It is not true! Miss Brawne was my mother's great friend, and I knew her well up to the time I was almost fifteen, when she left England. She was a very striking, dignified woman; . . . very clever, and most brilliant in society. I remember my mother saying she was a most lovely girl, but that she lost all her beautiful colour in an illness [after Keats's death]."

[28] See I, cvi.

[29] *Letters*, pp. 520, lxi.

[30] So Sharp, pp. 38f., but in October, 1845 (No. 181), Severn told Milnes that she was "devotedly attached to Keats & his fame." Again in the *Union Magazine*, February, 1846 (I, 157), he wrote that Keats's "was a real and honourable love, which, but for the separation occasioned by his direful illness, would have been blessed in a happy and advantageous marriage."

[31] *Papers*, I, 11.

asserted that Fanny had made all the advances to the poet "without really caring much for him," and that she and her mother could and should have gone with him to Italy. The whole Reynolds family were hostile to her—"that poor idle Thing of woman-kind," Reynolds called her—and they rejoiced when the journey to Italy freed him from her grasp.[32] "My friends laugh at you!" Keats himself said; "I know some of them—when I know them all I shall never think of them again as friends or even acquaintance. . . . These Laughers, who do not like you, . . . who were plying me with disencouragements with respect to you eternally." [33]

Colvin, then, is but partially right in saying that "the very few" of Keats's friends who knew of the love affair "seem to have been agreed, although they bore her no ill will, in regarding the attachment as a misfortune for him." [34] So desperate a passion for any woman would be a misfortune to any man who was dying of an incurable disease—and no less unfortunate for the woman if, like Fanny, she reciprocated it. Sir Charles Dilke [35] was not alone in thinking that Keats " 'gave in' to a passion which killed him as surely as ever any man was killed by love."

Fortunately for her reputation today, Fanny Brawne in September, 1820, came to be a friend of Keats's sister, at first by a correspondence that he had made her promise to initiate, and then by years of intimate personal association; so intimate, indeed, that after her mother's death she moved next door into the Llanos' house, where she remained until they left England sometime before March, 1832. The thirty-one letters she wrote to Fanny Keats in 1820–1824, after a long and not wholly ex-

[32] See I, cxx, 156.
[33] *Letters*, p. 500.
[34] Page 331.
[35] *Papers*, I, 7.

plained sojourn among the manuscripts of F. Holland Day in Massachusetts, were printed in 1936.[36] In them, as M. B. Forman [37] phrases it, she "emerges from some obscurity to refute silently and with dignity the unkind things that have been said about her in bygone days." Edgcumbe,[38] too, justly remarks that they show her "as a young woman of remarkable perception and imagination, keen in the observance of character and events, possessing an unusual critical faculty, and intellectually fitted to become the wife of Keats." That she grieved deeply for Keats, that she "cared for" him, is no longer questionable. "Dear Fanny," she wrote in May, 1821, "no one but you can feel with me—All his friends have forgotten him, they have got over the first shock, and that with them is all. They think I have done the same, which I do not wonder at, for I [have] taken care never to trouble them with any feelings of mine, but I can tell you who next to me (I must say *next* to me) loved him best, that I have not got over it and never shall." Probably in spite of her marriage she never did get over it.

Whether or not Fanny Brawne was beautiful (something difficult to believe when looking at her miniature) is a question of no importance. She was beautiful to Keats (as to Severn and Gerald Griffin [39]), and his love has made her immortal. A biog-

[36] Day had tried to secure permission from Herbert Lindon to publish these letters in 1891, only to be flatly refused. Earlier (October 6, 1889) Lindon had forbidden him to publish a reproduction of his mother's miniature and had requested him not to publish a photograph of her grave. Day gave the original letters to the Keats Museum in 1934, and the rough first proofs, supposedly unique, of a printed text of twenty-one from Day's abortive edition, plus two typewritten copies of the other ten, were bought by the Harvard Library around the same time. Publication of the manuscript, typewritten, and printed texts was interdicted until 1961. See Adami, pp. 233-235, 239-242, and Rollins, *PMLA*, LIX (1944), 203f., n.

[37] In Edgcumbe, p. vi.

[38] Pages xxviii f.

[39] See I, cix, 286, and *Letters*, p. lx.

raphy of Keats that ignored his letters to her and her letters to his sister would be like *Hamlet* with Hamlet, or at any rate Ophelia, omitted.

CHARLES (ARMITAGE) BROWN

On November 14, 1889, F. Holland Day, of Norwood, Massachusetts, wrote to Charles Brown, Jr. ("Carlino"), at Taranaki, New Zealand, asking about a portrait of his father, Keats's friend. Major Brown replied on January 2, 1890, forwarding a photograph of the bust by Andrew Wilson, which is now in the Keats Museum, Hampstead. Day wrote again on March 3 and March 11, requesting biographical details, and Major Brown replied on July 12, enclosing a so-called "Memoir" (likewise dated July 12) which was seen and to some extent used by Lowell, but which has not been printed. In its compilation Major Brown made use of Sir Sidney Lee's sketch in the *DNB*, repeating a few of its errors and adding others of his own. But the sketch has some new material and is genuinely interesting. It follows:

Charles Armitage Brown

Born, June 1786 in Grey's Walk, now Regent St— Lambeth. The house was large, and isolated, a hundred and forty houses having since been built on the property. He was the sixth son, and as the others <had to go> went out into the world, he had to take his turn at defending the house from burglars, with a blunderbuss, his <mother> mother, who was always on the alert, turning him out to accompany her. On one occassion he stopped the washing copper and chain from going over the garden wall, and on another occassion the burglars were boring holes in the front door, to take a piece out, and insert a boy to undo the fastenings, before they were stopped.

At fourteen, he was occupying a stool in a merchant's office, at a salary of forty pounds a year; and at eighteen he [*page 2*] was

liv

a merchant in Peter[s]burg, assisted by the firm he <had> left, and in partnership with his elder brother John, who represented the firm in London. While in Petersburg, he became engaged to a Miss Kennedy, <a> whose mother was governess to the Grand Duke Michael;[1] the lady jilted him for an apparently wealthier english merchant, who became a bankrupt and died, a year or two after. Brown received an intimation afterwards at Hampsted, through a mutual friend, that he could be introduced to the <lady> widow, if he desired it, but he had suffered too keenly to forget or forgive the injury; and it was his intention in after life, to gibbet the lady in a novel that he commenced, but which was not completed. After some years of prosperity, in which the firm accumulated some £20,000 of capital, the firm, in anticipation of the war, in which Russia [*page 3*] joined France against us,[2] invested largely beyond their means in bristles; Brown said that he had reason to deplore the inventive faculties of John Bull, for while the firm held the bristles for a high price, someone invented splitting whalebone as a substitute, and <while> before the worthles[s]ness of the substitute was discovered, the acceptances of the firm matured, were dishonored, and the firm became bankrupt. He suffered great privations after this, as he was too independant to ask for any assistance, often living on one meal a day, where he got it for four pence, and the knives and forks were chained to the table; until his brother James in India, with whom he was a favorite, appointed him his agent in London. James, through the influence of Sir Stamford Raffles,[3] was a Resident at Crowes under the East India Coʸ [*page 4*] on the return of James to England, in a dying state, from Malay poison, administered in India, he kept up his attachment to his brother Charles, and when he died, a few months later, he left him the competence which allowed him to lead a <literary life after-

---

[1] Youngest son of Czar Paul I, born in 1798 (see Pierre Morane, *Paul Iᵉʳ de Russie* [1907], p. 289).

[2] Alexander I concluded a treaty with Napoleon at Tilsit in July, 1807, and in the following October broke off relations with England. For a contemporary account see H. E. Lloyd's *Alexander I* (1826), pp. 115f.

[3] On Raffles (1781–1826) see Sir Reginald Coupland, *Raffles of Singapore* (1946). Lowell, I, 470, remarks that James Brown "was one of that corps of local 'residents' set up by the East India Company in those various districts of India under its control."

wards> life of literary leisure afterwards. In 1814, he wrote a comic opera, entitled "Narensky or the road to Yaroslaff" [4] with music by Braham and Reeve,[5] it was produced at Drury Lane on 11 Jan 1814, and its success was sufficient to reward him with £300, and free admission for life to Drury Lane Theatre, but he said, that he got more than it was worth, and destroyed every copy of the <libet> libreto that he could get hold of. Some time after this,[6] he made the acquaintance of Keats and his brothers, through Charles Wentworth Dilke, who was his [*page 5*] neighbour at Hampstead, and had been a schoolfellow of his. In July 1818 Brown and Keats made a walking tour in the North of Scotland; some of the letters that Brown wrote to Dilke, from time to time on this trip, appear in Dilke's "Papers of a Critic" [7]—he also wrote an account of the trip under the title of "Walks in the North" which appeared in the "Plymouth Journal"—(between 1836 & 1840) [8] On their return from Scotland, in August,[9] Brown and Keats joined in housekeeping, in Brown's house, Wentworth Place, Hampstead, and there the former introduced Keats to Mrs Brawne and her daughter Fanny. While here, Keats wrote the play of "Otho"—of which Brown supplied the plot. In April 1819, Keats wrote some verses on Brown, which appear in the various editions of his works.[10] In August 1819, when [*page 6*] Brown left Keats at Winchester, he went over to Ireland and married Abigail Donohoo, a handsome woman of the peasant class; the marriage was performed by a catholic priest, and therefore not legal, but as she was a bigoted catholic, and Irish, she was

[4] In the preface, dated at 16 Clement's Inn, January 13, 1814, Brown says the opera "was written nearly five years ago. The Plot is founded on an event which occurred in Russia, during my residence there."

[5] John Braham (1774?-1856), singer, and William Reeve (1757-1815), actor and musical composer.

[6] According to his own statement (see II, 57), Brown was introduced to Keats "in the latter part" of the summer, 1817, "on the Hampstead road."

[7] This sentence follows *DNB* closely.

[8] *Plymouth and Devonport Weekly Journal*, October 1, 8, 15, 22, 1840.

[9] So *DNB*, which is closely followed in this sentence and the two subsequent sentences. Actually Keats began to live with Brown after Tom's death on December 1, 1818.

[10] "Character of Charles Brown," *Letters*, pp. 324f., Garrod, p. 497.

satisfied with the blessing of the priest, and cared not for the illegality. In 1820 Keats left for Rome, Brown had hurried back from another pedestrian tour in Scotland, to see Keats before he left, but was too late; the ships in which the two friends were, were, unknown to each other, at anchor off Gravesend, the same night.[11] While he was absent in Scotland, his son was born, in July 1820. Owing to the mother's bigotry, and peculiarities of temper, Brown feared that she might appeal to Chancery to <deprive him of his boy> give her legal custody of the [*page 7*] boy, on the same grounds that Shelley had been deprived of his children. He therefore transferred himself, with his boy to Italy. From Paris, he travelled with Mrs Edwards and her boy, who was going to join her husband, Capt Edwards, in Turkey or Egypt. Mrs Edwards was a daughter of Hope, the author of "Anastasius" [12]— On their way, they stopped with Prince Duboin,[13] at Chambery, a friend of Hope, or of Capt. Edwards. Either here, or shortly after, they parted, and when Brown reached <at> Milan, he fell in with a Mr Tupper, he proved to be Lord Charles Murray,[14] <he> Brown felt very great sympathy with

[11] See II, 79, and No. 73.

[12] Thomas Hope (1770?–1831), F.R.S., F.S.A., patron of Canova, Flaxman, Chantrey, and Thorwaldsen, published *Anastasius, or Memoirs of a Greek* anonymously in 1819, at which time it was thought worthy of Byron.

[13] Not mentioned in P. L. Lainé's *Dictionnaire véridique des origines des maisons nobles* (1818) or N. Batjin's *Histoire complète de la noblesse de France* (1862).

[14] Lord Charles Murray was the sixth son of John Murray, fourth Duke of Atholl (1755–1830), by his second wife, Margery Forbes, widow of John Mackenzie, Lord Macleod. Charles was born in London on March 11, 1799, and died at Gastouni, Greece, on August 11, 1824. (Felicia Hemans tried to immortalize him in one of her miscellaneous poems called "To the Memory of Lord Charles Murray, Son of the Duke of Atholl, Who Died in the Cause and Lamented by the People of Greece.") His half-brother John, the fifth duke (born 1778), became *non compos mentis* in 1798 and died in 1846. See Sir James Balfour Paul, *The Scots Peerage*, I (1904), 498; Vicary Gibbs, *The Complete Peerage*, I (1910), 320f.; and the biographical sketches in *Blackwood's*, October (XVI, 390), and the *Gentleman's Magazine*, November, 1824 (XCIV, 465f.). The last account says that Murray's "death was occasioned by a most violent pain in the head."

lvii

him, as he believed him to be perfectly sane; from Lord C. Murray's account, he had escaped from a private lunatic asylum in <Auckland En> England, and had begged his way to Bristol, from whence he worked his way in a <s> vessel to one of the northern ports of Italy, he then made his way to Milan, [*page 8*] under the name of Tupper; he there received an intimation that it would be desirable for him to leave Lombardy as the "Code Napoleon" was still in force there, which dealt severely with all persons assuming an alias. They went on to Pisa, where they resided with a worthy Italian family of the name of Gordini. Lord Charles Murray subsequently went on to Greece, and it is believed, <was> died, or was killed there. When at Pisa, Brown became acquainted with Trelawny and Lord Byron, on one occassion he had to thank the latter for setting something right in reference to the "Liberal," when Brown for the first <on> and only time, gave him his title, which Byron immediately noticed by a quick glance. Leigh Hunt was also at Pisa, who was an old friend of Brown's, he afterwards moved to Maiano,[15] near Florence. Leaving his boy with the Italian family at Pisa that he [*page 9*] had been stopping with, he went to Rome to see Keats's resting place, learn from Severn, and acquaint himself, with the last reminiscenses of his friend Keats. He then went to Naples and Venice, visiting Verona, and learning all he could on the spot, of Romeo & Juliet, the Montegue's and Capulets; it is believed that Severn and Brown travelled together on this occassion. After about a twelvemonth,[16] he called at Pisa for his boy and went on to Florence, where he resided till he left Italy. Here, Hazlitt wished to make the acquaintance of Walter Savage Landor, and as the latter bore the character of being stern, and unapproachable, Hazlitt was very nervous about it, and asked Brown to manage it for him, which he did by taking Hazlitt to Landor's house, and introducing Hazlitt and himself, as having come to see him; Landor [*page 10*] soon put Hazlitt at his ease.[17] The friendship thus commenced be-

[15] Some two miles from Fiesole.

[16] *Apparently* twelvementh.

[17] John Forster, *Walter Savage Landor* (Boston, 1869), p. 434, tells another story, quoting Seymour Kirkup forty years after Hazlitt's call was made early in 1825: "He wished to pay Landor a visit, but was advised not, unless he was well introduced. Armitage Brown, who was Landor's greatest friend here, offered him a letter; but Hazlitt said he would

tween Brown and Landor, lasted for the remainder of their lives.
Before Brown left England, he often wrote the musical critiques in
the Examiner, and contributed to Colburn's New Monthly Magazine, to which he also contributed from Florence. In Italy he wrote
two papers in the "Liberal"—"Les Charmettes and Rousseau" signed
Carlone, and "Shakespeare's Fools" signed Carluccio, he also wrote
a tale that appears in <that portion of> the Literary Examiner,
under the name of "La Bella Tabaccaia" [18]— Leigh Hunt was so
impressed with it, that he was going to Pescia to see the hero and
heroine, when Brown told him that they had no existence. For
some years, Seymour Kirkup,[19] the artist, joined Brown in housekeeping, and when that ceased, Trelawny took Kirkup's place.
About 1828, Brown rewrote for Trelawny, for publication, "The
Adventures of a Younger [*page 11*] Son"—M[rs] Shelley had tried it,
and given it up.[20] Trelawny recognized Brown's assistance, by divid-
ing with him the proceeds of the two editions that were published.
Trelawny, <on the arriv> soon after the arrival of his little girl,
Zella,[21] from Greece, set up housekeeping on his own account.

When his boy was fourteen, he thought it time to complete
his education in England, and accordingly removed to Plymouth

---

beard the lion in his den," went alone "one winter's morning," was
well received, and often returned. P. P. Howe, *The Life of William
Hazlitt* (1922), pp. 377f., merely quotes Forster. Incidentally, Brown in
October, 1830, related "anecdotes of Hazlitt's personal cowardice, as well
as of his slovenliness, and says he was the worst-tempered man he ever
knew" (Edith J. Morley, *Henry Crabb Robinson*, I [1938], 387), while
Landor quarreled with Brown over the latter's bringing "up his boy on
the principle of letting him do what he liked" and declared "Brown's
son to be the wickedest boy he had ever known, but the father was a
kind man, he said" (the same, pp. 387f.).

[18] So *DNB*. The three works named are reprinted in M. B. Forman's
Some Letters, pp. 59-108.

[19] See I, 227n.

[20] Published anonymously in 1831. Mrs. Shelley did her editing and arranged for the publication after both Brown—whom Trelawny (*Letters*,
ed. Forman [1910], p. 140) called "a plain downright Cockney critic"—
and Landor had seen the manuscript.

[21] Born about June, 1826; by his Greek wife Tersitza (or Tarsitsa)
Kamenou.

in 1834; [22] but he found himself very much disappointed in his son, who he hoped would have been a companion to him in his literary and artistic tastes; the bent of his mind being mechanical, though, subsequently, after Brown's death, the son, by the force of circumstances in New Zealand, had to abandon his engineering experience, and for many years, to make use of his pen.

[*Page 12*] While at Plymouth, he completed a translation of the first five Cantos of Boiardo's "Orlando Innamorato"—which Lord Houghton spoke of as "admirable." His best known literary work is, "Shakespeare's Autobiographical Poems, <&c—"> being his Sonnets clearly developed, with his Character drawn chiefly from his Works"—London 1838.[23] Brown dedicated the book to Landor, with whom he had <discussed> first discussed its subject in Florence in 1828. It is Brown's endeavour to show that Shakespeare's sonnets conceal a fairly complete autobiography of the poet, and although Boaden had suggested a similar view in 1812, Brown was the first to treat it with adequate fulness or knowledge. Brown often illustrates Shakespeare from Italian literature, with which he was widely acquainted. Lord Houghton says that Keats learnt from Brown [24] all that he knew of Ariosto [*page 13*] and that Brown let scarcely a day pass in Italy without translating from the Italian. Various references to Brown in the letters of his literary friends, among whom Hazlitt and Leigh Hunt are to be included, prove that he was at all times excellent company. Leigh Hunt is believed to refer to him in the 'Tatler' [25] for 14 Jan 1831 as 'one of the most genuine wits now living.' [26] He assumed the name of "Armitage" a family name on the mother's side, when he published 'Shakespeare's Autobiographical Poems &c"—bearing in mind what Trelawny said to him, 'Brown, your name is that of a tribe, not of a family'— <At> He wrote very effectively in the "Plymouth Journal" during an election, in support of Mr Bewes, also some doggerel verses, and

---

[22] *DNB* says he returned in April, 1837. [23] See II, 33.

[24] Forty-eight stanzas of Canto I of Brown's Boiardo are reprinted by M. B. Forman, *Some Letters*, pp. 124-138, from the *West of England Magazine*, November, 1838. Milnes's comments (II, 50) were annotated by Dilke: "I do not believe that Brown could, at the time, read ten lines without a dictionary."

[25] II, 454.

[26] Most of the paragraph to this point follows *DNB*.

political skits, that were very telling and successful, so much so, that after Mr Bewes was elected, [27] Brown received the offer, through [*page 14*] the proprietor of the Journal, of a clerkship in the Customs for his son; he left it to his son to decide, who declined it.

In <July> 1840 he decided to emigrate to New Zealand, his health had been failing for some years, he felt annoyed at the fancied or real, clerical intolerance of a provincial town, as an avowed freethinker and <radical> liberal; several severe accidents had happened in the factory where his son was working in Sussex, to whom he was much attached; he felt his growing loneliness, and determined on becoming a settler under the Plymouth Co^y of New Zealand, from whom he purchased land orders in their settlement of New Plymouth, which proved to be in the Taranaki district. He sent his son out in the early part of 1841 [28] to prepare for his arrival, and wished his son [*page 15*] marry before he left, but the son declined to take a wife to a country that he had no wish to go to himself; [29] <he> Brown finally left <New> England about the middle of 1841 for his new home. For a short time, he rather enjoyed the change, but when he realized the want of congenial society; of new books and periodicals, with not even a newspaper, and that he had destroyed his son's prospects to no purpose, he determined to return to England, leaving his son in New Zealand; before however he could complete his arrangements, he died on his birthday, in June 1842 of apoplexy [30] at the age of <42> 56—

He was a very fair artist, with his pencil, and with watercolors. He was methodical, hospitable, kind hearted, and very cool in the presence of danger. At one [*page 16*] time, when the bargemen on the Arno, were in straits through a long drought, and stopped belated persons, <near> in the vicinity of Florence for money, he always refused to take any firearms, but if he had no

[27] Thomas Bewes, M.P. for Plymouth, first appears in the *Royal Kalendar* for 1833, p. 77.

[28] See Nos. 164 and 168.

[29] Brown himself (see II, 50f.) supports this statement.

[30] An anonymous writer in *TLS*, June 6, 1942, p. 284, says he died on June 5. Trelawny (*Letters*, p. 215) said in 1858: "Our old friend Brown was subject to those attacks for many years—but then he was a huge feeder." He calls them epilepsy. Sharp, p. 175, speaks of both apoplexy and epilepsy,

money <he> would borrow a few dollars to satisfy the necessities of the bargemen, who he considered ought to be pitied, and not shot. He had a great dislike to hereditary distinctions and as he said, he "Would never put his legs under a Lord's table"— When Sir Robert Lawley was made Lord Wenlock,[31] to pass the Reform Bill, he said he hoped Brown would make an exception in his favor, but they drifted apart.

Landor suggested to the son, in 1848, that he should collect, and publish, a collection of Brown's writings, but when it was mentioned to Trelawny, the latter said [*page 17*] that they were only of interest at the time, and not worth republishing, that his friends would subscribe for the book, because they would not like to refuse; these remarks prevented any further action.

A number of Keats's manuscripts were in Brown's possession on the poet's death, and Brown determined to publish some of them with a memoir by himself. He printed a few of Keats's unpublished works in the 'New Monthly Magazine" but a short biographical sketch which he wrote of his friend was refused by the booksellers, and by the 'Morning Chronicle"— On leaving England, Brown made over all his manuscripts relating to Keats to R. Monckton Milnes, afterwards Lord Houghton, whom he first met at Landor's house at Fiesole in 1833. In his [*page 18*] well known book on Keats, Lord Houghton made a free use of Brown's papers.[32]

Included in the foregoing, are two extracts from the life of Brown in the "Dictionary of National Biography"
N.P—N.Z.   C. Brown
12/7/90

Brown was for about two years Keats's most intimate associate. Of his kindness and devotion there can be no doubt, just as there is no doubt also that he regarded Keats's presence in Wentworth Place—where the great odes and "La Belle Dame sans Merci" were written—as a business affair. When Keats was ill, Brown acted as nurse. The poet told his sister, on March 13,

[31] Lawley (1768–1834) was created second Baron Wenlock on September 10, 1831.
[32] This paragraph comes from *DNB*. Milnes refers to meeting Brown at Landor's in the opening sentence of his preface.

1819, that Brown, a friend "of two years standing" had been "very kind to me in many things when I most wanted his assistance," and on October 16 that "without him I should have been in, perhaps, personal distress." [33] But, illness or no illness, Brown followed his custom of renting the house during the summer, so that in July, 1819, Keats was forced to go to the Isle of Wight with Rice, and thence with Brown to Winchester; and, characteristically, after Keats's death, Brown presented a bill for board and room to George Keats, who paid it (No. 277).

Life with Brown can scarcely have been unalloyed bliss: his unconventional domestic affairs must have given considerable emotional disturbance to the hopeless lover of Fanny Brawne. Lowell,[34] following "Carlino," tells a very confused story of Brown's illegal marriage to Abigail Donohue. She says that during "three weeks" in September, 1819, he visited Chichester and Bedhampton, and then went to Ireland, where a Catholic priest performed the ceremony. She says further that "Brown never seems to have had any intention of acknowledging the marriage, or of living with his wife," that a son Carlino was born to them probably in June, 1820, and that "for two years Brown left him with his mother." She is also "certain" that "Keats himself . . . never knew of Brown's marriage, or of the birth of his child." Her certainty is ill-founded. There is no proof that Brown went to Ireland (even if he *could* have gone to Chichester, Bedhampton, and Ireland and back in less than three weeks), and, indeed, all the evidence points to his having married Abigail in London.

Brown's granddaughter, Mrs. Mona Osborne, wrote from New Zealand in 1939 [35] that Abigail was for a time Brown's

---

33 *Letters*, pp. 288, 437.

34 I, 471f., II, 311, 409n. Askwith, p. 242, asserts that Brown took Abby to Ireland in April, 1820, and then married her.

35 See Askwith, pp. 277-280. Abigail was probably "Our irish Servant" who "piqued" Keats in January, 1820 (*Letters*, pp. 452f.).

housekeeper at Wentworth Place, that he "sometimes . . . went to Abigail's domain downstairs to provoke" her "great gift of repartee" (other reasons may be suspected), and that when he decided to marry her "some of his friends tried to persuade him not to." Keats may very well have been one of the objecting friends, as Rice certainly was,[36] and it is at least possible that one of the "sundry reasons" [37] for his decision to live at 25 College Street, Westminster, was his dislike of sharing Wentworth Place with Brown and Abby.

Carlino gave the date of his own birth as July, 1820, and, since he had a copy of the birth certificate, which was seen by Mrs. Osborne,[38] July needs no questioning. It follows that Brown and Abigail were living together, not in September, but in October or November, and it appears certain that she was an inmate of Brown's house, to which after a few days in College Street—around October 16—Keats returned, "being induced to it by the habit I have acquired of this room," by a desire of avoiding "any petty attentions to a diminutive house-keeping," [39] and of course by his longing to be near Fanny Brawne. Here he lived from mid-October to early May, and that he knew all about Abby and her son is sufficiently obvious from the coarse expressions in Brown's letter of December 21, 1820: "I must tell you Abby is living with me again, but not in the same capacity,—she keeps to her own bed, & I keep myself continent.

[36] See M. B. Forman, *Some Letters*, p. 26, for Rice's comments to Brown and his alleged gossip about Brown and Abby during 1822–1823. Thomas Richards (the same, pp. 7, 9-11, 25f.) and the Dilkes also knew all about Abby and Carlino.

[37] *Letters*, p. 431.

[38] Askwith, p. 278. The certificate spelled her name as "Donaghue," whereas Mrs. Osborne says that Carlino and the family used "O'Donaghue." In the "Memoir" Carlino has "Donohoo"; M. B. Forman, in *Some Letters*, gives it as "Donohue" and Lowell as "Donohue" or "Donahue."

[39] *Letters*, p. 437.

. . . Our child is very well. She [Abby] behaves extremely well, and, by what I hear from Sam [Brawne], my arrangements prevent the affair from giving pain next door" [40]—that is, to Mrs. Brawne and Fanny. Keats may possibly refer to both the Browns when in his final letter to Fanny Brawne (August [?], 1820) he says, "wherever I may be next winter in Italy or nowhere Brown will be living near you with his indecencies." [41]

During Keats's serious illness of February, 1820, Brown was unremitting in his attentions. That Abby likewise did some of the nursing may be inferred from a statement made by Carlino in his letter of July 12, 1890: "My father told me that my mother several times carried Keats from one room to another, at Hampstead." One might have supposed that Brown would have spent the summer of 1820 in Hampstead to look after his desperately ill friend. Instead, he rented the house, packed Abby off somewhere to bear her child, and started for Scotland after telling Keats goodby forever on May 7. The unhappy poet moved to Kentish Town to be near, and later with, the Leigh Hunts. On August 12 he was back at Wentworth Place, this time in the Brawnes' half of the house, already having been advised by the doctors to spend the winter in Italy. Even "speaking to an unaccostomed Person" suffocated him, while the mere thought of the "Journey to Italy wakes me at daylight every morning and haunts me horribly." These things made him forget that a month or so earlier he had written to Fanny Brawne about her flirtations with Brown: "Brown is a good sort of Man—he did not know he was doing me to death by inches . . . and . . . though he has done me many services, though I know his love and friendship for me, though at this moment I should be without pence were it not for his assistance, I will never see or speak to him until we are both old men, if we are

[40] *Letters*, p. 529.
[41] The same, p. 503.

to be." [42] Instinctively and confidently he wrote, asking Brown to be his traveling companion.[43]

In the only available texts of two letters [44] Brown carefully deleted these requests. In the biography he presents his own conduct in the best possible light, and says, "I contented myself with preparing to follow him very early in the spring, and not return should he prefer to live there." Fanny Brawne, too, believed that he would follow Keats "in a very few weeks,"[45] but obviously he had no intention whatever of resuming his role of nurse-companion, this time in a foreign land. As Dilke noted in 1848: "Keats *died* Feby 1821 and Brown *started* for Italy in July or August 1822! fifteen or sixteen months after he was *dead!*" [46] In his last letter Keats speaks of his "love" for Brown, just as some eight weeks earlier he had written, "I should think of—you in my last moments." [47] Brown thought first of himself, though he was foot-loose. "So you still wish me to follow you to Rome?" he wrote on December 21, three months after Keats had left London; "and truly I wish to go,— nothing detains me but prudence. Little could be gained, if any thing, by letting my house at this time of the year, and the consequence would be a heavy additional expence which I cannot possibly afford,—unless it were a matter of necessity, and I see none while you are in such good hands as Severn's." [48] Brown was apparently staggered at the news of Keats's death. Shortly thereafter, he recovered sufficiently to assume, no doubt with Taylor's approval, some of the functions of an executor; he drew up a list of Keats's books (No. 122), and distributed them

[42] *Letters*, pp. 508, 496.
[43] See also his letter of August 23 to Haslam printed by Hewlett, p. 425.
[44] See II, 77-79.
[45] Edgcumbe, p. 4 (September 18, 1820).
[46] Bodurtha, p. 116.
[47] *Letters*, pp. 526, 521.
[48] The same, p. 528.

among the dead poet's eighteen closest friends, including himself and Fanny Keats, omitting George Keats and Haydon.

Although in December, 1820, Brown and Abby were living together in Wentworth Place, the ménage was soon broken up, for he wrote on November 15, 1821, to Thomas Richards, "my poor boy is kept aloof from me by his obstinate Mother." [49] By the following March, however, he had charge of Carlino, and was considering leaving him with the Richards'. But Abby "rather *entreated*" Brown to take the child to Italy,[50] and he did so shortly thereafter. Whether Abby played any further role in his life does not appear. He speaks of her with the utmost callousness, and his remarks were almost equaled by those of her son. The latter, with impersonal detachment, informed Day, a complete stranger, "from what my father told me, he chose her for her splendid physique, for the sake of the offspring." He added a further detail: about 1828, when Brown was forty-two, his son eight, "Lady D King asked my father to join housekeeping with her, in North Italy; he talked it over with me, as he did almost everything, and I said, that with the two incomes (hers was double my father's) that they could live more comfortably, my father replied 'Yes, that is true, and of course the understanding would be, that it was a platonic arrangement, but I doubt if it would continue so, and *that* would not be good for your interests'—and he declined it, she was a very fine woman of 40."

During his twelve years in Italy Brown often thought of writing a biography of Keats, a project that Taylor had publicly announced in 1821 and 1822. On this matter the Keats circle was hopelessly split. As a biographer Taylor was opposed by Brown, Severn, Richards, Hunt, and for a time Dilke,[51] while

---

[49] M. B. Forman, *Some Letters*, p. 7.
[50] The same, pp. 9-11.
[51] Sharp, pp. 110-112.

Taylor, Woodhouse, Reynolds, George Keats, and ultimately Dilke were even more hostile to Brown. The unhappy squabbles of these former friends may be followed in the pages of Sharp and Bodurtha. Here it will suffice to say that in 1829 Brown finally made up his mind to write the life, and communicated his decision to, and asked for help from, Hunt, Dilke, Fanny Brawne, and Severn. Unluckily, Dilke and Brown had never seen eye to eye about George Keats's financial transactions, though they must have discussed the subject amicably when Dilke was in Italy. At any rate Dilke left his son Charles for more than a year (1826–1828) in Brown's keeping. Soon afterwards they came to a definite parting of ways. Dilke wrote George (February 12, 1833): "As to Brown . . . the correspondence about *your brother's* life has put a stop [to] all communication. I expressed my opinion on the subject with that straightforwardness which our whole life's intimacy justified, & he has in consequence broken off all further correspondence with me. —I regret this because our intimacy & friendship *was of five & thirty years standing.*" Then in 1838 even their "formal civility terminated." [52]

The enmity of Dilke and George was in itself enough to check Brown, who, however, for seven weeks in the autumn of 1832 entertained Woodhouse, now a powerful ally, in his home near Florence, and promised him "to write the life of Keats . . . during this winter." [53] But Brown did not write, and shortly after he had returned to England and settled at Laira Green, near Plymouth, George empowered Dilke to enjoin the publication of any of his brother's works.[54] The threatened injunction put a stop to Brown's plan of publishing the poems he had collected, but in the summer of 1835 he determined to begin

[52] See II, 33.
[53] Sharp, p. 170.
[54] The same, pp. 177, 186f.

writing a biographical sketch. This he managed to complete in time for a public reading in Plymouth on December 27, 1836 (No. 154). The sketch, which is brief and in nearly all respects disappointing, is printed below (No. 166), and its subsequent history may be followed in Sharp [55] and in Nos. 168-170. With no idea of its shortcomings and limitations, Brown made several unsuccessful efforts to secure a publisher. When early in 1841 publication did become available, he was busy in preparations for his migration to New Zealand. By that time, furthermore, George had waived his legal rights to the "literary remains." [56] Passing deliberately over all Keats's friends, and choosing a man who had never seen the poet, in March Brown asked Milnes to write the book and, when the latter promptly accepted, forwarded all the manuscripts in his possession. He then sailed from Plymouth, and a year later died.

Brown was a strange mixture of coarseness, kindliness, cold-bloodedness, and calculation. The finest tribute ever paid him is the comment written in 1848 by his enemy Dilke:[57]

He was the most scrupulously honest man I ever knew—but wanted nobleness to lift this honesty out of the commercial kennel. He would have forgiven John what he owed him with all his heart —but had John been able and offered to pay, he would have charged interest, as he did to George. He could do generous things too—but not after the fashion of the world and therefore they were not appreciated by the world. His sense of justice led him at times to do acts of generosity—at others of meanness—the latter was always noticed, the former overlooked—therefore amongst his early companions he had a character for anything rather than liberality— but he was liberal.

[55] Pages 186f., 191-197. On May 6, 1837, Severn told Crabb Robinson (Edith J. Morley, *Henry Crabb Robinson*, II [1938], 520) that Brown "is to write a life" of Keats, who "was fleeced by Haydon and Leigh Hunt."
[56] Sharp, p. 191.
[57] In his copy of Milnes (Morgan Library). The passage is printed in *Letters*, p. li. See also George Keats's sketch (No. 151).

BIOGRAPHICAL SKETCHES

DR. (SIR) JAMES CLARK

Clark was born in Cullen, Banffshire, in 1788, and educated at the University of Aberdeen. He became a member of the Edinburgh College of Surgeons in 1809, served for some time in the Royal Navy as an assistant surgeon, and received the degree of M.D. from the University of Edinburgh in 1817. In the next year he accompanied a consumptive patient to France and Switzerland, and in 1819 began to practise at Rome. Presumably Dr. Darling made arrangements for him to look after Keats, who wrote Brown in August, 1820:[1] "I am to be introduced, before I set out [for Italy], to a Dr Clarke, a physician settled at Rome, who promises to befriend me in every way." Clark secured the Spanish Steps rooms, opposite his own house, for Keats and Severn. About a week after their arrival he told a friend in London:[2] Keats is "too noble an animal to be allowed to sink without some sacrifice being made to save him. I wish I were rich enough his living here should cost him nothing. . . . I feel very much interested in him."

His kindness and attention were unfailing. He called two or more times daily, and often scoured Rome for special food, which his wife cooked and brought to the two young men. Though modern writers have sometimes expressed horror or disgust at his diagnosis and treatment, Severn all his life had nothing but praise for Clark; and Milnes,[3] who also knew him, likewise eulogized "this distinguished physician, who seems to have felt it a moral duty to make his own scientific eminence the measure of his devotion to the relief and solace of all men of intellectual pursuits." Clark was not present when Keats actually died,[4] but he took charge of the funeral arrangements,

[1] See II, 79.
[2] See I, 172.
[3] II, 80f.
[4] Sharp, p. 95.

assisted in the autopsy, followed the corpse to the grave, and forced a reduction in the exorbitant charges levied on Severn for fumigating and renovating the deathroom.

Later he became physician to the king of the Belgians, the Duchess of Kent, and Queen Victoria.[5] He had resumed practise in London during 1826. Though in January, 1839, a great outcry arose because he had supposedly diagnosed as pregnancy a tumor that seven months later killed Lady Flora Hastings, lady of the bedchamber to the queen's mother, and though as a result friends and patients dropped away, he remained in favor with the queen and the prince consort. The former had created him a baronet in 1837, and when he retired in 1860 gave him a house at Bagshot Park. He died there in 1870.

Lowell[6] calls Clark "a poor doctor, with a kindly heart and a pleasant bedside manner"; Hewlett[7] agrees that he was "a poor doctor," "a pleasant doctor who prescribed pleasant tasting medicines"; and J. H. Pershing[8] condemns "his diagnosis and treatment" as "singularly inadequate, even under the then existing standards." A more generous and authoritative opinion is given by Sir William Hale-White,[9] consulting physician to Guy's Hospital: Clark was "a sound, shrewd physician, who kept abreast of the times and showed much wisdom," and whose article on consumption in the *Cyclopaedia of Practical Medicine* (1833) "is admirable; indeed, considering the time at which it was written it could hardly be bettered."

[5] He was also the physician of Charles Eliot Norton, who preserved (among the Harvard Library papers) one of his prescriptions as well as a list of drugs (laudanum, paregoric, and the like) with directions for their general use.

[6] II, 501.

[7] Page 410.

[8] *PMLA*, LV (1940), 809.

[9] *Keats as Doctor and Patient* (1938), p. 78.

BIOGRAPHICAL SKETCHES

CHARLES COWDEN CLARKE

Clarke has told in Nos. 187 and 264 the story of his relations with Keats, so that little need be said about them here. Born on December 15, 1787, he greatly influenced the literary tastes of Keats, who was seven years his junior, inspired him to write poetry, and introduced him to Leigh Hunt. In the epistle "To Charles Cowden Clarke," September, 1816, Keats apostrophizes "friend Charles," saying, "Ah! had I never seen, Or known your kindness, what might I have been? . . . And can I e'er these benefits forget? And can I e'er repay the friendly debt?" The earliest letter of Keats's yet found was written to Clarke in October, 1816;[1] also the third, fourth, seventh, and tenth (March, 1817), but there the correspondence ends. It is worthy of note that Keats addressed him as "My daintie Davie,'' "C.C.C.," and (twice) "My dear Charles," whereas he addressed all his other male friends by their surnames. Nonetheless, Clarke passed out of the Keats circle fairly early. He helped to read the proofsheets of *Endymion* in the spring of 1818, but on February 4, 1819, Keats sent through another correspondent "my particular greeting to him; with the assurance of my constant idea of him—notwithstanding our long separation and my antipathy . . . to letter writing." Just a few days later he wrote, "I have not seen . . . C.C.C. for God knows when." [2] With that remark Clarke ceases to have much interest for Keats's biography until 1846. According to his own statement, he saw Keats for the last time in 1819, apparently in February.[3] How little he knew of the poet and his friends after 1817 is shown by the fact that he met Woodhouse for the first time in

[1] In *Letters* it is dated a year too early: see I, 4.
[2] *Letters*, pp. 282, 298.
[3] Keats read him his "last finished" poem, "St. Agnes" (see II, 151).

August, 1823,[4] and only then learned the details of Keats's departure from London.

After his father's death in December, 1820, Clarke moved to London, where he and Henry Hunt set up a publishing and bookselling business at 38 Tavistock Street, Covent Garden, as successors to John and Leigh Hunt. When it failed in 1829, Clarke turned to publishing music with Alfred Novello, son of Vincent Novello, the celebrated organist and musical composer, whose house Keats had sometimes visited. Clarke had married Vincent's daughter Mary Victoria in July, 1828, and moved into the Novello house, Craven Hill Cottage, Bayswater. Henceforth he and his wife knew nearly everybody worth knowing in literary and musical circles. From 1834 to 1856 he was an accomplished and popular lecturer on literary subjects. With his wife, who in 1845 published her once valuable concordance to Shakespeare's plays, he collaborated in the so-called *Shakespeare Key* (1879) as well as in an edition of Shakespeare's works. Both husband and wife wrote many other volumes before and after they moved to Nice (1856) and then to Genoa (1861). In the Villa Novello at Genoa Clarke spent the remaining years of his life, dying, about ninety, on March 13, 1877. Mrs. Clarke, after further publications, which included *My Long Life* (1896), died there at the age of eighty-eight on January 12, 1898.

Clarke, who late in 1821 had been "thinking of writing a memoir" of Keats,[5] was of great assistance to Milnes, and he read the Keats biography with delight, finding it *"all* I could have wished for his monumental fame." [6] He never lost his admiration for the "noble-hearted" poet. In 1853, when a passage about Keats's intemperance was made public in Haydon's autobiography, he sent a spirited refutation of it to the *Examiner*

---

[4] See I, 274.
[5] The same, p. 110 (quoting Brown).
[6] See II, 235.

(July 9).[7] Then in January, 1861, he published in an American magazine his own "Recollections" of Keats.[8] Presently he felt that "there ought to be a better life of him" than Milnes's. He urged Severn to write it and to incorporate therein "my reminiscences," offering to "see the book through the press for you." [9] Severn hesitated, so that in 1875, a year after he had reprinted the "Recollections" in an English magazine, Clarke decided to issue it in book form "with some additions" and various illustrations. He died before the book could be prepared. Late in 1877 Mrs. Clarke told Severn that she hoped "to see this intended book of my dear Charles's published according to his long-cherished strong desire," [10] but her hope was unfulfilled, and in 1878 she issued the "Recollections" of Keats, not greatly changed since 1861, in the *Recollections of Writers* by herself and her husband.[11]

DR. GEORGE DARLING

Darling had an office at 29 Brunswick Square and had a large practise among men of letters and artists. He was the physician of Taylor, who presumably sent him to Keats, and his name frequently turns up in the correspondence of Taylor, Hessey, and other members of the Keats circle. Among his patients were John Scott, Hazlitt, Clare, David Wilkie, George Darley, Sir Francis Chantrey, Sir Thomas Lawrence, and Haydon. In July, 1820, Haydon wrote Keats about Darling, "on

[7] See No. 264.
[8] See II, 319n.
[9] Sharp, p. 256.
[10] The same, pp. 258, 260.
[11] A charming and valuable sketch of the Clarkes is Mrs. James T. Fields's "Two Lovers of Literature and Art," *Century Magazine*, May, 1899 (LVIII, 122-131).

whose skill I have the greatest reliance—certainly I was as bad as any body could be, and I have recovered." [1] In the memoir prefixed to Richard Ayton's *Essays* (1825) Darley observes that "with a liberality that characterizes him" Darling attended Ayton "unremittingly and gratuitously at his lodgings," calling "two or three times every day." Darling published in 1814 *An Essay on Medical Economy,* which he dedicated to Sir James Mackintosh,[2] and in 1846 a pamphlet called *Instructions for Making Unfermented Bread.* He died at the age of eighty on March 30, 1862.

Darling first examined Keats on June 22, 1820.[3] Some two weeks [4] later he called in for consultation Dr. William Lambe; and, upon the joint advice of the two physicians, Keats presently set off on the disastrous voyage to Italy.

PETER DE WINT AND WILLIAM HILTON [1]

Henry De Wint, son of a wealthy Dutch-American merchant, was born in New York City and educated in Holland. Going to London, he studied medicine and married a Miss Watson, a Scotswoman, in 1773, whereupon his father disinherited him. Henry (died 1807) settled at Stone, Staffordshire, as a physician, and there the fourth of his twelve children, Peter, was born on January 21, 1784.

On April 1, 1802, De Wint went to London as an appren-

---

[1] *Letters,* p. 509.
[2] See Nos. 31 and 36.
[3] Lowell, II, 421f.; Hale-White, *Keats as Doctor and Patient* (1938), p. 55.
[4] Lowell, II, 429f.
[1] The most reliable account of these artists is Harriet (Mrs. Peter) De Wint's *A Short Memoir of Peter De Wint and William Hilton, R.A.,* privately printed (n.d., but around 1912?), with a postscript by her granddaughter Harriet Helen Tatlock. It was used by Sir Walter Armstrong for his *Memoir of Peter De Wint* (1888).

tice to John Raphael Smith, painter and engraver, in whose house, 31 King Street, Covent Garden, he met William Hilton, a lad some two years his junior. His friendship with Hilton was "one of the longest and truest friendships in the history of art." [2] Both managed to get released from their apprenticeships in May, 1806, and shared expenses, selling pictures when they could. After a summer visit to Lincoln, where De Wint fell in love with Hilton's sister Harriet, they took rooms together in Broad Street, Golden Square, and in the autumn of 1809 moved to Norton Street, Portland Road. On June 16, 1810, De Wint married Harriet Hilton, took a house at 10 Percy Street, Rathbone Place,[3] and joined the Society of Painters in Water Colours, where he exhibited regularly for some forty years. During some of this time he was exhibiting at the Royal Academy as well. His paintings are characterized by the Redgraves as original works with "a fine sense of colour" by "a very indifferent draughtsman," a representative of "the middle-period of water-colour art." [4] On the other hand, Sparrow says, "he takes rank, both in water-colour and in oil, as a leader in modern art. . . . He is a born master of the brush, an original colourist, a genuine *painter*." [5]

Hilton, who was born at Lincoln on June 3, 1786, lived with De Wint from 1802 to 1827, when he moved to chambers in Somerset House. He exhibited paintings at the Royal Acad-

[2] W. S. Sparrow in Charles Holmes's *Masters of English Landscape Painting* (1903), p. iv. Mrs. De Wint (pp. 6f.) and Armstrong (p. 9) say that in 1803 Hilton ran away from Smith, and that when De Wint refused to reveal his friend's whereabouts Smith had him jailed. He was badly treated before Hilton, hearing of Smith's action, rushed back to resume his apprentice duties.

[3] Sparrow, p. vii (who correctly says they lived there for seventeen years); *The Picture of London, for 1815,* pp. 321f.; Mrs. De Wint, pp. 9f.

[4] Richard and Samuel Redgrave, *A Century of Painters* (2d ed., 1890), pp. 402f.

[5] Page xvi.

emy as early as 1803, and won his first prize of fifty guineas at the British Institution in 1810 for "The Citizens of Calais Delivering Their Keys to King Edward III," as well as a second prize of some £122 in 1811 for "The Entombment of Christ." In 1813 he was elected an associate of the Royal Academy, in 1819 [6] a full member, and in 1827 keeper, all the while, says Samuel Redgrave,[7] "continuing to paint great works." Hilton was a friend of most of the members of the Keats circle; he often visited Keats's publishers, and in 1822, along with Rice, Woodhouse, Taylor, Hessey, and others, he attended Reynolds' wedding.[8] He married Justina,[9] eldest daughter of Reverend G. D. Kent, of Lincoln, in February, 1828, and set up housekeeping in Somerset House. His mother died on April 12, 1835, his wife on the following October 8. Hilton never rallied from the depression caused by these deaths. Still quartered in a Royal Academy apartment (since 1836 in Trafalgar Square), he rapidly declined; he moved back to the De Wints' on December 3, 1839, and died on December 30. The Redgraves [10] call Hilton "a man of more talent than genius, and not inclined to depart from precedent; but his reputation will be maintained if his works endure." They were said to be suffering from a too lavish use of asphaltum.

One cannot help regretting with Hessey [11] that there is "no Memoir of poor Hilton—His beautiful, retiring, aimable character, and his decided genius, would form a nice subject, and it is a thousand pities that such a man should have had no

[6] So Armstrong, p. 22, and William Sandby, *The History of the Royal Academy of Arts*, I (1862), 363.
[7] *A Dictionary of Artists* (1874), p. 204.
[8] H. C. Shelley, *Literary By-Paths* (1906), p. 325.
[9] Cosmo Monkhouse in *DNB* says he married De Wint's sister.
[10] Page 250.
[11] See II, 316.

record of him preserved." Had Taylor followed Hessey's suggestion by writing such a memoir, we should know much more about both Keats and Severn than we know today.

From 1827 till his death on June 30, 1849, De Wint lived at 40 Upper Gower Street. Whereas Hilton was a man of homely habits and delicate health that kept him from enjoying "society," De Wint was a favorite with the gentry and nobility. In death he was not separated from his friend. He was buried in the churchyard of the Royal Chapel in the Savoy in the same tomb with Hilton and Hilton's wife and mother. His widow erected to the memory of him and her brother a font in the Savoy Chapel and an altar monument in Lincoln Cathedral. She died in November, 1866.

Evidently Keats met De Wint and Hilton through either Taylor or Hessey, and he was more intimate with them than readers of the *Letters* would suppose. According to M. B. Forman, he mentions the De Wints only once, Hilton three times. Actually, however, five messages in 1818 to "Percy Street," which Forman peculiarly misinterprets as referring to the Hesseys, were written about De Wint, his wife, and Hilton:

January 10 to Taylor (91 Bond Street): "Remember me to the Fleet Street Household [the Hesseys, who lived at No. 93]— And should you see any from Percy Street, give my kindest regards to them."

February 27 to Taylor: "Remember me to Percy Street."

March 21 to Taylor and Hessey: "My respects to Mrs Hessey and to Percy Street."

April 24 to Taylor: "Remember me to Hessey—Woodhouse and Percy Street."

June 21 to Taylor: "Remember me to Percy Street," after which he gives specific messages for Hilton, De Wint, and

Mrs. De Wint before sending further remembrances to Hessey and Woodhouse.

In December, 1819, when Keats was dining at De Wint's, the group of artist-guests were gossiping about Severn's having been awarded the Royal Academy medal for "The Cave of Despair." One of them spoke of Severn as "an old fellow" who had frequently tried for the medal, which at last had been granted "out of pity and not for any merit." Keats waited for De Wint or Hilton to contradict the falsehood. As they remained silent, he rose indignantly, declaring (so Severn tells) "that he would not any longer sit at the same table with such traducers and snobs," "that, as they well knew, I was a young man, and that the picture was my first attempt for a prize of any kind." Then he "abruptly left the party." [12] The incident rankled in Keats's mind. When he narrated it in Rome, he expressed fear lest Hilton would try to injure Severn and his artistic career. The fear was groundless: as Haydon [13] testifies, "A more amiable creature never lived, nor a kinder heart." Not only did Hilton make a "fine, if too precise, chalk drawing" [14] of Keats, but both he and De Wint were among the five personal friends who in 1821 contributed £10 each to a subscription for his expenses in Italy. Furthermore, in November, 1821, Hilton took the leading part in securing for Severn a three-years' pension from the Academy ("he said many things to better my unfortunate cause"), and received him "kindly" on his return to England in 1837 ("the lesson Ke[ats] gave by leaving the table must have been effectual"). [15] Yet Severn never tired of repeating Keats's story; and in August, 1838, as a guest

[12] Sharp, pp. 65f.
[13] Penrose, p. 141.
[14] Sharp, *Century Magazine*, LXXI (1906), 545, who dates it "about 1819–20."
[15] See I, 266; II, 233.

with Mrs. Shelley and Crabb Robinson at Samuel Rogers', he "told a curious anecdote of De Wint's malignity towards him." [16] As late as 1868 he spoke of Hilton's chalk drawing as "not only not like Keats" but as making "a sneaking fellow of him." He added the remarkable statement, "Keats himself thought that Hilton had some spite at him in this draw^g." [17] No doubt Severn also disliked the portrait Hilton painted "twenty years or more after Keats's death," because it is "an obvious 'fake' " from his own miniature "and is in almost no respect faithful to recognized detail." [18] A critic in the *Athenaeum* [19] stigmatizes it as "a standing disgrace" to the National Portrait Gallery.

THE DILKES

Charles Wentworth Dilke—born December 8, 1789—at an early age entered the Navy Pay Office, Somerset House, and worked there until in 1836 it was abolished and he was retired on a pension. Meanwhile, around 1808,[1] he had married Maria Dover Walker, by whom he had one son, Charles, or "Charley" (1810–1869), afterwards Sir Charles, first baronet. In 1814–1815 he brought out his useful six-volume edition of *Old English Plays*, a continuation of Robert Dodsley's *Select Collection* of 1744. In the winter of 1815–1816 with Brown, an old schoolfellow, he built in John Street, Hampstead, a double house

[16] Edith J. Morley, *Henry Crabb Robinson*, II (1938), 552. Armstrong, pp. 39f., comments on De Wint's extreme irritability "in his latter years."

[17] See II, 329. The drawing is reproduced in the 1841 (Smith), 1867 and 1871 (Moxon), and undated (W. M. Rossetti, 1872?) editions of Keats's poems.

[18] Sharp, *Century Magazine*, LXXI, 545.

[19] November 16, 1895, p. 687. Williamson, p. 105, also calls it "a very inadequate and unsatisfactory likeness."

[1] Gertrude M. Tuckwell, *Life of the Rt. Hon. Sir Charles W. Dilke*, I (1917), 6.

called Wentworth Place, which became a social center for Reynolds, Hunt, Severn, Taylor, the Brawnes, and other members of the Keats circle.

Dilke's "most affectionate friendship," says his grandson,[2] was with Keats, but the date of their meeting is uncertain. Lowell[3] put it "some time during the Winter of 1816–17," Adami[4] "early in 1817." Perhaps it was Dilke who introduced Brown to Keats "in the latter part" of the summer, 1817.[5] In any case, Dilke was on friendly terms with him before September, 1817. In the following January Keats remarked, "I and Dilk are getting [to be] capital Friends," and in February, "I am a good deal with Dilke and Brown, we are very thick; they are very kind to me."[6]

Dilke was six years Keats's senior, strongly opinionated, utterly devoted to his wife and son, and it was but natural that the younger man should become somewhat critical of him. In a remarkable bit of analysis he concluded in September, 1819, "That Dilke was a Man who cannot feel he has a personal identity unless he has made up his Mind about every thing. . . . Dilke will never come at a truth as long as he lives; because he is always trying at it. He is a Godwin-methodist."[7] Dilke could be, as Brown said, "forbidding."[8] On the contrary, Maria Dilke was kind and generous and charming to all the Keats family. She evidently had much to do with the fact, stated by her husband in 1841 (No. 170), that the three Keats boys (before June, 1818) "were with me three times a week, often three times a day." From Kentucky George sent warm regards to "the merry

[2] *Papers*, I, 2.
[3] I, 466.
[4] Page 60.
[5] See II, 57.
[6] *Letters*, pp. 76, 107.
[7] The same, p. 426.
[8] See II, 50.

Mrs. Dilke," and wistfully mentioned her dancing; John referred to her as often as to her husband, always with liking, paying watchful attention to her health, sending her love to Fanny and the George Keatses, telling how she and he had "a battle with celery stalks." [9] Fanny, whose drab life she tried to brighten, was occasionally permitted to see and even to visit her.[10] When Tom, in the summer of 1818, was sick and alone, she and her husband were very attentive. At the doctor's request Dilke wrote, urging John to return home, but the latter, plagued with a sore throat, had already given up the walking tour and sailed for London. He arrived at Hampstead on August 18, and called immediately on Mrs. Dilke to express his thanks. "Charming dear Mrs Dilke" seems, in short, to have been a gay, warmhearted, likable woman, and there is small wonder that Brown and Keats, in January, 1819, wrote their mock-love-letter to her.[11]

From August 18 till April, 1819, it is probable that Keats "was daily with" [12] the Dilkes, who introduced him to Fanny Brawne. On April 3 they moved to Great Smith Street, Westminster, in order to be near Charles, whom they had placed in Westminster School (1819–1826). Keats visited them occasionally, though he criticized Dilke severely for talking about almost nothing but "My Boy": Dilke has "a sort of parental mania," he is "entirely swallowed up in his boy," worry about whom "makes his face pale, his society silent and his vigilance jealous." [13] Brown similarly complained (September, 1819) "of the great alteration the Disposition of Dilke has undergone. He thinks of nothing but 'Political Justice' and his Boy." [14] No

---

9 *Letters*, p. 269.
10 Adami, pp. 6of., 99.
11 *Letters*, pp. 279-281.
12 See I, xlvi.
13 *Letters*, pp. 320f., 403.
14 The same, pp. 425f.

doubt, too, Keats felt that the Dilkes (for reasons now obvious) disapproved of his engagement, and hence during his final months in England he saw little of them. When Dilke called in 1820, he "gave me a very great deal more pain than pleasure," Keats told Fanny Brawne; "I shall never be able any more to endure the society of any of those who used to meet at Elm Cottage and Wentworth Place. . . . I will indulge myself by never seeing any more Dilke or Brown or any of their Friends." [15]

Earlier Keats had had very friendly relations with other members of Dilke's family: with Dilke's parents, Mr. and Mrs. Charles W. Dilke, of Chichester, whom he visited for a few days in January, 1819; with his brother William (1796–1885),[16] who lived for a time in Wentworth House adjoining Wentworth Place, and who apparently disliked Fanny Brawne (No. 279); and with his sister, Mrs. John Snook. He visited the Snooks at Bedhampton for "nearly a fortnight" in January, 1819, and there, too, with Severn he passed his last night in England (No. 73). All the Dilke family realized Keats's greatness. Maria, for example, who thought him "a very odd young man, but good-tempered, and good-hearted, and very clever indeed," [17] wrote to her father-in-law in 1820: "I am anxious to learn what success Keats' new poems have. . . . If the public cry him up as a great poet, I will henceforth be their humble servant; if not, the devil take the public." [18]

After Keats's death Dilke more than anyone else kept in touch, personally or by correspondence, with members of the Keats circle. He supervised the financial affairs of Fanny Keats and the Brawnes as a trustee and looked after George's English property as a friend, while his wife took Fanny Brawne and, so

15 *Letters,* pp. 502f.
16 This brother is addressed in *Letters,* p. 64 (November, 1817), though the editor does not recognize his existence.
17 *Papers,* I, 8.
18 The same, I, 11.

far as possible, Fanny Keats under her social, if very unpunctual, wing. Distrusting Llanos' judgment, he guarded Fanny Keats Llanos' money, and kept more or less in touch with her so long as he lived. Though he had a temporary misunderstanding with George over money (No. 146), it was quickly cleared up. George expressed "endless gratitude" for his help, and called him "the best Friend I have in the world," "the man of all others to whom I am most closely allied in feeling." [19] George also empowered him to invoke the copyright laws against any attempt by Brown or others to print Keats's poems or letters; several times urged him to visit Louisville (William Dilke, on a journey to the United States and Canada around 1824, had been unable to get in touch with George); and confidently expected to visit him, as Georgiana Keats had visited him in 1828.

In 1825 Dilke moved to a house in Lower Grosvenor Place,[20] and in the next year took his son to Italy. In Rome they saw Keats's grave, and were deeply moved.[21] During 1826–1827 Charles lived in Florence with Brown and Carlino, and in the autumn of 1828 he entered Cambridge University, where in 1834 he received the degree of LL.B. His doting father bought partial control of the *Athenaeum* in 1828, complete control in 1830, and made the literary weekly successful and respected (No. 150). He relinquished the editorship, but not the ownership, in 1846, and for a time managed the *Daily News*. Maria Dilke died in 1850, Mrs. Charles Dilke in 1853. In this latter year Dilke moved into his son's home at 76 Sloane Street. In his final years he wrote a number of important studies, particularly on the Junius letters and Pope. Retiring to a Hampshire village

[19] See I, 315f.
[20] His grandson says (*Papers*, I, 16) that he edited the *London Magazine* around 1825.
[21] *Papers*, I, 17.

in 1862, he died on August 10, 1864, highly esteemed by all who knew him.

Long before, Brown had broken off relations with Dilke after quarrels over George Keats's alleged misdeeds, and had turned over his biography of the poet to Milnes. Through Severn it came to the attention of Dilke, who read it with disapproval (No. 170); but his criticisms made little impression on Milnes. Still he aided Milnes, so says the preface, "with letters and remembrances." In a letter of thanks to the author he praised the *Life* of 1848 with certain reservations (No. 243), and he printed two lengthy reviews of it in the *Athenaeum*.[22] The incisive notes and comments he jotted down in his own copy, now in the Pierpont Morgan Library, show that he could have done an infinitely better job than Milnes. He was, except for Woodhouse and Bailey, the most scholarly member of the Keats circle, the one best fitted to give an accurate, factual biography (George rightly thought him in "every way Competent" to write his brother's life [23]), and it is a great pity that he failed to do so. He would, to be sure, have omitted many of Severn's and Milnes's details as too personal or painful, but he would also have settled dates and other problems that still perplex students. W. J. Thoms, an old friend, wrote of him in 1864: "The distinguishing feature of his character was, his singular love of truth; and his sense of its value and importance, even in the minutest points and questions of literary history." [24] It was this love of truth, his sense of justice, that dictated the memorable sketch of Brown [25] and that made him determined to vindicate George Keats from Brown's and Haslam's slanders. Although he did not wholly convince Milnes in 1848, his letters and pa-

[22] See II, 261.
[23] See I, 288.
[24] *NQ*, August 13, 1864, p. 140.
[25] See I, lxix.

pers passed to his grandson, Charles (1843–1911), the second baronet, who continued the fight. Sir Charles had his ups and downs in life, but all students of Keats are greatly indebted to him. He defended George Keats (No. 276); kept in touch with Fanny Llanos, Severn, and other aging survivors of the Keats group, as well as Houghton and Brown's son; tried to prevent the publication of the love letters to Fanny Brawne; opened the columns of the *Athenaeum* to correspondence and articles about Keats; edited some of his grandfather's work with a memoir, *The Papers of a Critic* (1875); and willed his invaluable collection of Keats books, letters, and other relics to the Hampstead Public Library. This collection by itself makes the Keats Museum, the old Wentworth Place, a research library as well as a literary shrine.

WILLIAM HASLAM

Comparatively little is known of the life of Haslam, one of the most engaging and devoted of Keats's friends. Perhaps born in 1795, the same year as the poet, he was, according to Brown,[1] a schoolfellow of Keats, who held him "dearly." Likewise Severn testifies[2] that he "was very intimate with Keats" during the latter's stay at St. Thomas' Hospital. Upon the death of his father in March, 1819, Haslam, a solicitor, succeeded to the position his father had held with Frampton and Sons, wholesale grocers, 34 Leadenhall Street. Keats noticed with satisfaction (April 15) that the "Framptons have behaved well to him"; and with his customary dissatisfaction where engagements of his men friends were concerned (September) that Haslam is "very much occupied with love. . . . His love is very amusing." Severn had painted a portrait, or a miniature, of the

[1] See II, 52.
[2] See II, 160.

lady in question, and, characteristically enough, to Keats it represented a woman "though not very cunning, too cunning for" her fiancé. Holding such sentiments, Keats naturally saw for a time little of Haslam, who married on October 16. Unlike him, Severn calls Mrs. Haslam "your lovely partner," [3] and when he painted her portrait around July, 1820,[4] Brown also saw there a "fair face." [5]

The words "jealousy" and "change" were not in Haslam's vocabulary. He loved Keats as a boy, he loved him as a man, he considered him in many respects a rival of Shakespeare. He was a constant, competent, always obliging friend to whom in emergencies Keats and many of his acquaintances turned for help. My "oak friend" Severn termed him.[6] His kindness to Tom "during my absence and since my return," the poet said, "has endeared him to me for ever." During Tom's final illness he was "excessively Kind" and "always doing me some good turn." He loaned Keats money in September and apparently in November, 1819. He forwarded Keats's letters to his brother in America, and to that brother wrote the news of Tom's death. He arranged, almost at the last moment,[7] for Severn to accompany Keats to Italy, being prevented from going himself because his wife had had, or was about to have, a child, and because he was "miserably oppressed" with business as an executor.[8] He played a considerable part in making the financial arrangements for the journey, acting with Woodhouse as a witness to the copyright assignment of *Endymion* [9] that provided £100; and there is every reason to assume that he was

3 See I, 241, 252.
4 See I, 122.
5 See I, 159.
6 See I, 150.
7 No. 63.
8 See his letter to Severn of December 4, 1820, in Sharp, p. 73.
9 See I, 144.

one of the two unnamed friends [10] who gave Taylor £50 for the poet's use. Though M. B. Forman [11] deprives him of that distinction, Haslam was one of the five men (one of three personal friends) who sailed to Gravesend with Keats and Severn—and then dashed back to London for the passport Severn had forgotten.[12] Fanny Brawne wrote to Fanny Keats on September 18 [13] that his "kindness [to John] cannot be described," and that "in Mʳ Haslam you will see the best person in the world to raise your spirits, he feels so certain your brother will soon recover his health."

While Haslam had once been an intimate friend of George Keats, by 1820 his contempt for George equaled that of Brown, and to him he sent goading, taunting letters.[14] His opinions of George's brutality and dishonesty were frankly expressed to Severn, whom he told: "Avoid speaking of George to him [the poet]. George is a scoundrel! but talk of his friends in England, of their love, their hopes of him. Keats must get himself well again, Severn, if but for us. I, for one, cannot afford to lose him. If I know what it is to love, I truly love John Keats." [15] When the news of Keats's death reached Brown, he wrote at once, asking Haslam to convey it to Fanny Keats and Abbey.[16]

On October 6, 1822,[17] Mary Haslam died at Alton,

[10] See I, 207n.

[11] *Letters*, p. 527.

[12] See I, 150.

[13] Edgcumbe, pp. 4f.

[14] See I, 329.

[15] Sharp, pp. 72f.

[16] See I, 231.

[17] *Gentleman's Magazine*, XCII, 478. At the very last moment I find a transcript by Louis A. Holman of the tablet in the Alton Parish Church, Hampshire.

"To the memory of Mary the beloved wife of Mr. William Haslam of Greenwich in Kent, Gentleman whose mortal remains are buried in

Hampshire. Severn was deeply grieved, and he forwarded the widower a hearty invitation to share his quarters and his poverty in Rome.[18] Years later, in May or June, 1838, Brown dined with Haslam, and found him living prosperously with a wife and daughter, Annette Augusta, "the latter a nice girl of about sixteen." [19] Whether Annette was the daughter of the first Mrs. Haslam or the second (her name also seems to have been Mary) does not appear.

Haslam was of considerable assistance to Milnes in the composition of the Keats biography, giving him "letters and remembrances," and searching parish registers and Chancery documents for relevant facts. It is an odd contradiction that, careful and reliable as he was in other respects, he was careless about preserving letters. Keats himself ruefully tells of getting back from him in May, 1819, a letter from George "torn into a thousand pieces," and Keats's own letters to him [20] "were so well, or intended to be so well taken care of" that only three [21] are known today. Fortunately he did preserve many written to him by Severn, and they are the most interesting, indeed an invaluable, record of the poet's last days.

---

this church. She was given to him on 16th Oct. 1819, & died in this parish on the 6th of the same month in 1822, in the 27th year of her age.

> "Sweet spirit who in loveliest mortal form
> Did'st win & wean me from the world & charm
> My heart, my nature every thought of mine,
> To seek its origin, or end in thine
> Who mortal were to me the source, & test
> Of all that dignified, or truly blest
> Man's mortal nature! Deign to guard me still.
> Now mould me Mary to thy heavenly will."

[18] No. 130.
[19] Sharp, p. 186.
[20] See II, 189.
[21] Hewlett, p. 425, adds one that is not in *Letters;* it is printed also in the Hampstead Keats, VIII, 239.

Haslam died on March 28, 1851, broken down by the pressure of business and financial straits, but "his end was peace." [22]

BENJAMIN ROBERT HAYDON

Haydon (1786–1846), the painter, plays a comparatively small part in the letters that follow. The second of them, however, throws light on the date at which he met Keats. "Very glad am I at the thoughts of seeing so soon this glorious Haydon and all his creation," Keats wrote to Clarke on October 31, 1816, and it has been generally assumed, as by Lowell,[1] that he was "anticipating an initial meeting." Clarke himself says that "at Haydon's own request, I introduced . . . [Keats] to him." [2] Haydon, however, declared that he met Keats at Leigh Hunt's, and, although Lowell challenges the statement, she admits that Haydon spent "some weeks in October [1816] at Hampstead, seeing much of Hunt." He likewise saw a good deal of Reynolds and Keats, as No. 2 proves. He was then about thirty-one, apparently an established artist, the friend of the great, and the triumphant defender of the Elgin Marbles. He was also "most affectionately & ardently attached" [3] to Keats—as ardently as his vainglory and selfishness permitted, and Keats almost worshiped him. It is noteworthy that nearly all the twenty-two letters Keats sent him have such conclusions as "Your's affectionately," "Yours ever," "Your's eternally," "Your everlasting friend," and contain such extravagant statements as "[I] would sacrifice every thing I have to your service," "your wellfare and

---

[22] Sharp, p. 205, quoting Mrs. Haslam. The *Gentleman's Magazine*, n.s., XXXV (1851), 566, gives his residence as Roupel-road, Upper Tulse-hill, and his age as 53.

[1] I, 194f.

[2] See II, 319.

[3] *Letters*, p. 279.

fame is and will be a chief pleasure to me all my Life," "eve[r]y day older I get—the greater is my idea of your achievements in Art." [4]

Keats was especially interested in the huge painting, "Christ's Entry into Jerusalem" (now in Mount Saint Mary's Seminary in Norwood, Ohio), wherein his face appears along with Wordsworth's and Hazlitt's. He was disturbed, however, by Haydon's quarrels with Hunt and Reynolds, and in time suspected that his idol had feet of clay. When his own finances had reached a low ebb, he asked Haydon to repay a loan of £30. Not only was the painter unable to do so, but he "let me go without my money with almost non-chalance when he ought to have sold his drawings to supply me." As a result, Keats said angrily, "I shall perhaps still be acquainted with him, but for friendship that is at an end." [5] Forman detects in the letters following this outburst "a certain reserve of tone." [6] Soon Keats was writing, "I never see him"; [7] but in March, 1820, he attended the private showing of "Christ's Entry" and stood "up in a corner, really rejoicing" with Hazlitt,[8] and in one of his last letters he expresses a desire that Haydon will call on "Your affectionate friend." [9] Several calls were made, but were not successful. Haydon admits that Keats "grew irritated because I would shake my head at his irregularities, and tell him that he would destroy himself." [10] Another cause of irritation was a special messenger sent to bring back a book Haydon had lent— and the book was not returned for another month.[11]

[4] *Letters*, pp. 272, 30, 79.
[5] The same, p. 419.
[6] The same, p. 431n.
[7] The same, p. 450.
[8] Penrose, p. 242.
[9] *Letters*, p. 504.
[10] Penrose, p. 260.
[11] *Letters*, pp. 509f.

Haydon's later unhappy career is well-known. Towards the end of 1845 he began to correspond with Moxon and then directly with Milnes in order to secure a fitting niche for himself in the forthcoming biography. He sent copies of the two Elgin Marbles sonnets, asking that they be included, as they were,[12] and once he cut out of his memoirs a letter of Keats that he had transcribed so that Milnes could use it.[13] He committed suicide on June 22, 1846. His autobiography, published in 1853, told how Keats was driven into dissipation by the Cockney-School reviewers: "For six weeks he was scarcely sober, and . . . he once covered his tongue and throat as far as he could reach with Cayenne pepper, in order to appreciate the 'delicious coldness of claret in all its glory.' " [14] Needless to say, this passage, which was reprinted in Haydon's *Correspondence and Table Talk*, edited by his son in 1876, outraged many of the poet's friends and some of his relatives.[15]

WILLIAM HAZLITT

The name of the famous essayist and critic Hazlitt (1788–1830) turns up often in Keats's letters, beginning with March 9, 1817. References to occasions on which they met and dined together are fairly common. Keats attended many of Hazlitt's public lectures (on one night arriving an hour late to find the lecturer and his audience leaving the hall). "Hazlitt's depth of Taste" seemed to him one of the "three things to rejoice at in this Age." He read and quoted the vitriolic *Letter to William Gifford* with enthusiasm, describing it as "in a style of genius," and saying that Hazlitt "hath a demon, as he himself says of

12 No. 184; Milnes, I, 27f.
13 No. 193.
14 Penrose, p. 259.
15 See No. 264 and Adami, pp. 178-180.

Lord Byron." Hazlitt, he once remarked, "is your only good damner and if ever I am damn'd—damn me if I shoul'nt like him to damn me." Actually the reviewers damned both writers as members of Hunt's Cockney School, and more abuse was lavished on the "pimpled" essayist than on the apothecary versifier. The two men apparently met for the last time on March 25, 1820,[1] the first day of the exhibition of Haydon's "Christ's Entry into Jerusalem," but Keats sent him an inscribed copy of the *Lamia* volume. In the suppressed *Select British Poets* (1824) Hazlitt wrote: "Mr. KEATS is also dead. He gave the greatest promise of genius of any poet of his day. He displayed extreme tenderness, beauty, originality and delicacy of fancy; all he wanted was manly strength and fortitude to reject the temptations of singularity in sentiment and expression. Some of his shorter and later pieces are, however, as free from faults as they are full of beauties." [2]

LEIGH HUNT

The story of Leigh Hunt (1784–1859) is as familiar as that of Keats himself. Whatever his defects as man and writer (and they have sometimes been grossly exaggerated), there is no denying his kindness and devotion to Keats, whom he loved next to Shelley. Though Hunt was the first real critic of Keats's poetry and a continual propagandist for it, his influence was, on the whole, unhappy. Keats soon realized how disastrous to

[1] P. P. Howe, *The Life of William Hazlitt* (1922), pp. 295f.

[2] Page xv. Keats's poems are printed on pp. 760-770. Clarence D. Thorpe, in a recent essay on "Keats and Hazlitt" (*PMLA,* LXII [1947], 487-502), remarks: "The relationship between Keats and Hazlitt . . . was one of mutual respect and friendship. Toward Keats Hazlitt was gracious, kindly beyond his wont, and after the poet's death he became a sort of self-appointed watchdog of his fame and avenger of the wrongs he had suffered at the hands of the critics."

his reputation (and to his style) the association had been—how it had fastened on his poetry the pernicious label of Cockney. Soon, too, he found much to criticize in Hunt's behavior, but it was surely temporary pique that led him to describe Hunt in December, 1818, as "vain, egotistical, and disgusting in matters of taste and in morals." [1] It is a pity that only two letters Keats wrote him are preserved. There must have been more (though Hunt told Milnes, "I hardly received above three or four letters from him in all" [2]), and they would have given a truer idea of Keats's real opinions. It is pleasant to know that in 1820 he considered publishing *Hyperion* jointly with poems by Hunt; [3] and that after he had left Hunt's house in a rage in August, 1820, he wrote, "I feel really attach'd to you for your many sympathies with me, and patience at my lunes." [4] And it is pleasanter still to read the kindly farewell to Keats that Hunt published in the *Indicator*,[5] September 20, 1820, and the beautiful and generous letter he sent on March 8, 1821, to Severn, unaware of his young friend's death:

Tell him—tell that great poet and noble-hearted man—that we shall all bear his memory in the most precious part of our hearts, and that the world shall bow their heads to it, as our loves do. . . . tell him we shall never cease to remember and love him. . . . Tell him he is only before us on the road [to immortality], as he was in everything else. . . .[6]

The man who wrote thus was not a Cockney.

Hunt published the first life of Keats in *Lord Byron and Some of His Contemporaries* (1828). Several of his comments offended George Keats, and are even deemed offensive by cer-

1 *Letters*, p. 252.
2 See II, 170.
3 See II, 234.
4 *Letters*, p. 510.
5 Forman, IV, 199f.
6 Milnes, II, 95-97; Forman, IV, 220-222.

tain writers today, but he told the truth as he saw it and indulged in his usual praise. In the same year he wrote the second life of Keats—this time for John Gorton's *General Biographical Dictionary* which his nephew Henry Hunt and Charles Cowden Clarke published—an altogether remarkable biographical and critical sketch [7] that forever established Keats in such works of reference. In his subsequent periodicals he spoke beautifully and copiously about the dead poet, especially in *Leigh Hunt's London Journal,* where he expressed the critical judgments that today are generally accepted. "Thousands of your Readers," J. W. Dalby and one R. H. told him, had their eyes opened to the real beauties of "The Eve of St. Agnes" by his reprint of that poem with a critical commentary.[8] Among the "Thousands" may have been even *Blackwood's* Cockney-baiting reviewers. At any rate, "Christopher North," in August, 1834,[9] praised both Hunt and his *London Journal;* in March, 1840,[10] he rejoiced in Hunt's "success as cordially as his best friends can do—for he deserves it," and discussed enthusiastically *The Legend of Florence.* Had Keats lived till 1834 he would have found intimate association with Hunt no longer a liability. With all these critical activities in mind Milnes remarked, "Mr. Leigh Hunt had already laid his offering on the shrine of his beloved brother in the trials and triumphs of genius, and could only encourage me by his interest and sympathy." But Hunt naturally called to Milnes's attention the eulogistic sonnet

[7] It is signed only as an Original Communication, but Hunt's authorship is unmistakable. Probably its composition antedated that of the chapter on "Mr. Keats" in *Lord Byron and Some of His Contemporaries* where Hunt says (p. 268), "I venture to prophesy, as I have done elsewhere, that Mr. Keats will be known hereafter . . . as *the Young Poet."* G. G. Cunningham reprinted the Gorton sketch in his *History of England in the Lives of Englishmen,* VIII (1853), 252-254, as the best yet written.

[8] See the issues for January 21, March 4, March 18, 1835, pp. 17-20, 71, 82.

[9] *Blackwood's,* XXXVI, 273.

[10] The same, XLVII, 303-318.

"On Leigh Hunt's Poem, 'The Story of Rimini' " (No. 191), he provided the texts of his, Keats's and (what he thought was) Shelley's sonnets "On the Nile" [11]—and he asked Milnes's aid in getting a pension on the Civil List.

He read the *Life*, as he tells in his *Autobiography* (1850),[12] "with extreme pain." From its letters he learned that Keats "suspected both Shelley and myself of a wish to see him undervalued"; "it appears, by Mr. Milnes's book, that all his friends dissatisfied him in the course of those trials of his temper." It is impossible to keep from sympathizing with Hunt, who was shocked to the soul to read that one of his *Examiner* papers had "so much egotism of that drivelling nature that pleasure is entirely lost." [13] Perhaps he would have been wiser—students today certainly would be—if he had not objected so strongly to a second, revised edition that none was made until eight years after his death.

GEORGIANA WYLIE KEATS JEFFREY

Georgiana Augusta Wylie is described [1] as the daughter of James Wylie, Adjutant of the Fifeshire Regiment of Fencible Infantry. She was born about 1797 or 1798, but practically nothing is known of her or her family before she appears in Keats's letters on February 21, 1818. Her brothers Henry and Charles G. are first mentioned on June 28 and October 14 respectively, while to her mother Keats addressed his first of three letters on August 6. She married George Keats in the preceding June.[2] Keats had then known her for "some time"

[11] See II, 182.

[12] II, 202-204.

[13] Milnes, I, 92; *Letters*, p. 70.

[1] *Letters*, p. xxxvi.

[2] Lowell, II, 7, dates the marriage on or about May 28; Naomi J. Kirk (Hampstead Keats, I, lxxxv) and M. B. Forman *(Connoisseur,* September, 1945 [CXV, 8]), June 4.

and "was very fond of her." "I like her better and better," he told Bailey, "—she is the most disinterrested woman I ever knew —that is to say she goes beyond degree in it." [3] Against his opinion may be set that of Dilke, who in 1848 [4] called her "a pretty, lively ignorant girl, unaccustomed to society." The migration of George and Georgiana to America was disastrous to the health, fortune, and happiness of the poet. With Brown he accompanied them to Liverpool on June 22, 1818, before starting on the ill-advised walking-tour of Scotland, and to them his longest, brightest, most revealing letters are addressed.

Georgiana Keats had eight children:

1. Georgiana Emily, 1819–1855, who married Alfred Gwathmey.

2. Rosalind, born December 18, 1821, died around March, 1826.

3. Emma Frances, 1823–1883, who married Philip Speed, the son of Judge John Speed and the brother of James Speed, Lincoln's attorney general, and became the mother of John Gilmer Speed, the American editor of Keats's letters and poems.

4. Isabel, born February 28, 1825, died October 29, 1843.

5. John Henry, 1827–1917.

6. Clarence George, 1830–1861.

7. Ella, 1833–1888, who married George N. Peay.

8. Alice Ann, 1836–1891, who married Edward M. Drane.

Miss Naomi J. Kirk [5] asserted that George's descendants [6] disagreed "as to the number of George Keats's children. Were

[3] *Letters*, p. 152.

[4] Note in his copy of Milnes (Morgan Library).

[5] *Filson Club History Quarterly*, VIII (1934), 94.

[6] Evidently some of them informed the Louisville correspondent of the New York *World*, June 25, 1877, that there were only seven children. Forman, IV, 385n., took the correspondent to task for omitting "Rosalind, who died early."

there seven or eight? Was Isabel Rosalind one child, or two daughters born two years apart?" On the basis of a burial entry in the Louisville First Unitarian Church she decided, wrongly, that there were only seven children, that Rosalind and Isabel were the same child.[7] The entry runs: "1843. Oct. 20. Miss Isabel R. Keats, aged 16, daughter of George Keats. Her death was caused by discharge of a gun." The entry (or perhaps the transcript) is incorrect: Rosalind was dead by May 7, 1830, in 1843 Isabel was not sixteen but eighteen and a half, and she died on October 29.[8]

The details may be worked out from George's letters. On January 6, 1821, he names his two children, Georgiana and Rosalind; on February 7, 1825,[9] he tells of the birth of his fourth daughter, and on April 20 enumerates Georgiana, aged 6, Rosalind, 4½, Emma Frances, 2½, Isabel, 8 weeks. On May 7, 1830, George lists his five children, Georgiana, Emma, Isabel, John, Clarence (aged 3 months). Here he started to name the third child as "Rosa[lind]" but changed it to "Isabel." By November 23, 1833, he had six children, Ella being 6 months old, and by March 14, 1836, seven, Alice being 2 months old. All seven are again mentioned on March 1, 1838.

As for the unfortunate Isabel, her fate is told at length, evidently by the editor, G. D. Prentice (see No. 230), in the Louisville *Daily Journal* and in the *Boston Almanac for the*

[7] But in the Hampstead Keats, I, xcvii, she correctly gives the number of children as eight.

[8] According to the Louisville *Daily Journal*, October 30, of which Miss Kirk says that no copy "has been located." Under the heading "DIED" it says: "Yesterday morning, Miss ISABEL R. KEATS, daughter of the late George Keats, aged about 17 years. The friends of the family are invited to attend her funeral at the house of Mr. John Jeffrey, on Walnut Street, at 10 o'clock, this morning." According to J. J. Piatt, *Every Saturday*, December 30, 1871, p. 635, her name was given on the monument of George Keats in Western Cemetery as "Isabella Rosalind."

[9] See Forman, IV, 401, who possibly misdates the letter.

Year 1844 [10] compiled by Samuel N. Dickinson, under the date [11] of October 30, 1843. Prentice's account runs thus:

DISTRESSING OCCURRENCE.—Among our obituary notices, today, we record the death of MISS ISABEL R. KEATS. The circumstances of the death of this lovely and interesting young lady were extremely melancholy and distressing. On Saturday night, she sat with the other members of the highly respectable family, of which she was an ornament, until about 10 o'clock, conversing with her accustomed gaiety. At that hour, the family retired, but she, after going to her room, returned to the parlor to procure something to allay a toothache. Shortly afterwards, a loud report and a scream were heard, and the family, on rushing into the room, found her weltering in her blood upon the floor, and a gun, which had stood in the room, lying near her. The discharge had lacerated her breast and neck dreadfully. The first impression was, that the poor girl had committed suicide, and her half-frantic mother exclaimed: "Oh, Isabel! what made you do it?" She replied: "I did not mean to kill myself! Indeed, mother, I did not mean to kill myself!" The

[10] Page 61 (noted by Dorothy Tyler in the *Saturday Review of Literature*, January 31, 1942, p. 11):
    "Miss Isabel R. Keats, of Louisville, Ky., on Saturday night, after conversing as usual with the family till about 10 o'clock in the evening, retired; but shortly after returned to the parlor, the family having left, to procure something, it is said, for the tooth-ache. Shortly after there was a report of a gun. Persons immediately rushed into the room, and found her weltering in blood. The charge had dreadfully lacerated her neck and breast. She persisted in saying that she did not mean to kill herself, while she lived, which was several hours. How came she to have the gun? This is a point not satisfactorily explained. She was a niece of John Keats, an English poet of some celebrity."
    A special correspondent of the New York *World*, June 25, 1877, wrote: "Isabel at the age of sixteen met with a most mournful death. One of her brothers returning from shooting laid his loaded gun on a sofa. Shortly afterwards a report was heard, and Isabel was found lying upon the sofa. She was a beautiful girl, and showed promise of poetic talent. The late George D. Prentice was warmly attached to her, and addressed to her some of his best verses."
[11] October 30 was Monday, and Saturday October 28.

best medical skill was instantly called in, but she died at an early hour in the morning. She was able to converse for several hours, and she seemed calm, though much distressed at the thought of parting from the members of her family whom she dearly loved. Her repeated and earnest asseverations can leave no doubt that the fatal occurrence was entirely accidental.

All, who knew Miss Keats intimately, will long and deeply deplore her early death. She was a niece of John Keats, the young English poet, who was the friend and the peer of Coleridge and Shelley, and in her features she was remarkably like him. She was a girl of genius, and her heart was the home of all the high and pure and beautiful affections. The following lines, given her in her early girlhood by a friend [Prentice] whose years more than doubly numbered hers, may possibly be worth recording in connection with her memory:

I know a little girl
  With a spirit wild and free,
And it ever seems a blessing
  With that pretty one to be—
To mark her ringing shout
  And her ever-joyous words
Like the gushing of a fountain
  Or the cadences of birds.

That joyous little girl
  Is as wild as a gazelle,
Yet a poet's name and lineage,
  Are thine, sweet Isabel!
And although thy wild heart seemeth
  All-heedless of the lyre,
Within that young heart dwelleth
  The poet's gift of fire.

But 'twas a fearful gift
  To that noble child of song,
Whose glorious name and lineage
  To thee, bright one, belong:

c

For it turned his heart to ashes
  Where its centred light was flung,
And he perished in his morning—
  The gifted and the young.

Ay, he perished in his morning,
  That child of light and gloom,
But he left a name that glitters
  Like a star above his tomb;
And I deem *thou* hast a genius
  Like that which won *his* fame;
Thou hast his name and features—
  And why not his soul of flame?

Georgiana Keats visited England once after her marriage. She sailed in May, 1828, and in addition to visiting her family and seeing many old friends, carried out various business commissions for her husband. She was back in Louisville before March 19, 1829. In her second marriage, January 5, 1843, to John Jeffrey, a Scotsman some twenty years her junior, Georgiana fell, at least for a time, on evil days.[12] Not long thereafter Jeffrey's supposed brutal conduct and his unfaithfulness were graphically detailed to his brother Alexander in a letter of

[12] According to a letter of Jeffrey's, December 10, 1872 (see the *Athenaeum*, January 4, 1873, p. 17), the marriage took place "about a couple of years" after George's death. Miss Kirk, *Filson Club History Quarterly*, VIII, 93, says Mrs. Keats remarried "in little more than a year"; M. B. Forman, *Connoisseur*, CXV, 9, "a year after George's death." But the marriage books of Jefferson County, Kentucky, now in the custody of the Filson Club, Louisville, contain the original marriage bond, January 5, 1843, of £50, or $166 and "two-thirds cents," signed by John Jeffrey and H. P. Needham, for the marriage of Jeffrey and "Georgiana A Keats Widow of Geo Keats dec^d" and the marriage license, certified and returned on January 5 by John H. Heywood, pastor of the First Unitarian Church, Louisville. The marriage is also recorded, January 5, 1843, in the record book of that church, p. 73, under "MARRIAGES./ (During Mr. Heywood's ministry.)." A short notice of the wedding appeared in the Louisville *Daily Journal*, January 10.

Georgiana's (No. 179). Jeffrey volunteered to help Milnes with the life of Keats (Nos. 175, 177, 178). After enumerating the invaluable letters and autograph poems of which he "had become possessed," he made and forwarded copies, all grossly, though unintentionally, inaccurate, and his reward was the following comment in Milnes's preface: "Perhaps the most valuable, as the most confidential communication I received, was from the gentleman who has married the widow of George Keats, and who placed at my disposal, with the consent of the family, the letters George received from his brother after he emigrated to America."

Apparently Georgiana's later years were happy and serene. The Lexington *Kentucky Gazette,* April 5, 1879, reported under "DEATHS":

In this city on the 3d inst., Mrs. Georgiana Augusta Jeffrey, wife of John Jeffrey, Esq., and sister-in-law of the poet Keats.
Cincinnati Commercial and Louisville Courier-Journal please copy.

On the preceding day the *Courier-Journal* had announced:

Died: Jeffrey, April 3, at Lexington, Mrs. Georgiana Jeffrey, wife of John Jeffrey, who will be remembered by many of our citizens as Mrs. George Keats.
Due notice of funeral will be given.

It then published on April 6 a notice that "The funeral of Mrs. John Jeffrey will take place on Monday morning at 11½ o'clock from the residence of her son-in-law, Mr. Philip Speed," and the next day she was buried in the Philip Speed lot in Cave Hill Cemetery, Louisville. An unidentified newspaper clipping in the Harvard Keats Collection, after telling of Georgiana's death, goes on to say: "She was a woman of the most sprightly, and, in her later years, the most caustic wit, and retained the unusual qualities of mind that made her famous among Kentucky women to the very last, and she was nearly 80 at her death. . . .[13] By George Keats she had seven children, of whom four are still living, and John—a civil engineer in Missouri—is the only one of his relatives that bears the poet's name." [14]

John Jeffrey died at Lexington on February 18, 1881, aged sixty-four, after having been "in bad health since the death of his wife, which event greatly depressed and grieved him." [15] Sufficient information about him appears in the Lexington *Daily Press,* February 20:

Obituary.

John Jeffrey, who has jast [*sic*] passed away from among us, was the youngest son of John Jeffrey, solicitor of the Supreme Court, Edinburgh, Scotland. As a civil engineer his career was varied. He was with Napier, of Glasgow, when he constructed the engines for the first ocean steamers; served under Sir J. Brunell during the construction of the Thames Tunnel. When with Stevenson he volunteered on the speed trial trip, when the rate of over eighty miles an hour was made, the subordinates on which occasion were paid a high premium, and Stevenson agreed to pension their families in case of accident. He was with Sir John Rennie and Mr. Logan in the deepening of the Clyde, which was the making of Glasgow, and also on the government pier and light house at Port Patrick.

[13] Apparently she was over eighty (see I, xcvi).

[14] A list of "living descendants of George Keats in America" is given in the *Southern Literary Messenger,* August, 1942 (IV, 356).

[15] The *Kentucky Gazette,* February 19. This notice was obviously furnished and perhaps written by Alexander Jeffrey. It tells that John lived and died in the Phoenix Hotel, and says: "He was a man of varied and extensive information, and a most genial companion. . . . He was entirely free from selfishness and would not consent to live in a private house where he would have been most tenderly cared for when frequently urged by his brother to do so, for fear of giving trouble and marring the cheerfulness of one of the brightest homes in Lexington, where sick or well, he had always had a cheerful welcome. His death is a terrible grief to his brother, Alex. Jeffrey, Esq., between whom there has always existed the most cordial fraternal affection and intimacy."

Since he came to the United States he constructed over thirty gas works, commencing with Louisville, Ky. Of late years, after the death of his wife, who was the widow of the brother of John Keats, the poet, he has resided in Lexington, and not even his most intimate friends were aware of the eventful career of one so quiet and unassuming. He set free and settled in Canada all the slaves he acquired by his marriage.

Jeffrey, too, was buried in the Speed lot at Louisville.[16] He had left no will, and the Fayette County Court in February appointed two administrators, one being his brother, and three appraisers to dispose of his property. According to the appraisers' return, March 9, 1881, his estate amounted to $41,292, of which $3,127 was in cash, the remainder in gas and bank stocks.

GEORGE KEATS [1]

George Keats was born on February 28, 1797,[2] some sixteen months after his poet-brother, in the Keats lodgings over the Swan and Hoop at 24 (or 28), The Pavement, Moorfields, near Bethlehem Hospital. He was christened along with his younger brothers Tom and Edward at St. Leonard's, Shoreditch, on September 24, 1801. In 1803 George and John were sent to John Clarke's school at Enfield. By 1810 the deaths of

[16] The monument gives the dates of his birth (June, 1817) and death, whereas none are given for his wife. Jeffrey was instrumental in having the bodies of George Keats and his two daughters removed from Western Cemetery to Cave Hill, where he erected a monument "To the Memory of the Keats Family in America."

[1] The best account of George is that by Naomi J. Kirk in the Hampstead Keats, I, lxxiii-xcviii.

[2] But his tombstone in Western Cemetery, Louisville, according to several newspaper writers, bore the date March 1, 1778 or 1798. See J. J. Piatt, as quoted in *Every Saturday*, December 30, 1871, p. 635.

their father, mother, and maternal grandfather caused the grandmother, Mrs. Jennings, to appoint as guardians Abbey and Sandell, and hence, while John was apprenticed to a surgeon, George was set to work by Abbey at 4 Pancras Lane. In 1816 George, after a quarrel with Abbey's junior partner, withdrew from Abbey and Cock's countinghouse, and lived with his two brothers at 76 Cheapside and then at the postman Bentley's, 1 Well Walk. According to Miss Kirk,[3] "George became the family housekeeper, the companion and nurse of Tom, the copier of poems and the business agent for John's work," and it was he who first met and then introduced to John most of the friends who made the Hunt-Keats circle "one of the most famous in literary annals."

George took Tom to Teignmouth in the winter of 1817. By January, however, he had decided to migrate to America with the idea of recouping the family fortunes in Morris Birkbeck and Sir George Flower's colony. He married Georgiana Wylie in June, and, after raising what money he could with Abbey's help, set out with his bride, Brown, and John for Liverpool on June 22. Sailing shortly thereafter, and landing at Philadelphia, the George Keatses traveled by horse and carriage to Pittsburgh, down the Ohio River by boat to Shawneetown, Indiana, and thence overland to Princeton, the post office of the Birkbeck colony. They met the famous naturalist, John James Audubon, who persuaded them to live for several months in his home at Hendersonville, Kentucky, and who swindled George (so at least he believed) in a boat speculation.

George's financial affairs were, as a result, desperate. He moved to Louisville, where his first child was born early in 1819, about the time he heard the news of Tom Keats's death. Realizing that part of Tom's estate was his due, he borrowed money from his friend William Bakewell, and set out on the

[3] Pages lxxxi f.

only journey he ever made to England, a journey that threw a cloud over his relations with Keats himself and with many of his former friends. George reached London before January 13, 1820. Working rapidly, he collected his own share of Tom's estate plus, as Brown and others believed, a considerable part of John's. He then left London for Liverpool on January 28, and sailed for New York on February 1.

It is unnecessary to comment further on George's financial transactions, for much of the relevant material dealing with them is contained in the letters here printed. Taylor, Brown, Haslam, Severn, and for a time Fanny Keats were sure that he had deliberately taken money belonging to John, leaving his brother ill, pinched by poverty, and dependent on the charity of his friends; and the first three "goaded" him with "taunting" letters. On the other hand, Dilke, Abbey,[4] and eventually Fanny Keats [5] and Milnes completely exonerated him of all wrongdoing. More remarkable, however, are Fanny Brawne's judicious comments. Though George "is no favorite of mine and he never liked me," she wrote Fanny Keats in 1821,[6] "he is more blamed than he should be." He was "surely a very indirect and accidental" cause of the "dreadful consequences" that befell his brother. Keats had said in 1818, "George has ever been more than a brother to me, he has been my greatest friend," and in 1819, "George always stood between me and any dealings with the world." [7] It is pleasant to learn that Fanny Brawne, who should have known the facts, refused to believe that Keats had any real ill feeling towards his brother: "They tell me that latterly he thought worse of George, but I own I do not believe it."

[4] So George says, but Brown (see Sharp, p. 147) tells another story.
[5] See her letter of August, 1824, in Adami, p. 108.
[6] Edgcumbe, pp. 33f.
[7] *Letters*, pp. 208, 345.

Ultimately George paid all the debts left by John. There seems no reason to doubt that he was, as James Freeman Clarke [8] and others insisted, an honest, high-minded man; but the fact remains that, harassed as he was by his own financial difficulties, he failed his gifted brother, who died in Rome, almost friendless and saved from dire want only by the charity of certain English friends. Knowing all this, George tried for years, but in vain, to get one of those friends—not Brown—to write John's biography and to publish his works.

As time went on, George became one of the wealthiest and most influential citizens of Louisville. He put his money into a lumber mill, a flour mill, and real estate. The firm of Smith and Keats, lumber merchants, was located on Main Street between First and Brook Streets, and in 1835 George built on Walnut between Third and Fourth Streets a mansion [9] that was a cultural center. As early as 1831 "the only Society formed professedly for literary improvement," the Louisville Lyceum, had George as one of its three curators.[10] The *Louisville Directory,* 1838, lists him as president of the Louisville Charitable Society, treasurer of the recently organized (March, 1838) Kentucky Historical Society,[11] and director of the Bank of Kentucky. He served as councilman from the Fourth Ward for several years, and in May, 1840, took a big part in establishing a new and fine public-school system [12] and in having the first bridge built across the Ohio River.[13] Still further examples

[8] See Nos. 286, 287.

[9] Paul Nafe, in the Louisville *Courier-Journal,* April 25, 1943, section 3, p. 9, gives a picture of the "castle," which sold for $166,000 in 1924, along with a popular account of George's activities. Pictures both of the house and the Keats monument in Cave Hill Cemetery, Louisville, are in the *Connoisseur,* September, 1945 (CXV, 12).

[10] *Libraries and Lotteries* (Cynthiana, Kentucky, 1944), p. 11.

[11] John Rowan was president, Wilkins Tannehill recording secretary.

[12] J. S. Johnston, *Memorial History of Louisville* (n.d.), I, 236, 647.

[13] Nafe, p. 9.

of his activities, literary as well as religious and financial, are given by Miss Kirk.

Just as his first financial disaster resulted from an unwise investment in a boat, so his final one came from a note he had endorsed to enable William Bakewell, Audubon's brother-in-law, to buy a shipping business. Already ill with a cold, says Miss Kirk, "in a desperate effort to salvage something from the crash, he overworked. The family disease, tuberculosis, developed with startling suddenness." George made his will on December 21, and died on Christmas Eve, 1841.

The Louisville *Daily Journal* on Christmas Day said:

DIED,

Yesterday, the 24th inst., Mr. GEORGE KEATS, a native of England, but for many years past a resident of this city, in the 44th year of his age.

Mr. Keats was a younger brother of John Keats, the distinguished British poet, and possessed much of the genius, and all of the philosop[h]y, benevolence, and enlarged philanthropy, of the lamented bard. The suavity of his manners and the charm of his conversation endeared him to all who knew him, and his enterprise and public spirit rendered him an inestimable member of society. There is not a man in our community whose death would be more deeply and universally mourned. When such a one passes away from among us, every heart feels a mysterious chill, as if touched by the awful shadow of the tomb.

The friends and acquaintances of the deceased are invited to attend his funeral, from his late residence on Walnut street, to-day, at half past 2, P. M.

FANNY KEATS LLANOS [1]

Fanny Keats was born in a Craven Street house on June 3, 1803, and christened at St. Botolph's Without, Bishopsgate.

[1] The only complete account of the Llanos family is that given by Adami.

on June 17 as Frances Mary Keats. Following the death of her grandmother, Mrs. John Jennings, in 1814, she was under the strict control of Richard Abbey, guardian of all four Keats children, who after sending her to school for three years, took her into his own household. John was devoted to her, though, thanks to Abbey's distrust of him and his friends, during his last years in London he saw comparatively little of her, and he was forced to leave for Italy without telling her goodby. The letters he sent her (forty-eight have been preserved) are tender and beautiful, even if, reading them years later, Severn had dismissed them as not worth publishing.[2] In the last letter, almost the last sentence, he wrote, Keats sadly referred to "my sister—who walks about my imagination like a ghost—she is **so** like Tom."

When Fanny became of age in 1824, she called upon Dilke, who henceforth acted as her trustee, to force Abbey to turn over her share of her grandmother's and her dead brothers' money. When the Court of Chancery proceedings ended early in 1825, Fanny had, according to her biographer, a fortune of some £4,500. Soon after, on March 30, 1826, she married at St. Luke's Church, Chelsea, Valentin Maria Llanos y Gutierrez.

Severn says nothing about it, but, according to the Irish novelist and playwright Gerald Griffin, Llanos "was intimate" with Keats in Rome and "spoke with him three days before he died."[3] Llanos was about the same age as Keats. Adami describes him as the youngest of the twelve children of a wealthy Valladolid merchant. After the accession to the Spanish throne of Ferdinand VII in 1814, he left Spain to wander over the Continent till 1821. Dilke insisted that he came to England *"for his education";* that possibly "the revolution prevented his return [to Spain], & compelled him to get a living by teaching

2 See II, 327.
3 See I, liii.

languages—but he was certainly in this country before the Revolution." [4] Llanos apparently met Fanny Brawne and Fanny Keats in the summer of 1821—certainly before October 8. Miss Brawne wrote Fanny Keats: Llanos "is everything that a Spanish Cavalier ought to be. . . . he is extremely gentlemanly and well behaved." [5] Mrs. Brawne was his "intimate friend"; [6] Charles Cowden Clarke, years later, described him as "a man of liberal principles, very attractive bearing, and of more than ordinary accomplishments"; [7] and others give equally favorable opinions. Dilke and George Keats (who never saw him) held less flattering views because of the way in which he squandered his wife's money on a foolish bridle-bit patent. Before that time, he had published two poor novels, *Don Esteban, or Memoirs of a Spaniard* (1825) and *Sandoval; or, The Freemason* (1826). Another novel, "The Spanish Exile" (1828), remains unpublished.

The later lives of the Llanos family need only a rapid summary. After a visit to the Continent in 1826–1828, Fanny and Valentin moved into the half of Wentworth Place which had been the old home of Keats and Brown. There they remained till the end of 1831 or the beginning of 1832. Of their subsequent adventures and misadventures in England and Spain perhaps enough details are given in Nos. 150, 157, 243, 263, 269. They had six children:

> Irene Louisa, September 5, 1827–January 8, 1833.
> Louis Mariano, July 25, 1829–August 15, 1834.
> Juan Henrique, September 18, 1831–September 21, 1905.
> Rosa Matilde, November 2, 1832–November 11, 1905.

[4] See II, 175.
[5] Edgcumbe, pp. 44, 46f.
[6] See I, 298.
[7] Clarke and Mary C. Clarke, *Recollections of Writers* (1878), p. 122.

Isabel Beatriz, later Countess Brockman, February 28, 1839–1926.

Luis Jorge, born December 9, 1843, died ——?

In 1861 Severn, then English consul in Rome, met Fanny Llanos for the first time, and they became devoted friends during her four-years' residence there. Thanks partly to his suggestion, but mainly to the efforts of Sir Charles Dilke, Houghton, and Forman, in 1879 Fanny received a grant of £150 from the Queen's Bounty Fund. During the next year a public subscription of some £300 was raised for her, and the government granted her a pension on the Civil List. Valentin Llanos died on August 14, 1885; Fanny, aged 86, on December 16, 1889. They were buried in the same grave in the cemetery of San Isidoro, Madrid.

Juan Llanos y Keats painted Fanny's portrait in 1879–1880 for Forman, who reproduced it in *John Keats and His Family* (1933). A copy made by Juan and sent to Fanny's American niece, Mrs. Philip Speed, was reproduced by J. G. Speed [8] in *McClure's Magazine,* October, 1895.[9]

RICHARD MONCKTON MILNES, FIRST BARON HOUGHTON

Milnes was born in London, June 19, 1809, and educated at Trinity College, Cambridge, where he was about the most brilliant of the so-called "Apostles"—Henry Lushington, R. C. (Archbishop) Trench, John Sterling, Tennyson, Arthur Hallam, and six other undergraduates. Somewhat prophetically, in 1829 Hallam and his group arranged for the publication in London of *Adonais,* while with Milnes and the fine Cambridge

[8] Who wrongly described it as an original. See the *Athenaeum,* December 7, 1895, p. 798.
[9] V, 460.

Union orator Thomas Sunderland [1] he debated at Oxford on the superiority of Shelley as a poet to Byron. "Their enthusiasm for *Adonais*," as Colvin remarks, "implied enthusiasm for its subject, Keats, as a matter of course." Leaving Cambridge in 1831, Milnes traveled through Germany and Italy, seeing Landor at Florence, and then with Christopher Wordsworth toured Greece. In 1842–1843 he visited Egypt and the Levant.

From 1835 until his death he was a prominent social leader and host, a politician of minor importance, an author and helper of authors. His poetry appeared in volumes called *Memorials of a Tour in Some Parts of Greece* (1834), *Memorials of a Residence on the Continent* (1838; enlarged, 1844), *Poems of Many Years* (1838), *Poetry for the People* (1840), *Poems Legendary and Historical* (1844), and *Palm Leaves* (1844). In the forties Milnes had such a high reputation as to be talked of as Wordsworth's successor as laureate. Landor is said to have maintained "that Milnes was the greatest poet then living and writing in England." Tennyson, however, rapidly eclipsed him, and "it was, in fact, he who recommended Tennyson for the Laureateship." [2] By the time a collected edition was made—in 1876—his verse was largely forgotten in England, and the visit he paid to America in 1875 failed to revive the memory of it there.

On July 30, 1851, Milnes married Annabel Crewe, by whom he had a son (created Earl of Crewe in 1895 and Marquess of Crewe in 1911) and two daughters, and who died in 1874. He himself became the first Baron Houghton in July, 1863, and died at Vichy on August 11, 1885. Reid [3] eulogizes

---

[1] Frances M. Brookfield, *The Cambridge "Apostles"* (1906), p. 325, calls him "perhaps the greatest scholar Cambridge has ever seen," which is sufficient praise. He became insane shortly after leaving Cambridge but lived till June, 1867 (Reid, I, 75f.).

[2] Brookfield, p. 235.

[3] II, 466f.

his life as "now made fragrant by the best of all the memories which can surround the name of the dead. . . . It was his greatest delight to give . . . the rich fruits of sympathy and love to all who stood in need of them. 'Write me as one that loved his fellow-men' was an epitaph . . . [which] may justly be claimed for him."

Houghton knew everybody worth knowing, and he was long spoken of, in Reid's fashion, as a gracious and indefatigable host; a charming and generous benefactor of literary men, like Tennyson, Hood, and David Gray; a tireless traveler; an enlightened politician interested in the betterment of the poor and other liberal causes. More recently he has been pictured as the possessor of a celebrated library of erotica and a man of unedifying tastes. In *The Romantic Agony* (1933),[4] for example, Mario Praz tells how he introduced Swinburne in 1860 to the works of the Marquis de Sade. Milnes, he goes on,

used his friends, in fact, as instruments, in order to put together some strange, cruel comedy, from which he, as spectator, would derive the greatest possible enjoyment, nor did he much care whether the spiritual welfare of the actors gained anything from it. The youthful Swinburne . . . showed the promise of abnormal tendencies; Milnes, to satisfy his mind, opened to the poet the *enfer* of his library—and a very rich *enfer* it was, with a European reputation.

Brown, who had met Milnes at Landor's Florentine house, gave him the "Memoir, with Literary Remains" in March, 1841, expecting him to publish it intact with notes and comments.[5] But even before the news of Brown's death reached him, Milnes, especially after reading Dilke's objections (No. 170) to the "Memoir," must have found such a procedure impracticable. Not before 1845 did he really get to work on his

[4] Pages 215f.
[5] See II, 102.

own biography. In the next three years he consulted nearly all
the poet's friends and from them received aid and encouragement, even from Reynolds, who at first had flatly forbidden the
use of his manuscripts. Much of the material which he re-
worked into the biography is herein printed. It proves him to
have been a far from scholarly writer who was careless about
reproducing texts and quotations exactly and frequently too
lazy to verify dates and other biographical details. He omits,
condenses, or shifts the order of his correspondents' words,
phrases, or sentences, as in Mrs. Procter's letter (No. 192), without notice. Yet, on the whole, his work is excellent for the
period (it is far more accurate than that of his friend and admirer Carlyle), and the two-volume *Life, Letters, and Literary
Remains, of John Keats* (1848), announced in the *Athenaeum*,
August 5, as "Just published," [6] and dedicated to the poet's belated admirer Lord Jeffrey, is pleasantly written, though, oddly
enough, he himself had a poor opinion of it. "It is," he wrote,
"the biography of a mere boy . . . and therefore the literary interest is but small. . . . I cannot expect any reputation for the
book." [7]

In his preface Milnes fully acknowledged the debts he
owed to Brown, Severn, Clarke, Reynolds, and others: "I received from the friends and acquaintances of the poet the kindest assistance." All helped him except Hunt, who "could only
encourage me by his interest and sympathy," and Bailey, whom
he thought dead. When he sent out gift-copies, all but Hunt
commended the work in flattering and cordial language. Reynolds 'loved' it; poor Mathew found it "most beautiful and in-

[6] Page 761.
[7] Walther Fischer, *Die Briefe Richard Monckton Milnes'* . . . *an Varn-
hagen von Ense* (1922), p. 122. Reid himself gives the *Life* almost no
attention.

teresting"; Dilke, except for reservations about the veiled attack on George Keats, thought the "spiriting kindly" and read with "eagerness and pleasure"; Haslam was overcome with emotion at the admirable portrait of his friend; Holmes praised the author's "great judgment & . . . discriminating hand"; Clarke without reservations said the volumes contained *"all I could have wished for his [Keats's] monumental fame"*; while Bailey, writing (in a hand as dreadful as Milnes's own) to resurrect himself from the dead, was deeply moved by the narrative. In short, all Keats's friends, except Hunt, were satisfied and, indeed, were titillated by the reflected glory the book threw on them; and they wished for an immediate second edition with corrections and additions. But Hunt, whose feelings were hurt by certain expressions in Keats's letters, objected so strenuously that, as Milnes told Bailey, a new edition was out of the question. Even after Hunt's death in 1859 it was still deferred.

Coventry Patmore had given Milnes, as Colvin [8] phrases it, "some measure of secretarial help," which apparently consisted only of transcribing Keats's letters.[9] As a paid amanuensis he was not mentioned in Milnes's preface. One hopes that remarks he made to his friends were misinterpreted. At any rate, in 1864 Clarke, who had forgotten his enthusiastic notes of 1848 (No. 236), wrote Severn that "there ought to be a better life of him [Keats]. *Between ourselves,* Holmes told me that Coventry Patmore was the writer of the so-called 'Life of

[8] Page 532.

[9] See Nos. 218, 220, 232. Perhaps Milnes discovered too late that Patmore was an inaccurate copyist. In volume I of what is thought to have been his own copy of the 1848 *Life* the printed texts were collated by Moxon with the original letters and dozens of errors and omissions noted. Only part of them were corrected in the 1867 *Life*.

Keats.' " [10] Holmes and Clarke were ill-informed, and their gossip can hardly have pleased Severn, since he regarded himself as Houghton's chief collaborator. He liked Houghton, and he liked the book—"Lord Houghton's [biography] or rather yours, where all has been said, and said well," as Fanny Llanos described it to him in 1877.[11] As recently as 1921 Arthur Severn referred to Houghton's "memoirs of Keats, most of which he got from my Father." [12] But all this is an exaggeration. Severn was an invaluable helper, but he had no more to do with the planning and composition of the biography than Patmore had.

In 1867 [13] Houghton issued in one volume *The Life and Letters of John Keats*, wherein he incorporated some new material and corrected various errors (Severn, Dilke, and Bailey were his chief helpers) and omitted the "Literary Remains," which he promised would soon appear "printed uniform" with the *Life*.[14] This time the dedicatee was Mrs. Bryan Procter. His edition of Keats's poems with a memoir had been issued in 1854, and it reappeared many times, as in 1856, 1858, 1861, 1863, 1864, 1865, 1866, 1868, 1869, 1871, 1876. In 1856 he published *Another Version of Hyperion,* and in 1876 the Aldine Keats with a new biographical sketch. Keats and his present-day biographers owe much to Lord Houghton. The *Life* is still far too frequently cited as an authority, but that is only natural in view of its numerous reprints, as in 1906, 1927, 1928, and 1931.

[10] Sharp, p. 256.

[11] The same, p. 254.

[12] *The John Keats Memorial Volume*, p. 168.

[13] An intermediate edition of 1852, listed by Ernest de Sélincourt in the *Cambridge Bibliography of English Literature*, III (1941), 221, seems to be a ghost. If not, it escapes mention in the British Museum and the Library of Congress catalogs, in all biographies and all other bibliographies of Keats.   [14] See II, 328n.

THE PROCTERS [1]

Early in 1820 "Barry Cornwall," or Bryan Waller Procter (1787–1874), persuaded Hunt to take him to call on Keats,
whom he found "very pleasant, and free from all affectation in
manner and opinion. . . . I never encountered a more manly
and simple young man." Two or three further meetings only
confirmed his first impressions.[2] In February Procter sent Keats
autographed copies of his *Dramatic Scenes* (1819), *Marcian
Colonna* (1820), and *A Sicilian Story* (1820), the last based on
the tale of Boccaccio which is the source of *Isabella*. In a note
accompanying the second of these Procter requested him to
"set me the example of leaving off the word 'Sir.' " In telling of
the gift Keats described it as "a specimen of great politeness,"
but the poems teased him: "they are composed of Amiability—
the Seasons, the Leaves, the Moon &c. upon which he rings . . .
triple bob majors." Nonetheless, in turn he sent Procter an
inscribed copy of the *Lamia* volume, now in the Victoria and
Albert Museum.[3] As a contributor to the *London Magazine*,
Procter learned of Keats's illness and death through letters that
its editor, Taylor, showed him. He was greatly touched, and he
composed for the magazine, April, 1821,[4] a fine tribute to the
dead poet that was widely copied and quoted in England and
America.[5]

Mrs. Procter, the former Anne Skepper (1799–1888),
stepdaughter of Basil Montagu, had an even more casual connection with the poet; so casual, indeed, that she merely saw

[1] See R. W. Armour, *Barry Cornwall* (1935).

[2] The same, *The Literary Recollections of Barry Cornwall* (1936), p. 104.

[3] *Letters*, pp. 470f., 477.

[4] III, 426f. It is signed "L.," but Procter's authorship is vouched for by
Taylor in a letter of March 28 (see Olive M. Taylor, *London Mercury*,
XII [1925], 260).

[5] See *Keats' Reputation*, pp. 7f., 107.

him twice at Hazlitt's lectures of 1818.[6] But all the rest of her life she recalled his face as "one of singular beauty and brightness" with "an expression as if he had been looking upon some glorious sight." That she remembered his eyes as blue, his hair as auburn, thereby misleading Milnes and starting a protracted word-battle, is a detail of small importance. Mrs. Procter was a celebrated wit and hostess who knew almost everybody of importance. To her Houghton dedicated the revised edition (1867) of his biography, calling her "A poet's wife, a poet's mother, and herself of many poets the frequent theme and valued friend"; and Colvin [7] somewhat inaccurately remarked that she "—staunchest, wittiest, and youngest-hearted defier of Time that she was—" and her husband "were the only two persons I have known and spoken to who had known and spoken to Keats."

JOHN HAMILTON REYNOLDS [1]

Reynolds, often called Keats's dearest friend, was born at Shrewsbury on September 9, 1794. He entered Shrewsbury School in 1803 and, after the family had moved to London, St. Paul's School on March 4, 1806. Early in 1810 he withdrew from school to serve as a junior clerk in the Amicable Insurance Office. Through Rice he became an intimate friend of Bailey and of the three Leigh sisters at Sidmouth before the end of 1815. Apparently Reynolds had been in love with a girl, now unknown, who died before January, 1815, and whose features were accidentally reproduced by Haydon in "Christ's Entry

6 See No. 192.
7 Pages 321f., n.
1 The chief printed authority on Reynolds is Marsh; the fullest account of his life, Pope's (see I, xlii n.)

into Jerusalem." [2] He had also published various things, including *Safie, An Eastern Tale* (1814), *The Eden of Imagination* (1814), and a pamphlet called *An Ode* (1815). He was introduced by the Leigh girls to Eliza Powell Drewe, of Exeter, and by late summer, 1816, was in love with her,[3] though their marriage was postponed until August 31, 1822. Meanwhile, on December 25, 1816, Reynolds and Bailey had presented to Thomasine Leigh their manuscript "Poems by Two Friends"— twenty-five poems by the one, thirty-two by the other.

Reynolds met Keats at Leigh Hunt's no later than October, 1816.[4] They were kindred spirits. By September, 1817, Keats was telling Jane Reynolds that "henceforth I shall consider as mine" "your Brother John"; and by July, 1818, was assuring Reynolds, "upon my soul, I have been getting more and more close to you every day, ever since I knew you." [5] Reynolds introduced Keats to Brown, Rice, Bailey, Taylor, Hessey, and others; [6] favorably reviewed the *Poems* (1817) in the *Champion* (March 9); [7] talked about poetry with him and in a large measure counteracted the bad influence of Hunt; inspired him to write various poems like "Robin Hood" and *Isabella;* prevented him from publishing the first tactless, indeed reckless, preface to *Endymion*; [8] and defended this last poem against its savage reviewers in an Exeter newspaper article that Hunt reprinted in the *Champion.*

Unquestionably Reynolds was a good influence on Keats, although except for *The Fancy* (1820), his own literary produc-

[2] See II, 281.
[3] Pope, pp. 633f., 646.
[4] See No. 2 and II, 177.
[5] *Letters*, pp. 43, 178.
[6] Including, he says, Dilke (see II, 177).
[7] See *Letters*, pp. 13f., and Rollins in *Studies in Honor of A. H. R. Fairchild* (1946), pp. 163-166.
[8] See II, 178.

tions—*The Naiad: A Tale* (1816), a successful farce with the curious title of *One, Two, Three, Four, Five: By Advertisement* (1819), and a parody of Wordsworth, *Peter Bell, A Lyrical Ballad* (1819)—were none too promising. But literature was only his avocation, since in November, 1817,[9] he had taken up the study of law. Reynolds entered this "dreary profession" at the urgency of Rice,[10] who paid the fee—about £110—that his relative Fladgate demanded before accepting Reynolds as "an Articled Pupil," and promised upon succeeding to his father's business to take Reynolds as a partner, a promise that he kept faithfully.[11] In November, 1819, Keats observed that Reynolds "has settled in Lodgings very near to Rice's and seems set in for the Law." [12]

Keats became more and more critical of Reynolds' family, but his affection for Reynolds himself remained constant. He called Reynolds "the playfullest" of the "three witty people" in his set, one who "makes you laugh and not think." [13] That the friendship lasted is remarkable, since Reynolds had a very low opinion of Fanny Brawne, that "poor idle Thing of woman-kind," and her mother.[14] Keats, indeed, probably knew and resented Reynolds' attitude towards Fanny Brawne, and, if so, that would explain Brown's insistence in 1821, "the fact is, he was no dear friend to Keats, nor did Keats think him so." [15] Noticeably, too, he did not consider going with his sick friend to Italy, but he was dubious about Severn's qualifications; [16] nor did he try to find any substitute, although in the

9 *Letters*, p. 62.
10 And also that of Eliza Drewe, says Marsh, p. 20.
11 *Letters* (quoting Dilke), p. 177.
12 The same, p. 442.
13 The same, p. 454.
14 See I, 156.
15 Sharp, p. 109.
16 See I, 157.

previous year he had exerted himself in the behalf of Henry Worsley, a young man who wanted to travel abroad as a companion.[17] He even failed to make the kindly gesture of sailing on the boat to Gravesend, and he supplied none of the money that Taylor *used* to cover Keats's expenses in Italy.[18] There may be some significance in the fact that Keats wrote to him for the last time, so far as is known, on February 28, 1820.

After Keats's death he published *The Garden of Florence; and Other Poems* (1821) and contributed to the *London Magazine,* the *Athenaeum* (of which he was part owner from 1828 to June 8, 1831), and other magazines. With his brother-in-law Thomas Hood he wrote the anonymous *Odes and Addresses to Great People* (1825). His membership in the Garrick Club (1831) resulted in his composing a *New Entertainment* (1833) and, with George Dance, a farce called *Confounded Foreigners* (1838). In the meanwhile, as a member of the firm Rice and Reynolds he had done a good deal of legal business, poorly they thought, for Fanny and George Keats. He had likewise almost entirely dropped his old acquaintances in the Keats circle. As early as November 20, 1827, Taylor reports, "Reynolds has been ill of a Fever, but I have not seen him for this three Years nearly." [19] Again, on January 9, 1835, he wrote: "Reynolds . . . has lost a Child—but she was his only Child, a Daughter, 10 years of age, and I understand he grieves much for her Loss." [20] Some twenty years later Hessey lamented that Reynolds had withdrawn from his and Taylor's society, "I scarcely know how & why." [21] Long before that time Reynolds had grossly mismanaged the Llanos' money. His own affairs,

---

[17] See I, 72f.

[18] See I, 207n.; Sharp, pp. 100f.; Pope, p. 734.

[19] Blunden, p. 185.

[20] The same, pp. 199f.

[21] See II, 475. In a letter of October 31, 1837 (No. 347), to Taylor, Reynolds lamented the fact that we are "now strangers."

Dilke said in February, 1833, had "been long desperate," a bit of news which led George Keats to express the fear that "he may be even now obtaining money from Abbey on my account." [22] The 'desperation' probably explains why, at some unspecified date, Reynolds gave up the law business turned over to him by Rice.

All along Reynolds had played with the idea of being Keats's biographer, but he procrastinated. After Brown had arranged for Milnes to begin the work, Reynolds, angered by what he considered Taylor's duplicity, at first declined to allow any of the valuable manuscript material in his possession to be used. That situation was changed by tactful letters from Milnes, to whom he turned over all his papers,[23] and hence Milnes not only thanked him in the preface to the *Life* (1848) [24] but also inserted in the book a flattering remark about the "invaluable worth of his friendship to Keats" and his own "remarkable verse." There seems to be some justice in Brown's charge (1821) that Reynolds "wished he should shine as the dear friend of poor Keats." [25] He himself protested to Milnes (No. 204) about Taylor's suggestion "that none of my letters should be printed— & 'that my name should not be mentioned in the Memoir!' " —"It would be playing Hamlet, without Laertes!"

Reynolds was extremely enthusiastic about the *Life,* and he promised to send corrections and additions for the second edition which, he said, *"must* come." [26] The publication of Milnes's book marked his last moment of near-greatness. The

[22] See II, 9, 14.

[23] Except his copy of the *Poems* (1817), in which Keats had written four sonnets. A writer in the London *Times,* May 18, 1914, p. 10, says he "deliberately suppressed this volume," whereas Garrod, p. 527, thinks he "must have forgotten" it.

[24] I, 31, and note.

[25] Sharp, p. 109.

[26] See II, 239.

end of his life was as depressing as its beginning had been promising. In 1861 William Robson, author and translator (1785–1863), wrote: "I did not see Reynolds for many years before his death, but when I asked Mr. C. Kemble, with whom I was very intimate, after him, he always shook his head, and said—'Brandy & Water! Brandy & Water,' and what was still worse, I was warned if I met him, *not to play at cards with him!*" [27]

Equally depressing is the statement of Lord Ernle (R. E. Prothero):

Lord John Russell . . . in 1847, appointed him assistant clerk of the newly established County Court at Newport, in the Isle of Wight. In Newport Reynolds lived for the five years that elapsed before his death in 1852. He was buried in the churchyard of the town,—a broken-down, discontented man, whose great literary abilities had brought him no success in life. Few, probably, of the islanders were aware that the assistant County-Court clerk, who professed himself an Unitarian and a bitter Radical, and whose drunken habits placed him beyond the pale of society, had promised to be one of the stars of English literature at the period of its poetic revival. [28]

Pope [29] shows that Ernle has somewhat blackened the facts, and that the *Hampshire Independent,* reporting Reynolds' death,

[27] Blunden, p. 222.

[28] *The Works of Lord Byron. . . . Letters and Journals,* III (1922), 46n. The *Athenaeum,* April 20, 1901, p. 501 (see also April 27, p. 531), published a letter in which he said: "As to the later days of Reynolds in Newport, . . . his drunken habits were, in my childhood, the talk of the neighbourhood, and the legends of his doings innumerable. My father, who was a clergyman within three miles of Newport, knew him well, and the fact is incontestable." Mrs. Procter disposed of Reynolds more charitably when she wrote to Thackeray (*Letters,* ed. G. N. Ray, III [1946], 127): "Poor John Hamilton Reynolds is dead— He had long been very poorly—and died very quietly conscious that [he] was leaving this world."

[29] I cite a reprint from *Wessex,* III (1935), 9-11.

called him "highly respected." On his tombstone in the cemetery on Church Litten is now inscribed his highest distinction: "In memory of John Hamilton Reynolds who died November 15th, 1852. Aged 58 years. The friend of Keats." [30]

REYNOLDS' FAMILY

George Reynolds, the father of Keats's friend, was born in London probably in December, 1764, or early in January, 1765. For some six years (1774–1779) he was a pupil at Christ's Hospital. From about 1794 to 1806 he served as a writing master or schoolmaster at Shrewsbury. Returning to London in 1806, he held various positions, among them master of the Lambeth Boys' Parochial School, writing master to the Female Asylum, Lambeth, and writing master to Christ's Hospital from May, 1817, to March, 1835, at which date he retired on a pension. He died on July 29, 1853. A pen sketch "depicts him as a quaintly garbed, jolly old gentleman." [1]

Keats never mentions George Reynolds, but for a time he was a frequent visitor at the Reynolds house in Little Britain, and in letters he often sends his love to Mrs. Reynolds and her two oldest daughters. Charlotte Cox Reynolds was born on November 5, 1761,[2] and died on May 13, 1848. In 1827 under the pen name of Mrs. Hamerton she published a story called *Mrs. Leslie and Her Grandchildren.* George and Charlotte Reynolds had at least five children: Jane, John Ham-

[30] See the obituaries in the *Athenaeum*, November 27, 1852, p. 1296, the *Annual Register* for 1852, p. 330, and the *Gentleman's Magazine*, n.s., XXXIX (1853), 100f.

[1] H. C. Shelley, *Literary By-Paths* (1906), p. 223 (see also p. 349). Shelley also reproduces sketches or paintings of J. H. Reynolds and his mother, sister Marianne, wife, and sister Jane (pp. 222, 224, 226, 231, 354).

[2] Walter Jerrold, *Thomas Hood* (1907), p. 204. In *Letters*, p. xli, the date is given as November 15.

ilton, Marianne, Eliza, and Charlotte. Jane (1791–1846) became the wife of the poet Thomas Hood in 1825, and with her children Thomas and Frances Freeling (Mrs. John Somerville Broderip) figures in Nos. 348, 349, and 350. Marianne (1797–1874), an especial favorite with George Keats, after being proposed to and then more or less jilted by Bailey, married H. G. Green before 1833, and was the mother of the artists Charles and Townley Green. Eliza (born 1799) married Dr. George Longmore of Upwell, Norfolk, in February, 1822, and died before December, 1870, when her son William sent the first of three letters to Houghton (Nos. 273, 275, 281). Charlotte (born 1802) lived till 1884, unmarried, and gave much information about her family and Keats to Forman.

For some time Keats was on friendly terms with the Reynolds family, as were Bailey, Rice, the Dilkes, and Charles Lamb. Mrs. Reynolds, Jane, and Marianne were among his correspondents. At their house he wrote the sonnet beginning "Spenser! a jealous honourer of thine," which he gave to Eliza. Mrs. Reynolds' cat suggested the sonnet of that name. Charlotte told Forman "that she sometimes played to Keats for hours," and she is supposed to have inspired the poem, "I had a dove," [3] and "Hush! hush! tread softly." For Jane he wrote "O Sorrow! why dost borrow" and "On a Leander Gem Which Miss Reynolds, My Kind Friend, Gave Me." Jane, Marianne, and Charlotte are thought [4] to be addressed in "To the Ladies Who Saw Me Crown'd." Marianne apparently had two of Keats's autograph manuscripts, which she bequeathed to her son Townley.[5]

But if Keats usually disliked the girls with whom his friends were in love, the Reynolds women in turn made spite-

---

[3] *Letters*, p. 266n.
[4] Finney, I, 180.
[5] The same, II, 775.

ful remarks about the sweethearts of their men friends. By October, 1818, though Keats admitted that the "Miss Reynoldses are very kind to me," he added, "but they have lately displeased me much," particularly by their derogatory comments on the "east indian," or Jane Cox, whom he admired.[6] In September, a year later, he confesses that except for John Hamilton Reynolds he is prejudiced against "all that family." [7] Though for some time he had found the "Miss Reynoldses . . . all very dull," he continued to see them occasionally, as at Mrs. Dilke's "hop" of January 11, 1820, but at that party they were not "very enticing," and he was "affraid to speak to [them] for fear of some sickly reiteration of Phrase or Sentiment." [8] Mrs. Reynolds called during Keats's illness of February, 1820.[9] Probably she was none too welcome, for her dislike of Fanny Brawne, who lived next door, must have been obvious to Keats. Certainly Fanny knew the sentiments of the whole family towards her. Telling Fanny Keats in November, 1821, that Mrs. Dilke had quarreled with the Reynolds', she added: "If you live [to] the age of the Methuselem and I die tomorrow never be intimate with the Reynolds. . . . Every day I live I find out more of their malice against me." [10] Rice, however, remained a steadfast friend of the Reynolds women, and as late as 1860 Hessey spoke (in the past tense) kindly of them all and wondered "whether any of them are still alive."

JAMES RICE, JR.

All readers of Keats's letters know and admire James Rice, but few details of his life are preserved. Pope [1] has shown that

---

[6] *Letters*, p. 232.
[7] The same, p. 400.
[8] The same, pp. 297, 450, 453.
[9] The same, p. 458.
[10] Edgcumbe, pp. 48f.
[1] Page 39f., 629-638. See I, xlii n.

he met the Leigh girls in Sidmouth, which he was visiting for his health, on June 26, 1814, and that to them he introduced Bailey and, before the year ended, Reynolds. The three young men were intimately associated with the three girls, to whom they addressed various poems, nine by Rice being known.[2] Thomasine Leigh's silhouette and miniature of him are now in the Keats Museum, Hampstead.

Reynolds introduced Rice to Keats[3] sometime before April 18, 1817,[4] and their acquaintance rapidly grew into close friendship. "I have had a great deal of pleasant time with Rice lately," the poet said in January, 1818, and many other letters mention him with admiration and affection—"a friend . . . to whom I am greatly attached."[5] They spent a month together during the summer of 1819 in the Isle of Wight, and more or less got on each other's nerves. As Keats explained, "He was unwell and I was not in very good health: and I am affraid we made each other worse by acting upon each other's spirits. We would grow as melancholy as need be."[6] But this natural re-action did no permanent damage to their friendship. A short time afterwards, Keats spoke of Rice as "the most sensible, and even wise Man I know—he has a few John Bull prejudices; but they improve him."[7] Again he calls him "the wisest" of "three witty people" in his set: he "makes you laugh and think."[8]

Early in 1821 Rice was one of the five friends who sub-scribed £10 to Taylor's fund for Keats,[9] and later in that year Brown included his name in the list of those among whom

[2] Pope, pp. 42-47, reproduces them.
[3] See II, 177.
[4] See *Letters,* p. 22.
[5] The same, pp. 74, 346.
[6] The same, p. 364 (and see p. 522).
[7] The same, p. 400.
[8] The same, p. 454.
[9] See I, 235.

Keats's books were to be divided.[10] Pigot's *Commercial Directory*, 1823–1824, includes James Rice and Son as attorneys, 62 Great Marlborough Street, with James Rice living at Poland Street, Oxford Street, and James Rice, Jr., at 50 Poland Street, presumably identical addresses. In 1825 "James Rice, Junr." was one of the witnesses at the wedding of Thomas Hood and Jane Reynolds.[11] Several years earlier, he persuaded Reynolds to enter the "dreary profession" of law and "ultimately . . . into partnership." [12] The partners, Rice and Reynolds, acted as Fanny Keats's solicitors after her marriage, and handled business for her and George in a fashion that pleased neither, on one occasion seriously embarrassing George by refusing to honor a draft.[13]

For all his gayety and wit Rice had for years suffered with some incurable ailment. His life, indeed, was nothing but "a long lingering" ever since Keats first met him,[14] and it was some time before his parents, Keats wrote, were "able to appreciate him better than they did in his first youth" and became "devoted to his comfort." [15] He may have retired before May, 1832, when George Keats mentioned Reynolds', but not Rice's, mismanagement of the Llanos affairs.[16] He died before February 12, 1833, the day on which Dilke characterized him as "the best of all who formed the associates of my early life— the best man indeed I ever knew." [17] George Keats [18] agreed that "he was indeed a noble fellow," while Reynolds years later

10 See I, 260.
11 *Letters*, p. xl.
12 See II, 178.
13 No. 141.
14 See II, 10.
15 *Letters*, p. 360.
16 See II, 5.
17 See II, 10.
18 See II, 16.

testified, "For every quality that marks the sensible Companion —the valuable Friend—the Gentleman and the Man—I have known no one to surpass him." [19]

JOSEPH SEVERN [1]

Today Severn is the best-known of Keats's friends. He was born, the son of James Severn, a musician, at Hoxton on December 7, 1793. At an early age he was apprenticed to an engraver named William Bond, in whose service he spent seven or eight unhappy years copying works of art. He managed, however, to attend classes in painting at the Royal Academy, and determined to become a famous artist. When or where he met Keats cannot be determined. In one of several contradictory statements he set the date, far too early, in 1813, but it is not improbable that Haslam, his lifelong friend, introduced him to Keats, then a student at Guy's Hospital, in October or November, 1815, and very likely that the introduction came no later than the spring of 1816. Keats first mentions Severn in a letter of December 17, 1816, wherein he says that Severn "yesterday" promised to visit him that night, and in the letter Forman, perhaps wrongly, detects a reference to a portrait Severn had painted of him.[2]

The first meeting, whenever it occurred, delighted Severn, though Keats seems to have regarded him more as a casual acquaintance than a real friend. It raised me, Severn later wrote, "to the third heaven. . . . A new world was opened to me, and I was raised from the mechanical drudgery of my art to the hope of brighter and more elevated courses." [3] For a

[19] See II, 178.
[1] In spite of the biographies of Sharp and the Countess of Birkenhead (*Against Oblivion*, 1943) a satisfactory life of Severn is still to be written.
[2] *Letters*, p. 12.
[3] Sharp, p. 19.

time the artist was on closer terms with George Keats than with the poet, and the four letters the latter wrote to him are polite, friendly, though somewhat reserved and formal. On the other hand, his copy of the 1817 *Poems*, now at Harvard, was inscribed, "The Author consigns this Copy to the Severn with all his Heart." Keats was interested in art and artists; he admired Severn's portraits and his fair musical skill; but he never admitted him to the intimacy which he shared with Hunt, Clarke, Brown, Reynolds, Bailey, or Dilke. Remarkably enough, Severn knew nothing of his passion for Fanny Brawne until the poet had left England, though as early as July, 1819, Keats was jealous of the attention Fanny paid *him*.[4]

Severn was a gay companion. Fanny Brawne could hardly believe that anything could make him unhappy, for she never saw him serious for ten minutes at a time.[5] Now and then the poet enjoyed this gayety. After Charles Wells and Severn had dined with him on January 4, 1818, he wrote his brothers: "We had a very pleasant day. I pitched upon another bottle of claret —Port—we enjoyed ourselves very much were all very witty and full of Rhyme—we played a Concert from 4 o'clock till 10— drank your Healths the Hunts and N.B. Severn Peter Pindars." [6] On other occasions, as in March, 1819, Keats "took a turn" about the British Museum or the National Gallery, with Severn as a guide to point out the beauties of the Elgin Marbles or the paintings of Titian.[7] In April of that year Severn's miniature of Keats and his painting "Hermia and Helena" were exhibited at the Royal Academy with no acclaim. In December, however, the Academy awarded him a medal in a students' competition for "The Cave of Despair," and when the award was ridiculed

[4] *Letters*, p. 362.
[5] Edgcumbe, p. 13.
[6] *Letters*, p. 74.
[7] The same, p. 311; Sharp, pp. 28f.

by certain other painters Keats tactlessly but loyally defended his friend.[8] Severn saw Keats "many times" in the first half of 1820 and thereafter visited him "twice a week."

Ordered by the doctors to Italy, Keats at once wrote to Brown, asking for his company, but getting no reply. For a time it appeared as if he would have to go alone.[9] The boat was to sail on September 17, and Keats went to Taylor's house on September 13 to make final preparations. Fortunately, Haslam had talked to Severn during the preceding night, and hence on the thirteenth he informed the delighted Taylor of Severn's decision to accompany the poet. That decision was the most important Severn ever made, as he himself fully realized, even if the reasons behind it have often been misinterpreted or adversely criticized. Milnes,[10] for example, said: "Entirely regardless of his future prospects, and ready to abandon all the advantages of the position he had won, Mr. Severn at once offered to accompany Keats to Italy." Actually, as B. I. Evans [11] remarks: "Quite apart from Keats he had his own motives for going: for in Rome he might work for the Royal Academy travelling scholarship, his only chance of maintaining himself in his years of training as a painter."

Unquestionably Severn did think of his own future as much as of Keats's dire need, but what man would or could have thought in any other way? Reynolds, once Keats's best friend, who did not even toy with the notion of making the journey, described Severn as "scarcely the resolute, intelligent or cheerful companion" the sick man needed; [12] Dr. Clark, too,

8 See I, lxxix, and Milnes, 1, 73 (who dates the incident in "the winter of 1817–18").
9 Edgcumbe, p. 4.
10 II, 70.
11 His interpretation of Severn's motives and character, *London Mercury*, August, 1934 (XXX, 337-349), is the best yet written.
12 See I, 157.

at first felt that, though very attentive, he was "not the best suited for his companion"; [13] and various contemporary writers have expressed severer judgments. But few people in the 1820's would, and few now will, even if relatives by blood, condemn themselves to be shut up for months with a sick person. Like everyone else, Severn had faults and limitations. The fact remains that he was the only acquaintance of Keats's even to consider going to Italy; that he left in spite of the violent objections (extending to physical assault) of his father; [14] and that, in short, he attended his friend with a devotion and kindness seldom equaled. Like many other sick persons Keats could hardly endure a strange face or voice, and there was only a handful of strangers in Rome who made any effort to go to Severn's aid. For weeks he acted as nurse, cook, cleaner, secretary, entertainer, spiritual consoler, and confidant to the sick poet, who died in his arms. He deserves all the bouquets and few of the brickbats that have been thrown at him.

Many of the letters in which Severn describes the final months of Keats's life are herein printed. They present him in a good light, and it is certainly not to his discredit that after writing a touching letter to Haslam or Brown he penned gay, gossipy letters to members of his own family. The best nurses, the only ones who hold out, are those who can in off-hours put aside all thought of their patients—and Severn had few off-hours.

Money could never have bought service as devoted and unremitting as Severn's, who expected and got no money at all. It is, then, only poetic justice that, immediately after Keats's death, the artists and the English society leaders in Rome promptly took him up. While he was painting "The Death of Alcibiades," a work which in November, 1821,

[13] See I, 172.
[14] Sharp, pp. 51f.

brought him the Royal Academy's three years' traveling pension of £130 and a refund of his travel expenses to Rome, he was rejoicing, somewhat naively, in "the most polite attention" he was receiving from a "party of English Noblemen," from a group of "kind and good" artists, and from two lords and titled ladies and "many others of the English gentry" (No. 116). Lowell [15] finds it "unpleasant to feel, as we must, that although his love [for Keats] was undoubtedly sincere, he made capital of it. . . . What began as genuine admiration ended as advertisement. . . . Severn was a weak and a vain man." She should have remembered that practically all artists are vain, that as a matter of course they advertise themselves frankly and without shame, and, further, that while Severn was trying to make his own reputation as a painter he was incessantly trying to establish that of Keats as a poet. Few artists today would criticize his remark of June 27, 1823, to his sister Sarah (though some might possibly be less candid), "I make a point never to know anyone who is not superior to me in fortune or ability, or some way or other, that I may still be raising myself and improving, even in moments of pastime." [16] Again, when he told Maria Severn on October 4, 1824, "My coming with Keats and friendship for him will be a never fading Laurel. For everyone knows it, as Keats' name is rising and everyone respects my character for it," and Tom Severn on November 21, 1825, Keats's "Friendship and death are so interwoven with my name that it will be ever an honour [to] me," [17] he was merely predicting a state of affairs that has long since existed. How can Severn be blamed for his pride in Keats's friendship? Great poets keep alive the memories of many totally obscure people—and Severn certainly was not obscure. If he exaggerated his early intimacy

[15] I, 106f.
[16] B. I. Evans, p. 348.
[17] The same.

with Keats, that is a venial error in a man who was Keats's only attendant and confidant during the final dark, painful months. The anxious friends in London who read Severn's letters with sorrowful interest and copied and passed them around to one another—or all except the elusive Mrs. Isabella Jones [18]—gave no thought to his vanity. George Keats always spoke gratefully of Severn, and Fanny Keats to the end of her days looked upon him as a benefactor, almost a brother. Holmes and Hunt and Clarke,[19] Taylor, Haslam, and Hessey were similarly grateful. Hunt [20] considered him an ideal companion because of his "old acquaintanceship, great animal spirits, active tenderness, and a mind capable of appreciating that of the poet." In 1826 Dilke, after seeing the tomb Severn had erected at his own expense, remarked, "I always liked Severn, and shall like him the better as long as I live," [21] and in 1848 he noted that "no friendship could for the time have been more severely tried & no friend found more nobly self-devoted. For that Severn deserves all honor—and I for one shall always honor him for that devotion—but I did not & cannot see the wonderful sacrifice of going on a Journey to Italy." [22] Brown wrote on January 15, 1821, "I feel . . . all your attentions to my unhappy Keats as if they were shown to myself," [23] and in March, "I feel towards you as a brother for your kindness to our brother Keats." [24] Two years later he found nothing important to criticize in Severn except his "vile trick of mingling" English and Italian words: "Bating this fault . . . ," he told Thomas Richards,[25] "I think him quite

18 See Blunden, pp. 97f.
19 Sharp, pp. 127, 130, 258.
20 *Autobiography*, II (1850), 211.
21 *Papers*, I, 17.
22 Note in his copy of Milnes.
23 See I, 200.
24 Sharp, p. 88.
25 M. B. Forman, *Some Letters*, pp. 39f.

a perfect fellow. He has a generous way of thinking on all occasions and an independence of spirit that I seldom saw equalled." The "Apostle" (later Archbishop) Trench wrote in 1830: "He is a very fine fellow, and I like him amazingly," "he cherishes most affectionately" Keats's memory.[26]

As the fame of "poor Keats" slowly developed, that of Severn automatically and justly kept pace. Many Victorians grew sentimental in discussing the "sacred friendship" of the two, as when W. M. Rossetti remarked: "In the annals of watchful and self-oblivious friendship there are few records more touching than the one which links with the name of John Keats that of Joseph Severn." [27] But whatever Severn's demerits as man and artist, his fame will continue so long as *Adonais* and biographies of Keats and Shelley are read. Shelley's prayer, "May the unextinguished Spirit of his illustrious friend . . . plead against Oblivion for his name!" long ago was answered. It is true that his later artistic career was not successful. His numerous paintings found, as M. B. Forman says,[28] "a certain acceptance for the sake of the poet at whose deathbed he had attended so devotedly," but are usually ignored in most works on art today. His name does not even appear in Richard and Samuel Redgrave's *A Century of Painters* (1890). On the other hand, his miniatures, sketches, and portraits of Keats, Reynolds, and the Severn family are still highly esteemed.

For twenty years after Keats's death Severn lived in Italy. In 1828 he married Elizabeth, daughter of General Lord Archibald Montgomerie (died 1814), and ward of his patroness, the Countess of Westmorland, who violently opposed the marriage. Of his six children three, Walter, Arthur, and especially Ann Mary (Mrs. Charles Thomas Newton), were artists of distinction.

[26] Maria Trench, *Richard Chenevix Trench*, I (1885), 51.
[27] *Life of John Keats* (1887), pp. 54, 63.
[28] *Letters*, p. xlv.

Early in 1841 Severn returned with his family to England. In a letter of March 21 Brown welcomed him home and announced his decision of giving to Milnes the "Life and Literary Remains" of Keats for publication.[29] Thereafter Milnes frequently consulted Severn, and he says in his preface that without the artist's help "I should probably have never thought of undertaking the task." [30] For years after 1848 Severn supplied Milnes with new (and old) details and anecdotes, often inaccurate and conflicting. But the debt Milnes and subsequent biographers owe to him cannot be overstated. Mrs. Pidgeon, the Cotterells, Captain Walsh, the English nurse, Ewing, Lieutenant Elton, Llanos, and the few others who saw Keats outside England have left almost no records of the poet. But for Severn's letters and reminiscences nearly all that we would know about Keats's last days would come from Dr. Clark's three brief notes (Nos. 80, 87, 91).

Aside from helping Milnes, Severn "enjoyed an uneventful and industrious art-life in London" [31] until 1860. In that year Charles Thomas Newton resigned the consulship at Rome to resume his work as keeper of classical antiquities at the British Museum. Probably Newton, who married Ann Mary Severn in April, 1861, suggested that her father apply for the post. Though he was overage—sixty-seven—he was backed by Gladstone, Houghton, and Ruskin, and he was appointed consul in January, 1861. Mrs. Severn, too ill to accompany him to Rome, died at Marseilles in April, 1862.

The remainder of Severn's life was placid and useful. He met Fanny Llanos in April, 1861, saw much of her until her return to Spain in the fall of 1864, and both in 1864 and 1877

[29] Sharp, pp. 193f.
[30] In the 1867 edition, p. 328, Houghton pays him a graceful compliment on "the self-devotion of his youth."
[31] Sharp, p. 201.

tried through Houghton to have her pensioned by the British government. In 1872 he retired from the consulship on a pension. Where a modern writer says that his association with Keats "was his only claim to fame," [32] Ruskin had different ideas. In *Praeterita* [33] he gives a charming sketch:

> There is nothing in any circle that ever I saw or heard of, like what Mr. Joseph Severn then was in Rome. He understood everybody, native and foreign, civil and ecclesiastic, in what was nicest in them, and never saw anything else than the nicest. . . . He forgave the Pope his papacy, reverenced the beggar's beard, and felt that alike the steps of the Pincian, and the Araceli, and the Lateran, and the Capitol, led to heaven, and everybody was going up, somehow; but might be happy where they were in the meantime. Lightly sagacious, lovingly humorous, daintily sentimental, he was in council with the cardinals to-day, and at picnic in Campagna with the brightest English belles to-morrow; and caught the hearts of all in the golden net of his good will and good understanding.

Baron Bunsen, the Prussian minister at Rome, likewise characterized him as having "peculiar fitness" for his job, as "universally useful and popular among the English residents" and acceptable to "Romans of all classes," and as having more "*practical* knowledge and ability" than any other artist he had ever known.[34]

Almost to the end of his life Severn continued to paint. In February, 1879,[35] when he was a sort of legendary figure, he was eulogized by Sir Vincent Eyre at the unveiling of the memorial tablet on the Keats House in the Piazza di Spagna. He died about five months later, August 3, 1879, aged eighty-five, and was buried in the new Protestant cemetery. Sentiment

[32] Lowell, I, 106.
[33] *Works*, ed. E. T. Cook and Alexander Wedderburn, XXXV (1908), 278.
[34] Sharp, p. 216.
[35] See II, 369n.

prevailed: funds for a suitable monument were quickly raised in the United States by a committee headed by Richard Watson Gilder [36] and endorsed by Lowell, Longfellow, and other literati; while in Great Britain Houghton, Archbishop Trench, D. G. Rossetti, and many more celebrities did their share. Permission was secured from the Roman government, and in 1881 Severn's body was reinterred by the side of Keats. There could be no lovelier or more suitable last resting place for him whom the tombstone describes as "devoted friend and deathbed companion of John Keats. . . . An artist eminent for his representations of Italian life and nature. . . . In recognition of his services to freedom and humanity."

JOHN TAYLOR AND JAMES AUGUSTUS HESSEY [1]

Keats was lucky in having his last two volumes published by Taylor and Hessey, a firm perhaps more distinguished for its intimate associations with authors and artists than for its book list, which, however, included, along with the Reverend Harvey Marriott, of Claverton, and the Reverend Francis Hodgson, of Bakewell, the names of Coleridge, Landor, Carlyle, De Quincey, Hazlitt, and other celebrities. Both were fond of him personally. They made him welcome in their homes, introduced him to many interesting men, defended him stoutly against the reviewers, loaned him books and money, and, indeed, helped him in every possible way. Both were convinced of his greatness. As Taylor phrased it in December, 1818, "Keats will be the brightest Ornament of this Age," and in June, 1820, "I am sure of this, that for poetic Genius there is not his equal living, and I would compare him against anyone with either Milton or

[36] *Century Magazine*, February, 1906 (LXXI, 551f.).
[1] The chief biographical sources are Olive M. Taylor, *London Mercury*, June, July, 1925 (XII, 158-166, 258-267), and Blunden.

Shakespeare for Beauties"; [2] while Hessey said of *Lamia* and the rest: "I think no single volume of Poems ever gave me more real delight on the whole than I have received from this." [3]

John Taylor was born at East Retford, Nottinghamshire, on July 31, 1781. His father, James, himself a bookseller, had other children—Ann, Sarah, Elizabeth, James, William, Jane, Henry—who are mentioned in the ensuing correspondence, in particular James (1788–1863), a banker at Bakewell, Derbyshire. John Taylor went to London in 1803, where he worked for the publishers Lackington and Company. In their employment he met "an Apprentice, of very genteel and wealthy Connexions," [4] James Augustus Hessey, who was his junior by four years (he was born on August 28, 1785 [5]), and who became his lifelong friend. By April, 1804, he was working for another publishing house, Vernor and Hood (Hood was the father of the poet), and in 1806 he and Hessey established their own firm in a house [6] at 93 Fleet Street. There, too, they lived in rooms, which they shared with Frederick Falkner and F. W. Haden, [7] overlooking St. Bride's Church graveyard; but, after his marriage to Kate Falkner, Hessey took over the Fleet Street house, as Blunden says, "for a time," while Taylor moved to a Hampstead Heath inn and, later, to 91 Bond Street, and then back to 93 Fleet Street. [8] The Fleet Street shop with its accompanying living

[2] See I, 69; Olive M. Taylor, XII, 259.

[3] Blunden, p. 73.

[4] The same, p. 23.

[5] In *Letters*, p. liii, the month is given as July on the authority of Archdeacon J. A. Hessey, the publisher's son. But see II, 416, 421.

[6] There is a description and a picture of it in H. C. Shelley's *Literary By-Paths* (1906), p. 252.

[7] See II, 377.

[8] H. C. Shelley believed that Keats spent his last days in England at 93 Fleet Street with Taylor; Lowell, I, 289, that Taylor was then still in Bond Street. Blunden, p. 34, is vague on the matter. Olive M. Taylor, XII, 260, is clearly wrong in asserting that "Some years previously

rooms became the haunt of Barry Cornwall, De Quincey, Lamb, Reynolds, Woodhouse, Hood, Darley, Severn, De Wint, Hilton, as well as Keats and numerous friends and relatives of the publishers from Bath, Bakewell, Claverton, and Retford.

Keats respected and liked Taylor and Hessey, who by April 15, 1817, had agreed to become his publishers.[9] Five of his letters to the firm and two to Hessey have been preserved. Elsewhere he has casual references to a dinner and a visit with Hessey, to whom (once as "Mistessey") and his wife he several times sent remembrances and regards.[10] Fifteen letters to Taylor are now known. The fact that Taylor was (as he remained) unmarried, while Hessey had a wife, children, and many visitors who were provincial relations-in-law no doubt helps to explain Keats's preference for the former's company. Both partners behaved very kindly to him in financial matters, among other things making the Italian journey possible, although the sales of his books before and after 1821 were small. Their chief money-makers were, instead, such now-forgotten authors as Jane and Ann Taylor, of Ongar, whose edifying books for girls could hardly be kept in print.

After Keats's departure for Italy the partners waited with the greatest anxiety for Severn's letters, which Hessey often copied and passed around among interested friends. At least

---

[to 1820] the Hesseys had removed from Fleet Street to a house in the suburbs as the air of Fleet Street was found to be injurious to the health of Mrs. Hessey and her young family. It therefore became necessary for John Taylor again to take up his abode at the place of business." To be sure, Hessey wrote on September 5, 1818, of taking a house in Brixton, three miles from the business, but he was apparently still at 93 Fleet Street in August, 1819 (see I, 78, 90). According to Olive M. Taylor, XII, 264, the Hesseys returned to that address and Taylor moved to Waterloo Place "at the close of the year 1822."

[9] Olive M. Taylor, XII, 258.

[10] His relations to Hessey are exaggerated in *Letters* because the references therein to "Percy Street" are wrongly explained. See I, lxxviii f.

twice, also, he wrote Severn what Sharp [11] sneers at as "the kind of epistle one would expect from a clergyman of the most pronounced evangelicalism," expressing "a regretful remembrance of having heard poor Keats utter the most extraordinary and revolting opinions." But as Keats, a professed non-believer, was on his deathbed, and as Hessey was devoutly religious, the "epistles" reveal the concern any orthodox Christian might be expected to have for the soul of a dear and dying friend. Severn, Haslam, Clarke, Bailey, R. C. Trench, and others in 1821 or later manifested a like concern. When it became certain that Keats was dying, Taylor and Hessey were concerned about more earthy matters, and they made speedy and somewhat drastic efforts to have the money they and others had donated for the poet refunded by George Keats (Nos. 102-104) and Abbey (No. 114).

Meanwhile the famous *London Magazine*, edited by John Scott and published by Baldwin, Cradock, and Joy, had made its first appearance in January, 1820. Taylor and Hessey were old friends of Scott, whose poem *The House of Mourning* (1817) they had published. He, in turn, and his wife were acquaintances and admirers of Keats. Indeed it was his defense of Keats and others, his onslaughts against Lockhart and *Blackwood's Magazine*, that led to the duel, February 16, 1821, in which he was mortally wounded.[12] In April Taylor, who presently set up a new publishing establishment at 13 Waterloo Place, and Hessey, who continued to preside over the Fleet Street shop, bought the *London Magazine*,[13] and their first issue appeared in July. Taylor himself was the editor, Thomas Hood the sub-editor, while Hessey gave able and loyal assistance. The

[11] Pages 86, 90. Keats, who could scarcely bear to look at a letter from England, read at least one from Hessey without emotion: see I, 183.

[12] See I, 233.

[13] In July they also bought Gold and Northhouse's short-lived *London Magazine.*

early issues of the magazine are a Who's Who of famous writers, De Quincey, Hazlitt, Landor, and Lamb among them. Later issues deteriorated, and the firm itself was losing money, so that with deep regret Taylor and Hessey dissolved their partnership on June 30, 1825, selling the magazine to Henry Southern.[14] Hessey remained in the bookselling business at 93 Fleet Street until he became bankrupt on May 19, 1829,[15] and then started over at 279 Regent Street as a bookseller and auctioneer of books, prints, pictures, "etc." [16] By July, 1834, he was in charge of a school at Hampstead, in which John and George, John Taylor's nephews, were pupils.

Taylor was a man of learning with a fondness for philology.[17] Before 1818 he had written several books identifying Sir Philip Francis as Junius, and later in life he wrote a number of volumes on currency, banking, and Scriptural subjects, as well as antiquarian articles in magazines. Regarding himself as a man of letters, almost automatically he planned to be Keats's biographer. Hence after writing to James Taylor on March 28, 1821, "I believe I shall try to write [Keats's] Life—it is the Wish of his Friends, and was Keats's Wish also," [18] he inserted in the *New Times*, March 29 and April 9, a Taylor and Hessey advertisement, "Speedily will be published, with Portrait, Memoirs and Remains of John Keats." Hence, too, in April he asked Severn for the dead poet's papers, and confidently expected the artist's help. The latter respected Taylor's "talent and good heart," and called him "a most noble friend" who "loved Keats." [19] Nevertheless, he forwarded Keats's papers

14 From May, 1825, till it died in 1828 it was published by Hunt (Leigh Hunt's nephew Henry) and (Charles Cowden) Clarke.
15 Blunden, pp. 188f.
16 The *Post Office London Directory*, 1830.
17 See I, 80, 87, 97, 155.
18 Blunden, p. 90.
19 Sharp, pp. 99, 110.

to Brown. But without quibble or delay Bailey sent Taylor all his Keats letters as well as various notes. In June, 1822, Taylor inserted in the *London Magazine* an announcement of the proposed "Memoirs of . . . [Keats's] life . . . to be accompanied with a selection from his unpublished manuscripts." [20] Brown and others thought him incompetent for the task. Brown said, "I shall always be the first to acknowledge Taylor's kindness to Keats," though, "in my opinion, Taylor neither comprehended him nor his poetry," while "towards me his conduct has been ungracious and even unmannerly." [21]

Taylor dallied with the idea of the biography, aided and abetted by Woodhouse, but by 1832 it was obvious to the latter that he would never write it, and that Brown was the logical biographer. He did, however, retain his personal interest in Keats. In 1840 William Smith published the first English edition of Keats's works (following the piratical Paris edition of the Galignanis), evidently after an arrangement with Taylor, for in the reissue of 1841 it had as a frontispiece Hilton's sketch of Keats "Published by Taylor and Walton, . . . 1841." When Milnes's biography was announced Taylor wrote, on February 13, 1845, to Edward Moxon, offering to sell his copyrights for an edition of the poems which Milnes should equip with critical remarks, and expressing a preference for Reynolds to write the life (No. 174). On September 30 he sold Moxon an equal right with himself to publish Keats's poems and letters (No. 180). Thereafter Taylor fully cooperated with Milnes, too fully thought Reynolds, who in November, 1846, flatly forbade Moxon to publish any of *his* Keatsiana that Woodhouse had copied and Taylor had turned over to Milnes. The two old friends, Reynolds and Taylor, quarreled bitterly, but Milnes

[20] V, 591.
[21] Sharp, p. 109.

pacified the former, and the biography proceeded.[22] In his preface he speaks of his indebtedness "to the enlightened publishers Messrs. Taylor and Hessey . . . for willing cooperation."

The later lives of Keats's publishers are outside the province of Keatsian studies. Taylor, first as Taylor and Walton, then as Taylor, Walton, and Maberly, continued in business for years, centering most of his efforts on educational publications. He and Hessey remained on the warmest terms. Both gave some aid to Hood's son and daughter in the preparation of *Memorials of Thomas Hood* (1860), and both read the volumes with interest and some nostalgia for the past (Nos. 349, 350). Taylor retired in March, 1853, and for a few years lived in Kensington as Hessey's neighbor. He died on July 5, 1864. Hessey moved to Wiltshire in 1861, and died on April 7, 1870.

RICHARD WOODHOUSE, JR.[1]

Woodhouse, one of the most interesting and about the most foresighted of Keats's friends, was born in Bath, December 11, 1788, the oldest in a family of fourteen children, two others of whom slightly figure in the correspondence below. The father, Lowell says, was owner or part owner of the White Hart Inn, and he and various other members of the family had business relations with Spain and Portugal, presumably as wine importers. Richard himself lived in those countries for over two years after his education at Eton, while his brother James was in Cadiz as early as 1813 and again during the revolution of 1820.[2]

Woodhouse attended no university, but he was a scholar

[22] Nos. 196, 199, 200, 204.
[1] For his portrait as a boy see the list of illustrations. Lowell, Blunden, and *Letters* are the sources for his biography.
[2] See I, 108, II, 409.

cxliv

with a sound knowledge of the ancient as well as various modern languages. In 1815 he published *A Grammar of the Spanish, Portuguese, and Italian Languages.* Though at least three of his brothers proceeded from Eton to Oxford, he turned to the law; and when he was introduced to Taylor and Hessey in March, 1811, by his Bath schoolfellow George Stothert, he was "a lawyer—at present with a Conveyancer in the Temple," [3] living at 11 King's Bench Walk. Woodhouse at once became a member of Taylor's little group of debaters and essay writers— the so-called Philological Club that met at the Queen's Arms Tavern during 1812–1814—and a literary and legal adviser to Taylor and Hessey. The former described him in 1811 as learned, remarkably abstemious, industrious, self-effacing, and strictly religious.

Keats met Woodhouse at 93 Fleet Street probably soon after he had been introduced to the publishers by Reynolds.[4] Woodhouse, obviously impressed by the 1817 *Poems*, discerned in the author of *Endymion* a genius equal to that of the young Shakespeare. Like the magazine critics he realized that *Endymion* had faults, and in particular that Keats's diction was frequently bad. Nonetheless, by October, 1818 (No. 23), he was eager "in all places, & at all times, & before all persons" to express "my high opinion of his poetical merits— Such a genius, I verily believe, has not appeared since Shakspeare & Milton." If *Endymion* be compared with *Venus and Adonis,* "Keats's poem will be found to contain more beauties, more poetry (and that of a higher order) less conceit & bad taste and in a word much more promise of excellence than are to be found in

---

[3] Blunden, p. 29.
[4] Finney, I, 343f., thinks he first met Keats in February, 1818, whereas Colvin, p. 134, places the meeting between March 3 and mid-April, 1817. Hewlett, p. 123, suggests that Woodhouse introduced Keats to Taylor and Hessey.

cxlv

Shakspeare's work." Woodhouse's "admiration . . . of Keats,"
was, as his brother George said,[5] "unbounded." He managed to
communicate it to his sister Nan, who in April, 1820, delighted
in "the countless beauties" of *Endymion* and the "beautiful
and grand Sonnet to the 'Sea' ";[6] and perhaps also to his cousin
Mary Frogley, of Hounslow—but not to the man she married,
Dr. William Henry Neville, of Esher.[7]

Woodhouse was a fine critic—his comments on Hunt are
penetrating—but quite as remarkable as the "deliberate opinion" of Keats quoted above was his realization that some day
all "Keatsiana," a term he actually uses at least twice, would be
invaluable. Hence he devoted much time and effort to copying
every Keatsian manuscript, poem, and letter he could lay his
hands on. Late in life Reynolds asserted that "the Copies of the
letters addressed by Keats to me, & of the Poems contained in
them—were unauthorizedly made by a Mr Woodhouse, to whom
I lent them in confidence for perusal only." The fact is, however, that he authorized the copying (No. 37), for which he
should have been grateful. In the most recent edition of Keats's
correspondence seventeen of the twenty-one letters addressed to
Reynolds (and one to his sisters Jane and Marianne) are printed
from Woodhouse's 'unauthorized' transcripts.[8] But for Woodhouse's copying, and in 1818–1819 Reynolds knew and en-
couraged his penchant for Keatsiana, the latter's place in the
Keats circle would seem comparatively unimportant. Hence it
is pleasant to read in a second letter that "a Mr Woodhouse"
(with whom he had been closely associated for years [9]) is characterized as "a good & enthusiastic friend of Keats. *He* meant

[5] See II, 221.
[6] See I, 108.
[7] See I, 54-57, 108.
[8] As are also two letters to Taylor and one to Hessey. Other texts transcribed by him are herein printed from the Morgan MS.
[9] *Letters*, pp. 328, 383, 385.

nothing cringing towards money." [10] Six or seven minor poems in Garrod's edition are likewise known only through Woodhouse's copies.

It is odd that just three letters of Keats to Woodhouse (and three from Woodhouse to Keats) are in the *Letters*. There were certainly more, and the methodical lawyer must have treasured them like diamonds. In his will he bequeathed to Taylor among other manuscripts "all papers I have in the handwriting of Keats." Possibly the "papers" will turn up yet—if they escaped burning. In 1885 Richard Garnett [11] asserted that to Woodhouse "were the heart-rending communications of Severn from Italy most commonly addressed." Apparently Garnett had actually seen these "communications," but they "unhappily perished in the conflagration which in 1883 destroyed the premises of the publishers," Kegan Paul, Trench and Company.

At first Keats thought of Woodhouse as a mere agreeable business acquaintance, and in writing to Taylor and Hessey he often sent regards to him.[12] But the kindness of the lawyer, who loaned him books and magazines,[13] made suggestions (sometimes bad) about proofsheets, verses, and prefaces, offered to introduce him to celebrities like the Porter sisters,[14] and on occasion listened respectfully—with tongue in cheek—to his "rodomontade," [15] soon won Keats's respect and gratitude. As late as February 13, 1819, he knew so little about Woodhouse's personal affairs as to write, "I stood by in doubt whether it was

[10] See II, 173.
[11] In his edition of De Quincey's *Confessions of an English Opium-Eater*, p. xix.
[12] *Letters*, pp. 135, 154, 223, 273, 373.
[13] The same, pp. 218, 511.
[14] The same, pp. 245, 251; No. 32.
[15] See I, 92.

cxlvii

him or his brother, if he has one," whereas he had seven.[16] Soon, however, Woodhouse was buying him a bottle of claret in a public house; [17] and two months later the poet and Brown entertained Taylor, Reynolds, and Woodhouse at dinner, after which they all played cards from nine "till very daylight." Shortly thereafter Keats and Woodhouse spent "a quiet Sort of pleasant" Sunday at Taylor's.[18] As time went on, Brown took "one of his funny odd dislikes" to Woodhouse, but Keats remarked, "I'm sure he's wrong, because Woodhouse likes my Poetry—conclusive." [19]

Despite Keats's apparent reservations about Woodhouse, who never was an intimate friend, the latter was merely stating a fact in reminding Taylor of "my good wishes towards Keats, as well as their complete disinterestedness." What people often say they wish they could have done for Shakespeare and Chatterton, I, he told Taylor, would "(with due regard to certain expediencies) do for Keats." Hence tactfully he explained away actions or expressions that had ruffled Taylor's feathers, and gave him money to loan to the poet, saying, "my friendship for the poor fellow wo^d willingly go, if need is, greater lengths than merely lending you money to lend him." [20] He arranged the copyright transfers that provided money for the Italian journey, and was one of the small party who went as far as Gravesend to see Keats and Severn begin their voyage—and he cut off a lock of the poet's hair, now in the Morgan Library. A few days earlier, with fine generosity, if with typical 'regard for expediencies,' he had authorized Keats to draw on him in Rome for money, expressing "more than a brotherly Interest in your wel-

16 *Letters*, p. 297; Lowell, I, 291.
17 *Letters*, p. 302.
18 The same, pp. 328f.
19 The same, p. 394.
20 See I, 83f.

fare," and signing himself "very sincerely and affectionately" (No. 66). Of his sincerity and affection there can be no doubt (in 1838 Brown testified to "the love he bore Keats" [21]), although Charles Cowden Clarke, whom he first met on August 21, 1823,[22] and who himself had contributed nothing towards Keats's trip, said to Hunt: "I should have had no fault to find with him, had he not told me that he desired Keats, when he took leave of him at Gravesend, to draw upon him for what money he might want!!" "I fear," Clarke added with an uncharacteristic lack of generosity, probably with some jealousy, "he panted to impress me with his spirit of munificence." [23]

After Keats's death Woodhouse's efforts to advance the poet's fame were redoubled. Expecting Taylor to write the biography (how admirably he could have written it himself!), he added poems, letters, facts to his Keatsiana, sometimes looking up Keats's friends and acquaintances himself, at others encouraging Taylor to make the visits. He also commissioned Hilton to paint the portrait now in the National Gallery and Giuseppe Girometti to make the beautiful medallion now in the Keats Museum. Meanwhile, he was associated with the famous group of writers for the *London Magazine*—De Quincey, much of whose conversations he jotted down with Boswellian fullness,[24] Hood, Lamb, Barry Cornwall, Cary, Reynolds, and others. As the years passed by with the biography unwritten, Woodhouse developed the disease that had killed his friend. In a vain search for health he lived in Madeira during 1829–1830.[25] In 1832 [26] he was in Italy, and he spent seven weeks with Brown

[21] Sharp, p. 166.
[22] See Nos. 129 and 131.
[23] Blunden, *Shelley and Keats* (1925), p. 94.
[24] H. A. Eaton, *Thomas De Quincey* (1936), pp. 278-285.
[25] Blunden, p. 189, who says (p. 197), "In September 1830 . . . he went from Lisbon to Rome."
[26] So Sharp, p. 170, who dates Brown's letter in the autumn.

LETTERS AND PAPERS 1816–1830

Numbers 1-148

GEORGE KEATS TO JOHN AND TOM KEATS
August (?) 1816 [1]

My Dear Brothers

I take the advantage of enclosing my thanks for two letters, one from each of you received this Morning in a Frank of
Our Friend Wells [2]— To your's My Dear Tom I will answer on
Monday or Tuesday{.} John's shall be attended to at the beginning of next Week. I most fortunately met Briggs [3] this Morning, who informed [me] C.C.C. was living with Mr Towers. I
shall endeavour to see him—. What may occur at our meeting
shall be communicat'd in my next. Wagtail is waiting & I am
not over-quick or you should have more from

Your Affectionate

{George}

[1] This letter, from which the signature has been cut off, is important in
correcting certain biographical details. Both Colvin (p. 37) and Lowell (I,
155) agree that after Keats passed his examination at Apothecaries' Hall,
July 25, 1816, he went alone to Margate for part of August and September. George's letter shows that, at least during some of the time, Tom
was with John. The reference to C. C. Clarke as living with his
brother-in-law, J. Towers, a chemist, at 6 Little Warner Street, Clerkenwell, is also interesting. Colvin (pp. 34, 40) and Lowell (I, 84) date
Clarke's moving about October, 1815. Clarke himself is vague on the
matter. The third of Keats's own letters to be preserved, dated October
31, 1816, is addressed to Clarke at Towers', Warner Street.
   On the back of this one-page letter is Keats's first draft of the sonnet
"Written in Disgust of Vulgar Superstition." At its end another hand,
apparently Tom's, has added: "J Keats/ Written in 15 Minutes." In his
copybook Tom provides another version of the sonnet, which he dates
"Sunday Evening Decr 24 1816." Neither December 24 nor December 23
(the date given in the transcript of the sonnet made for Milnes before
1848) was a Sunday, and Lowell (I, 233-236, II, 532) corrects the date to
December 22.   [2] Charles J. Wells: see II, 114.   [3] See I, 281, 283.

⇶ 2 ⇷

B. R. HAYDON TO J. H. REYNOLDS

October 1816 [1]

1

Come thou Poet!—*free* and *brown!*
Next Sunday to Hampstead Town
To meet John Keats, who soon will shine
The greatest, of this Splendid time
That e'er has woo'ed the Muses nine.*

Note 1

* Quite original— "Muses nine" we never recollect having seen
them in any Poet ancient or modern Ed.[2]

[1] In his autobiography Haydon (Penrose, p. 217) seems to say that he met Keats in November, 1816, at Leigh Hunt's cottage in the Vale of Health, Hampstead. That date (on or after November 1 and before November 19) is accepted by Colvin, p. 64, M. B. Forman (in *Letters*, p. xxix), and Lowell, I, 191, 195. The last, however (and she is followed by Finney, I, 143f.), thinks that his statement about Hunt is "undoubtedly the trick of a faulty memory," and that Haydon first saw Keats at his London studio. She bases her opinion on a letter of October 31 (*Letters*, pp. 8f.) in which Keats tells Clarke, "Very glad am I at the thoughts of seeing so soon this glorious Haydon and all his creation." But, as Garrod remarks, p. lxxv, "the obvious meaning" is that Keats is hoping "to visit Haydon with Clarke *at Haydon's studio*." What has been called "the most disputed problem" in Keats's biography (Finney, I, 130f.) is the date of his meeting with Hunt. Finney decided that it was "in the latter part of October 1816"; Garrod, p. lxxv, "not much after October 9 [the real date of the first letter in *Letters*, pp. 3f.], and certainly before the end of October"; Blunden, *Leigh Hunt* (1930), pp. 107f., and Clarke Olney, *PMLA*, XLIX (1934), 258, 260, on December 1; and R. D. Altick, *NQ*, October 7, 1944, pp. 159-162, sometime between October 9 and December 1. The present letter throws some light on both meetings. Haydon (*Correspondence and Table-Talk*, ed. F. W. Haydon, I [1876], 309) wrote to David Wilkie on October 27, 1816: "I have been at Hampstead

2

Dear Reynolds! this to you I say
Because you know the other day
You said the same ¶———
And as I feel thy heart is free
From Envy, in a great degree
Pleas'd I it repeat to thee—

3

It's evident from this small bit,
For Painting I am much more fit
So now adieu! Thou Poet sweet
At ½ past two
Both Keats & you
     Next Sunday I do hope to meet.

¶— This Poem [3] is peculiarly sublime—

P. S.

                              Post[s]crip[t]

Lest you might go, quite far beyond
I beg to say the Street is Pond
Turn to the right along the road
You soon find out my still abode—[4]

---

this fortnight. . . . The greater part of my time has been spent in Leigh
Hunt's society." He already knew Reynolds, who had dedicated to him
The Naiad, published in August, and during this October fortnight he
met Keats as well as Reynolds, and got to know them so well that he
felt free to write a doggerel-verse invitation to dinner at his house,
22 Lisson Grove—in all likelihood including Hunt among "the others"
who were not to know of it. As he says he was introduced to Keats at
Hunt's, those two poets surely had met, as Garrod argues, shortly after
October 9.

[2] Doubtful word.

[3] Doubtful word.

[4] A line after this is canceled.

The number's seven————
Now Reynolds it'll, be just as well
If that, you dont to others tell!—
The kindest Compliments from me
Do give to your fair Sisters three.

You Rascal— In verses do you answer, write
Or I will— d— with all my might—

—»» 3 «←

BENJAMIN BAILEY TO J. H. REYNOLDS [1]
21 September 1817

Address: Mr J. H. Reynolds. Little Britain Christs Hospital London.

Sunday Even⁵

My dearest Reynolds,

I had certainly purposed writing you by this post—but
as Keats told me he should give you a Letter, I have deferred it
until to morrow. It will be more pleasant to you I have much
to say to you & of a different character from what Keats would
write: *our* Communications with each (other) are centrally
seated in the heart from whence they issue and to where they
are borne—they are of deep interest; I mean we are two beings
in the bosom of dark and stormy waters, my Friend we *have
been* rather—for I am flung upon a desart shore after much
tossing:— *You* are yet on the waters:—may you be wafted to a
quiet and sunny harbour! [2] Dont be alarmed my good fellow,

1 Written on "the doublings" of Keats's letter of September 21, 1817, to
Reynolds (*Letters,* pp. 44-48). Both letters are known only from Woodhouse's Book of Transcripts of Keats's Letters (Harvard), p. 49. Like
everyone else, Woodhouse had great trouble in deciphering Bailey's
hand, as numerous changes in his readings show.
2 Perhaps a flowery reference to their respective love affairs with Marianne Reynolds and Eliza Drewe.

at this strange sort of language & imagery. it is my nature, I have more to tell you of my own affairs, than yours— But enough now —By to morrow's post you shall hear from me—not a syllable can I find Rice has written any one. I have not heard from Little Hampton [3] since their return from Mrs Snookes [4] Jane owes Keats a Letter. Have you written? Give my love to your Mother and believe me Dr Reynolds Ever with affection & fidelity

Your friend
P [5] Bailey

P S. There is one passage of Keats's 3^d Book which beats all he has written. It is on *death*.[6] He wrote it last night— Tell me if you agree with me when you hear it.

→» 4 «←

BENJAMIN BAILEY TO JOHN TAYLOR

22 February 1818

Address: John Taylor Esqre/ 91 New Bond Street/ London. *Postmark* (*part illegible*): OXFORD. Morgan MS. Printed in part (with some curious misreadings) by Blunden (*B*), pp. 45-47. Finney, I, 320, quotes a few sentences.

Oxford. Feby 22. 1818.

My dear Sir

I am much obliged & gratified by your friendly & entertaining Letter. The liberal spirit of it claims my especial admiration, and increases my personal regard for you. However, I trust, first & last you shall not be a sufferer for this; and in

---

[3] Jane and Marianne Reynolds had visited a Mrs. Earle at Littlehampton, Sussex. See Keats's two letters, September 5 and 14, addressed to them at Mrs. Earle's (*Letters*, pp. 35-37, 41-44).

[4] See I, lxxxiii.

[5] *Sic.*

[6] Presumably lines 766-806.

regard to the Sermon [1] I shall not suffer you to be eventually a loser. As to what I happened to let fall about reviewing I did not intend that you should give yourself any trouble, or that it should excite in you any anxiety on *my* account. For yourselves I could wish the thing had been a more vendible commodity. Do not, my dear Sir, give yourself any trouble about so paltry a thing. That a stray bundle of my speculations should fall still-born from the Press excites in me very little wonder. Indeed I find I have an odd and useless sort of mind. I have brooded over my pregnant thoughts, and nursed their offspring. I have, to *my own* perception, done this with much *regularity*. My *first* perceptions have become more strong by the greater maturity of time and thought and knowledge. As far as my weak mortal eye-sight will carry me I have seen, from my first glances, an analogy, conformity, & unity in all things; or, to speak more intelligibly perhaps, the two last are perceptible *by* analogy. I have thought that this principle is the governing one of the universe, and that I have equally perceived it in nature, external & internal—in the minds of men as reflected through the best authors—and (as far as we can glimpse) in the eternal mind—of which every thing that exists, it seems to my apprehension, is but the image of the Decree—the word, the Logos. Now all this (which were I to indulge myself I could write on to the end of time almost)—all this, I say, *to me is clear as noonday*. But, I dare say, I have not made my notions more clear to you than at best a sort of dusky twilight. Well—and so it is, I find, with every one. I share the same fate with all the world that "Paradise Lost" did with the mathematician who, you may recollect, had but *one* fault to find with it, but it was [a] radical one—that it *"proved nothing!"*— "Ay me, I fondly dream!" [2] for this is pre-

---

[1] See I, 20, and *Letters,* p. 111. No copy of Bailey's sermon is in the British Museum catalog (1934), but one is in Bodley.

[2] *Lycidas,* line 56.

cisely *my* case. I am asked to *prove* what I can but *see,* not *reach.* As the stars of Heaven I could die upon it, but I can *see* many most glorious truths: but I can no more *demonstrate* (a logical pick-axe, that word.) *how,* than I can trace "the path of an eagle through the air" ³ and the other mysteries which Solomon proposes. I have been reading Plato whom I can sufficiently follow to fill my mind with his fine abstractions without deluding me with his errors. I have been reading Aristotle, or rather I have begun to read him; and I confess I am puzzling about "specific differences" and such kind of hard words[?], which others understand at a glance, whilst I could have read and followed 50 pages of Plato upon *"one"* & *"other."* ⁴ The fact is this:—my mind seems of no earthly use. I dig for diamonds, and take "the wings of the morning" ⁵ to adore the Goddess of Truth which I burn after like a man in a fever. The more prudent hands sow & reap, & spin & weave: and I am laughed at. Aristotle was doubtless a wonderful man, and perhaps a more *generally* useful one than Plato; but it seems to me that he looked very *im*perfectly *beyond* this world, but *very* perfectly *in* it. But being a choleric sort of animal I lose all patience when I hear him exalted above Plato as though "high on a throne exalted." ⁶ Plato had "the vision and the faculty divine." ⁷ He looked into "adyta," the "penetralia," the inmost recesses of Truth; and wanted but the eye of Revelation to see *clearly* into the mysteries of Christianity, which he saw shadowed in the twilight. In the *greatest* Truths, in a word, Plato saw correctly—and Aristotle *in*correctly. Aristotle could not miss [?] of the unity & eternity of the godhead with his vast intellectual energy, for I deny it

³ Compare Proverbs 30:19.
⁴ He refers to *The Sophist* with its criticism of Parmenides' One Real Being.
⁵ Psalm 139:9.
⁶ *Paradise Lost,* II. 1, 5.
⁷ Wordsworth's *Excursion,* I. 79.

not that he was a giant: but it was for Plato to see the non-eternity of matter, which the other could not comprehend, but held the eternity of what is but a feeble echo or prototype of the Divine Intelligence.—I have now done—and beg pardon for having detained you so long which I no more intended than a visit to the moon.—By the bye I wish you could get me <a trans> translations of some of Plato's works. I have but a patch-work collection of his works—Greek & English. I have Taylor's Translation of 4 dialogues—and 2 little volumes *from the French London 1749.* of a few dialogues.[8] I want his *Republic* very much—and any other of his dialogues & works which you may chance to light on which I have not. Will you think of this? I am in great hopes your second edition [9] will sell. It ought. It is a very clear book. You possess a great deal of the useful along with your finer parts of mind. I wish I did.—

I have had a most eccentric letter from Coleridge [10] at last. I can only say it is the oddest thing I ever read. He however speaks very handsomely of the notice taken of himself, and *generally* so of the Discourse, of which "in toto he thinks very highly." He moreover promises to write in the spirit of a friend what he thinks are Errors, or as he says it more delicately to give hints of experience{.} He speaks very highly of your house, and of your civility with respect to his Lectures. He had not seen you, but he had Mr Hesse[y], whose handsome conduct he says has redeemed the name of Bookseller & Publisher. He seems sorely shackled by his present publishers. And if you have any desire to be his Publishers I am sure you may. I don't suppose you do—but *should* you think it worth your while I know a

[8] Thomas Taylor actually translated all the known *Works,* 5 vols., London, 1804. See I, 21, 36. The two "little volumes" are a translation from Anne Lefèvre Dacier, perhaps the so-called third London edition, 1772.

[9] Of *The Identity of Junius,* the preface of which is dated February 12, 1818.   [10] To whom Bailey had sent his printed Sermon.

word [11] will effect it. After his "friend" is published he will leave Gale & Co,[12] he declares: [13] so you would not behave ill to a brother in the Profession. This is but a hint of course. Because if you chose to follow it up I might serve you; & this is why I thought it worthy mention. He will leave his first 2 Lectures [14] at your house for me—which you will of course send me.

I will take a Copy of Hazlitt's work be what it may.[15]— It is odd that he and Coleridge should be holding forth from the same *drum-head,* as it were, at the same time.

Keats I expect here in his way to Devon. I am sorry you are disappointed with his 2ᵈ book, because I think very highly of it. Nevertheless I own there is much justice & good sense in what you say. But I have no room, as you will perceive, to canvass the matter.

I do not say I have a chance that can be called a good one of Taylor's MS.[16] After all it may not be true that it is in existence—of which Doubts will, in spite of me, come across me. When however it is decided one way or other, I think, we had better come to some sort of determination whether or not it would be adviseable to try to get names for his works. I have got *one* name should we *ever* do it. I long to set about it.

I take it, you are snugly settled in your new abode. "Peace be with you!" [17] I address this thither. For you will never have leisure at Fleet Street to make out my scrawl, upon which I

[11] *B misreads* I know [I] could easily.

[12] Gale and Fenner published his *Lay Sermon* (1817); Rest Fenner, *The Friend* (1818).

[13] *For* published . . . declares *B reads* published [ ] Rest, Fenner Gale & Co. are declining.

[14] Coleridge delivered fourteen lectures on general literature from January 27 to March 13. All that is now known about them will be found in T. M. Raysor's *Coleridge's Miscellaneous Criticism* (1936), pp. 3-228.

[15] See I, 27.

[16] On Jeremy Taylor's manuscript see I, 211f.

[17] Genesis 43:23, etc. (Vulgate).

ought to apologize as often as I write my friends. Yet I do not. I must be taken as I am—warmly theirs, and, my dearest Sir, Ever your most sincere & faithful friend

My compts to Mr Hesse[y].   B Bailey

A course of Bampton Lectures [18] is begun against the Unitarians. I heard the 2ᵈ today. It is careful [19] not great. [. . .] [20] *I* think masterpieces— Do read & recommend them, if you like them—

⟶⟫ 5 ⟪⟵

J. A. HESSEY TO JOHN TAYLOR [1]

6 March 1818

Address: Mʳ Taylor/ 91 Bond Street. Morgan MS. The first paragraph is quoted by Lowell, I, 597, and Finney, I, 371.

Dear John

George Keats called here to day to say that his Brother the Poet is gone into Devonshire & has left the third Book [2] with him—he will leave it here either to morrow or on Monday— The Proofs he wishes to have sent to Mʳ Charles Clarke, 6 Little Warner Street, Clerkenwell— Keats went off on the night of the Storm on the *outside* of the Coach.[3]

---

[18] Charles Abel Moysey, M.A. of Christ Church, published his eight John Bampton sermons as *The Doctrines of Unitarians Examined* (Oxford, 1818).

[19] Doubtful word.

[20] Three or four words illegible.

[1] Finney (I, 371) calls it a transcript by Woodhouse.

[2] Of *Endymion*.

[3] Lowell, I, 597f., takes a page to argue that this was the night of Sunday, March 1, or Tuesday, March 3, and Finney, I, 379, accepts the latter date. A glance at the Meteorological Table in the *Gentleman's Magazine*, LXXXVIII, 286, shows that March 1 was "showery," March 3 fair, while on March 4 there was a violent storm. As the *New Monthly Magazine*, April, 1818 (IX, 264f.), phrases it, "On the night of March 4th the

Hazlitt sent two corrected proofs [4] here to day just before dinner time & said he would send copy this Evening—he desired to see Revises—

I have not seen or heard of Reynolds to day— Mrs H. I think is rather better to day— I took her out a little way into the Country for a Ride this Morning

Enclosed is a letter from Retford

Y^rs very truly.

J A H

Mar. 6. 1818

⇢⟫ 6 ⟪⇠

GEORGE KEATS TO MARIANNE AND SARAH JEFFREY

March 1818 [1]

Address: For the/ Misses. Jeffries.—/ p^r favor of J. K. Lowell, I, 599, prints a brief extract.

Hampstead: Saturday.—

My dear Girls

What think you of my impudence? where have I picked up assurance to write to you without the slightest intimation

---

metropolis, in common with almost the whole kingdom, was visited by a hurricane more violent than has been remembered for many years past, which did considerable mischief in many places." The *Scots Magazine*, March, 1818 (LXXXI, 283f.), gives further details, as that "Several mail and stage coaches and waggons were blown over, and the drivers and passengers more or less injured; in some cases lives were lost. . . . Indeed, there are few people who remember a storm having so extensive a range, and so long a duration." Keats begins a letter of March 14 (*Letters*, p. 113), "I escaped being blown over and blown under & trees & house being toppled on me."

[4] Of his *Lectures on the English Poets* (1818). See I, 11, 27.

[1] Keats left for Teignmouth in the first week of March, 1818. George's letter was written before Tom's serious illness of March 13 (*Letters*, p. 113), probably on Saturday, March 7. On Mrs. Jeffrey, of Teignmouth,

that a letter would be welcome, or without even the excuse of having something interesting to communicate. Having no apology, its reception must [2] decide upon its criminality. Suppose I speculate a little upon probabilities.—— Enter the letter— Sarah half anxious and half laughing looks very enquiringly at Marianne to whom the letter is delivered, who opening it hurryingly says on looking at the signature, "From George Keats." Sarah (quickly) "I was sure he'd think of *me*—correcting herself suddenly—of *us,* what does he say, make haste, I'm bursting with curiosity" Marianne "Well you shall hear, don't be in such a hurry; what can he have to write about?"—Sarah. "As if you did not know now"—M "he has already sent us word that he has delivered those drawings—S—"Do read the letter, does he say anything about my Eyes, or my hair, or my arms, or my speech, or my voice, or my manners, or, lord! Marianne how provoking you are, I never saw such a slow creature in my life." M— "he surely cannot have any thing to say about the drawings," S. "why now Marianne I protest you are enough to put Job himself into a passion, read the letter or let me read it; to see what he has written is the way to ascertain what he had to write about— M. reads to herself— Sarah. after a pause says—"Well what does he say?" M. "Nothing!" S. "Nothing; what's the matter with the Girl, you have read through a whole page and yet he says nothing." M. "that I can understand at least." S. "Let me try"—snatches the letter—after reading some time continues— "Well to be sure he says but very little that is at all intelligible, there's something about being impudent—I never found him

---

and her daughters Sarah and Marianne see *Letters,* pp. lvi-lix. Marianne later became Mrs. I. S. Prowse, but I have no means of telling whether there is any connection between her husband (who apparently lived at Torquay) and the J. S. Prowse, merchant, ship and insurance broker, 31 Botolph Lane, who is listed in the *Post Office London Directory* for 1822.

[2] *Written* must must.

14

so, did you? Marianne again takes the letter and says— "He then goes on about Marianne & Sarah and Sarah & Marianne; what can he mean? a long pause during which Marianne cons the letter, then Sarah says in an under voice "Marianne may well say he says nothing, since its so little to the purpose, nothing at all interesting, he does not even say that he sometimes thinks of me, he might have"—Marianne interrupting reads out— Oh! Sarah I cannot with all my endeavours drive from my waking thoughts, or sleeping dreams the image of your blue Eyes, sparkling through your long hair, and I feel with the greatest satisfaction that I have in my possession a lock of this same hair. This is the best of all remembrances, since always beautiful, and only valuable to the party to whom it is given. Pray Marianne send me one by my Brothers, when they come up, let it [be] taken from a part which you are in the habit of curling: indeed to speak properly I should ask for a *curl* of your hair.— I shall ever remember with pleasure the many pleasant walks we have rambled together; I fear much from the present posture of my affairs that I shall never again pass my arm in that of the steady, quiet Marianne, and laughing thoughtless Sarah. I think with infinite regret that you should be obliged to look up to a Person so every way inferior to you, however fate seems to have ordered it, and enables you to bear with it.—How is your Mother? Tom mentioned a most lamentable accident that had befallen her. I hope she is not the worse for it— And pray Sarah why don't you take more care? however since the accident has happen'd I insist that you don't move about much untill you have completely recovered from it; lameness for life frequently attends those accidents, and how would you like to hobble in your walk? Set still, never mind about losing your colour for a time. I think you may venture to my Brothers if you walk gently. How do you like John? is he not very original? he does not look by any means so handsome as four months ago, but is

15

thoughts he has appeared nearly in good health, every answer I have given to enquiring Friends, has been, "much better" and "improving every day" I can hardly beleive this melancholy news, Having [2] so long accustomed myself to think altogether otherwise—I hope and trust that your *kind* superintendance will prevent any violent bleeding in future, and consequently that this alarm may prove in the end advantageous; Tom must never again presume on his strength, at all events untill he has *completely* recover'd. John Reynolds is little better, in many respects worse, he has a very bad rheumatic Fever, and suffers constant pain: it is not said that he is dangerously ill, but I cannot help thinking that so many evils acting upon his most irritable disposition; deadening his hopes of his advance in business, consequently all his hopes, must make this illness somewhat dangerous.—I called yesterday but he was not sufficiently well to be seen.[3] His Sisters are well— Your letter [4] was most welcome to him— Bailey's in Town for a few days, on business for Glegg [5]— I have not seen him.— Mrs Scott [6] desires her compliments to you and Tom, I have repeatedly called on Taylor & Hessey and have never found them at home, or you should long since have known the progress of your book. Brown has I understand written to you and given you the pleasant information that the printer's are in immediate want of the Fourth book and preface. By the time you have received this I have no doubt but T & H will have received them—the inclosed 20 pounds N° 834 dated 3rd Feb^y—1818. will reach you before you are quite aground. I am about paying your's as well as Tom's bills, of which I shall keep regular accounts and for the sake of justice and a future proper understanding I intend calcu-

[2] *Written over* I have.
[3] See *Letters*, pp. 120f., n.
[4] See the same, pp. 113-115.
[5] See I, xliii.
[6] Wife of John Scott: see I, 233.

lating the probable amount Tom and I are indebted to you,
something of this kind must be done, or at the end of two or
three years we shall be all at sixes and sevens. let me know when
you want Money. I have paid Hodgkinson [7] who desires his
best rem⁵—I'll write Tom soon give my love to him—rem⁸ to
Miss M & C—and love to the Miss J's [8]—Miss Wylie [9] as usual
desires her *respects* to you, and *best wishes* to Tom—R Draper
has been teazing throughout the writing of this to my great an-
noyance—

    Goodbye for the present

                        Your most affectionate Brother

                                    —George.

→» 8 «←

BENJAMIN BAILEY TO JOHN TAYLOR
9 April 1818

Address: John Taylor Esqᵗᵉ/ 91 New Bond Street/ London. *Postmarks:*
OXFORD 9 AP 9; B 10 AP 10 1818. Morgan MS. A few sentences are
quoted by Blunden (*B*), pp. 47f., and Finney (*F*), I, 320, 382.

                             Oxford. April 9. 1818.

My dear Sir

    I wrote the slovenly scrawl on Sunday Evᵍ at the sugges-
tion of my friend, Gleig, though I guessed at the meaning, and,
I will add kind delay of your letter. I am much obliged to you
for the exertions you have made, as, I can assure you, is my
friend, however we may regret your ill success. I wish most
earnestly I could get any other situation, which was pretty

---

[7] Partner of Abbey: see I, xl.
[8] See I, 13f., n.
[9] Later Mrs. George Keats.

respectable, & where he could be boarded during the term of his apprenticeship for a moderate premium. If you hear of any thing of this nature I know I need not ask you to interest yourself for me. Nor will you forget the situation of the Eldest, should any thing of the sort occur.—To a man of your friendly disposition & correct feeling I should insult you by making apologies for thus troubling you, when the service of an unhappy & afflicted fellow creature is involved.—I hate sentiment; so much is it abused to the mockery of straightforward manly feeling & sympathy for one another: but really the misery, *ex*ternal alone (not to take in the flashing pangs of agony of the "[. . .] [1] spirits" "thick as the motes that people the sunbeam."—[2]) scattered as it is in hearts over the world, when collected into a mass is so painful to the imagination that "our hearts burn within us while it speaks." [3] But lest I should fall into that sentimentality, which I have condemned, I will quit the subject.

I am glad Endymion is so near the commencement of his Pilgrimage into & through the world of letters. Your remarks are very just. I have now & then a few & far-between-angel-like visits [3a] of poetical feelings I once possessed, which, I own with sadness & humility, a long series of bodily sickness, *heart*-sickness, utter [4] disappointments of golden hopes has almost effacced from my mind. Yet there is something so etherial in Keats's Poetry that it pierces the cloud. It no longer mantles my spirits when I am in his fairy world. Nothing but the finest poetry can now touch me, but that *does* touch me in the most secret springs, the "resting-places calm & deep," [5] of my soul. Keats's is

[1] One word, possibly "unwanted" or "wounded," illegible. Compare "wounded spirit," Proverbs 18:14.   [2] *Il Penseroso*, line 8.

[3] Compare Luke 24:32.   [3a] Compare Thomas Campbell, *The Pleasures of Hope*, II.378, "Like angel-visits, few and far between."

[4] *Or perhaps* bitter (*so B and F*).

[5] Wordsworth, "Song for the Wandering Jew," line 4.

of this power.—You know, as far as I am able, I shall be most happy to answer any attack upon him. Or, if required, I will write a Review of Endymion. If I can serve you, command me; but if I cannot, have no delicacy in leaving me out of the question. I see no papers, nor periodical publications; but if any appear which you think I can answer, & will send me, I will with pleasure do it.

Dilke wrote the article in the Champion upon my Sermon.[6] He intended it as a kindness:—but for the sake of the book, &, I think, for his own, he had better have let it alone. He is at best a Sceptic in his principles;—& it rather arises from too much passion,[7] & too little knowledge, than any cause which can assume the shape of rational conviction.[8]

I am, like yourself, interrupted, & though I had much to say, must defer it until another time. I shall be in London about the end of the month or the beginning of May, but for a very few days. If I can get a Curacy & Title in the Diocese of Carlisle before July or Aug^t, the Bishop of C——[9] has promised to ordain me. Could you serve me at all in this? I know your will is good towards me, & scruple not asking this. I must con-

[6] See I, 8. The review in the *Champion*, March 22, 1818, p. 186, of "*A Discourse Inscribed to the Memory of the Princess Charlotte Augusta. By an Under-graduate of the University of Oxford*. Taylor and Hessey, 1817," is unsigned. Among other things it says: "The writer of this sermon is evidently an amiable man, not only well read in the best of our divinity, but intimately conversant with our poets; a zealous lover of truth, with a poetical imagination, and an enthusiastic spirit. This is easily enough discoverable. His theological and poetical knowledge is impressed, somewhat too strongly perhaps, on every page; his imagination sometimes leads him into the mystical; and his keen search after truth into the abstract and metaphysical. This last is the greatest objection we have to the work. . . ."

[7] *F reads* pride [?].

[8] *F reads* criticism.

[9] Samuel Goodenough (1743–1827).

clude with assuring you how since{re}ly I return your good wishes in subscribing myself, my dear Sir,

Your faithful friend

B Bailey

P S. Have you ever enquired what you could get a set of Taylor's Plato [10] for? And what is the price of the Biponti [11] Ed^{n} of his works in the original.

9

TOM KEATS TO MARIANNE JEFFREY [1]

17, 18 May 1818

Address: Miss Mary Ann Jeffrey/ Teignmouth/ Devonshire. *Postmarks:* [?] o'Clock MY. 19 1818 N.T.; MY 19 C 1818. Part printed by Lowell (*L*), II, 4f., and *Letters,* p. 146n.

Hampstead Sunday [2]

May 1818

My Dear Maryann

We received your Mothers Letter by Mrs Atkins which prevented my writing so soon as I had intended that the Letter might accompany the Book John promis'd you, and be deliver'd by M^{rs} A on her return— I thank you all for your kind solicitude—the rest of the journey pass'd off pretty well after we had left Bridport in Dorsetshire— I was very ill there and

10 See I, 10.

11 Ed. Exter and Embser, 11 vols., 1781–1787.

1 See I, 13f., n. The letter has the embossed seal of "Albert Forbes Sieveking. F.S.A. 12 Seymour Street W."

2 May 17, 1818, was Sunday. The postscript was added on Monday the eighteenth. No effort has been made to identify all the Teignmouth persons herein mentioned.

lost much blood—we travell'd a hundred miles in the two last [3] days—I found myself much better at the end of the journey than when I left *Tartarey* alias Teignmouth—the Doctor was surprised to see me looking so well, as were all my Friends— they insisted that my illness was all mistaken Fancy and on this presumption excited me to laughing and merriment which has deranged me a little—however it appears that confinement and low spirits have been my chief enemies and I promise myself a gradual recovery—this will be grateful news to you— Our leave-taking was more formal than it might have been: and at the time I cursed the Doctor,[4] but now I think it better as it hap- pen'd— I was at the Window to stop you as you return'd from the Cottage but you did not come our way—it did not require John's assurance to convince me that you felt our departure— Your Sister must indeed have been au desespoire that she could not eat a Bun—she lost her appetite and that was not all—the Bun lost an honor: instead of being masticated by a pair of *Ivory Teeth* it was destined perhaps to some hungry pityless voracious maw, or perhaps to a more fearful destiny—there are a thousand arguments for a sophist for and against— It may be cowardly to attack a poor unfortunate lumped Combination of Doe and flour—but as it has to do with a point in Philosophy I must put in this opinion: that, as material Bodies sometimes feed upon the things they nourish, so Miss S. J. may one day find herself, by the treacherous machinations of this son of paste, prematurely possessed of an unpleasant compliment of hollow teeth; which to carry on the discussion may be argued for and against—in their * favour we might say—they tend to the maintenance of a very respectable class in Society the Den- tists, Barber, and whatnot—the greatest objection to them is * The Buns

[3] *L* last two.
[4] William Turton, M.D., F.L.S. (1762–1835).

that they bring on Lisping and denote old age which as * Chaucer calls it an affectation in a coarse old monk cannot but be still more despiseable in a Young Lady— I hope Mr Stanbury vet.[5]—is elected to twenty Pounds a year and that Waltzing will be admitted to the Teignmouth and other Town and Country Ball rooms in Sarah's time.—I calculate it will be by then she has attained the age of Fifty Six and that's no age at all— Convey my Compliments to Miss Mi[t]chell and thank her for the present—remember me to Captain Tonkin and Mr Bartlett [6] if he should Come in your way in the Labyrinthe of Teignmouth—tell Captain T if he <puts> goes his projected Tour to Italy we may perhaps meet—this leads me to a developement of my plan which I am fond to think about if I should alter it— in {five} [7] weeks I shall be here alone and I hope well— John {will} have set out on his Northern Expedition George o{n his} [8] Western and I shall be preparing for mine to the South Johns will take four months at the end of that time he expects to have atchieved two thousand miles mostly on Foot— George embarks for America— I shall either go by vessell to some port in the Adriatic or down the Rhine through Switzerland and the Alps into Italy most likely to the Town of Paiva—[9] there to remain untill I have acquired a stock of Knowledge and strength which will better enable me to bustle through the world— I am persuaded this is the best way of killing time— now if I should go by vessel and the port of Plymouth has

* Somewhat he lisped for his Wantonnesse
To make his English Sweet upon his Tongue [10]

[5] Doubtful reading. *L* has &ct.
[6] Captain (later Sir Warwick) Tonkin married Miss Mitchell: see *Letters*, p. 149n. Bickford Bartlett was a surgeon at Teignmouth.
[7] Torn out with the seal.
[8] *L has* on this (*unbracketed*).
[9] *For* Pavia.
[10] *Prologue* to *The Canterbury Tales*, lines 264f.

Communication with that part I will take Teignmouth in my way thither and see you once again—it will be some atonement for the abuse I have lavished on your Native Town

till then I will bid you farewell—my Love to your Mother and Sister— I insist upon the former's thinking for herself as well as for others—tell her selfishness is fashionable and she is not so much out of the world as to be able to do without it—

Believe me Your Sincere Friend   Tho⁵ Keats

P S— George has been busily occupied in preparing for his Journey they both ¹¹ desire their Love—perhaps John will write —he is also very much engaged with his Friends— I am the only idler—in regard of Idleness I fear you will say this letter out-Herods Herod ¹² 　 **T. K.**

Monday.

John will write to you shortly. 　 **T. K.**

⇢⇢⇢ **IO** ⇠⇠⇠

BENJAMIN BAILEY TO JOHN TAYLOR

20 May 1818

Address: J. Taylor Esqʳᵉ/ 93 Fleet Street/ London. *Postmarks:* OXFORD 20 MY 20 1818; B 21 MY 21 1818. Morgan MS. Extracts are quoted by Finney (*F*), I, 223, 320f., and Blunden (*B*), pp. 48f.

Oxford May 20. 1818.

My dear Taylor

I am very much obliged to you for your kind remembrance of my friend.¹ But you have ever been much more kind to me than I had a right to expect. I will tell him your success

---

¹¹ George Keats and Georgiana Wylie.
¹² *Hamlet,* III.ii.15f.
¹ Gleig: see I, xliii, 27f.

24

with regard to the quarterly, & put it to him whether he will immediately write something, as Mr Gifford has suggested, or have you apply to Roberts about the British,[2] about which you will not therefore do any thing until you hear from me.

A few copies of Endymion have already been sold upon the strength of my recommendation to the booksellers. I have written an account of *Keats,* as much,[3] & perhaps more, than of Endymion. I have said bold things, &[4] would excite the *curiosity,* though I cannot interest[5] the hearts of these learned men. I wish[6] they would some of them answer me in the paper,—& attack Keats. This would give me a right, in a manner, to another column of the paper: and I feel so strong upon the subject that I fear nothing that can be brought against him. I am prepared to concede his *real* faults, but I do not expect to have them attacked, but what I feel to be his beauty & his power. I have read over the Poem[7] two or three times with *great* attention since my return. The 4th book, which I at first thought inferior,[8] I *now* think as fine, & perhaps finer than any. You will stare at this. Nor do I think the abrupt conclusion so bad—it is *rather,* but not *much* too abrupt. It is like the conclusion of Paradise Regained.— I will send a copy of the paper on Sunday for Keats to *you* at Fleet Street. You will of course have read it before you give or send it him. I send it you for that purpose.—

I have invited Keats to come &[9] spend some time with

---

[2] William Gifford (1756–1826) edited the *Quarterly Review* and William Roberts (1767–1849), barrister, the *British Review.*

[3] *F* Keats,—[as a man (?)]. Bailey's "account" was published in the *Oxford University and City Herald,* May 30, June 6; it is reprinted in the Hampstead Keats, II, 237-243.

[4] *F* x—.

[5] *B* criticise.

[6] *F* men. Since.

[7] *F* Poems.

[8] *F* Infamous.

[9] *B* to come to Oxford and.

me. I wish he would. I understand he is not the better for having been with his brother, Tom, so long.—I have promised to assist him in his Greek, as much as so bad a scholar can, if he will come. I earnestly desire it.

Well— I have written two long essays, one upon *Moral* [10] *Principles,* the other upon "the relative state of man & woman" which is the longest & the best. I am upon the 3ᵈ—which is an enquiry into *"What is Power."* This & one upon *"The Unity of Nature"* [11]—are my greatest speculations. These 4 will contain a good deal of *space,* if not matter. I hope before the end of this month to have these 4 completed. "The *Insufficiency* of *Language—*" & "Considerations previous to reading an author," I have thought of following—& to end the whole of this "eventful (or rather event*less*) history" [11a] with my first essay on Paradise Regained, *re*written, an essay on "the moral beauty of Poetry" —and at last an essay upon *Keats's Poetry* alone.—Now if I complete all this, I think it will be worth something. This is saying too much perhaps—but unless I feel it so, I will not trouble my friends, & certainly not the public with it. I have abundance of matter, which makes it more difficult to throw my speculations into form than if I had infinitely less. Indeed I find it much more difficult than I expected. To *begin* is "the rub." [12] I am convinced writing a large volume upon one subject is much less difficult than treating several subjects, especially if they be deep & elemental truths, in the form of separate essays. You must say much in a little space—& the composition must be complete in its parts— It must have a beginning, a middle & an end, like a little Epic Poem. *Purpose* must be constantly kept in view. Consequently I have to write my beginnings two or 3 times

[10] *F* the Casual.
[11] *F* Nations."   [11a] Compare *As You Like It*, II.vii.164.
[12] *Hamlet*, III.i.65.

over before I am satisfied with them. When I next am in London we will go over these things together; & if you think them worth publishing, why we will talk about it. As to the *interested* part of the proposition we will say no more upon it. I am ashamed of having made it. But I give you my honour my *self* never would have put such a suggestion into my head & heart. God bless you.[13]

When you are more at liberty, I shall expect a long letter from you. You sent me the *"Characters"* instead of the *["]Lectures"* [14] by mistake, but Munday [15] has changed it for me. I was quite vexed at first for I so burn to read the Lectures. Farewell.

Yours affec^y

B Bailey

→≫ I I ≪←

BENJAMIN BAILEY TO JOHN TAYLOR

9 June 1818 [1]

Address: J. Taylor Esqre/ 93 Fleet Street/ London. *Postmarks (both blurred):* OX[FORD]; B 10 [JU] 10 1818. Morgan MS.

Tuesday Ev^e

My dear Sir

I have but just time to say that I have this morning had a letter from my friend Gleig. He desires me to present his best

---

13 The rest of the letter is written on the back outside fold.

14 Taylor and Hessey published in 1818 both Hazlitt's *Characters of Shakespear's Plays* (2d ed.) and his *Lectures on the English Poets.* See I, 11, 53.

15 Joseph Munday, Oxford bookseller, 1802–1833.

1 Tuesday was June 9 (see the postmark), and this letter was obviously written soon after No. 10, of May 20.

thanks to you. He shall be very happy to engage with the Quarterly, if he can, and forego the British.[2] Would or could you ask Gifford if there be any particular work he would like to be reviewed? This, my friend would wish to know, as he would not desire to pay much attention to a thing indifferent. Pray give me an answer to this.

I did not send you the first Oxford paper in which I wrote about Keats, because I happened to have occasion to write Keats at the same time—& the letter was trifling. I desired one to be left you last Monday. You will see, I think, that I could say no more in a newspaper. To attempt a regular criticism were out of the question in a newspaper—and it was a favour that I got so much space allowed me. I shall have an extract inserted in next week's I believe.[3]

I am, *next to a certainty*, likely to be ordained next month or early in August by the Bishop of Carlisle.[4] He has written very handsomely of me to Bishop Gleig, both from the report of his son here, and my own interview with him.

My Essays go *slowly* on. I have not been in spirits to write —& am oftentimes tempted to burn what I *have* written. I shall see you before long,—and if we have half an hour together I will show you one, and take your opinion whether it will be worth while to go on. I shall not have much time for some time, as I must now read for my ordination which is elementary & unpleasant.

God bless you— In great haste.

Yours faithfully & truly

B Bailey

[2] See I, 24f.
[3] See I, 25n., and *Letters*, p. 151.
[4] See I, 20.

→≫ 12 ≪←

GEORGE KEATS TO JOHN TAYLOR

About 18 June 1818 [1]

Address: —— Taylor Esqr/ Messrs Taylor & Hessey/ Fleet Street. Lowell, II, 12f., quotes the postscript.[2]

28 Judd St—Brunswick Sq^r

My dear Sir

I am infinitely obliged for the perusal of these letters; [3] they raise my spirits (if it were possible for them to be higher), they certainly make my sanguine hopes appear somewhat more reasonable. In one respect however I must be disappointed; by what he says it appears clear I cannot be a very near neighbour, and since all his land is gone that he could recommend, it is hardly likely that he will make a fresh entry for my 640 acres; that not being done of course there will be no house to receive us: however the disappointment is not immense; when I thought these things might be done the advantage seemed great, but when I consider the having to do them myself, I only feel an addition of pride to undertake and accomplish the whole task myself— You were so kind as to offer a letter to a Friend [4] at Philadelphia as well as another to Birkbeck I should be obliged if you would send them to me before Monday; I will call on Saturday but perhaps you may not have time to write

[1] George Keats and his bride took the Liverpool coach on Monday, June 22 (Lowell, II, 13). He wrote this letter before Saturday, June 20. The paper is watermarked "Reese & Turners/ 1817."

[2] She (like Finney, II, 765, and M. B. Forman, *Connoisseur*, September, 1945 [CXV, 8]) says the letter was sent from "29 Brunswick Square," which was the office of Dr. Darling.

[3] Morris Birkbeck's *Letters from Illinois*, published by Taylor and Hessey in 1818.

[4] Michael Drury: see I, 100, 217.

29

by that day noon. I start from lad lane at 11½ Monday Morning [5]—Comp[s] to M[r] Hessey and beleive me

Your Friend (most obliged)

George Keats.

Reynolds will be with me this Evening can you come, I think
John likewise, you must see M[rs] Keats since you are physiog-
nomist [6] and discover if the lines of her face answer to her
spirit.

ex scrawl

-»» 13 «<-

TOM KEATS TO JOHN TAYLOR [1]

22 June 1818

Address: John Taylor Esq[r]/ Messrs Taylor and Hessey/ Fleet Street.
Postmarks: TwoPyPost Unpaid SOHampstead; 12 o'Clock JU.2[2] 1818
NT. Lowell, II, 73, prints the postscript.

Hampstead 22nd June 1818

Dear Sir—

My Brother in the hurry of his Letter forgot to mention
to you that he intended M[r] Severn to have a copy of his Poem—
M[r] S will call at your house for one

I am

Your humble Serv[t]

Tho[s] Keats

P S On consideration it strikes me that you will not be able
to let me have books to read—your stock being as I should think
mostly new—and modern Books—

[5] According to the *Post Office London Directory* for 1819, stage coaches
for Liverpool, 206 miles away, left from the Swan-with-Two-Necks, Lad
Lane, at 9 A.M., 6 P.M., 7:30 P.M. I have not seen a 1818 directory, but
that for 1820 lists a 11:30 A.M. coach.

[6] *Lowell has* physognomick.

[1] This letter (see also the next) is supplementary to that Keats wrote to
Taylor on June 21 (*Letters*, pp. 153f.). He left for Liverpool on June 22.

→》》 14 《《←

TOM KEATS TO JOHN TAYLOR

30 June 1818 [1]

Address: John Taylor Esqr./ Messrs Taylor & Hessey/ Fleet Street. *Post-marks:* TwoPyPost Unpaid SOHampstead; 2 2 o'Clock JY.1 1818 NT.

Hampstead
Tuesday Evening

Dear Sir

I received the parcell of Books I like Eustaces Tour [3] very much, and should be glad of the other Books you have mentioned— I had a Letter [4] this morning from Kendal—my Brother is delighted with what he has hitherto seen— I have sent it to John Reynolds—if you are desirous you can see it there, as also the subsequent accounts I may receive—

I am

Your humble Servt

Thos Keats

→》》 15 《《←

BENJAMIN BAILEY TO JOHN TAYLOR

29 August 1818

Address: John Taylor Esqre/ 91 New Bond Street/ London. *Postmark:* G 1 SE 1 1818. Morgan MS. Brief extracts are quoted by Lowell, I, 398, II, 76, 118f., by Finney, I, 321, II, 433, and by Blunden, pp. 51f.

Mr Fairbairn, Court Square, Carlisle.
August 29. 1818.

My dear Taylor,

I have long intended writing you, but you know what it

[1] Tuesday was June 30. See the postmarks and the letter preceding.
[2] *Or perhaps* 12.
[3] J. C. Eustace, *A Classical Tour through Italy* (1st ed., 2 vols., 1813), 4th ed., 4 vols., 1817.
[4] Dated June 25–27. See *Letters,* pp. 154-157.

is to put off from day to day, and (in Young's words) "resolve &
reresolve, then *do* the same." [1] But I have had a *fillup* this
morning, and am really determined not to lose another Post. I
shall surprize you perhaps when I tell you an old friend of
your's breakfasted with me this morning. This was M[r] *Collett* [2]
of or near Bath. He is related to M[r] *Fletcher's* family of Dalston
near Carlisle, from whom I have received great kindnesses since
I have been here. M[r] F—— first introduced me to him that we
might share a chaise to Ross Castle (the Bishop of Carlisle's) [3]
on Thursday, & to M[r] F's yesterday, at both which places we
dined together. And this morning he was so good as to take a
batchelor-breakfast with me; & I discovered him to be your
friend by a singular circumstance. He brought *Keats's Endymion* under his arm to shew me, as he said, it was published
by an old friend of his. "Indeed—it is both written & published
by friends of mine." The explanation ensued. We had been
fellow-travellers, likewise about a month ago in Scotland. He
desired me to present his best regards to M[r] Hesse[y] & yourself. M[rs] Collet has been very ill at Carlisle, but is sufficiently
recovered to go to M[r] Fletcher's for a few days on Monday, &
then they start for the South. This is my *preface*

You of course know I am ordained, and a poor northern
Curate—"passing rich with *60*[l] a year." [4] I have travelled a
vast deal since I saw you in London. I have been up into Scotland to visit Bishop Gleig, about 35 miles North of Edinburgh.
And I preached my *maiden sermon* in the Bishop's Chapel. It is
a glorious country. Stirling is but on the *edge* of the Highlands,
but the valley is the richest in Scotland. The Grampians are in

[1] Adapted from *Night Thoughts*, Night 1 (*Poetical Works*, Aldine ed.,
I, 14).
[2] Probably the partner in Collett and Falkener, of Bath, in whose care
Reynolds addressed to Taylor his letter of July 4, 1820.
[3] See I, 20n.
[4] Compare Goldsmith, *The Deserted Village*, line 142.

view, and in the golden sunset, are "cloud-capt towers, & gorgeous palaces." [5] One can only suppose them the habitations of unearthly beings, genii & fairies. But *you* perhaps have not seen them & *I* cannot describe them. "From the sublime to the ridiculous is but a step"—said Bonaparte (or somebody [6] for him). I heard so ridiculous a parody of the hackneyed beginning of the speech in Douglas [7] that I cannot better descend to the earth from the clouds of imagination than by it. A gentleman of the name of *Trotter* who lived in the Grampians taught a little boy of his to mouth this speech with this appropriate alteration:

"My name is *Trotter:* on the Grampian hills
   My father feeds his *flock* &c

This is a *"Sic vos non vobis,—"* [8] if there ever were one, for it cannot be imitated or supplied.

I have had a letter [9] from Keats which travelled from Inverary to my father's in Cambridgeshire, & from thence back again to Carlisle. Since the receipt of this I have heard of poor Tom's situation who, I suppose, is dead ere this. I hope John would reach home before he died. I do not well know what to think, whether good or bad of the death of this young man, if it happen. It looks harsh to say it is happy; & yet from his character he must have lived a life of discomfort to himself & those with whom he was connected, if the character I have heard of him be just. [10] Happen as it will, I am *religiously* persuaded, all

5 *The Tempest*, IV.i.152.
6 Compare Tom Paine, *The Age of Reason* (1795), Part II, note (New York, 1898, p. 92n.): "One step above the sublime makes the ridiculous, and one step above the ridiculous makes the sublime again."
7 John Home's *Douglas* (1756), II.i.42f.
8 "Lines on Bathyllus," claiming the authorship of verses by Virgil, "sic vos non vobis mellificatis apes." See Norman W. DeWitt, *Virgil's Biographia Litteraria* (1923), pp. 87f.
9 Of July 18–22: see *Letters*, pp. 191-197.
10 Bailey never saw Tom: see II, 279.

is for the best, though a thousand "Candides" rise up in derision of a truth which is the only real comfort of life.—I have something to tell you respecting *Endymion:* but it must be *in your ear.* That is, I do not wish it to be repeated to Keats, it being my determination to do him all the good I can without creating mischief. I fear Endymion will be dreadfully cut up in the Edinburgh Magazine (Blackwood's). I met a man [11] in Scotland who is concerned in that publication, & who abused poor Keats in a way that, although it was at the Bishop's table, I could hardly keep my temper. I said I supposed then he would be attacked in Blackwood's. He replied "not by *me*"; which would carry the insinuation he would by some one *else.* The objections he stated were frivolous in the extreme. They chiefly respected the *rhymes.* But I feel convinced *now* the Poem will not sell; & I *fear* his future writings will not. In Scotland he is very much *despised* from what I could collect. In the Edinburgh Magazine I can get an article inserted; and I will certainly write one in his defence if he be *grossly* attacked. As a *man of Genius* I know Keats is defensible, let him be abused as he may. And I hope they may attack him in this point. But the quarter I *fear,* & cannot defend, is the *moral* part of it. There are two great blotches in it in this respect. The first must offend *every* one of proper feelings; and indelicacy is not to be borne; & I greatly reproach myself that I did not represent this very strongly to him before it was sent [12] to the Press—not that I apprehend it would have had any great effect; but it would have been more [13] *self*-satisfaction. The *second* book, however, was concluded before I knew Keats. The second fault I allude to I think we have noticed— The approaching inclination it has

[11] For Bailey's retelling of his conversation with Lockhart see I, 245-247, II, 286-288.
[12] *F, L* it went.
[13] *F* some.

to that abominable principle of *Shelley's*—that *Sensual Love* is the principle of *things*. Of this I believe him to be unconscious, & can see how by a process of imagination he might arrive at so false, delusive, & dangerous conclusion—which may be called "a most lame & impotent conclusion." [14] If he be attacked on these points, & on the *first* he assuredly will, he is *not* defensible. Poor Keats! He shall not be deserted if he be destined to [be] disappointed [15] in his poetical career; & he shall be constantly supported & defended by me when he is at all to *be* defended. My Taste has been called *"perverted"* [16] in relation to him. No matter. I must first be *convinced* by *proof,* & not by names. I think this had better not be mentioned to Keats. I certainly cannot in person, & would not, if I could, give up any names on the opposite side of the question. I account it fortunate that I have accidentally been thrown in such a situation as that I can best defend him, & without doing any mischief.

Bishop Gleig has recommended to me, in a course of Theological Study, some books, which you may perhaps assist me in procuring. I will write <them> down their Title's on the folds of this letter. Therefore *Turn over. Cotelerius's Edition of the Apostolic Fathers.* This is the Title: "*S. S. Patrum Qui Temporibus Apostolicis floruerunt &c Opera edita et inedita, vera et supposititia. I. B. Cotelerius Societatis Sarbonicæ Theologus ex Mss Codicibus &c &c.* It is in 2 vols fol: Bishop Gleig's edition was published at *Antwerp 1700.*[17] Also *Reading's Edition of the Church Histories,*—*Eusebius, Socrates, Theodoret* &c Also, *Cave's Historia Literaria 2 vols fo. 1740.* There are *other* editions—but this is the *best.* And *Cave's Lives of the Apostles.* I have but an abridgment. If you cannot meet

---

[14] *Othello,* II.i.162.
[15] *F* to a disappointment.
[16] Doubtful word, but certainly *not* parasitic (*as in B*).
[17] First ed., Paris, 1672.

with the original of the first (Cotelerius) get *Archbishop Wake's Translation* & *Johnson's Vade Mecum*.[18] These are not books in fashion, and I hope are to be met with not very dear. If you can get them for me I shall thank you. And at the same time could you get Taylor's Plato [19] without laying the money down, for I cannot now afford 9¹ which, I believe, is the price? If you can procure the above, write me before you think of sending them: because you must try to make a bargain to send them by *water,* & such as they must keep, for I have been sadly cheated in my packages from Oxon.—

 I draw large congregations [to] my little church at present, & have been fortunate enough to gain the goodwill of the people, and am endeavoring to *humanize* a set of *boors,* who are sadly ignorant. Time will shew whether it be *novelty* only that draws them—very likely. I live at Carlisle—about 5½ miles from my Cure. Best compts to Hesse[y] & all friends. Believe me, with much regard, my dear Taylor, your assured friend

B Bailey

P S. Write soon, & I hope we may correspond as usual.[20]

Eusebius &c Reading—best Edit. Cam 1720 3 V folio 4/14/6—
 Ogle 1800
Cotelerius, Patres Apost.—best Ed.—Amst 1724 2 V fol. 4/4/6—
 dº 1778
Cave's Hist. Literaria, best Edit. Lond 1740—2 V fol. 2/12/6
 dº 1966
——Lives of the Apostles 2 V. fol. 1677—1/11/6—dº 3873
Plato

18 William Wake, *The Genuine Epistles of the Apostolical Fathers,* London, 1710, 1719, 1817; John Johnson, *The Clergyman's Vade-Mecum,* London, 1706 (6th ed., 1731).
19 See I, 10.
20 What follows is written across the outside folds in Taylor's hand.

->>> 16 <<<-

J. A. HESSEY TO JOHN TAYLOR

5 September 1818

Address: Mr John Taylor/ Messʳ Johnson & Taylor/ Bakewell. *Postmark:* SE C 5 [1]818. A few sentences are quoted by Blunden, p. 54.

Fleet Sᵗ Sep. 5. 1818

My dear John

I send you annexed the two Statemᵗˢ you wished to have— You will observe we do not at present owe sufficient to Montgomery [1] in the way of Profit on his Book to make any Division practicable— I have opened a regular Account of Sales for the Books of our publishing—those which we sell retail are not included in the Statement   I thought you would have been at Retford before this time & I sent thither for you Blackwoods Magazine which contains a cruel attack on poor Keats and some sad low abuse of Hazlitt— It is really time these fellows were put down and I should like very much to see a severe philippick against them in some of our English Magazines— I have not seen Keats since the Mag. appeared, but Hazlitt has been here and he is very much moved— He thinks & so do I that he had better remain quiet and let them take their Course— William & Dick Falkner [2] are in Town—they arrived last Night, and Mr Marriott [3] is in London also— Mrs Hessey left Teignmouth last

[1] James Montgomery (1771–1854). I have not seen Samuel Roberts' *The Blind Man and His Son, A Tale for Young People*, which Taylor and Hessey published in 1816, and the author of which, says the *Monthly Review*, May, 1817 (LXXXIII, 102) "ushers his performances into the world under the auspices of Mr. Montgomery." According to John Holland and James Everett's *Memoirs of . . . James Montgomery*, III (1855), 105f., it was dedicated to Montgomery and contained a poem by him.
[2] Relatives of Mrs. Hessey.
[3] Reverend Harvey Marriott, Claverton rector, five of whose works Taylor and Hessey later published (Blunden, p. 27).

Friday week (yesterday week)—she is now at Nursted, very much improved in Health—she will stay there I suppose about a <week> Month longer— I have seen a House at Brixton about 3 Miles from hence very pleasantly situated, that I think will just suit us—the Rent is 50£ a Year—what do you think of it— I cannot meet with any thing more reasonable that is large enough for our family and respectable in itself or I should have been glad to have a lower rent—but as this House is quite new, in a good neighbourhood, in a very airy healthy Situation, & in a pleasant Country I feel very much disposed to take it— Wright was in Town for two days last week—he rode up on Horseback so you may suppose he is not very ailing— Mrs W.[4] is pretty well— Percival [5] is also very well & so is Woodhouse— he kept me up the other night till nearly 3 in the morning talking and reading & poetizing—so you see it is a different thing to preach and to practise, and so you may tell me when I preach again— We have had no rain here of any consequence nor at Bath or Teignmouth either till to day When it has rained ever since 8 o'Clock till 3—very steadily & heavily—it is now fine again & we are going to walk to Brixton— I shall be glad to hear from you soon— Moyes is waiting for the Introd. to Hale [6]—but don't trouble yourself about it— Remember me most kindly to all your Circle, & my brothers desire their kind regards—

Believe me Dr John Yrs ever   H

[4] The Wrights turn up frequently in Hessey's letters (see the Index), but I have not identified them.

[5] Reverend John Percival, Fellow of Wadham College, intimate friend of Taylor and Hessey and a warm admirer (see I, 235) of Keats.

[6] J. Moyes, Greville Street, printer. Hale is, I presume, Sir Matthew Hale, seventeenth-century Lord Chief Justice, from whose manuscripts Taylor and Hessey published *The Counsels of a Father . . . to His Children* (1816, 1823) and *A Letter of Advice to His Grand-Children* (1816, 1823).

→»» 17 «««

B. R. HAYDON TO JOHN KEATS [1]

25 September 1818

Address: John Keats Esq/ Well walk/ Hampstead/ London. *Postmarks* (*partly illegible*): BRIDGEWATER 150; 10 o'Clock SP. 26; D 26 SE 26 1818. Printed in the *Century Magazine*, October, 1895 (L, 953), at which time it was owned by W. H. Arnold, of New York, and in *Letters*, p. 219, from the W. H. Arnold sale catalog, New York, May, 1901.

Bridgwater Sep[r] 25th

My dear Keats

Here I am as Shakespeare says "Chewing the cud of sweet & bitter fancy," [2] solitary in the midst of society with no human being to exchange a notion with except my sister [3]—and she begins to be so occupied with her little brats that if I attempt to quote Shakespeare to her—I am ordered into silence— for fear I should wake the Children.—I came here for repose of mind—as I am now getting better I am again on the rack to be again in the midst of all the objects of my ambition.—I am getting about again my hero—and I hope to God I shall yet finish my picture [4] to the satisfaction of all of you.—I am longing to be among you—and hear your account of your last Tour [5]—if it has done as much good to the *inside* as the outside of your head you will feel the effects of it as long as you live.—I shall leave this place tomorrow—or Monday & hope to be in Town by Wednesday at furthest. I hope your brother Tom does not suf-

---

[1] Only the signature and the postscript are in Haydon's hand. Endorsed by Tom Keats, "Haydon to John."

[2] "Chewing the food," etc., *As You Like It*, IV.iii.102.

[3] Keats sent a message to Harriett Haydon on May 11, 1817 (*Letters*, p. 33). She married James Haviland, of Bridgwater, in 1815.

[4] "Christ's Entry into Jerusalem" was finished in 1820.

[5] Keats got back to London on or about August 17 (Lowell, II, 77f.).

fer much—poor fellow—I shall never forget his look when I saw him last.—I can never say as much when I dictate a letter as when I write it myself—and this I hope will be a sufficient excuse for not writing a longer one to you—at any rate this is better treatment than you gave me when you went on your Tour.[6] —Believe me my dear Keats most affectionately & sincerely

Yours ever

B R Haydon

P. S. to give you an idea of the elegant taste of this place the other day, in company when I illustrated something by a quotation, one of the company said with great simplicity, "Lord Mr Haydon, you are full of *scraps!*"—adieu—my eyes will not permit me.

→» 18 «←

BENJAMIN BAILEY TO JOHN TAYLOR

5 October 1818

Address: John Taylor Esqre/ 91 New Bond Street/ London. *Readdressed.* Mr James Taylor's/ Market Place/ Retford/ Notts. *Postmarks:* CARLISLE 5 OC 5 1818; G 8 OC 8 1818. Morgan MS.

Court Square, Carlisle

Octr 5. 1818.

My dear Sir

I wrote you so long ago that I begin to think you never intend to answer my letter, or have any desire to renew or continue our Correspondence. And if it at all put you out of your way, I am sure I do not desire it. But I wrote upon *business* then and am going to do so *now*, or I should not look for an answer. Be so good however as to notice *this*. I write in ye name

---

[6] No letters from Keats to Haydon are known between April 8 and December 22, 1818, but Tom turned over at least two of John's letters for him to read (*Letters*, p. 239n.).

& on y⁰ behalf of my friend, Gleig, who wants to engage with
some Bookseller, on whom he can depend, for the translation of
one of two *Greek Fathers*—either *Eusebius's Ecclesiastical History*, which is not a very long book, being but 10 books, about
y⁰ size of a small 4ᵗᵒ Volume. This he would prefer. The other
he would *do,* if it was much preferred. This is *Philo's Life of
Moses.* I do not know the size of this book, having never seen
it; but it is a work held in very high esteem, and quoted by all
sound divines. To Eusebius Bishop Gleig would assist his Son
in y⁰ notes; and he would likewise be assisted herein by y⁰ Latin
translation to which there are notes. I believe there is no Translation of this Father in English, so considerably as he is quoted
& referred to. I have an *abridgement* in English.¹ Would y⁰
Translation of one or other of these books be a Speculation *you*
would like to enter into? Gleig is a good Greek Scholar; and as
his father would revise it, you are sure of a good translation. Of
course it would not be undertaken without a stipulated sum
previous to y⁰ undertaking. The Bishop suggested it to his son
as a thing wanted. Would you think of this; & though you
should not like to undertake such a thing yourselves, would you
ask any bookseller whom you could think would. *Longman's*
house has been applied to. If you can serve me in this, you will
much oblige me.

I have been able to borrow "Caves Lives of y⁰ Apostolic
Fathers" ² from y⁰ Diocesan Library in this place. But I should
like to know if you have heard about those other books I wrote
you concerning. If you cannot meet with them before I visit
London again, I must ferret them out myself.

I have been misled as to my hope of getting any article in

¹ The works of Philo Judaeus had to wait till 1854–1855 to be translated by C. D. Yonge. Bailey's abridgment with notes by Valesius was
published at London in 1661, 1698, at Cambridge in 1692.
² See I, 35f.

Blackwood's Magazine. They attack people, but do not leave their columns open to defence. Unwillingly therefore I have applied to Constable's [3] upon whom I called when I was in Edinburgh about 10 days ago. I have sent an article against Blackwood's Magazine, bringing Keats forward as an instance. I hav{e} not time now to do yͤ subject Justice, were I to enter upon a regular defence of Keats's Poetry. Besides it would not be admitted; & God knows whether what I *have* written will. I have done yͤ best I could, of which you must judge when you see it, if it be printed. If not, you must allow my *intention*.

I was introduced to Blackwood who told me he had seen you, and that he was sorry on his return to find the attack on Keats. I told him it was *"infamous."* He did not like to be told so—but no matter for that. He is a great poet. I fear Endymion don't sell.

I have given up all thoughts of publishing those Essays I once thought of.[4] 'Tis an age of speculations & authors. I will not be one to be charged with vanity & a thousand other accursed [?] things of which as I am innocent, I will avoid yͤ imputation. Farewell. Pray answer this as soon as you can satisfactorily & decisively—and with best respects to Hesse[y], & Love to *Keats* when you see him, believe me dear Taylor, yours most sincerely

B Bailey [5]

Eusebius, Socrates & Evagrius by Wells [6]—tran—fine copy LP
     1/4—1709.
Philo's Moses—unknown

[3] Probably the *Scots Magazine*.
[4] See I, 26-28.
[5] What follows is written on the outside folds in Taylor's hand.
[6] Edward Wells, *The History of the Church* (1709).

⇶ 19 ⇷

J. H. REYNOLDS TO JOHN KEATS
14 October 1818 [1]

Address: Mr John Keats/ N° 1 Well Walk/ Hampstead. *Postmarks:* 4 o'Clock OC.14 18{18}; Two Py Post Unpaid EOStrand. Partly printed by Colvin, pp. 312f., and Lowell, II, 105f., and almost entirely in *Letters,* pp. 223f. (which followed the W. H. Arnold sale catalog of May, 1901). Two sentences are quoted in *Harper's New Monthly Magazine,* LV (1877), 361, and the whole letter, then owned by Arnold, is printed in the *Century Magazine,* October, 1895 (L, 953).

My Dear Keats

I was most delighted at seeing you yesterday,—for I hardly knew how I was to meet with you, situated as you are, and confined as I am. I wish I could have stayed longer with you. As to the Poem I am of all things anxious that you should publish it, for its completeness will be a full answer to all the ignorant malevolence of cold lying Scotchmen and stupid Englishmen. The overweening struggle to oppress you only shews the world that so much of endeavour cannot be directed to nothing. Men do not set their muscles, and strain their sinews to break a straw. I am confident, Keats, that the Pot of Basil hath that simplicity and quiet pathos, which are of sure Sovereignty over all hearts. I must say that it would delight me to have you prove yourself to the world, what we know you to be;—to have you annul the Quarterly Review, by the best of all answers. When I see you, I will give you the Poem, and pray look it over with that eye to the *littlenesses* which the world are

---

[1] Lowell, II, 105, says that Reynolds visited Keats "on Thursday, October thirteenth," carried off the manuscript of *Isabella,* and wrote this letter "the next morning." But it is dated Wednesday and postmarked October 14. The thirteenth was Tuesday. The letter is endorsed by Tom Keats, "Reynolds to John."

so fond of excepting to (though I confess with that word altered which I mentioned, I see nothing that can be cavilled at)— And let us have the Tale put forth, now that an interest is aroused. One or two of your Sonnets you might print, I am sure— And I know that I may suggest to you, which,—because you can decide as you like afte{rward. You} will remember that we were {. . . } [2] together—<but> I give over all intention and you ought to be alone. I can never write anything now—my mind is taken the other way:— But I shall set my heart on having you, high, as you ought to be. Do *you* get Fame,—and I shall have it in being your affectionate and steady friend. There is no one I am more interested in—and there is no one that I have more pleasure in communicating my own happiness to. You will gratify me much by letting me have, whenever you have leisure, copies of what you write;—for *more than myself* have a sincere interest in you. When shall I see you—& when shall I go with you to Severn's

Your ever affection{ate}

Wed^y Morn^g   J. H. Reynolds

→≫ 20 ≪←

RICHARD WOODHOUSE: NOTES ON THE CRITIQUES ON
Endymion IN THE *Quarterly Review* AND
Blackwood's Edinburgh Magazine

October 1818

Note.[1]

In the Quarterly review for April (publish^d about the 27 Sep^r) 1818 is a most unjust & illiberal criticism upon Endym-

[2] *Lowell has* we were [to] pu[t out], *Colvin* we were to print. The *Century reads* [Nobody] will remember that we were [to write].

[1] From Woodhouse's Book of Transcripts of Keats's Letters (Harvard), p. 10. These incomplete notes were presumably made about the middle of October while Woodhouse (see the following letter) was at Bath.

ion— The critic first objects that the work is not written in couplets— This objection can require no answer, tho' it is very natural that one, who has been all his poetical life employed in tagging couplets together, should be unable to conceive a poem to be good, that is written otherwise.—He next makes a ridiculous objection about the rhymes suggesting the ideas: which, if true, would be no fault in the poem, but which may be shewn to be unfounded by the simple process of changing the final words of the lines, so as to destroy the rhyme; notwithstanding which, the sense & picture of the descriptions &c remain— He then finds fault with the versification, in such a manner as to shew he is quite ignorant of the very grounds & rudiments of English heroic verse— He next objects to certain compound words which have been in use with every bard that ever rhymed in our language—from Chaucer down to himself— And he ends with accusing Keats of coining several specified words—the majority of which are found in Shakespeare or Spencer.— To crown the whole, he professes to have read only the 1ˢᵗ Canto.—

In Blackwood's Edinburgh Magazine,[2] a work as infamous in Character as the man whose name it bears,[3] are a series of attacks upon nearly all the English poets of the day, (apparently with a view of leaving the Scotch in possession of the field of fame) & upon Keats among the number. There is nothing worth notice in it.

The poem has also been noticed in the [4]

[2] August, 1818 (III, 519-524).
[3] See I, 42, 133-137.
[4] The note ends thus.

45

⇛ 21 ⇚

RICHARD WOODHOUSE TO JOHN KEATS

21 October 1818

A draft, printed in part by Lowell, II, 97-99, and Finney, II, 475f., and entire, except for the cancelations,[1] in *Letters*, pp. 225-227.

My dear Keats,

Whilst in the country, from whence I am but <just> lately returned, I met with that malicious, but weak & silly article on Endymion in the last Quarterly Review.[2] God help the Critic, whoever he be! He is as ignorant of the rudiments of his own craft as of the Essentials of true Poetry[.] [3] * I take it the precious article in question once formed a portion of the critique in the <preceding> former Nº upon L. Hunts foliage.—[4] That the reviewer, in a <fit> moment of compunction, changed his plan, & <determined to> reviewed <L> Hunts work by itself, intendᵍ to leave you alone; tho' the scissors with which this sentence <operation> of divorce was <performed> carrᵈ into effect left in the earlier article a few traces of the origˡ union.—But that the Editor, finding himself at a loss for a few pages of matter to eke out his presᵗ Nº, bethought himself

1 Most of the canceled words or passages are here given, but others cannot be deciphered or else defy any intelligible system of reproduction. For Keats's reply to the letter actually sent see *Letters*, pp. 227-229.

2 April (XIX, 204-208). Elsewhere (see note 7) Woodhouse names the reviewer, who actually was J. W. Croker, as Gifford. Keats himself (see *Letters*, p. 250) believed Gifford the author.

3 This sentence originally ran: "He is as much to seek in the rudiments of his own craft, as he is ignorant of the essentials of true poetry.—" and was then changed to: "He is as ignorant of the rudiments of criticism as of those of true poetry."

* The remainder of the paragraph is written at the bottom of the last (fourth) page, to be here inserted.

4 January (XVIII, 324-335 .

46

of the fragments of his former review, which he has cooked up
afresh, <& garnished out for> as a side dish [5] for his readers.—

That his *very equitable* censures [6] may have the effect of
scaring from the perusal of the Work some of the "Dandy"
readers, male & female, who love to be spared the trouble of
judging for themselves, is to be expected— But with men of
sense, <like> (as the example of J. S. in the Chronicle [7] proves)
the effect must be the reverse— The Criticism <carries in it the
sufficing cause of its own destruction> is felo de se— It bears on
its [8] front the sentence of its own condemn[g] <on its front>:
for the Reviewer in <the sheerness of his> his undiscrimina-
ting stupidity, has laid his finger of contempt upon passages of
such beauty, that no one with a spark of poetic feeling can read
them without a desire to know more of the poem.—"If"—said
a friend of mine at Bath, who had <read> seen the critique,
but not the work, "these are the worst passages, what must the
best be."—To be praised in the same review that slabbers with
its eulogy Barretts woman [9] would have been damnation Such

[5] After "dish" is canceled something like "as the finest banquet he could
provide."
[6] Originally, "That his unjust censures," then "But his edifying censures."
[7] J. S.'s letter to the *Morning Chronicle*, October 3, 1818, is reprinted by
Forman, III, 381-383. Woodhouse also copied it into his Book of Transcripts of Keats's Letters (Harvard), pp. 11f., adding the following notes:

"N.B. The reviewers above alluded to are 1st Gifford, the author of the
Baviad & the Aeviad [*sic*]—& translator of Juvenal—who is the Editor
of the Q: Rev: & most probably author of the critique in Question—
The 2d is Mr [*or apparently* Wm] Southey Poet Laureate & Editor of K
White's remains. & the 3d is Jn Wilson Croker, Secretary of the Ad-
miralty, & author of a poem on the battle[s] of Talavera.—R.W.

"N.B. Other Letters & Extracts from the work appeared in the Chronicle. The Sun—the Day or New Times. the Examiner & other papers. all
speaking favorably of Endymion."
[8] Here "own cond" is canceled.
[9] E. S. Barrett's *Woman: A Poem* (second edition, revised), 1818, **of**

a pestering insect may annoy <one> for <an hour> a moment, but its impotent attacks can <give> cause no permanent uneasiness.—And I am happy to <find from> see by the daily papers,[10] that the crying injustice of the decision has roused <the> indignation <of> in a few who "do look with a jealous eye <to> on the honor of English literature." [10a] But enough of such a <bungling> cobbling, carping, <shallow> decasyllabic, finger-scanning—criticaster.—His hour of <bustling poking about, is nigh done> "brief authority" [11] must be nigh over—His blindness will soon work its {own w}ay into the earth.—

  The appearance of this "critical morsel," however, determines me to address you on the subject of our late conversation at Hessey's,[12] on which I have often since reflected, and never without a degree of pain— I may have misconceived you, —but I <then> understood you to say, you thought there was now nothing original to be written in poetry: that its riches <were being> were already exhausted, & all its beauties forestalled—& That you should, consequently, write no more<: but continue increasing your knowledge, merely for your own gratification without any attempt to make use of your Stores>.—I cannot <agree with you in> assent to your premises, and I most earnestly deprecate your conclusion.—For my part I be-

---

which the *Quarterly*, April, pp. 246-250, said: "Mr. Barrett has evinced both talent and genius . . . and sustained a flight far above the common level." The first edition is reviewed in the *Monthly Mirror*, July, 1810 (VIII, 51).

[10] See Forman, III, 373-383.

[10a] Preface to *Endymion*.

[11] *Measure for Measure*, II.ii.118.

[12] Originally this ran: "Before the appearance of this critical morse" and "I have several times lately reflected with some pain upon the Conversation we had together at Hessey's, the day before I left Town; and the appearance of this critical morsel determines me to address you on the subject."

lieve most sincerely, that the <beauties riches> wealth of
poetry <are> is unexhausted & <indeed> inexhaustible—
The ideas derivable to us from our senses singly & in their
various combin^ns with each other store the mind with endless
images of natural beauty & perfection—the Passions add life &
motion—& reflection & the moral Sense give order relief unity
& harmony to this mighty world of inanimate matter.[13]—It is in
the gleaning of the highest, the truest & the sweetest of these
ideas, in the orderly grouping of them, & arraying them in the
garb of exquisite Numbers, that Poetry may be said to consist.—
It is then for the Poëta factus, the imitator of others, who sings
only as has been sung, to say that our measure of poesy [14] is full,
& that there is nothing new to be written, thus charging [15] upon
"most innocent nature" [16] <the faults arising out of his own
dullness> a dearth exist^s only in <the [*word illegible*] of his>
his own dull brain— But the poëta natus, the true born Son of
Genius <& the Muse>, who creates for himself <a> the
world in which his own <Imagination> fancy ranges <wherein
he may wander, &> who culls from it fair forms <samples> of
truth <&> beauty & purity & apparels them in hues <of his
own choosing> chosen by himself, should hold a different language— <He> he need never fear that the treasury he draws
on can be exhausted, nor [17] despair of <always> being always
able to ma{ke} an original selection.

[13] Woodhouse first wrote: "The ideas of beauty & perfection, natural as
well as moral, derivable to us from our own senses only are most numerous—and those suggested by all our senses separately, & by them in combination one with another must be almost infinite in variety. Add the
passions, and a world arises before you." The stages of revision inter-
vening between this original version and the final one are not here
recorded.

[14] Changed from "poetry."

[15] Changed from "to charge."

[16] Milton, *Comus*, line 761.

[17] A second "nor" with the *n* canceled appears here.

It is true that in this age, the mass are not of soul to conceive <of themselves> of themselves or even to apprehend when presented to them, the truly & simply beautiful <in> of poetry.—A taste vitiated by the sweetmeats & kickshaws of the <last> past century may be the reason <of this> of this. Still fewer of this generation are capable of properly embodying <what> the high conceptions they may have—and of the last <few> number few are the individuals [18] who do not allow their fire & originality to be damped by apprehensions of <contemptible> shallow censures from the groveling & the "cold hearted."

In these "evil days" however & amid these "Evil tonges" [19] (in the spirit of truth & sincerity & not of flattery I say it) I believe there has appeared *one* bard [20] who "preserves his vessel" in purity independance & honor—who judges of the beautiful for himself, careless [21] who thinks with him—who <steers> pursues his own selfappointed & selfapproved course right onward [21a]—who stoops not from <the height of> his <high> flight to win sullied breath from the multitude—and who "leans away" for highest heaven, and sings, pointing for his [*word illegible*]—to a standard of excellence dimly visible as yet even to himself & scarcely free from the shadows in which from unknown time it has been vested [22] and of which the meaner

[18] Originally: "and of these <not> scarce are there two or three individuals."   [19] *Paradise Lost,* VII.25f.

[20] Originally: "If the spirit of truth & sincerity and not of flattery, (for I should despise myself If I flattered) I say, that I know but one bard." Intermediate revisions not recorded.

[21] Changed to "reckless" and back to "careless."   [21a] Compare Milton, sonnet 22, lines 9f., "still bear up and steer / Right onward."

[22] This phrasing is the result of much revision of the original: ". . . multitude—and who appeals for justification in his [*word illegible*] to a standard of excellence set up by himself, & scarcely yet free from the shadows in which it has [*word illegible*] long rested, or discernible by the clearest eye." Woodhouse quotes *Endymion,* IV.568.

spirits of his day seem to be without even a conception—²³ And shall such a one, upon whom anxious eyes are fixed, at whose noble aspirings "unnumbered souls breathe out a *still* applause," ²⁴ be dismayed at the yelpings of the tuneless, the envious, the malignant or the undiscerning? or shall he fall into the worse error of supposing that there is left no corner of the universal heaven of poesy unvisited by Wing? ²⁵ Shall he subtract himself from the <gaze> expectations ²⁶ of his country; and leave its <palled> ear & its soul to be soothed only by the rhymers & the coupleteers? Shall he let "so fair a house fall to decay" ²⁷—and shall he give the land which let Chatterton & K. White die of <neglect &> unkindness & neglect,— but which yet <had> retained the grace to weep over their ashes, no opportunity of redeeming its Character, & paying the vast <great> debt it <yet> owes to Genius?—Your conduct, my Dear Keats, must give these Questions an answer.—

"Know thine own worth, and reverence the lyre"!—²⁸

The world, I hope & trust, is not quite so dead dull and ungrateful as you may have apprehended—or as a few malevolent spirits may have given you reason to imagine— It contains, I know, many who have a warm "affection for the cause Of stedfast Genius toiling gallantly," ²⁹—many who, tho' personally unknown to you, look with the eye of hope & anticipation <at> to your future course—but very few who in <earnest>

---

²³ Here is canceled some such remark as "What conduct [*or course?*] should he pursue?"

²⁴ Keats's sonnet "Addressed to Haydon," line 13.

²⁵ Compare *Paradise Lost*, III.13.

²⁶ Lowell reads "caputations," a word unknown to *NED*.

²⁷ Shakespeare, sonnet 13, line 9.

²⁸ James Beattie, *The Minstrel*, I.59.

²⁹ Keats's sonnet "Addressed to Haydon," line 10.

sincere wishes for your welfare, & passion for your fame, exceed,
Dear Keats,

Yours most truly,

Richd Woodhouse.

Temple <17> <21> 21st Octr 1818.

➤➤➤ 22 ◄◄◄

J. A. HESSEY TO JOHN TAYLOR

23 October 1818

Address: Mr John Taylor/ Mr Taylors/ Market Place/ Retford. Printed
in part by Blunden, p. 57.

London Oct. 23. 1818

My dear John

My chief reason for writing is to answer your Question
respecting Honour— She is, I believe, very honest & well disposed, and as far as she is able a good Servant—but she is not
quite so clean as people who are particular in that respect
would like, and as you know she is no great hand at cooking—
She can roast & boil Legs of mutton, & make rice pudding &
Batter pudding such as it is— But she certainly is not equal to
the preparing a Dinner fit for any Stranger to sit down to—
Whenever I have had any one to dine with me I have been
obliged to have Sally to cook, which is not pleasant & which I
would avoid in future for good reasons— If your friends should
know of a steady respectable trusty woman, who knows her
business thoroughly and may be depended on without looking
after I would advise you by all means to secure her— But till
you can find such a person you had better have Honour with
her good qualities & her Imperfections together than a Stranger—
I have much pleasure in saying that Endymion begins to move
at last—6 Copies have just been ordered by Simpkin & Mar-

shall [1] & one or two have been sold singly in the Shop—there is nothing like making a Stir for it—the papers have said so much about it many persons will doubtless be curious to see what it does contain—& here & there a man of taste may be found to admire its beauties   Keats was here last Evening & Hazlitt yesterday & to day—the latter of course came for more money which I was obliged to give him— He has got, he says, the first 4 Lectures written & much of the others— He begins next tuesday [2] week— Fairbairn [3] has ordered 25 Lectures & 15 Shaksp: [4] with many other things— I suppose you have seen the Times of to day with my Letter about Birkbeck [5] in it— I have sent it also to several other papers to turn the tide against the Quarterly in that Quarter as well as in the Poetry line—they are shameful fellows—

D[r] Symmons [6] has written to say that hearing of our liberality to Mr Carey he is disposed to give us an opportunity of being equally liberal to him in purchasing his translation of Virgil—much obliged, but won't do— Royal 4[to]!—he made his Book as much too large as Carey's was too small— Dante [7] is selling very well— We are both very well and desire our united kindest remembrances to all your Circle— Believe me Dear John

Yours very sincerely
J A H

[1] Booksellers, 4 Stationer's Hall Court, Ludgate.

[2] On November 3, when Hazlitt gave the first of his lectures at the Surrey Institution on the *English Comic Writers*.

[3] Perhaps John Fairburn, bookseller and publisher, 110 Minories.

[4] See I, 27.

[5] See Blunden, pp. 57f.

[6] Charles Symmons' translation of Virgil first appeared in London in 1817. The second edition, 1820, was published by N. Hailes, London.

[7] On H. F. Cary's Dante see I, 80.

⇒⇒ 23 ⇐⇐

RICHARD WOODHOUSE TO MARY FROGLEY [1]

23 October 1818 [2]

Morgan MS. Printed in *TLS*, April 16, 1914, p. 182 (by Colvin), and in part by Colvin, p. 368.

My dear Mary,

I returned from Hounslow late last night, & your mother desired me to forward to you the enclosed letter. I brought Endymion back, thinking you might like to have it in Town whilst with your friends.

You were so flattering as to say the other day, you wished I had been in a company where you were, to defend Keats.—In all places, & at all times, & before all persons, I would express, and as far as I am able, support, my high opinion of his poetical merits— Such a genius, I verily believe, has not appeared since Shakspeare & Milton: and I may assert without fear of contradiction from any one competent to Judge, that if his Endymion be compared with Shakspeare's earliest work (his Venus & Adonis) written about the same age, Keats's poem will be found to contain more beauties, more poetry (and that of a higher order) less conceit & bad taste and in a word much more promise of excellence than are to be found in Shakspeare's work— This is a deliberate opinion; nor is it merely my own— The Justice

[1] See I, 71, II, 217. A draft of this letter, varying from the final copy only in a few trivial details, is also in the Morgan MS., much damaged by crumbling of paper at the right-hand side of pages, so that the last words of each line are regularly missing. Lowell, II, 186f., printed part of the draft but, she says, consulted "the original letter published" in *TLS*.

[2] The references to "Gifford's" review of *Endymion*, which, though dated April, appeared in September (Lowell, II, 85), and to the "remonstrances" in "the daily papers" (see I, 48, note 10), together with "Friday" at the end, fix the date as October 23.

of which, however, can only be demonstrated to another upon a full review of the parts & of the whole of each work. I sh[d] not shrink from the task of doing it to one whose candour I was acquainted with, and whose Judgment I respected.

But in our Common conversation upon his merits, we should always bear in mind that his fame may be more hurt by indiscriminate praise than by wholesale censure. I would at once admit that he has great faults—enough indeed to sink another writer. But they are more than counterbalanced by his beauties: And this is the proper mode of appretiating an original genius. His faults will wear away—his fire will be chastened —and then eyes will do homage to his brilliancy. But genius is wayward, trembling, easily daunted. And shall we not excuse the errors, the luxuriances of youth? are we to expect that poets are to be given to the world, as our first parents were, in a state of maturity? are they to have no season of Childhood? are they to have no room to try their wings before the steadiness & strength of their flight are to be finally judged of?—So says M[r] Gifford of the Quarterly— But the world meted out a far different measure to his youthful Infirmities,—though he forgets it.— So said <Horace Walpole of Chatterton, So said> the Edinburgh Review<ers> of L[d] Byron— So said the Monthly [3] of Kirke White— So said Horace Walpole of Chatterton.[4] And how are such Critics now execrated <by> for their cruel injustice.—I see the daily papers teem with remonstrances against Gifford's arbitrary decision. An appeal to the Country is lodged against it. Perhaps this age,—certainly posterity,—will judge rightly— However the decision be, the competence of a poet to write, and of a Critic to Judge of poetry are involved in the dispute, and *one* reputation must suffer deeply. Had I any literary reputation I would stake it on the result. You know the side I

[3] *Monthly Review,* February, 1804 (XLIII, 218).
[4] See J. H. Ingram, *The True Chatterton* (1910), pp. 162-178.

should espouse. As it is,—I can only prophesy. And now, while Keats is unknown unheeded, despised of one of our archcritics, neglected by the rest—in the teeth of the world, and in the face of "these curious days," [5] I express my conviction, that Keats, during his life (if it please God to spare him to the usual age of man, and the critics not to drive him from the free air of the poetic heaven before his Wings are fullfledged,) will rank on a level with the best of the last or of the present generation; and after his death will take his place at their head.—

But, while I think thus, I would make persons respect my judgment by the discrimination of my praise, and by the freedom of my censure where his writings are open to it. These are the Elements of true criticism— It is easy, like Momus, to find fault with the clattering of the slipper worn by the Goddess of b{e}auty: but "the serious Gods" [6] found better employment in admiration of her unapproachable loveliness.—A Poet ought to write for Posterity. But a critic should do so too.—Those of our times write for the day, or rather the hour. Their thoughts & Judgments are fashionable garbs, such as they imagine a skinwise world would like to array itself in at second hand.—How is the great Johnson

"Fallen, fallen, fallen, fallen,
"Fallen from his high Estate," [7]

by the malice, the Injustice, & envy of his criticisms in that "Monument of his Mortality the lives of the Poets," and by his deadness [8] to the exalted & excellent in Poetry.

Adieu, my dear Mary;—I have mounted so far into the Clouds that I am, like Endymion, [9]

[5] Shakespeare, sonnet 38, line 13.
[6] *Endymion*, II.785.
[7] Dryden, "Alexander's Feast," lines 77f.
[8] *TLS* deafness.
[9] I.583f.

——"Become loth & fearful to alight
"From such high soaring;"
but when he did, it was to pay his respects to a divinity. In this
too I follow his example, kissing your poor *one* hand, and craving kind remembrances to the divine ones around you.

I am &c e^r [10] yours, Richd Woodhouse
Friday Morn^g

→>> 24 <<←

RICHARD WOODHOUSE: NOTES ON A LETTER FROM KEATS [1]

About 27 October 1818

Morgan MS. Printed in part by Lowell, II, 102-104. Finney, II, 492,
quotes a sentence.

I believe him to be right with regard to <the> his own Poetical Character— And I perceive clearly the distinction he draws
between himself & those of the Wordsworth School.—There are
gradations in Poetry & in Poets. One is purely descriptive <&>
confining himself to external nature & visible objects—˙Another
describes in add^n the effects of the thoughts of wh: he is conscious—<& the effects he has produced in others by such
like [?] thoughts> & wh: others are affected by— Another will
soar so far into the regions of imagination as to conceive of beings
& substances in situations different from what he has ever seen
them but still such as either have actually occurred or may possibly occur— <Such is the tragedian> Another will reason in
poetry—another be witty.—Another will imagine things that
never did nor probably ever will occur, or such as can not in
nature occur & yet he will describe them so that you <may>

[10] So apparently. *TLS has* as ever.
[1] For Keats's reply, October 27, to Woodhouse's letter of October 21
(No. 21) see *Letters*, pp. 227-229. Here Woodhouse analyzes its philosophy
of "negative capability." A few of his canceled words cannot be made
out.

recognize nothing very unnatural in the Descriptions when cert[n] principles or powers or cond[ns] are admitted— Another with [2] throw himself into various characters & make them speak as the passions wo[d] naturally incite them to do The highest order of Poet will not only <embrace> possess all the above powers but will have so high an imag[n] that he will be able to throw his own soul into <the> any object he sees or imagines, so as to see feel <&> be sensible of, & express, all that the object itself wo[d] see feel <&> be sensible of or express—& he will speak out of that object so that his own self will with the Exception of the Mechanical part be "annihilated."—and it is of the excess of this power that I suppose Keats to speaks,[3] when he says he has no identity— As a poet, and when the fit is upon him, this is true— And it is a fact that he does <create> by the power of his Imag[n] create ideal personages substances & Powers—that he lives for a time in their souls or Essences or ideas—and that occasionally so intensely as to <forget> lose consciousness of what is round him. We all do the same in a degree, when we fall into a reverie—
See below. x

If then his imag[n] has such power: and he is continually cultivating <& exercising> it, giving it <space to act> play. It will acquire strength by the Indulgence & exercise. <And as> This in excess is the Case <with> of mad persons. And this may be carried to that extent that he may lose sight of his identity so far <that as generally to> as to give him a habit of speak[s] [4] generally in an assumed character—so that What

---

x <To instance> The power of his Imagin[n] <It wo[d] be
[2] *Sic for* will.
[3] Woodhouse first wrote "that Keats speaks" and when he added "I suppose" and "to" he neglected to change "speaks" to "speak."
[4] *Originally* speak.

he says shall be tinged with the Sentiments proper to the **Char-**
acter which at the [5] time has possessed itself of his **Imagination,**
<and, thro' that, of his other faculties>—

This being his idea of the Poetical Character—he may
well say that a poet has no identity [6]—as a man he must have
Ident^y. But as a poet <it is> he need not <necessary>— And
in this Sense a poet is "the most unpoetical of Gods creatures."
<But> for his soul has no distinctive characteristic—it can not
be itself made the subj^t of Poetry that is another persons soul
can not be thrown into the poet's—for there is no identity
(separatedness) (distinctiveness) or personal impulse to be acted
upon—

Shaksp^r was a poet of the kind above ment^d—and he was
perhaps the only one besides Keats who possessed this power
in an extr^y[?] degree, <that> so as to be a feature in his works.
He gives a descr^n of his idea of a poet

The Poets eye &c [7]

Ld Byron does not come up to this Character. He can
certainly conceive & describe a dark accomplished vilain in
love—& a female tender & kind who loves him. Or a sated &

---

enough to read his vol of poems> is <will be> apparent in
Ev^y page of his Endym^n Θ—& He has affirmed that he can conceive of a billiard Ball that it may have a sense of delight from
its own roundness, smoothness <& very> volubility. & the
rapidity of its motion.—[8]

Θ Take p 69 [9] —only & look at the qualities with wh. in
that one page <69 End^n> he Endues inan^e beings & even
imagined <beings> ideas, as silence—<refreshment>[10] a channel of a stream, a sallow by water side & the Sense of refreshm^t.

[5] *Written* the the.   [6] *Written* idenitity.
[7] *A Midsummer-Night's Dream*, V.i.12.   [8] See No. 131, note 4.
[9] The reference is to *Endymion* (1818), II.340ff.
[10] Another canceled word follows.

palled [11] Sensualist Misanthrope & Deist— But here his power ends.—The true poet can not only conceive this—but can assume any Character Essence idea or Substance at pleasure. & He has this imaginative faculty not in a limited manner, but in full universality.

Let us pursue Speculation on these Matters: & we shall soon be bro^t to believe in the truth of every Syllable of Keats's letter, taken as a descript^n of himself & his own Ideas & feel^gs.

→» 25 «←

BENJAMIN BAILEY TO JOHN TAYLOR

9 November 1818

Address: Jno Taylor Esqre/ 93 Fleet Street/ London. *Postmark:* O 13 NO 13 1818. Morgan MS. Lowell, II, 91, summarizes the letter.

Carlile. Novr 9. 1818.

My dear Sir

I suppose you will be in London again before this arrives there. I am much obliged to you for your answers to my enquiries. I have, since I wrote & indeed since I received your letter which I did in Scotland, seen an old Edition of *Eusebius,* with one or two others translated into very old English. The Notes, with which ye Bishop would furnish his Son,[1] would be of this Nature: to compare the state of the ancient church with the church in ye present times. Will there be any chance of a translation, with such notes, which *in themselves* would I am sure be valuable, at all attracting y^e public? I own, I fear not, in this half-learned & irreligious age. But I wish you would give the matter some thought, & tell me your candid opinion when you write.

---

[11] *Originally* apalled.
[1] See I, 41.

CHARLES WENTWORTH DILKE

MARIA WALKER DILKE

There is no one translating any of y⁶ old fathers into English that you have heard of? Yet I have some glimmering remembrance of having heard something of y⁶ sort when I lived in London. May I trouble you to make this enquiry, if you can do it without putting yourself out of y⁶ way.

The copies of those books, the prices of which you have been so good as to ascertain & send me, I hope to meet with at much less. Bishop Gleig has them all; & he paid no such money for them.—I am ashamed of putting you to so much trouble. Whilst I am in business let me mention one thing which I have from time to time forgotten. I took away with me that copy of Jeremy Taylor's Sermons in fo: which you lent me at our first acquaintance. It is marked 10/6; & I have added that sum to a small account in which I stand indebted to you, & wᶜʰ after Xmas shall be discharged.—

I both wrote & sent y⁶ article, I promised,[2] on Endymion, to Constable's for insertion in their Magazine; but they have declined printing it, & sent it back without a word. It was *generally* severe, but with no personality. I attacked the *principle* of y⁶ Magazine, inasmuch as it's Criticisms were personal, instead of being confined to the works. Also that they confounded good men & bad men. That it had no respect for any individual's feelings. And much more than I can tell you (for I have destroyed y⁶ article now), but it was certainly written very severe. I brought forward the Review of Keats as an example of all that I had said. I am sorry they have rejected it, because it would have been some satisfaction to one's own mind to reflect I had done something for him, were it ever so little. But I beg you will tell him of my *intentions* in his favor. Give him my kindest remembrances; & say I shall be very happy to hear from him. I hope his brother is better.

[2] See I, 42.

61

You have seen the attack on [3] Blackwood's **Magazine, I** suppose, & have seen likewise the folly of ye Editors in exposing themselves. They must now personally answer their personal attacks. The work is ably written where it is not scurrilous. There is as fine a tribute to Pitt in ye last number as I ever remember to have seen to departed greatness: and the article on Moore's Poetry is very just & good.[4] If they would always write thus, they would *deserve* to succeed.

I have let my correspondence get ye head of me so much, having been in Scotland for nearly a month, that I am quite laboured to get it up. This must apologize for this slovenly letter.

I believe I shall not remain much longer here, being invited by the Congregation at St Andrews in ffifeshire to take charge of them. I have to get the Bishop's consent to leave this Diocese which I hope to be able to do, & to get into Priest's orders. If I accomplish one, I shall both. And I have little fear as to either. St Andrews is an old university Town, & the Seat of the famous Archbishop Sharpe.[5] In the church there is preserved the monument, on which is carved the several scenes of the murder—1st the attack of the Coach—2^d the Death of the Archbishop after he is <with> dragged out of his carriage—& 3dly the prayers of his daughter to the assassins. It is a curious Relic. The church has been rebuilt, but this was preserved. On the Scite of this church it was that John Knox incited the mob to destroy the Cathedral. It is now the finest ruin I ever saw. If ever you come into Scotland, & I am in St Andrews you must come & see it & me: For wherever I am I shall always be

[3] *Sic.*

[4] Keats was ridiculed as a member of the Cockney School in August, 1818 (III, 519-524), "Fox and Pitt" appeared in July (III, 456-459), and Moore was reviewed in October (IV, 1-5).

[5] James Sharp (1613–1679) was murdered by a band under John Balfour, third Baron Balfour of Burleigh.

happy to see and entertain you; for I am with much sincerity, my dear Taylor, yours very faithfully

B Bailey

⇟⇟ 26 ⇞⇞

RICHARD WOODHOUSE TO JOHN TAYLOR
23 November 1818

Address: Jnᵒ Taylor Esqʳ. Morgan MS. Printed in part by Lowell, I, 534, and Finney (*F*), I, 236, 346 (both misdate it 1820).

Temple 23. Nov 1818

Dear John,

I return you non sine gratiis actis <th> Reynolds's volume of Poetry [1]— I see there are a few variations in *his Edition* of the Sonnets on the sea, & on the Elgin Marbles, from the Copy I had. Perhaps he wrote them from Memory— I see he entitles the "Ode to Apollo" a fragment.—I need not have been so jealous of your Pointing out to me the *best* of those of Keats's new compositions which it contains—the thing speaks for itself— The subject had not been broached before— Some old writer (Horace I believe) seems to have regretted this in his time, if *my* reading of his line is correct,

Nile intentatum nostri liquere Poetae." [2]

There are two or 3 sweet sonnets of Reynolds's— I like those addressed to a Lady best (with the Exceptⁿ of that to Poetry)— I had no time to read Devon: [3] for I left it till last, as I understand it is to be published— It seems from the judgment to be formed by dippings into it to be the best.—

[1] A manuscript of some of Keats's and some of Reynolds' (and perhaps Hunt's) poems, but evidently *not* the Reynolds commonplace book (see I, 85n.) described by Garrod, pp. lxx f.

[2] Horace, *Ars Poetica,* line 285, "nil intemptatum," etc. Woodhouse may be punning on the sonnets "To the Nile."

[3] For the three poems see Marsh, pp. 152, 174f., 138-142. They were printed in *The Garden of Florence* (1821).

I can not like Leigh Hunts.—His thoughts have "Leaden Eyes which love the ground" 4—they do not come naturally: they seem as if they were pressed into the service, & brought into action before they were drilled.—And instead of <force or> power and range of Expression, he substitutes quaintness & conceit— It is the same in his prose—and both seem a sample of the heroics of the Servants' Hall—

I have tried unsuccessfully to admire the 3ᵈ stanza of "Drear nighted Decʳ" as much as the 2 first.—I plead guilty, even before I am accused, of an utter abhorrence of the word "feel" for feeling (substantively)— <But> But Keats seems fond of it. and will ingraft it "in aeternum" on our language 5— Be it so— I will conquer my dislike— But the great objection to the 3ᵈ stanza is that the 4 last lines are an excrescence—and ought to have had some connection with the 4 first which are an application of or rather antithesis to the 1 & [?] 2 Stanzas—6

I woᵈ not dream of entering into the lists with any poet that ever rhymed much less Keats. But as a specimen of the sort of Sentiment which shoᵈ terminate the Song in my opinion "See here" (ἔπεα πτερόεντα 7)

3

But in the soul's December
The Fancy backward strays,
And sadly doth remember
The hue of golden days:

4 Thomas Gray, "Hymn to Adversity," line 28, "With leaden eye, that loves the ground."

5 Line 21 in most of the manuscripts (see Garrod, pp. l-lii) runs, "The feel of not to feel it" (which J. M. Murry [*Studies in Keats* (1930), p. 65] calls "the true and authentic reading"). In three printed copies of 1829 it appears as "To know the change and feel it." For "feel" as a noun see "Calidore," line 139; *Endymion*, II.284, III.139, 496; *Otho*, II.i.63; "After Dark Vapours," line 6; *Letters*, pp. 31, 129, 255.

6 *Not, as F has it,* the last stanza.

7 Homer's "winged words" (*Iliad*, I.201).

> In woe, the thought appalling
> Of bliss—gone past recalling,
> Brings o'er the heart a falling
>> Not to be told in Rhyme, by yrs truly
>> R^d Woodhouse.

→»» 27 «««

RICHARD WOODHOUSE TO JOHN TAYLOR

November 1818 [1]

Address: Mr Taylor/ Fleet S^t. Morgan MS. Printed in part by Finney, I, 346f., II, 486, and in part (but in the guise of a complete letter) by Blunden, pp. 52f.

Dr John,

As soon as Dan Sol shall have warmed the atmosphere "a pretty while," [2] I shall send you one bottle of the same port you had in Bond S^t—wrapped up to avoid Chill, for I am sure your own will be "shaken, shaken, shaken, shaken, shaken from its Crusted state" [3] & thick as hogwash— Also two of my own sherry, which, tho' it wants age, will be still perhaps better "tipple" than you can procure at this short notice elsewhere

The following is what Ainsworth [4] says about H— S— "H. S. corruptly for L. L. S. a sesterce, being the fourth part "of their Denarius viz. two pounds denoted by the L L and S. "semis, a half; which, in the first times of the Empire, was "worth two pence in our Money."—

Do not forget to put in hand for me an Endymion, to be ½ bound in plain brown calf with very loose hollow back

---

[1] The sonnet referred to in paragraph 4 was sent to Keats by an unknown Teignmouth admirer, "P. Fenbank," under the date of November 9. See I, 146n., and Penrose, p. 218.

[2] Shakespeare, *Lucrece*, line 1233.

[3] Adapted from Dryden's "Alexander's Feast": see I, 56n.

[4] Robert Ainsworth, *Thesaurus linguae Latinae compendiarius* (London, 1746), introduction to "H." See I, 257, note 38.

& Interleaved—(same as you did his smaller Poems) **as little
of the Edges to be cut away as may be**— Give it to one of your
most Expeditious expediters, (ut expediatur, et ut expedit) let-
tered merely "Endymion."—[5]

Do you think you could manage to procure me a **Copy**
of the Sonnet you were talking of last night—as it is "a thought"
complimentary, Keats may not be disposed, out of his excessive
modesty, to give copies, and I would not wish to make **an unpleasant application to him**, but the circumstance is an interesting one, and I sho^d like to add that to my collection of
"Keatsiana"— Do try— Perhaps Reynolds will get one for himself, & it may be done easily thro' that Channel.—

Yrs truly

R^d W.
Tuesday

⇥»» 28 «««

CHARLES BROWN TO RICHARD WOODHOUSE

1 December 1818

Address: —— Woodhouse Esqre. Printed by Lowell, II, 117.[6]

Hampstead
Tuesday 1st Dec^r [7]

Sir,

Mr Keats requests me to inform you his brother Thomas

[5] Woodhouse's interleaved copy of *Endymion* is now in the Berg Collection, New York Public Library. It was used by Forman in preparing
his text for the 1883 *Poetical Works,* and by subsequent editors.

[6] Colvin, p. 320, had said that Tom died in "the first night of Decem-
ber." Lowell, II, 117f., corrects him. Tom was buried, not as she says on
December 3, but on December 7 (Pope, *TLS,* December 22, 1932, p. 977).
Woodhouse copied this letter in his Book of Transcripts of Keats's
Letters (Harvard), p. 25.

[7] *Another hand has added* 1818.

died this morning at 8 o'Clock quietly & without pain— M^r
Keats is pretty well & desires to be remembered to you—

I am, Sir,

Your obed^t hum Servt

Chas Brown.

→» 29 «←

JANE PORTER TO WILLIAM HENRY NEVILLE ¹

4 December 1818

Ditton Cottage Decr 4th 1818

Dear Sir,

As my mother is sending a messenger to Esher, I cannot but make the same the bearer of my regrets for not having had the pleasure of seeing you the morning you called at the gate— I had given orders to be denied; I was so very unwell with an ² adhesive cold: but had I known it was you I should have taken off the Interdict for a few minutes, to say how very much I am delighted with Endymion I had just finished the poem—and have now ³ done as you permitted, lent it to Miss Fitzgerald.

I regret you are not personally acquainted with the author; for I should have been happy to have acknowledged to him through the advantage of your Communication, the very rare delight my sister & myself have enjoyed from this first fruits of his genius— I hope the ill-natured review will not have

---

¹ A transcript by Woodhouse, enclosed in his letter (No. 32) of December 10. (He copied it again in his Book of Transcripts of Keats's Letters [Harvard], p. 26.) Keats himself copied this transcript in a letter of December 17 to George and Georgiana Keats. His verbal variants (*K*) and those supplied from the original letter (now in the Keats Museum, Hampstead) in *Letters*, pp. 251f. (*F*), are given in footnotes. For Neville see II, 217n.

² *K with my still.*

³ *K omits.*

67

damped [4] such true parnassian fire⸗It ou{ght} not: for when
life is granted [5] to the possessor, it always burns its brilliant way
thro' every obstacle. Had Chatterton possessed sufficient manliness of mind to know the magnanimity [6] of Patience & been
aware that Great Talents have a Commission from Heaven he
would not·have deserted his post—and his name might [7] have
posed [?] [8] with Milton.

Ever much yours
Jane Porter.

To

  H. Neville Esq[r]

Sh[d] you [9] be passing this Way tom[ro] or Sunday my Mother & I
are at home.

⇢≫ 30 ≪⇠

JOHN TAYLOR TO SIR JAMES MACKINTOSH [1]

5 December 1818

Morgan MS. A few sentences are quoted by Colvin, p. 313.

Extract of a letter to Sir JM—Dec 5 1818.

    If you have not seen Endymion (of which I also beg your
Acceptance) you will perhaps find some few passages in it worth
perusal.—Its Faults are numberless, but there are redeeming
Beauties in my Opinion, & the Faults are those of real Genius.
But whatever this Work is, its Author is a true poet— He is
only 22, an Orphan at an early Age, & the oldest of 4 Children,
one of whom, a Brother aged 19, died last Monday [2] of Con-

---

[4] *K* have damaged (or damped). (That is to say, *K*, like the editor, could
not read Woodhouse's hand here. *The original has* damped.)

[5] *K ends here.*

[6] *F* magnonimity.

[7] *F* might now.

[8] *F* posed.

[9] *F* <you>.

[1] See Nos. 31 and 36.

[2] "Last Monday" was November 30, but see I, 66.

sumption,—another Brother has joined B.[3] in America, & his Sister is a Girl at School. These are odd particulars to give, when I am introducing the Work & not the Man to you,—but if you knew him, you would also feel that strange personal Interest in all that concerns him.—M[r] Gifford [4] forgot his own early life, when he tried to bear down this young Man. Happily it will not succeed. If he lives, Keats will be the brightest Ornament of this Age. I cannot expect you to be of the same opinion, because you know nothing of *him* even when you have read the Book: & yet I think the Hymn to Pan p 12 &c—the Episode of Glaucus p. 114 &c & above all, the Triumph of Bacchus p 166 &c will justify this Prediction—

I remain &c

→≫ 31 ≪←

SIR JAMES MACKINTOSH [1] TO JOHN TAYLOR

7 December 1818

Madocks [2]

Dec[r] 7

Dear Sir

I received your books last night & I hasten to inform you that though I had a good collection of common Italian

---

[3] Probably Morris Birkbeck (see I, 29n.).

[4] See I, 25, 46.

[1] (1765–1832), philosopher and, during 1818–1824, professor of law and general politics in the college for civil servants of the East India Company at Haileybury. During this period his home was a few miles from the college at Mardock, near Ware. He was buried in the churchyard of the parish church of St. John's, Hampstead—the church wherein Anne Whitney's bust of Keats was placed by Americans in 1894. See the *Century Magazine*, October, 1895 (L, 904n.).

The letter (see also No. 36), a reply to No. 30, is a copy made for Milnes on paper watermarked 1861. If the index may be trusted, there is no mention of Taylor or Keats in R. J. Mackintosh's *Memoirs* (1835) of his father.

[2] *Sic.*

69

Books I had very few that are rare— I have therefore this day written to a Friend in London who has a very large library to beg that he will if he has it lend Guido Cavalcanti [3] to Mr Cary,[4] I had begged him to send it with Cancelliari [5] if he can find that to you under cover to Mr Cary.

Let me know in a few days whether you receive it for if I fail in this quarter, I am sure of procuring Guido for Mr Carey, from the Library of another friend, to whom I shall pay a visit in 2 or 3 weeks.—

I have not yet read Mr Keats's Poem the story of his family is affecting—he has been attacked in a most merciless manner in the scurrilous magazine published by Blackwood at Edinburgh—such attacks will interest every liberal mind in his success—

I am d^r Sir

Y^rs very truly

J. Mackintosh

→≫ 32 ≪←

RICHARD WOODHOUSE TO JOHN KEATS

10 December 1818

Letters, p. 245, prints Woodhouse's draft (Morgan MS.), which differs in some details from the letter actually sent to Keats and here printed.[1]

My dear Keats,

I have to thank you for a mark of kind consideration, shewn at a moment when an attention to such matters must

[3] Poet and philosopher (*ca.* 1250–1300), whose poems were printed at Florence in 1527.

[4] See I, 80.

[5] Francesco Cancellieri (1751–1826).

[1] It is an acknowledgment of No. 28 and an explanation of No. 29, and is discussed by Colvin, pp. 325f., Lowell, II, 122f., and Hewlett, p. 209. For Keats's reply see *Letters,* p. 270.

have been peculiarly irksome.[2]—Accept this late acknowledgment— Believe me, I deeply sympathised with you, though I
could not bring myself to interrupt the sacredness of recent
affliction with commonplaces of condolence. Your brother is
now, we trust, happier than we have ability to wish him; and
it is our duty to turn eyes of gratitude around for the many
blessings that yet remain to us.—It will please me to hear that
you are well, and are recovering from the Shock of your loss.

I send enclosed a letter which, when read, take the trouble
to return to me. The history of its reaching me is this.—My
cousin, Miss Frogley of Hounslow, borrowed my copy of Endymion for a specified time. Before she had time to look into it;
her and my friend Mʳ Hʸ Neville[3] of Esher, who was
house<hold> Surgeon to the late Princess Charlotte, insisted
upon having it to read for a day or two, & undertook to make
my cousins peace with me on account of the extra delay.—
Neville told me that one of the Misses Porter (of romance celeb-
rity)[4] had seen it on his table, dipped into it, & expressed a
wish to read it. I desired he would keep it as long, and lend it
to as many, as he pleased, provided it was not allowed to slum-
ber upon any one's shelf. I learned subsequently from Miss
Frogley that those ladies had requested of Mʳ Neville, if he
was acquainted with the author, that they might have the pleasure of an Introduction.—About a week back the enclosed was
transmitted by Mʳ Neville to my cousin, as a species of apology
for keeping her so long without the book. And she sent it to
me knowing it would give me pleasure.—I forward it to you,
for somewhat the same reason, but principally because it gives
me the opportunity of naming to you (which it would have been

[2] Tom Keats had been buried on December 7 (see I, 66n.).
[3] See I, 67, 108, II, 217.
[4] Jane (1776–1850), author of *The Scottish Chiefs* and *Thaddeus of War-
saw,* and her less famous sister, Anna Maria (1780–1832), author of *The
Barony, Don Sebastian, The Hungarian Brothers,* and so on.

71

fruitless to do before) the opening [5] there is for an introduction to a Class of society, from which you may possibly derive advantage as well as gratification, if you think proper to avail yourself of it.—In such case I should be very happy to further your wishes— But do just as you please— If you decline the overture, rely upon it no Intimation from me shall ever reach the quarter in question, that the letter enclosed, or any thing that has transpired has come to your ear.—The whole is entirely at present "inter nos."—I go out of town tomorrow for 3 or 4 days,—Do not therefore write to me till after Tuesday next.—Believe me, my Dear Keats,

Most sincerely yours,
Richd Woodhouse.
Temple 10 Decr 1818.

P. S. I believe you are not at Hampstead,[6] I shall therefore beg Taylor to forward you this.

Jn° Keats Esqr

⇛ 33 ⇚

J. H. REYNOLDS TO JOHN TAYLOR

12 January 1819

Address: Mr Taylor/ Taylor & Hessey/ Booksellers/ Fleet Street/ London. *Postmark illegible.* Morgan MS.

Dear Taylor

Will you excuse the trouble I am about to put you to?— The following advertizement I am desirous of having inserted in the Times, with the reference, if not disagreeable, to yourself. It is for the young Man of whom I once spoke to you, & who really is too good for so dense a city as this. He is very

[5] *Written* openening.
[6] Keats was staying with Charles Brown at Wentworth Place.

desirous of quitting it—and seeing "foreign parts" and I am sure his qualifications are such as to make him a desirable companion to any given young Gentleman in want of a clever and well informed associate. He knows all that the advertizement holds out—and more to boot. His direction is "Henry Worsley, Manly's Buildings, St Sidwell Exeter"— This is all the information you can require—as on application he will be ready, like Mr Croker's potatoes, to speak for himself.[1] I inserted it in the Times once with no effect, and therefore, as in all lotteries, I am tempted by the bad success to venture again. I make no apologies for troubling you thus, because I know your readiness to assist in any act of kindness:—If you would send it the day you get this, I should be obliged. TO PERSONS GOING ABROAD. A young Man aged 25 years, of respectable connexions wishes to accompany any Gentleman as a Companion to the Continent. He understands the French Language thoroughly, has a knowledge of music and of painting;—has been accustomed to sketching. He is also possessed of other acquirements which might be found useful in such a Situation— Address by Letter (postpaid) to H. W. at Taylor & Hessey Booksellers Fleet Street.[2]

The above I think will do, and a reference to a Bookseller looks more tempting to the eyes of the little-Learned. If you can do anything among your Friends or Customers it would be so much kindness carried to my account:—Though I

[1] Hazlitt, in the *Liberal*, July, 1823 (*Complete Works*, ed. P. P. Howe, XX [1934], 113), tells how Croker was introduced to Horace Smith, Prince Hoare, Richard Cumberland, and others, and how "he began to make a display of his native ignorance and impudence on all subjects immediately, and no one else had occasion to say any thing. When he was gone, Mr. Cumberland exclaimed, 'A talking potato, by God!' " Hazlitt elsewhere (the same, XII [1931], 101, 183n.) mentions "this *'talking potatoe'* " and "A certain *Talking Potatoe*."

[2] The advertisement appeared in *The Times*, Saturday, January 16, p. 1.

do not think your interest lies much amongst the pretty Gentle-men that escape from College [3] to Continent.

I expect to be home—indeed I am sure, that I shall re-turn,—by Saturday, when I will repay you for all but the trouble of this little task.—The Weather here is as changeable as a Woman (this is in the established style of manly comparison,—and therefore I adopt it.)—The sun now is as bright as though it had forgotten the Month, an{d} had put on its August Coat and Waistcoat. But I must also tell you; not to make you En-vious of our Devonshire Suns, which are a ray or two better than most County Suns,—that we have decent allowances of frost & rain, at handsome intervals.—And last night the Wind was so high, one might as well have lived in a pair of bellows with one's face to the snout.

I am much bounden to you for the Coat, which behaved in a truely friendly manner all the way down here,—you could not have taken greater care of me yourself. Remember me to Hessey,—and make my Compts to Mrs Hessey. If you see Keats tell him I am well, & not forgetful of him. I suppose by this,—you have received from Hilton a sketch for the Poem. I shall like to see it. Ever yours most sincerely

Exeter [4]   JHReynolds
   12 Jany 1819

[3] Perhaps Henry Worsley came from Oxford University. The name Worsley, from an Isle of Wight family, frequently turns up there.
[4] In December Keats wrote (*Letters*, p. 256): "Lately George Drewe ex-pired in a fit—on which account Reynolds has gone into Devonshire."

→»» 34 «←←

RICHARD WOODHOUSE TO JOHN TAYLOR

9 March 1819

Address: Mr Taylor/ Fleet St. Morgan MS.

Dr John,

I send you this Letter of Reynolds's.

Yrs truly

RdW. 9 Mar 1819.[1]

The greater ordinary Bazil riseth up usually with one upright
stalk diversely branching forth on all Sides with 2 leaves at
every joint which are somewhat broad & round yet pointed—
of a pale green Colour yet fresh a little snipp'd about the
Edges, & of a strong healthy scent— The flowers are small &
white standing at the tops of the branches with 2 small leaves
at the joints in some places green in others brown after which
come black seed.—Culpepper.[2]

The red whort or whortle berry or bilberry.[3] ed: <ibid>

W

---

[1] What follows is written at right angles to Woodhouse's note.

[2] To elucidate *Isabella* Woodhouse copied this passage from Nicholas Culpeper's *Complete Herbal* (1833 ed., p.27). He also copied it in his collection
of Keats's verse (Garrod's "Woodhouse Transcripts. Poems II," or "W2"),
folio 29v, substituting for everything after "black seed" Culpeper's sentence, "The root perisheth at the approach of winter, and therefore must
be new sown every year."

[3] See Culpeper, p. 37.

→» 35 «←

MRS. GREEN [1] TO RICHARD WOODHOUSE

29 March 1819

Address: Mr R. Woodhouse. Morgan MS.

> Duncan Terrace.   1819
> Islington   29th
> March

Mrs Colonel Green's Compliments to Mr Woodhouse and feels exceedingly obliged to Mr W—— for the perusal of *Endymion* and the other trifle— There are a great number of [2] beauties in the *former* which speaks highly for the authors growing Genius— A Stranger perhaps might fancy him too *wild* in some of his passages but Mrs G knowing the Author at a time when the *Fire* of his imagination appeared agitated with a *Thirst* for *fame*—can easily excuse him *for the—sudden bursts* [3] of en-*thusiasm* which *pervades* his *affectionate Constitution.* Should [4] Mrs G—— ever see the Author she certainly must rally him—for a great *Mistake*—commited in the Book of trifles and which *by this time he must* be *a very great* Judge. Mrs G begs to be kindly remembered to him and should at all times be happy to see both Mr Woodhouse and the Author of Endymion—

---

[1] Lowell, I, 114, supposes this lady "to have been the future mother-in-law of Marianne Reynolds," who married H. G. Green. The British Army Lists of the period give far too many Colonel Greens to provide any clue. The letter is rather inexactly printed by Hewlett (*H*), p. 209.

[2] *H* great many.

[3] *H* outbursts.

[4] Begins a new paragraph in *H*.

�>>> 36 ⇙⇙⇙

SIR JAMES MACKINTOSH [1] TO JOHN TAYLOR

19 July 1819

Mardocks near
Ware
19 July 1819

Dear Sir

When will the 8ᵛᵒ Edition of Mʳ Cary be published [2]— Excuse the impatience of a warm admirer— Have you any other literary novelties or news—? I very much admire your young Poet with all his singularities—where is he, & what high design does he meditate. I was so hurried during the last Session as not have a moment for literary indulgence

I am dear Sir
Yours truly
Js Mackintosh

You will do me a favour if you will write me a note on Wednesday Eve? [3] to say what the wild men of Smithfield have been doing— You are so near to the scene & to the G. Post Office that your intelligence may come down to a late hour in the Evening.—

---

1 See No. 31. Milnes, 1867, p. 251, quotes three sentences from "a letter still extant," but the copy made for him and here printed is on paper watermarked 1861. Presumably Lowell quoted her three sentences (II, 292) from Milnes, or perhaps from the *Century Magazine,* October, 1895 (L, 904n.).

2 See I, 80.

3 July 21. The *Gentleman's Magazine,* August (LXXXIX, 175), reported that at "the Smithfield Meeting" the "disaffected" had plotted to burn London and to murder *"all its peaceable inhabitants."*

≫≫ 37 ≪≪

RICHARD WOODHOUSE TO JOHN TAYLOR

August 1819 (?) [1]

Morgan MS. A few sentences are quoted by Lowell, I, 289, II, 274, 293, Finney, I, 374f., and Blunden, pp. 53, 61n.

My dear John,

And so you are at length clean gone from this scene of "Fumum, et opes, strepitumque," [2] & arrived (though we have had no letter to say so) at a spot where the pure breath of Heaven *can* <breathe> blow upon you; and are probably at this Moment (N.B. ½ p. 6 P.M) engaged in deep chat with the very individu[a]l,[3] who has been beaming looks of benignity from his canvas over Hessey, Mrs H., your humble, and a cold leg of Mutton— Happy rogue! "Tu Tityre lentus in umbrâ." [4]—But I shall be off soon, & gulp down pure breeze too, & show off as an olive branch round a paternal table. And so in the mean time I shall be patient, and partake in idea your happiness. I am glad to find from Hessey's account that he left you some way on your journey, in good heart & spirits; and I shall sport my person in Fleet Street tomorrow, in the expectation of hearing that you performed the latter part of your journey as well as you did the first. Hessey has brought home, as he usually does, a tanned face, and moreover a red angry pimple on his nose, whose glare takes off somewhat from the brownness of his face. I bethought me on Saturday of my promise about *"Isabella,"* and took the earliest opportunity (as there was a lady in the Case) of enquiring whether you had left out the Book in

---

[1] See note 6, below.
[2] Horace, *Odes*, III.xxxix.12.
[3] His father, James Taylor.
[4] Virgil, *Eclogues*, I.4.

which she was to be copied: but without the least idea that you
had done so. However William found it, and I have copied the
Basil pot in it & given it (but this is a prophecy—a narrative
preceding the fact—as Sir Philo says,—I *mean* to give it) to
Hessey along with this letter to forward to you— And if the
parcel sho^d be made up, why it will go <by> in the next.—Recollect that this is the 4th time I have written it over,[5] recollect
also that I could say<ing> it by heart with about 5 prompt-
ings; and if, as really was the case, I went through it with more
pleasure than ever, one of two conclusions is inevitable: either
that it is a noble poem, or that my judgment is not worth the
tythe of a fig;—And I am quite content to <stand> be set down
for a dolt in the opinion of that man who should deny the first
of the above alternatives— May <one and [?]> those to whom
you shew the poem derive as much gratification from it as I
did.—Reynolds is off (another prophecy) tomorrow— He promised, but one never builds upon his *promises*, that I should see
him before he went; he <has> has owed me 2 translated sonnets [6] of Keats's any day these 2 months, But I suppose I must
perforce now give him further credit till Michaelmas Term.—
I have just bought his "One two three four Five" [7] and paid
just that number of pence for it plus 3— It lies on my table un-
cut; If I had read it I would send it you: but your curiosity can
keep: and indeed I think I am doing an act<ion> of Charity
to those about you to keep back any thing that might abstract
your attentions from them, till you are pump'd quite dry of

[5] On Woodhouse's transcripts see Garrod, p. xxxiii.

[6] In an undated letter to Reynolds (in *Letters*, pp. 217f., M. B. Forman assigns it to September 22, 1818) Keats gives "a free translation of a Sonnet of
Ronsard," beginning "Nature withheld Cassandra." Reynolds probably
gave it to Woodhouse before the end of August, 1819 (see I, 85n.).

[7] A farce first produced at the English Opera House, the Lyceum in the
Strand, on July 17 and published in *Cumberland's British Theatre*. It had
some fifty other performances. See I, 87.

79

intelligence. It shall go in the next parcel.—I have seen, in the course of my peregrinations today, the back of a Boyd's Dante [8] markd 36ˢ bds— The d—ce (N.B. not the ace) is in it if Carey [9] can be dear at the same price— Did you ever see Fanshaw's translation [10] of the pastor Fido?—If not you shall when you come back. Hessey says you were far gone into the "Radicals" when he left you. I have a great respect for your powers of application & perseverance: but I question whether your principles of reform in our grammatical constitution will be ripe by the time you come back.—We are the creatures of habit & association. All my studies have such a rascally combination with my own 16 walls, & the Temple gardens & those interesting places of resort just in front of my "look out," that I really cannot study in <the> stone Buildings, or green fields. I then let my mind go to sleep, & call my limbs into action.—I dare swear it is the same with you. Indeed the thing is demonstrable; What does the proverb say of you, "All work & no play makes *John* a dull boy." [11]—put the train of reasoning into syllogistics— John always works & never plays in<t> Town <a>, But sometimes goes into the country.—But all work & no play <would> makes John a dull boy— Ergo John must either play when he is in the country or be a dull boy.—Now as I would be the last person in the world to make you blush, after having given over that practice 7 & 40 years,[12] I won't say which of these 2 alternatives is the true one.—But ask any body—or put it to the vote: and I'll undertake to make the majority eat the minority if any be found—

I would not make you pay postage for this nonsense for

[8] Henry Boyd's Dante, 3 vols. (1802).

[9] H. F. Cary's new edition (8ᵛᵒ) of Dante had gone to the press in July (Blunden, p. 60).

[10] Sir Richard Fanshawe's translation of Guarini's *Il Pastor Fido* (1647).

[11] Apperson, *English Proverbs* (1929), pp. 8f., cites examples from 1659.

[12] According to Blunden, p. 21, Taylor was thirty-eight in 1819.

the world— It would be a Sin to repent of for a twelvemonth.— But one may scribble stuff when it goes in a parcel.—I am piping hot from <reading> the perusal of Gray—a fellow that wrote more about nothing than any human being I ever met with.—He tells me "You may say any thing to a friend, in a letter, as I do." [13]—In my simplicity I took no notice of the last 3 words— But I begin to fancy it is not every one that CAN say *things to friends in letters* in the manner he does.—I dare say you have found this out too.—But if you have, I know you will keep your own counsel, and not tell one so to one's face.— Good bye (or God b'w'ye—which? Priscian?) Johnny— Remember me kindly to those of your family whom I do know—and Ditto to those I do not.—& believe me,

Yours very truly,

Temple Tuesday Ev^g   Richd Woodhouse.

P.S.— Having now exhausted all the topics

⤜ 38 ⤛

RICHARD WOODHOUSE TO JOHN TAYLOR

31 August 1819

Address: To,/ Jn⁰ Taylor Esqr/ [*In lower left corner*] R. W. Morgan MS. Printed in part by Lowell, II, 301-303, and Finney, II, 683f. A few words are quoted by Blunden, p. 70.

My dear John,

Though I have let a post elapse, I apprehend this letter, which will go in a parcel to you, will reach you as soon as Keats's answer.—I have read his Letter; [1] and I did it before I

---

[13] A remark somewhat resembling this is in Gray's letter of February 25, 1768 (*Correspondence*, ed. Paget Toynbee and Leonard Whibley, III [1935], 1018), to Walpole.

[1] Of August 23 (*Letters*, pp. 371-373).

had read yours, and with my usual disposition to understand his terms in the sense in which he uses them.—Now I apprehend his word Pride to mean nothing more than literary Pride,— that disposition which arises out of a Consciousness of superior & improving poetical Powers, & which would keep him, even in his present state of comparative imperfectness, from writing so as to minister to the depraved taste of the age.—It is not in my opinion personal pride, but literary pride which his letter shews;—That he has some of the former also, I believe; But his letter does not evince it, further than as it displays a solitary spirit. The Pride contained in his letter, as I understand it, is a noble pride, akin to that Indication which Milton pours forth in language of such "solemn tenour & deep organ tone" [2] at the beginning of his 2^d book on "the reason of Ch. Government." and for which I honor him. And I am not quite certain whether your Post Script was not added in consequence of a new ray of light breaking in upon you on this Subject.—Is he wrong to be dissatisfied with the Prospect of a mere "seat on the Bench of a myriad-aristocracy in Letters?" or to keep aloof from them and their works,—or to dislike the favor of such a "public," as be-praises the Crabbes, & the Barretts, & the Codruses [3] of the day.—I wonder how he came to stumble upon that deep truth that "people are debtors to him for his verses & not he to them for admiration."—Methinks such a conviction on any one's mind is enough to make half a Milton of him.

I agree with you in every syllable you say about Pride. But I do not think it applies to Keats, as he shews himself in his letter— And if you were [to] cull out a person upon whom to fit your summary of the whole [neither self praise nor man's praise can turn the scale either way,—nor can unmerited neglect

[2] *Hyperion*, I.48.

[3] For Barrett see I, 47; for Codrus, Virgil, *Eclogues*, V. 11, VII. 22, 26. It is interesting that Woodhouse put George Crabbe in such company.

or censure weigh a feather]⁴ I think, as far as Poetry is concerned, that very man would be Keats as evidenced in his letter.

Having complied with your wish of telling you what I
thought of his letter, I come now to his request.—I doubt
whether he will want so much as you mention. I apprehend 50ᵉ
or 60ᵉ would suffice him, but this his next letter will shew. I
think I mentioned to you how I was situated as to Cash, that I
had scraped all I could together, to pay my Father, whose two
calls lately had run him close. That I expected nothing till
winter, and had made my calculation upon wanting little till
that time. Under these circumstances I could not command
£100. But I can spare £50. which shall be at your disposal, at
what time & place you think proper.—You are well acquainted
with my good wishes towards Keats, as well as with their complete disinterestedness. Whatever People <say they> regret
that they could not do for Shakespeare or Chatterton, because
he did not live in their time, that I would embody into a Rational principle, and (with due regard to certain expediencies)
do for Keats.—But one's means are not unlimited, and one
would not wish to give rise to expectations, which should end
in disappointment, nor would one like to have the oats eaten
by other cattle. I wish he could be cured of the vice of lend-
ing⁵—for in a poor man, it is a vice.

I think with you about the offer of Brown's name, and
about the non use⁶ of the note.⁷—But would it be or not beneficial to K. that it should be taken? and is any part of the money
to go to Brown? The Sum will perhaps enable you to judge.

Hessey spoke about Keats's letter, & wants, & quoted your
intimation to him, so that I could not do less than say he should

⁴ Bracketed in the original.
⁵ In this instance, to Haydon.
⁶ *L and F* the nonsense.
⁷ Brown offered (*Letters*, p. 373) to go on Keats's note for the money Taylor
was asked to lend.

see the letter. He will not "peach" about the Tragedy,[8] and there is no other secret in it. I think to shew him your letter too, <and> perhaps he may think with me, and contrary to you, that the obligation to K. may prove beneficial to "the business."—

I can say nothing about what is best to be done, for K.— I am tempest tost [9] on the Subject, and even with the light of his next letter I may be as much in the dark.—I think (and you need not make a bow for the compliment) that you are the prudenter man of the two, to judge in this case.—But take this with you—1ˢᵗ I really can't spare more "As in presenti," than the sum I have named. And 2ᵈ my friendship for the poor fellow woᵈ willingly go, if need is, greater lengths than merely lending you money to lend him.—

I shall be out of town in about 10 Days, but I can send you (or Hessey) a draft from any place.—

It pleases me that the poor "Comforter" [10] is to have a chance of making good its title. I spoke my true opinion when I told you I regretted that it shoᵈ not be published. So I did, when I talked of my "natural disposition to melancholy," at which you or Hessey laughed. As a proof of it, I have just been embodying some of the principal events of my life in a "dream" <like> upon the Plan of Lᵈ Byron's [11]—and these I have made all melancholy.

I like Brown's few lines much.

I shall put what relates to the "Cub" in another sheet— He is an unLICKED one: and I could "do the needful" to him

---

8 *Otho*, the completion of which Keats asked to be kept secret.

9 *Endymion*, III.703.

10 A reference to Taylor and Hessey's *The Comforter: A Poem*, announced among new books in the *Eclectic Review*, May, 1820 (n.s., XIII, 495). It was reviewed in the same, June (n.s., XIII, 570-579), and in the *Monthly Review*, September (XCIII, 94-96).

11 "The Dream," July, 1816.

with pleasure. He shan't appear among this Good Company. I shall not take notice of his Marriage—I have not seen it in the papers, and don't mean to do so. If I can turn a period, about his wife, that shall be *all prickles,* & leave him ashamed of himself, & posed how to reply, I will.[12]—I shall write tomorrow, to say you are out of Town, and that I shall be so before his arrival.—If I can clear up matters of business here, I shall spend a Week at Weymouth, & thence with my Daddy to Bath.

Reynolds is off, but before he went he called and left me the Sonnet—& a letter he had received from Keats.[13]—I send it you: It will be a Comment on <his> parts of his to you. *Please return it me through the first Parcel you send*— If you have Milton's prose Works handy look at that ubi supra, It beats any organ. I shut up my windows, & held up my head, & spouted it aloud on Sunday Evening, con amore.

Remember me to all friends & believe me, Dʳ John,

Yours very affectionately,

Richᵈ Woodhouse.

Temple Tuesday Evᵍ

J. Taylor Esqʳ   31.Augᵗ 1819.

→» 39 «←

RICHARD WOODHOUSE TO JOHN TAYLOR

7 September 1819

Morgan MS. A few sentences are printed by Lowell, II, 275, 304f.

My dear John,

I was favored with your last on Saturday, & saw off a Bk.

12 See I, 86.

13 For the letter see *Letters,* pp. 373f. Possibly Woodhouse refers to the "P. Fenbank" sonnet (see I, 65n.) or else to the "translated sonnet" of Ronsard, for which see I, 79. This latter is included in the Reynolds commonplace book described by Garrod, pp. lxx f. (see I, 63n.).

p. Bill for 30¹ to Keats.—Hessey holds the rest [1] at his disposal.
The funds of this Beaumont & Fletcher pair,[2]

"Who with combined powers, their Wit employ'd

To raise a trophy to the Drama's Muses."   (Poems p. 53) [3]

were at a low,—verily at a silver, ebb. But, with your supply,
there came an announcement that some Cash was gone to
Chichester, by mistake, in payment of one of the Debts due to
K. so that he was quite flush: & he supposes some one, to make
a complete Midas of him, will send him down a pair of Ass's
ears by the Waggon. If Hessey sends you Keats's letter,[4] you
will have this Joke twice over: But it is too good to be lost.—
I roared aloud over it, to the astonishment of some male &
female "natives," [5] who were book buying in the back shop.
I had the gratification of hitting off in a neat way an intimation to the Captⁿ that I had been told of his marriage, but
that of course I could not believe it, having recᵈ a letter from
him that day without mentioning it.—He affects, in reply, to
remind me of his having told me in Town that after his marriage he intended setting off for Malvern & Cheltenham, and
as his letter went from the former place, & as he <told> talked
in it of *his Wife's* Trustees, he conceives he told me of his Marriage.[6] (or to that Effect, for Hessey has the letter.)—How
matrimony improves a man, where there is any room left for
it!—and what may not you & I expect from each other, when we
marry. Why he is what Sʳ P. Sidney [7] calls *a piece of a logician*

---

[1] That is to say, £20 (see I, 83). For Keats's acknowledgment to Taylor see
Letters, p. 379.
[2] Keats and Brown, who were collaborating on *Otho* at Winchester.
[3] Keats, 1817, "To George Felton Mathew," lines 6f.
[4] *Letters,* p. 378.
[5] A commonplace today, repeated below (see I, 93).
[6] On the captain, or cub, see I, 85, 90.
[7] In the opening paragraph of the *Defense of Poetry.*

already.—He regrets that I shall not be in Town when he comes; but supposes Mr Parsons [8] speaking to Hessey will do as well. And when he has settled this matter in Town he means to go over to France with his Rib. He will leave Cheltenham for London on the 13^(th)—

I culled out of a book in your shop something about the Welsh Language, which I enclose: It <shows> states that (all the radicals in that tongue) are monosyllabic: but that many monosyllabics are not primitives. It may give you a lift, if you want to reason by analogy.

I send also (if Hessey forwards it, which I have injoined him to do) Reynolds's one, two 3. 4. 5.[9]—Such a thing must be judged of, not as a literary production, but, by some golden rule, according to the purpose of the Author: It was written for the mouth of an imitator of an imitator.—How triumphantly it succeeded, I told you when I went in my <critic> theatro-critical Capacity to see it. There is much of Reynolds's kind of wit, half pun & half humour, in it.—But the parts that told best in the representation, as giving the actor [10] an opportunity of taking off the mannerism of his brethren, will have least effect in the perusal.

I wish you understood <the> French: I would copy you out a beautiful old balad, in the old French or semi-Provençal upon the same subject as the Scots "Balow my babe, lie still & sleipe." [11] But more tender, at least more endearing in its style, tho' perhaps less varied in its ideas. <than> I think It worth sending to Keats.—Try your teeth at this Stanza. If you like it, you shall have the whole.

[8] Mentioned later (see I, 90).

[9] See I, 79.

[10] John Reeve (1790–1838), formerly in the banking-house of Gosling and Sharp.

[11] See *The Roxburghe Ballads,* ed. J. W. Ebsworth, VI (1889), 575-579.

O cher enfantelet, vray pourtraict de ton pere,
Dors sur le seyn que ta bousche a pressé!
Dors, petiot; cloz, amy, sur le seyn de ta mere
Tien doulx œillet par le somme oppressé.—

I believe it has been modernized in part: and if so, I sho^d like
to make the moderni*z*er *eat it* for his pains.—It is by Marguerite
de Surville [12]—born 1405.—If my plans for the Summer were
not laid past alteration; I wo^d go upon a poetical spec: [13] into
France to pick up bits of Provençal & old Poetry &c.—Or wo^d it
not be better to "miser it" till next Summer <&> so as to
afford to take J. K. with me—and should you like to trust your
personage with us?—But we have plenty of time to think of it.

I am highly indebted to you for your encomiums upon
my *vers*atility of talent. But It certainly did not lie at the time
I rec^d yours in *verse* making. I pity you, and if I could in any
way help you to a rhyme or an idea on the Subject I would: But
it is impossible. I dare say however you are by this time out
of your Misery.

I think of going about the end of this week to Weymouth
or Bath. I have not yet determined which first. But I will let
you know, by the next parcel Hessey sends.—

I return you Keats's letter.[14]—

Remember me kindly to all ffriends around you & believe me

     my Dr John
Temple   Yours very sincerely
7. Sepr 1819.   Richd Woodhouse.

[12] *Poésies*, ed. Ch. Vanderbourg (Paris, 1804), p. 251. The attribution to
Marguerite Eléonore Clotilde Bérenger de Surville (1405–1495) is now dis-
credited.
[13] *Lowell has* spree.
[14] Probably that in *Letters*, pp. 377f.

>>> 40 <<<

RICHARD WOODHOUSE TO JOHN TAYLOR [1]

19, 20 September 1819

Address: To,/ Jn⁰ Taylor Esq./ East Retford/ Nottinghamshire. *Post-marks (part illegible):* WEYMOUTH 20 SE 20 1819; 21 SE 21 1819. Morgan MS. Printed in part by Lowell, II, 317-320, by Finney, II, 689-693, and by M. R. Ridley, *Keats' Craftmanship* (1933), pp. 169-171.

Weymouth Monday 20. Sepʳ 1819.

My dear John,

    I begin to find out that there is no getting pen to paper any where but in London. For tho' I do litterally nothing here {it} is as exclusionary an employment as I ever met with. God-win (whose life of Chaucer [2] I am skimming over) says there is no doing any thing in the writing way, out of one's own study:— What with the dearths of pens Ink paper, knives, wax &c, it is quite an attempt to begin a letter, and quite an achievement to have finished one.—I left Town on Sunday Evening (12ᵗʰ) & arrived here on the Monday about 1— I found the place, as it always was, and ever will be, very dull. to me this is a recommendation rather than otherwise: for I get bustle & bother enough in Town, & gladly hail *quietude* in the Country. I walk or run till breakfast time, after which I amuse myself with books for about 2 hours, and I am then at my Sister's disposal for the rest of the day, till 9 oClock, when the family go to roost; but I—generally keep my vigils till near twelve; thanks to those habits of *industry* you & I imbibed from Lord Sommers.[3]—I was very much out of order when I came down here:

---

[1] Answered in the letter next following.

[2] Two vols., London, 1803 (R. Phillips).

[3] Finney, I, 343, interprets this remark as meaning that Woodhouse met Taylor while both men were "in the service of Lord Sommers," presumably

but I am getting to rights gradually,—I have not bathed yet: the smell of the sea, & the air bath that blows from it have been sufficient for me.—Freeman is I suppose in Town by this time, & occupied in discussing with the Squire [4] the terms and times of his receiving that portion of 'his "existence" which is in your hands. I take it for granted he will have left England in regret for his departure before I return to Town.—Keats was in Town the day before I left. He came <in> into 93 unexpectedly, while I was in the midst of a recapitulation to Hessey of the strong points of the Matter between yourselves & the Capt[n] [5] for his government in case Parsons [6] should set himself to wonder & be astonished &c at any thing that has happened. In such Cases, a strong point, well put, & coming out pat, often does wonders.—K. came about his Chancery Suit that is to be: or rather that is not to be, if he succeeds in the object of his Journey to London; which is to dissuade some old aunt [7] from going into that Court.—He took his breakfast with me on the Sunday, and remained with me till I stept into the Coach for this place at 3 oClock. I was much gratified with his Company. He wanted I believe to publish the Eve of S[t] Agnes & Lamia *immediately:* but Hessey told him it could not answer to do so now. I wondered why he said nothing of Isabella: & assured him it would please more {than} the Eve of S[t] Agnes— He said he could not bear the former now. It appeared to him mawkish. This cer-

---

John Sommers (1760–1841), Baron Sommers of Evesham, who was created Viscount Eastnor and Earl Sommers in July, 1821; but in his biography of Taylor, Blunden has nothing about such service. I cannot explain Woodhouse's words. Can he be referring to Lord Chancellor John Somers (1651–1716), first Baron Somers, whose *Somers Tracts* Sir Walter Scott edited, 13 vols., 1809–1815?

[4] For other references to Freeman, of Farnham, by the Squire (Hessey) see II, 376, 414, 416.

[5] See I, 86.

[6] See I, 87.

[7] Mrs. Midgley Jennings.

tainly cannot be so. the feeling is very likely to come across an {au}thor on review of a former work of his own, particularly where the objects of his present meditations are of a more sobered & <ab> unpassionate Character. <Mawkishness seems to me> The feeling of mawkishness seems to me to be that which comes upon us where any thing of great tenderness & excessive simplicity is met with when we are not in a sufficiently tender & simple frame of mind to bear it: when we experience a sort of revulsion, or resiliency (if there be such a word) [8] from the sentiment or expression. Now I believe there is nothing in any of [9] the most passionate parts of Isabella to excite this feeling. It may, as may Lear, leave the reader [10] far behind: but there is none of that sugar & butter sentiment, that cloys & disgusts.—He had the Eve of S[t] A. copied fair: He has made trifling alterations, inserted an additional stanza early in the poem to make the *legend* more intelligible, and correspondent with what afterwards takes place, particularly with respect to the supper & the playing on the Lute.—he retains the name of Porphyro—has altered the last 3 lines to leave on the reader a sense of pettish disgust, by bringing Old Angela in (only) dead stiff & ugly.—He says he likes that the poem should leave off with this Change of Sentiment—it was what he aimed at, & was glad to find from my objections to it that he had succeeded.—I apprehend he had a fancy for trying his hand at an attempt to play with his reader, & fling him off at last— I sho[d] have thought, he affected the "Don Juan" style of mingling up sentiment & sneering: but that he had before asked Hessey if he co[d] procure him a sight of that work, as he had not met with it, and if the E. of S[t] A. had not in all probability been altered before his

---

[8] *NED* gives no example of the word with this meaning between 1751 and 1826. In all its meanings the word was rare.

[9] *Lowell omits* any of. (*So Ridley.*)

[10] *Ridley* sentiment.

91

Lordship had thus flown in the face of the public. There was
another alteration, which I abused for "a full hour by the
Temple clock." [11] You know if a thing has a decent side, I generally look no further— As the Poem was orig^y written, *we*
innocent ones (ladies & myself) might very well have supposed
that Porphyro, when acquainted with Madeline's love for him,
& when "he arose, Etherial flush^d &c.&c (turn to it) set himself
at once to persuade her to go off with him, & succeeded & went
over the "Dartmoor black" (now changed for some other place)
to be married, in right honest chaste & sober wise. But, as it is
now altered, as soon as M. has confessed her love, P. <instead>
winds by degrees his arm round her, presses [12] breast to breast,
and acts all the acts of a bonâ fide husband, while she fancies
she is only playing the part of a Wife in a dream. This alteration
is of about 3 stanzas; and tho' there are no improper expressions
but all is left to inference, and tho' profanely speaking, the
Interest on the reader's imagination is greatly heightened, yet I
do apprehend it will render the poem unfit for ladies, & indeed
scarcely to be mentioned to them among the "things that are." [13]
—He says he does not want ladies to read his poetry: that
he writes for men, & that if in the former poem there was
an opening for a doubt what took place, it was his fault for not
writing clearly & comprehensibly—that he sh^d despise a man
who would be such an eunuch in sentiment as to leave a
<Girl> maid, with that Character about her, in such a situa-
tion: & sho^d despise himself to write about it &c &c &c—and all
this sort of Keats-like rhodomontade.—But you will see the
work I dare say.—He then read to me Lamia, which he has half

11 Compare *1 Henry IV*, V.iv.151f., "fought a long hour by Shrewsbury
clock."
12 *Finney* proper.
13 Bartlett, *Familiar Quotations* (1922), p. 926n., cites Proclus Lycius, *On
Plato's Timaeus*, "I am the things that are."

RICHARD WOODHOUSE WHEN A BOY

CHARLES ARMITAGE BROWN

fair Copied: the rest is rough. I was much pleased with it. I can use no other terms for you know how badly he reads his own poetry: & you know how slow I am in Catching, even the sense of poetry read by the best reader for the 1st time. And his poetry really must be studied to be properly appretiated. The Story is to this effect— Hermes is hunting for a Nymph, when from a wood he hears his name & a song relating to his loss— Mercury finds out that it comes from a serpent, who promises to shew him his Nymph if he will turn the serpent into a Woman; This he agrees to: upon which the serpent breathes on his eyes when he sees his Nymph who had been beside them listening invisibly— The serpent had seen a young Man of Corinth with whom she had fallen desperately in Love— She is metamorphosed into a beautiful Woman, the Change is quite Ovidian, but better,— She then finds the Youth, & they live together in a palace in the Middle of Corinth (described, or rather pictured out in very good costume) the entrance of which no one can see (like the Cavern Prince Ahmed <was in> found in the Arabian Nights, when searching for his lost arrow) [14]— Here they live & love, "the world forgetting; of the world forgot." [15] He wishes to marry her & introduce her to his friends as his Wife, But this would be a forfeiture of her immortality & she refuses but at length (for says K.— "Women love to be forced to do a thing, by a fine fellow—*such as this*—I forget his name— *was*") she consents. The Palace door becomes visible—to the "astonishment of the Natives" [16]—the friends are invited to the wedding feast—& K. wipes the Cits & the low lived ones: of some of whom he says "who make their mouth a napkin to their thumb" [17] in the midst of this Imperial splendour.—The lover

[14] See "The Story of Prince Ahmed, and the Fairy Pari Banou," *The Arabian Nights' Entertainments*, III (London, 1821), 375-377.

[15] Pope, *Eloisa to Abelard*, line 208.

[16] Compare I, 86n.

[17] See *Letters*, p. 382.

had seen his tutor Appollonius that morning, while in a car with his Lamia; he had a scowl on his brow, which makes the hearts of the lovers sink: & she asks him, who that frowning old fellow was, as soon as A. passed.—He appears at the feast: damps the joy of the two by his presence—sits over against the woman: He is a Magician— He looks earnestly at the woman: so intently & to such effect, that she reads in his eyes that she is discovered: & <shri> vanishes away, shrieking.—The lover is told she was a "Lamia" & goes mad for the loss of her, & dies— You many suppose all these Events have <left> given K. scope for some beautiful poetry: which even in this cursory hearing of it, came every now & then upon me, & made me "start, as tho' a Sea Nymph quired." [18] The metre is <heroic> Drydenian heroic —with many triplets, & many alexandrines. But this K. observed, & I agreed, was required, or rather quite in character with the language & sentiment in those particular parts.—K. has a fine feeling when & where he may use poetical licences with effect— He very kindly reproach'd me with never writing to him. You may suppose I promised amendment, & stipulated (as Paddy says) "that all the reciprocity should not be on one side"— The last thing, as he shook me by the hand, he promised to drop me a line to Bath: "and if (said he) it {s}hould be in verse,[19] I dare say you will forgive me."—He parted with me at the coach door —I had the inside all to myself: and I amused myself with diving into a deep reverie, & recalling all that had passed during the 6 hours we were tête à tête.—I make no apology for stuffing my letter with these Keatsiana. I am sure nothing else I could say wo^d have half the Interest.—And I deem myself in luck to have such a subject to write about.—I shall leave this place for Bath on Wednesday, & be there to dinner— I shall remain in Bath till the end of the month—perhaps later. As soon as I get

[18] Misquoted from Keats's sonnet "On the Sea," line 14.
[19] Part of his letter of September 21 *was:* see *Letters*, pp. 386-392.

there I shall write to Reynolds. Let me have a line from you to "R. W. Jʳ 8 Duke Sᵗ Bath."—This letter tho dated on Monday was written thus far on Sunday night to the Music of some one snoring. This morning I have been taking a six or 7 mile walk round an Inland lake: It was a journey of discovery: but I found contrary to Expectation all the passages practicable. I am just going to break my fast. Our post leaves us at that unseasonable hour 10 oClock. So Adieu—& remember me kindly wherever remembrances will be acceptable. I suppose you are ere this returned to Retford. I have tried for a frank but there is no Member here into whose hand I can put a cover.—I am Dear John

Yours, as ever, most truly

<Temple>   Richᵈ Woodhouse.

P. S. Do not lose Keats's letter to Reynolds

→≫ 41 ≪←

JOHN TAYLOR TO RICHARD WOODHOUSE [1]

25 September 1819

Address: Richard Woodhouse Esq Junʳ/ 8 Duke Street/ Bath. *Postmark:* BAKEWELL 152. Printed in part by Lowell (*L*), II, 321f. (whence a few sentences are quoted by Blunden, pp. 71f.), and by Finney, II, 694.

Bakewell Saty. 25 Sep 1819

My dear Dick,

Your welcome Letter has just reached me, having been forwarded in a parcel from Retford, which place I left last Tuesday.—I sit down to reply to it, more perhaps to express my regret at what you tell me of the Changes in the Eve of St Agnes, than for any deliberate purpose of saying my say

[1] An answer to the preceding letter. Lowell decides that Keats destroyed the offending stanzas of "St. Agnes."

on things in general.—This Folly of Keats is the most stupid
piece of Folly I can conceive.—He does not bear the ill opinion
of the World calmly, & yet he will not allow it to form a good
Opinion of him & his Writings. He repented of this Conduct
when Endymion was published as much as a Man can repent,
who shews by the accidental Expression of Disappointment,
Mortification & Disgust that he has met with a Result different
from that which he had anticipated— Yet he will again chal-
lenge the same Neglect or Censure, & again (I pledge my Dis-
cernment on it) be vexed at the Reception he has prepared for
himself.—This Vaporing is as far from sound Fortitude, as the
Conduct itself in the Instances before us, is devoid of good
Feeling & good Sense.—I don't know how the Meaning of the
new Stanzas is wrapped up, but I will not be accessary (I can
answer also for H.[2] I think) towards publishing any thing
which can only be read by Men, since even on their Minds a
bad Effect must follow the Encouragement of those Thoughts
which cannot be rased without Impropriety— If it was so natural a process in Keats's Mind to carry on the Train of his
Story in the way he has done, that he could not write decently,
if he had that Disease of the Mind which renders the Perception too dull to discover Right from Wrong in Matters of moral
Taste, I should object equally then as now to the Sanctioning
of the Infirmity by an act of cool Encouragement on my part,
but then he would be personally perhaps excusable— As it is,
the flying in the Face of all Decency & Discretion is doubly
offensive from its being accompanied with so preposterous a
Conceit on his part of being able to overcome the best founded [3]
Habits of our Nature.—Had he known truly what the Society
and what the Suffrages of Women are worth, he would never
have thought of depriving himself of them.—So far as he is

[2] Hessey.
[3] *L* found.

unconsciously silly in this Proceeding I am sorry for him, but for the rest I cannot but confess to you that it excites in me the Strongest Sentiments of Disapprobation— Therefore my dear Rich^d if [4] he will not so far concede to my Wishes as to leave the passage as it originally stood, I must be content to admire his Poems with some other Imprint, & in so doing I can reap as much Delight from the Perusal of them as if they were our own property, without having the disquieting Consideration attached to them of our approving, by the "Imprimatur," those Parts which are unfit for publication.—

You will think me too severe again. Well then,—I will suspend my Judgment till I see or hear more, but if then [5] my present Views are shewn to be no Illusion I must act as I have described.—How strange too that he should have taken such a Dislike to Isabella— I still think of it exactly as you do, & from what he copied out of Lamia in a late Letter [6] I fancy I shall prefer it to that poem also.—The Extract he gave me was from the Feast. I did not enter so well into it as to be qualified to criticise, but whether it be a want of Taste for such Subjects as Fairy Tales, or that I do not perceive true Poetry except it is in Conjunction with good Sentiment, I cannot tell, but it did not promise to please me.—

Your Quotation in a former Letter on the Primitives [7] of the Welsh language will be of much use to me, *when* I go on with my Grammar, but I am "idling in the greenè Shaw," [8] or less agreeably & healthily in the Chimney Corner, all day long, and Shun Study as a Bargast [q{uery} Bear-Ghost] [9]—a word used here for an Hobgoblin— I have often wished for you

4 *L* Dick if.
5 *L* these.
6 See *Letters,* pp. 379-382.
7 See I, 87.
8 Keats, "Robin Hood," line 36.
9 Bracketed in the original, and one word hidden by the seal.

here.—The Scenery is of the most romantic & beautiful character— Open your Eyes & their Sense feels charmed as by a magic Touch— But I cannot enjoy it so much as I ought for Want of—what? I cannot certainly say what; but I see all Things around as in a Mirror and therefore when I turn away, I forget "what Manner of Scene it was."—The Fault is my own I know, & perhaps that Conviction may lead to the right Way of amending it.—

Since writing the above I have had a Letter from Hessey, containing Mʳ Parsons's [10] proposal: it is very liberal If I understand it correctly he proposes to give up all the profit, if F's [11] Capital is replaced with Simple Interest— This will make a Difference to us of about 500£.—I trust there fore that all this Business is now nearly brought to a Termination—but I will tell you more in a few Days— Write to me at Retford <if> as usual— If I am here the Letter will be forwarded—but I shall stay here till Saturday nex{t.} Ever my dear Friend Richard I am thine most truly J Taylor

➵➵➵ 42 ⬻⬻⬻

CHARLES BROWN (?): A POEM [1]

1819 (?)

Far down in the lowland of Scotland I've heard,
A philosopher liv'd, who stood high in renown;
He wore famous long whiskers, & a handsome grey beard;
He'd the soul of a monarch, tho' the garb of a clown.

[10] See I, 87, 90.
[11] Possibly Frederick Falkner, Hessey's brother-in-law.
[1] A transcript made by Charles Cowden Clarke at some unspecified date. Perhaps this is one of the coarse poems Brown put in his manuscripts of Keats's verse to prevent (see II, 103) ladies from borrowing them. The date 1819 is assigned purely for convenience.

The neighbours all swore that he dealt with the Devil,
Because his strange tricks they did not understand;
And they fled from his sight as the source of all evil,
When he shook his long whiskers, or wav'd his black wand.

At length, in the form of a female so fair,
Curiosity peep'd through his window one night;
And shocking indeed was the sight she saw there;—
A tall figure, slow moving about, all in white.
She look'd for a moment; the thing never vanish'd;
She wish'd to look on, but she dreaded some hurt;
But all fear of danger the maiden soon banish'd,
When it prov'd the philosopher dress'd in his shirt.

Curiosity still felt inclin'd to be peeping;
Impell'd by what motive I cannot well say;
But into his room, Sirs, she forc'd herself, creeping,
And all fear of danger fled far away.
The philosopher, rous'd, would have put on his breeches;
But the maiden admitted of no such delay;
For when a fair maid's curiosity itches,
Such kind of impediments prove in the way.

She told him she came entirely to learn, Sirs,
The arts, the sciences, all the fine things;
And, if so dispos'd, she'd show him in return, Sirs,
How gravity acted on Coblers and Kings.
But first, she would wish an experiment made
On air-pumps, electrics; (fine cures for the spleen)
And if he would only just lend her his aid,
She'd then take a shock from his electric machine.

99

The philosopher gave his immediate consent, Sirs,
His cylinder fix'd, his conductor was brought;
And about this fair maiden to shock her he went, Sirs,
And soon with his fire the fair maiden was fraught.
They studied together, as the neighbours all say,
And discover'd such things as before were scarce known;
He found where the centre of gravity lay;
And she— O, she found the "Philosopher's stone."

Although Keats gave me this, it is not in his hand-writing; and he made no observation in giving it. I trace nothing of his manner in the narration; and, unless for amusement, he intended to mimic the doggerel of such effusions, I should say decidedly he never wrote it. In humour and manner it is more like an effusion of Charles Brown's.

C. C. C.

⇶ 43 ⋘

JOHN TAYLOR TO MICHAEL DRURY

26 January 1820

Address: Mr M Drury/ Philadelphia/ By the Favor of Mr G. Keats. *Endorsed by Drury:* "Jno Taylor/ London Janry 26./ red Mar. 16."

London 26 Jany 1820

My dear Cousin,

I avail myself of the Opportunity afforded me by the Return of Mr George Keats, to thank you very sincerely for the kind Attentions you paid him on his Arrival in America.—I find by his Account that Business is as perplexing & as scarce on the other Side of the Water as on this, & I am sorry to hear it, but with you it cannot be long before it revives, your Burthens are so light compared with ours in England, & even we fancy we

see an Improvement here. But I am out of Love with Politics,
& shall spare you a Dissertation on the Subject.

I am much concerned to hear of the far-away Wanderings
of my dear Cousin your Sister Mary.—The Change since I last
saw her, seems more like a Dream than a Reality— But you are
all I hope only Absentees for a Season still retaining your Affection for Old England, & purposing at some Time to return
& remain here.—Our poor old King is thought to be dangerously
ill at this Time, & the Duke of Kent you will have heard is
dead,[1] but a Change of Kings will be an Event of little Consequence I think to us at present.—

If Mr K. can take it, I purpose sending over a Copy of
Clare's Poems, which your B. Edward was the chief Instrument
of bringing to Light,[2] & I have had the pleasure of editing.—Are
they worth selling the Copyright of in America provided they
take there as they seem likely to do here? I know nothing of the
Law on this Subject, but I suspect when the Right has been
purchased in America, from the Author or Proprietor, that the
Work may be reprinted in England from the American Edition,
& that would be highly undesirable— Therefore, say nothing
about selling the Right, even if you had the Opportunity which
I should much doubt.—

I should like to send over an Edition of 1000 Hazlitt's
Lectures on the Poets,[3] if I thought they would sell for more
than waste paper, exclusive of the Freight, for we have over-
printed that Work.—But perhaps we had better make a short
End of them in our own Hands.—

[1] George III died on January 29, the Duke of Kent on January 23, 1820.

[2] On Edward Drury, a Stamford bookseller, and Clare, see Blunden, pp. 65-
67. Clare's *Poems Descriptive of Rural Life* was published on January 16,
1820 (Blunden, p. 102), by Drury and by Taylor and Hessey, who also jointly
published his next book, *The Village Minstrel* (1821).

[3] Taylor and Hessey published a second edition in 1819, a year after
the first.

James [4] will tell you all the News {of} your Friends in Lincolnshire.—The rest of {our} Connections are all well—

With sincerest Wishes for your prosperity & Happiness, & kind Love to Mrs Ja^s Tallant [5] when you write, I remain,

Dear Michael

Your affectionate Cousin

John Taylor

➳➳➳ 44 ⸸⸸⸸

RICHARD WOODHOUSE TO JOHN TAYLOR

9 February 1820

Morgan MS.

Dr John,

I ought to have read & sent you this [6] before—but my sister occupied my Saturday & Sunday entirely—& Reynolds took up, with his agreable Company, my Monday Evening.—I think we agreed to say nothing to each <of> other about it till we had both read it— So Mum!—But let me recommend you *not* to do, as I did,—*Skim* it over first for the sake of the plot— I shall be wiser another time.—

As to writing down one's opinion upon it, I think it would be a good exercise—but it would take so much meditation, & going so often over it, that you & I should be talking ourselves into the same opinion long before I could be delivered of a written essay on the subject— The time of my gestation is longer than yours— I wish I could say as much for the vitality of what comes at last.—

Yrs very truly

R^d Woodhouse.

Temple 9 ffeb^y/20—

[4] James Drury, Michael's brother.
[5] Of Cincinnati. See I, 216f, 219.
[6] Possibly one of the poems ("Lamia"?) later published in the 1820 volume.

⇢≫ 45 ≪⇠

CHARLES BROWN TO JOHN TAYLOR
8 March 1820

Address: To/ Mr Taylor/ N° 93 Fleet Street. *Postmarks:* 7 o'Clock MR.8 18[20]; TwoPyPost Unpaid SOHampstead. Morgan MS. Printed by Lowell, II, 401.

Hampstead.
Wednesday 8th March

Dear Taylor,

Poor Keats will be unable to prepare his Poems for the Press for a long time. He was taken on Monday evening with violent palpitations at the heart, and has since remained too weak to get up. I expect Dr Bree [1] every hour. I am wretchedly depressed.

Your's sincerely,
Chas Brown.

If you come, do not let him hear your voice, as the slightest circumstance tending to create surprise, or any other emotion, must be avoided.

CB

P. S.

Since writing the above, Dr Bree has been here, and I am rejoiced to say, gives very favourable hopes.

CB

[1] Robert Bree (1759–1839), Fellow of the Royal College of Physicians, specialist in respiratory diseases, who lived in George Street, Hanover Square. For details of his life and work see Sir William Hale-White, *Keats as Doctor and Patient* (1938), pp. 74f.

→»» 46 «←

CHARLES BROWN TO JOHN TAYLOR

10 March 1820

Address: To/ Mr Taylor/ N° 93 Fleet Street/ London. Morgan MS. Printed by Lowell, II, 401f.

Hampstead.
Friday 10 March.

Dear Taylor,

After my dismal note I am glad to be able to give you good news. Keats is so well as to be out of danger. We intend, if the weather remain kindly, to go to the coast of Hants. He walked in the Garden to-day. You will suspect I gave you a useless alarm, but I wrote at the time I was told that it was possible he might suddenly be lost to us in one of those fits. Hessey's letter came, & I opened it, for Keats could not endure even the circumstance of a letter being put in his hands,—nor can he bear it even yet, tho' I consider him perfectly out of danger, & I am happy to tell you that we are now assured there is no pulmonary affection, no organic defect whatever,—the disease is on his *mind,*[1] and there I hope he will soon be cured.

Your's sincerely
Chas Brown.

Remember me to Mr Hessey.

[1] Sir William Hale-White, *Keats as Doctor and Patient* (1938), p. 54, remarks: "To us this seems incredible, when we remember the bleeding from the lungs a month earlier."

→≫ 47 ≪←

CHARLES BROWN TO JOHN TAYLOR

13 March [1] 1820

Address: To/ Mr Taylor. Morgan MS. Printed by Lowell, II, 404.

Dear Sir,

Keats has been slowly recovering; yesterday and to-day however he has been greatly altered for the better. He wishes his Poems to be published as soon as convenient to yourself,— the volume to commence with St Agnes' Eve. He was occupied yesterday in revising Lamia. It is not his intention at present to have a Preface,[2]—at least so we talked together to-day. He desires to be remembered. When will you come? for *he* must not venture to Town before we have mild weather,—& when? It is very pleasant at Hampstead—*in our parlour.*

Your's sincerely

Chas Brown.

Don't let any one take a Copy of Otho.—

→≫ 48 ≪←

J. H. REYNOLDS TO JOHN TAYLOR

March 1820 (?) [3]

Address: Mr Taylor or Mr Hessey/ 93 Fleet Street. Morgan MS.

Dear Taylor

Did you see Keats?—And how is he?—And what is "the cause of thunder"? [4]

Ever yours

JHReynolds

Wednesday Morng

[1] The date is a guess, based on the fact that Keats dined in town with John Taylor on March 14 (Blunden, *Shelley and Keats* [1925], pp. 72f.).
[2] See No. 53.
[3] A mere guess.
[4] *King Lear,* III.iv.160.

⇥⇥ 49 ⇤⇤

NAN WOODHOUSE [1] TO RICHARD WOODHOUSE

6 April 1820

Morgan MS. Finney, II, 445, quotes two sentences.

Esher April 6ᵗʰ 1820

My dear Richard,

Your ready and prompt compliance with *my* request of favouring me, with the details of the *Mill* between "Martin & C<ooper">abbage"—Cooper and Hickman" together with the technical jargon thereunto belonging—such as Tapping the Claret—shutting up their daylights &c [2] has absolutely so overcome me by the weight of obligation it has laid me under that I know not how sufficiently to thank you nor how to appreciate the favour enough—but joking apart when your charming long letter was delivered me by my Aunt on Sunday at dinner time before eight persons, "thinks I to myself" I wish you all farther that I might read my letter but no opportunity had I except of *peeping* into its contents till I went to my room, then if you could have seen the anxiety with which I glanced my eye over line after line and page after page in hopes of <my> meeting

---

1 Presumably the writer refers to herself in the third person as Nannie. For the use of her letter, the end of which is missing, in Reynolds' *Fancy* see I, 117. Finney, II, 445, 748, quotes two of her sentences, attributes the letter to Reynolds, and says that it was "Written by Miss Reynolds from her brother's dictation"; Hewlett, p. 209, refers to it as having been written by Charlotte Reynolds.

2 John Badcock, *Slang. A Dictionary of the Turf, the Ring*, etc. (1823), pp. 64, 119, 170, explains "daylights" as "the eyes," "millers" as "boxers," and "tapp'd his claret" as "gave a bloody nose." In *Boxiana* (1824 ed., vol. IV) Pierce Egan gives full details of the lives and fights of Tom Hickman (pp. 153-232), Jack Martin (pp. 418-446), Jack Cabbage, "the Iron-Armed Bristollian," whose real name was John Strong (pp. 447-461), and Jack Cooper (pp. 563-579).

with something that was intelligible and shall I add interesting?
lastly had you witnessed my disappointed looks on beholding
two whole sheets and *half a third* devoted to the same subject
you must in spite of yourself have pitied me   Can it be possible my dear Richard that you did derive from the exhibition all
the gratification you describe, and regret [3] that "It is not given
to poor human nature to forget such a sight at will, so as to
have the gratification arising from seeing the exhibition *for the
first time*, sixty times over"   Good Heavens! Why you are quite
enthusiastic, and on such a subject too— I could not help
mentally exclaiming why Richard is surely mad and so I really
think, a mania it certainly is which has seized you, how long it
will last, remains to be proved. the "Sonnet" [4] no doubt is very
clever but indeed I was too sick of the subject to enjoy it, I can
just fancy *your* astonishment at my want of taste and ingratitude
in returning you a letter full of complaints and grumbling after
the time and trouble you bestowed on yours   indeed it is too
bad and my conscience smites me for it and as a punishment
adaquate to my offence I deserve not to be written to again, but
remember no attribute so well becomes a Judge, as that of
Mercy pray therefore extend it to me, and write to me again as
soon as you have half an hour to spare.

I must now give my reason for not having written earlier
in the week, it is no less cogent a one than that I fully intended
to have answered it this day in person as Mary and Mr Neville [5]
intended to have been in Town   I should in that case have gone
up the same day but having been disappointed in that pleasure
I am commissioned to say that we are all to dine at Hounslow
on Sunday *next* therefore if you come down the following

[3] *Over* regret *is* "lament.
[4] Reynolds' "Sonnet on the Nonpareil" (John Randall), later printed in
The Fancy. See I, 116f.
[5] See II, 217.

<Sunday> Saturday your Cousin and Cousin-in Law [6] will be most happy to see you and amongst the number of the Esherites your Sister Nannie will not be the *least* delighted of the party to welcome you though perhaps she may not be able to greet you with the silvery tones of her dulcet voice having been minus in *that* department just one fortnight but I have not mentioned it in my letters home as it only annoys my Father, and does no good

The Review [7] shall be taken care of and returned when I see you—in your opinion of the Critique on Keats I perfectly coincide so far as that the author of it has not done him justice but like many others he does not understand him I was so vexed last evening to hear his Endymion so abused by some ladies who drank tea here and Mr Neville how much I wished for you to point out some of the countless beauties with which it abounds, but I think even your rhetoric would have been useless so prejudiced did they seem against the whole of his writings even that beautiful and grand Sonnet to the "Sea" [8] failed to interest them after that I gave them up as lost *muttons* With the Apollo Belvedere I am really delighted and interested in the explanatory tale. [9]

I am and shall be uneasy until we hear (on poor James' account), [10] owing to the horrible massacre there has been in Cadiz [11] my blood ran cold while reading it and dear Jane [12]

6 See II, 217.

7 Probably that of *Endymion* in the *London Magazine*, April, 1820 (I, 380-389).

8 Published in the *Champion*, August 17, 1817.

9 Possibly she refers to Woodhouse's sonnet "To Apollo. Written after reading Keats's 'Sleep and Poetry'" (1818), on which see Finney, I, 344.

10 Perhaps her brother James, who in 1830 lived at 17 Bedford Square, London (Blunden, p. 28n.). He was in Cadiz as early as 1813 (see II, 409).

11 During the revolution of 1820, in which King Ferdinand VII was imprisoned there.

12 Perhaps the writer's sister or sister-in-law.

used always to say my brain was more fertile in conjuring up
and anticipating troubles than in any other employment I hope
when they hear in Town I shall know of it he has been very
unfortunate since his residence there I should like to hear if M^r
Domecy is liberated

No letters yet from our dear Jane is it not strange, my
patience is quite exhausted at least five weeks since we heard
of her safe arrival and yet no letters from herself— I was surprised to see Henry looking so well after so much suffering as
he has gone through

You say you have received some unintelligible messages
from some of us the fact is this that Mr Neville told us before
we reached this, that he had engaged you to dine here the Sunday after we arrived not seeing you then I depended on

*   *   *

->> 50 <<-

GEORGE KEATS TO FANNY KEATS

25 May 1820, 6 January 1821

Address: Miss Keats. The January 6 letter is printed in *Letters*, p. 515.

{Louis}ville May 25th 1820.

My dear Fanny

You will have seen the letter I sent John containing an
account of my journey and safe arrival at Home; of the sickness
of your little neice,[1] and her recovery; in fact it was altogether
so exactly what I have now to say to you that I must refer you
to it that I may not repeat. It will not I hope be many years
before we meet again when our communications will be as
frequent as our affections will prompt; in the mean time think

[1] Georgiana Emily.

of me as a Friend and Brother who loves you, and who will always be ready and willing to serve you. You cannot fail to like Mrs Keats, she has good sense, an excellent temper, and good taste enough to dislike this country. She is much pleased with your present and desires her love. We look anxiously towards England. I would talk about your little neice but that all Fathers talk of their darlings in the same strain, she cannot be otherwise than beautiful the most obvious recommendation to a baby and the most easily distinguished; I am told she "is too intelligent to live long," this is a sort of flattery intended to be beleived, and to create pleasure at the same time, would you suppose it possible? and yet it is not altogether injudicious since the praise is the highest that can be administered, the death uncertain and not imputable to the discovery of the merit of the child. It is said that Princes and men in affluent circumstances never hear the truth, I should like to know who is not flattered in his turn, or hears the truth often enough to profit by it: I cannot help thinking my child both beautiful and intelligent for her age and am My dear Fanny

Your most affectionate Brother
George.

Give my respects to M^{rs} and Miss Abbey and love to John.

Jany 6—1821— I wrote the inclosed for a private opportunity of which I was disappointed; I have now another. You have now my dear Fanny another neice,[2] she was born on the 18 Decr See how fast I'm becoming an old Man your Sister and Child are both well. I am informed you feel disappointed at not hearing from me, the date of this will show you, you were not forgotten, nor will you ever be forgotten altho' you may not hear from me very frequently, my letter could only inform if we are

[2] Rosalind: see I, xcvii.

well or ill, with politics you cannot be interested, what then must make up my epistles when the chances of the posts and the necessary distance of time between writing each letter will make a regular correspondence or interchange of ideas so difficult if not impossible. I should be more anxious to keep up a frequent communication by letter, if I did not one day expect to give you assurances of my affection in Person. Your entire leisure may make this appear a mere evasion, that a letter is easily written, but you will find it otherwise when you may have constant and perhaps important occupation. I have by me copies of letters of immense length built on nothing and written without trouble, but now my mind after a certain stretch will revert to my daily avocation, and writing letters instead of being as formerly a pleasure is now become a task. Under these feelings I procrastinate untill it seems almost useless to write; after having delayed writing six months another delay of a month seems nothing. I don't pretend to say that this is sufficient excuse for not writing, but you will see that my silence is not a want of affection and that I am still altho lazy

Your very affectionate Brother
George.

I hope to have time to write to John in [3] this packet. Your Sisters love.

[3] *Written over* by.

111

→≫ 51 ≪←

RICHARD WOODHOUSE TO JOHN TAYLOR

June (?) 1820 [1]

Address: To, Jn⁰ Taylor Esqʳ/ Fleet Sᵗ. Morgan MS. Printed by Garrod
(G), p. xxx.

Lamia p 13.[2]

was heard
And a soft voice *swell'd out* upon the air
Muttering, "Where art thou, Lycius! [3] Ah Where?"

═══

Dʳ John,

    <Pre> If the above will not do, pray "hit off Something
Better" as Sʳ Philip says.[4]—But at all Events do not let the poem

[1] The address is on the first page of the folded sheet. On the second page,
upside down at the top, in Keats's autograph is

    Shore Shore Shore Shore
    Jane Jane

followed by a number of scattered drawings. Woodhouse's letter is on the
third page. Taylor had evidently objected to *Lamia,* I.168f., the proofsheets
of which (with Woodhouse's autograph and the date "May/ June 1820"),
now at Harvard, read:

    And her new voice, soft luting in the air,
    Cried, "Lycius! gentle Lycius, where, ah where!"

In the proofs the last three words were inked out, and an exclamation point
inserted after the second "Lycius." As finally printed the lines run:

    And in the air, her new voice luting soft,
    Cried, "Lycius! gentle Lycius!"—Borne aloft.

Garrod, p. xxxi, has interesting speculations on the meaning and significance of the letter.

[2] G pt 3.

[3] G Lamia!

[4] Not found. I do not know whether the reference is to Sidney or to Sir
Philip Francis, whom Taylor in *The Identity of Junius* (1816) identified
with Junius.

be published incomplete. "Rather than so," I would let it remain as he had written it.

Yrs ⁵ R^dW.

"Whose senses all were straight benumb'd, and *stark*." ⁶

Spenser.

→» 52 «←

GEORGE KEATS TO JOHN KEATS

18 June 1820

Printed in *Letters*, pp. 494f.

Louisville June 18th 1820

My dear John

Where will our miseries end? so soon as the Thursday ¹ after I left London you were attacked with a dangerous illness, an hour after I left this for England my little Girl became so ill as to approach the Grave dragging our dear George after her. You are recovered (thank [God] I hear the bad and good news together) they are recovered, and yet I feel gloomy instead of grateful. Perhaps from the consideration that so short a time <is necessary to> will serve to deprive me of every object that makes life pleasant. Brown says you are really recovered, that you eat, drink, sleep, and walk five miles without weariness, this is positive, and I beleive you nearly recovered but your perfect recovery depends on the future. You must go to a more favorable clime, must be easy in your mind, the former depends on me the latter on yourself. My prospect of being able to send

---

⁵ *Possibly* Yr's *or* Yrs—.
⁶ G no italics. Spenser, *Faery Queen*, I.i.44. Woodhouse is perhaps illustrating *Lamia*, II.298, which originally ran, "Corinthians! A Serpent, plain and stark!"
¹ February 3, 1820. George left London on Friday, January 28.

113

you 200£ very soon is pretty good, I have an offer for the Boat which I have accepted, but the party who lives at Natchez (300 miles only near New Orleans) [2] will not receive information that I have accepted his offer for some weeks since the Gentleman who was commissioned to make it has gone up the Country and not yet returned, the only chance against us is that the purchasing party may change his mind; this is improbable since he has already purchased one fifth and to my knowledge is very anxious to obtain mine, but it is not impossible. I will direct my Agent at New Orleans to send you 200£ instantly on receiving the proceeds of the sale, and should no unexpected delay occur it will arrive within 2 or 3 weeks of this letter, It shall be addressed to you at Abbey & C⁰'ˢ the first of exchange directly from New Orleans, the second and third by way of New York and this place. I have no other means of raising anything like that Sum, scarcely a Man in the Town could borrow such a sum. I might suggest means of raising the money on this hope immediately but Brown being on the spot will advise what is best. Since your health requires it to Italy you must and shall go. Make your mind easy and place confidence in my success, I cannot ensure it, but I will deserve it. I have a consignment of goods to sell by commission, which helps me a little, if this parcel does well I shall have more. When I have received the price offered for the Boat I shall have been no loser by the purchase. This considering the alteration in times is doing wonders. George desires her love and thinks that if you were with us our nursing would soon bring you to rights, but I tell her you cannot be in better hands than Browns, she joins me in grateful thanks to him. I will write to him next post repeating what is important in this, lest one should miscarry. Our love to Fanny and Mʳˢ W [3] and Brothers. Yesterday's Post with

[2] Above the last three words is inserted "300 miles only."
[3] His mother-in-law, Mrs. Wylie.

114

Brown's letter brought us one from Henry Wylie acquainting us with the death of M⟶ᵣˢ Miller. our love to Mary Miller [4] if you should see her, George will write her in a few days. I will write again soon. I made up a packet to Haslam containing letters to Fanny, Mᵣ Abbey and Mᵣˢ W.[5] to go by private hand, the Gentleman has postponed his voyage. Take the utmost care of yourself my dear John for the sake of your most affectionate and alarmed Brother and Sister.

I am

Your very affectionate Brother

George.

⟶≫ 53 ≪⟵

RICHARD WOODHOUSE: DRAFT OF THE "ADVERTISEMENT"

TO *Lamia*

June (?) 1820 [1]

Morgan MS.

Italics.

† ‡ † The Publishers <of this volume> think it right to state, that it was not the wish of the Author [2] that the ensuing fragment should <be pu> meet <appear before> the public eye.—He commenced the Poem just before the publication of his Endymion; and he abandoned the <idea> [3] intention of proceeding with it, in consequence of the reception

---

[4] The Millars, of Henrietta Street, London, were "George's" cousins.
[5] Mrs. Wylie.
[1] A guess based on the fact that the book was published on July 1 or 3 (see I, 121). The "Advertisement" actually printed differs entirely in wording, and may have been written by Taylor. It was disowned by Keats (see Lowell, II, 424f.).
[2] *Originally* the Author's intention [*changed to* wish].
[3] Another word before this is canceled.

115

that work experienced from some of the reviews.—The fragment remains therefore in the same state in which it was originally written; and the Author's health is not at pres^t such as
to enable him to make ^{4} any corrections. The Publishers have
however prevailed upon him to allow of its <being printed in>
form^g a part [of] this volume: and they are Content to take upon
themselves whatever blame may attach to its publication.

>>> 54 <<<

RICHARD WOODHOUSE TO JOHN TAYLOR

30 June (?) 1820 ^{1}

Address: To,/ Jno Taylor Esqr/ Bath. Morgan MS. Two sentences are
quoted by Lowell, II, 428.

Dr John,

You have, I dare say, ere this handed over to my Sister
a Copy of K's poems, which I desired Thomas to put into your
Parcel— Thank you, by anticipation.—"If you have ribs, prepare to shake them now." ^{2}—i. e. as soon as you see the review
of Peter Corcoran's executor's work in Blackwood. Where the
d—ce could the Scotsman have purloined so much wit & humour
from? Did you hear that Miss Drewe ^{3} had been at Bath &
spent a day at Duke S^t ^{4}—where she saw the Fancy lying on the
Table— And (being in the Secret herself) she had much amuse-

---

^{4} *Woodhouse first wrote* in a [*changed to* that] state to allow of his making.
^{1} The *Lamia* volume was published on July 1 or 3 (see I, 121), and the
review of Peter Corcoran's or Reynolds' *Fancy* appeared in the June
issue of *Blackwood's* (VII, 294-306). Woodhouse may (as Lowell suggests)
have been referring on Friday, June 30, to an advance copy of Keats's
book. On that very day (see Blunden, *Shelley and Keats* [1925], p. 76)
Taylor sent "a copy of Keat's [*sic*] New Volume" to John Clare.
^{2} Compare *Julius Caesar*, III.ii.173.
^{3} See I, cxix.
^{4} Woodhouse's father lived at 8 Duke Street.

ment in making malicious enquiries, & hearing my sister wonder how her letter could have got into the Book [5]—& declare that I must have some hand in the book She sent an account of it to Reynolds, who read it to me. I wish when you can spare Blackwood for a day, you would take an opportunity of letting her see the Review. I dare say you will be repaid in the fun you will have: and if you can leave it doubtful whether Corcoran is not a real personage, & was not an acquaintance of mine, so much the better.—Barry Cornwall's article [6] on P. C. is a very tame one in comparison; what will you bet about the work coming to the fag end of a 2^d Ed^n?—Master Blackwood to be sure has been full lavish in his extracts— But Reynolds forgives him.—

Barry Cornwall praises the Sonnet about "Lilies lying uneasily at rest" as being *very prettily* [7] *written notwithstanding the Editor's note*. This is capital!—& pleases John Hamble-

[5] In *The Fancy* (1820), pp. xx f., Reynolds used Miss Woodhouse's letter of April 6 (see No. 49) thus:

"About this time he [Peter Corcoran] wrote a slang description of a fight which he had witnessed, to the lady [Kate] while she was on a short visit at Esher, accompanied with his Sonnet to Randall. He received in return, as might be expected, a grave remonstrance. The lady says, with affectionate simplicity and frankness,—

" 'Could you have seen the anxiety with which I glanced my eye over line after line, and page after page, in hopes of meeting with something that was intelligible, and, (shall I add?) interesting; and had you witnessed my disappointment in beholding two whole sheets, and half a third, devoted to the subject of a "mill between Belasco and the Brummagem youth," you must, in spite of yourself, have pitied me.'——'Can it be possible, my dear Peter, that you *did* derive so much pleasure as you describe, and that you "lament that it is not given to poor human nature to forget such a sight at will, so as to have the gratification, arising from seeing such an exhibition for the first time, sixty times over"? Good heavens! you are quite enthusiastic! and on such a subject too!'——'I cannot thank you for the Sonnet. It is no doubt clever, but I was too sick of the subject to enjoy it.' "

[6] In the *London Magazine*, July (II, 71-75).

[7] *Actually* sweetly.

117

ton [8] highly.—We went to see the Showing yesterday: & today
have M[r] P. Egan's version of it in the New Times [9]— It
is a rich bit— Pierce has not perambulated Bath for nothing.

Miss Bonsor [10] has got a volume of Miss Vivian's Poetry
for you— I had the honor of Picking shrimps with her & his
Honor of Polesden yesterday evening— She has done a beautiful little bit of colour, in the shape of a Landscape, with which
you will be pleased.—

I got into your jacket just now, & think of building one—
But the hot weather is all gone. Today I have actually been
obliged to shut down my windows.—

I am taking tea with Hessey; & had commissioned him
to say my little say to you— But I thought it better to take up
a pen & go "step for step" with him, as Saturn did with Thea [11]
—so that whe{n} he ends, he finishes me too.

Have the goodness to make my kindest remembrances to
those who care about such an urban as your humble. Draw
that Blacksmith George Stothert [12] out of his shell, and tell
him to let his iron cool while he listens to a *Taylor's* news.—
And (if you can) bring him up to Town.

Hessey has subscribed 160 of Keats—& sold *one Endymion* today— So that the bard's works begin to get in request.—
Hessey makes motions of folding up— So no more at Present,
from

Yours very sincerely

R[d] W.   93, Fleet S[t]
Friday.

[8] *For* Hamilton (Reynolds).
[9] I find nothing in the *New Times* to explain this remark unless it means
that Egan reviewed a new opera.
[10] Probably a daughter of the stationer often mentioned in Hessey's letters
(see the Index).
[11] *Hyperion,* I.202.
[12] A Bath schoolmate who in 1811 introduced Woodhouse to Taylor (Blunden, pp. 29f.).

⇶ 55 ⫷

J. H. REYNOLDS TO JOHN TAYLOR

4 July 1820

Address: John Taylor Esq/ Messrs Collett & Falkener/ Bath. *Postmark:* JY 4 1820. Morgan MS. The third paragraph is quoted by Lowell, II, 424.

50 Poland Street
4 July 1820

My Dear Taylor

You will be astonished at receiving a Letter from me, but pray do not let it see you in those fustian clothes or it may be equally startled at you. The cause of my writing to you is this:—My Father among his various places of *emolument* hold[s] the place of Writing Master to the Asylum [1] & he *has* held it for the last 15 years.—Some of the Managers of this concern are now proposing to lop his trifling salary of £50 per annum down to £30—on the economy *lay.* He has gained great credit by his attention to the children as I am told,—and I really think it hard that he should be the only martyr to the saving system. What I want you to do is to write, if you do not mind such a thing, to Lord Radstock [2] who is a leading & an attending man and get him to oppose this reduction, if on inquiry he finds it causeless. If you could write to him by return of Post, he will get your Ansr on Thursday morning, the day of the meeting & decision.

I really would on no account have you write, if it will be thought an obligation and you know that I always thus freely ask you, because I have the confidence in your refusing anything that would be painful, unpleasant or impossible. I

[1] The Female Asylum, Lambeth.
[2] William Waldegrave (1753–1825), first Baron Radstock of Castletown, Clare's patron.

have not said a word to my Father of this letter, & therefore
your declining on the score of delicacy, will not be known, but
of course it would be a pleasure to me to be in anyway instrumental in preserving to him what he is really intitled to, & the
loss of which it would be an affectation to say he would not
feel. So much for this—

Poor Keats! You cannot think how much pain Hessey's
account [3] has given me:—for if ever there was a worthy fellow
& clever fellow on Earth—he is that fellow. His Book looks like
an Angel, & talks like one too. You have heard of the damn'd
Literary Gazette.[4]

What say you to Blackwood?—Is it not clever & apt.—I am
& have been really amused with it.[5]

This is no letter—but you, up to your eyes in Sun, want
no letters—and my heart strings are just at present, of red tape [6]—
Yours ever most truly

JHReynolds

[3] See Keats's own reference, June 23 (*Letters*, p.495), to his spitting of blood
and Hessey's letters, about the end of June, to Clare (Blunden, p. 73).
[4] On July 1 (p. 423) it mentioned Keats's book, "which is on the eve of publication," with one sentence of comment and various quotations from the
poems.
[5] See I, 116n.
[6] Referring to the pressure of legal business. The letter was written from
Rice's address (see I, cxxviii).

⇥⇥ 56 ⇤⇤

JOSEPH SEVERN TO WILLIAM HASLAM

12 (?) July 1820 [1]

A few sentences are quoted by Colvin, p. 466.

6 Goswell Str Road [2]

Wednesday M

My dear Haslam

I have been away from home until Monday—on a face-making expedition—so that your letter has been to Hampton Court—Tiddington [3] & Richmond before I received it—it shall be done as you say—next week————.

Poor Keats has been still nearer the next world—a Fortnight back he ruptured a blood-vessell in the Chest— I have seen him many times—particularly previous to this accident—once since—and it will give you pleasure to say I think [4] he will still recover—his appearence is shocking and now reminds me of poor Tom—and I have been inclined to think him in the same way—for himself—he makes sure of it—and seems prepossed [5] that he cannot recover—now I seem more than ever *not* to think so and I know you will agree with me when you see him—are you aware another volume of Poems was published last week—in which is—"Lovely Isabel—poor simple Isabel"— I have been delighted with this volume and think it

---

[1] Severn writes that the *Lamia* volume, which was published on July 1 or 3 (Lowell, II, 421-424, 428), came out "last week." Wednesday, then, was probably July 5 or 12.

[2] Sharp, p. 28, says that "early in 1819" Severn left his Goswell Street lodgings to live with his father in Hoxton, but this address indicates that he is wrong.

[3] Teddington, Middlesex.

[4] So apparently, *altered from* trust.

[5] *Sic.*

will even please the Million— Keats has been for some time at
Leigh Hunts on account of the attention he requires—most certain his body cannot be in better hands—but for his soul——
altho' I can see in Keats such a deep thinking—determined—
silent spirit—that I am doing him the greatest injustice to suppose for a moment that such a man as L—— H—— can ever
taint him with his principles *now*—or even school him with
his learning— I think the house is 13 Mortimer Terrace Kentish
Town—it is only a few doors from Keats's lodging (2 Weslyan
Place)— I shall continue to visit Keats very much at every opportunity—perhaps twice a week——

Now about your "dearer self"— I am quite ashamed that
I have not succeeded The white sattin gown looks most vile
after all my trouble—now if I may be favored with a sitting I
will succeed—to this purpose I think I can manage—some day
next week I shall be going to Deptford Dock Yard—say Thursday now I can call on M^rs H—— and regain my lost favor—
present my respects—and say that from any silk dress I can
paint white satin [6]—it is merely the light and shade and the
form I want— I met your Servant on Monday but I cou'd not
return from the East India Dock Y^d in time to call—try to see
me Sincer^ly yours

Jos^h Severn

No I'll give you another half sheet and fill this bit with self—
I have been very much occupied with my Miniatures—am at
home finishing 5 now— I cannot tell how they will turn out
for they are all new faces to me— I am glad to be going this
way altho' it takes me entirely from my other Painting—but

[6] Severn had painted the first Mrs. Haslam before September 17, 1819, when
Keats wrote (*Letters*, p. 401) that Haslam "show'd me her Picture by Severn.
I think she is, though not very cunning, too cunning for him." Perhaps the
new portrait here referred to was that seen by Brown before September 30
(see I, 159).

soon I begin and continue until the end of the year—my reputation is increasing most largly and nobly—and I hope soon
to reap much profit—tell Kent that the [*a sketch of a flag appears here*] are [7] being gilt— I expect them soon to be com-
pleate.

⇒ 57 ⇐

PERCY BYSSHE SHELLEY TO JOHN KEATS [1]

27 July 1820

Address: John Keats Esq[r]/ (to the care of Leigh Hunt Esq[r])/ Examiner Office/
Catharine Street/ Strand/ London/ [*At the left, in a line with* "Strand"]:
Angleterre. *Postmarks:* F P O AU.10 1820; LIVORNO.

Pisa— July 27. 1820

My dear Keats

I hear with great pain the dangerous accident that you
have undergone, & M[r] Gisborne [2] who gives me the account of
it, adds, that you continue to wear a consumptive appearance.[3]
This consumption is a disease particularly fond of people who
write such good verses as you have done, and with the assistance

[7] Presumably "the flags are," though I cannot explain the meaning.

[1] This famous letter is discussed and at least partly quoted in all the biographies of Keats and Shelley, and is included here only for completeness. It
is printed with almost entire accuracy in *Letters*, pp. 505f. For a photo-
graphic facsimile of Keats's reply, August 16, see R. Glynn Grylls, *Mary
Shelley* (1938), between pp. 126, 127, and compare the Hampstead Keats,
VIII, 233f. The incorrect text of the reply in *Letters*, pp. 506-508, is reproduced from Lady Shelley's *Shelley Memorials* (1859).

[2] John Gisborne and his wife Maria saw Keats at Leigh Hunt's on June 23
and July 12, 1820, and were painfully impressed, as Maria noted in her
journal, by his dreadful appearance and his being "under sentence of
death." See, among others, Colvin, pp. 466f., and Hewlett, pp. 340f., 343,
345f.

[3] Some sort of odd flourish, or possibly only a corrected punctuation mark,
comes between the *e* and the period.

of an English winter it can often indulge its selection;—I do
not think that young & aimiable[4] poets are at all bound to
gratify its taste; they have entered into no bond with the Muses
to that effect . . .[5] But seriously (for I am joking on what I am
very an{x}ious about) I think you would do well to pass the
Winter a{fte}r so {treme}ndous an accident in Italy, & (if you
thinks[6] it as necessary as I do) so long as you could find Pisa
or its neighbourhood agreable to you, Mrs Shelley unites with
myself in urging the request, that you would take up your residence with us.—You might come by sea to Leghorn, (France
is not worth seeing, & the sea air is particularly good for weak
lungs) which is within a few miles of us. You ought at all events
to see Italy, & your health which I suggest as a motive, might
be an excuse to you.—I spare declamation about the statues &
the paintings & the ruins—& what is a greater piece of forbear-
ance—about the mountains the Streams & the fields, the colours
of the sky, & the sky itself—

I have lately read your Endymion again <for> & ever
with a new sense of the treasures of poetry it contains, <bu>
though treasures poured forth with indistinct profusion— This,
people in general will not endure, & that is the cause of the[7]
comparatively few copies which have been sold.—I feel persuaded that you are capable of the greatest things, so you but
will.[8] I always tell Ollier to send you Copies of my books.—
"Prometheus Unbound" I imagine you will receive nearly at
the same time <of> with this letter. The Cenci I hope you
have already <seen> received—it was studiously composed in
a different style "below the *good* how far! but far above the

[4] *Sic.*
[5] *Sic.*
[6] *Sic.*
[7] *Altered from* of the coln (?).
[8] What follows is written on the back of the letter. Probably Shelley intended a new paragraph to begin here.

LEIGH HUNT

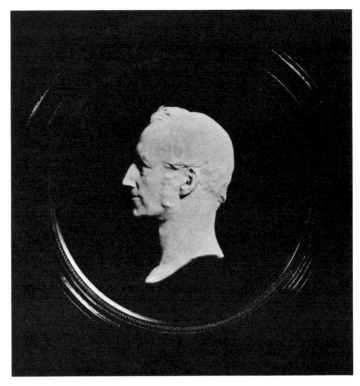

JOHN TAYLOR

great" [9] In poetry *I* have sought to avoid system & mannerism; I wish those who excel me in genius, <had> would pursue the same plan—

Whether you remain in England, or journey to Italy,— believe that you carry with you my anxious wishes for your health happiness & success, wherever you are or whatever you undertake—& that I am

Yours sincerely

P. B. Shelley

➸➸ 58 ≪≪

BENJAMIN BAILEY TO JOHN TAYLOR

27 July 1820

Address: J. Taylor Esqre / 93 Fleet Street. Morgan MS. A few sentences are quoted by Blunden, p. 87.

Dallington. July 27. 1820.

My dear Sir

I have been in the daily expectation, for the last fort-night, of a parcel from you with Keats's Poems &c. I desired Martin [1] to send some books he was to procure for me to you that they might be included in your parcel. I trusted you would excuse that liberty, though I did not mention it to you. But I have received none; & I will trouble you to put the in-closed for Martin into the twopenny post.

I send you the copy of Taylor's Sermons,[2] and am very sorry that I should have retained it, though under the impres-sion which I explained to you.

I hope shortly to receive the long expected parcel with

[9] The last line of Gray's "Progress of Poetry."
[1] Evidently a bookseller: see II, 311n.
[2] See I, 61.

125

poor Keates's Poems. Do not wait for any thing which Martin might send, for I shall tell him to dispatch it to me at once. You have surely been long in the publication beyond the time you expected the book to be out. I hope, from the bottom of my heart that it may succeed; but I confess my apprehensions of it are fully as powerful as my hopes. There are some principles which Keats has taken up, which have been adopted by many of similar powers of mind, and under similar circumstances, which I sincerely lament, and can make allowances for. He has abundant power, but little knowledge. He has good dispositions and noble qualities of heart; but, I think, we shall accord in one conclusion, that he has not kept the best society for one of his character and constitution. Many of his moral principles are consequently loose; his moral conduct not very exact; and the Phantom of *Honor* is substituted for the truth and substance of *Religion*.

Such at least was the bias of his mind when I knew and associated with him more intimately than I have had the opportunity of doing since I have been engaged in my present profession; and your knowledge of my sincere regard for him will, I am sure, readily excuse the freedom of these remarks. But to return to his book: I fear these traits will, nay they must appear in his book. I have thought more on his character and the comparative excellencies & defects of his mind since you & I were wont to talk of him; & I confess my confirmed apprehensions that these causes will operate to his great hindrance throughout his career in the literary world and as a moral agent.—Give my kind regards to him when you see him, & say I always cherish much good will and affection for him. I believe I wrote him last, but he does not show great alacrity in the continuance of my correspondence. But that does not at all offend me.

I have read Millman's book, and do not think so much

of it as the Quarterly Reviewers.[3] I agree with you that the scholarship swallows up the mind of the poet. The comparison with Milton must in every way tend to his disadvantage, and in none more obviously than in the learning displayed in their pages. Milton's immense weight of learning is but a light surface compared with his mind & real knowledge—the power of his imagination & the strength of his Judgment. But without his very inferior quantum of learning, Millman would have been either no poet at all—or a much more genuine one. For the feeble light of poesy is almost darkened by the cloud of words.

I have written you freely to encourage you to make a like return to, My dear Sir,

Yours very sincerely

B Bailey [4]

You will probably have heard that I am the father of a Son since I had the pleasure of seeing you. I shall be most happy to see you here.

[3] The *Quarterly*, May, 1820 (XXIII, 198-225), not only compared H. H. Milman's *Fall of Jerusalem* to Milton but promised it "whatever immortality the English language can bestow."
[4] What follows is written on the back outer fold.

⇒⇒ 59 ⇐⇐

RICHARD WOODHOUSE: CRITICISM OF A SONNET BY KEATS [1]

July (?) 1820

Printed in part by Lowell, I, 501f., and Finney, II, 532.

*   *   *

p 64. l.l. 7, 8— These lines <faintly [?] show> give <a fair [?]> some <idea of> insight into K's mode of writing Poetry. He has repeatedly said in convers^n that he never sits down to write, <until> unless he is full of ideas—and then thoughts come about him in troops, as tho' soliciting to be acc^d & he selects—one of his Maxims is that if P. does not come naturally, it had better not come at all.[2] the moment he feels any dearth he discontinues writing & waits for a happier moment. <He writes on> he is generally more troubled by a redundancy <of images> than by a poverty of images, & he culls what appears to him at the time the best.—He never corrects, unless perhaps a word here or there <in writ> sh^d occur<s> to him as preferable to an expression he has already used— He is impatient of correcting, & says he would rather burn the piece in question & write ano^r or something else— "My judgment, (he says,) is as active while I am actually writing as my imagin^n In fact all my faculties are strongly excited,

---

[1] A fragment, in which not all the cancelations can be read. The reference to "p 64" is to one of Woodhouse's books of transcripts where he copied "When I have fears that I may cease to be." Lines 7 and 8 there run:

    And feel that I may never live to trace
    Their shadows with the magic hand of chance.

Lowell, not understanding "p 64," thinks, perhaps wrongly, it "ridiculous to suppose" that "Keats ever said the things here attributed to him, as they stand."

[2] Woodhouse wrote "selects—*" and then added the sentence "*one of . . . at all" at the top of the page.

& in their full <state vigour> play— And shall I afterwards, when my imagination is idle, & the heat in which I wrote, has <cooled, sit> gone off, sit down coldly to criticise when in Poss^{on} of only one faculty, what I have written, when almost inspired."—This fact explains the reason of the Perfectness, fullness, richness & completion of <whatever> most that comes from him— He has <not often> said, that he has often not been aware of the beauty of some <of his writings> thought or exprⁿ until after he has composed [3] & written it down— It has then struck <it> him with <wonder & he has sca> as-tonishm^t—& seemed <like> rather the prodⁿ of another person than his own— He has wondered how he came to hit upon it. This was the case with the descrⁿ of Apollo in the 3 b. of Hypⁿ white melodious throat.[4]—Perhaps every one in the habit of writ^g <Poetry> verse or prose, may have <felt> had a somewhat similar feeling, that of the extreme appositeness & happiness (the curiosa felicitas [5]) of <some> an idea, of the <be> excellence of wh: he was unaware until he <had written it down> & came to read it over. It seems scarcely his own; & he feels that he c^d never imitate or hit upon it again: & he cannot conceive how it came to him— Such <was> Keats [6] s^d was his Sensation of astonishm^t & pleasure when he had prod^d the lines "His white melod^s &c— It seemed to come by chance or magic—to be as it were something given to him.—

<This was> It is probable that this was what he meant, & has <so happil> expressed in these lines so happily that they are an illustration of the very thing itself

[3] Woodhouse apparently wrote first: "until after he had composed them, when they have struck his eye"; then he began to revise the second clause, "& he has seen"; then he produced the version above.

[4] These three words from *Hyperion*, III.81, are written in shorthand.

[5] Petronius Arbiter, *Satyricon*, 118.

[6] *Originally* Keats's.

when I see upon the Nights starred face
Huge Cloudy Symbols of a high romance
And think that I may never live to trace
Their <magic> shadows with the <happy> magic
    hand of chance.[7]

<Did he> Had he in fact any <design> ideas of <making a>
romances suggested by the constellat[ns] or the lore connected
with them; of wh, to use his own expression
    "Some fainter gleamings over his fancy shot." [8]

*　　*　　*

➳➳➳ 60 ⬿⬿⬿

JOHN AITKEN [1] TO JOHN KEATS

17 August 1820

Lowell, II, 453, refers to the letter and quotes five words.

East Lothian Bank
Dunbar 17th Augt 1820

Sir

One, so enthusiastically fond as you are, of the early
poets, and poetry of your country, can pardon enthusiasm in
another, whether it be directed to those old worthies, who have
made us what we are,—or towards our bright con[s]tellation
of contemporary talent, which shall never put to shame immortal verse.—If I should express what I feel, of the rank which
I consider you to hold among your illustrious compeers, I

---

[7] "When I have fears," lines 5-8.
[8] "I stood tip-toe," line 178.
[1] A bank clerk (1795–1833), who later edited various editions of *The Cabinet*
(as 1825, 1828) and of *Constable's Miscellany* (1820–1834), and helped to
found the *Edinburgh Literary Journal*.

might perhaps be suspected of an intention to flatter, than which, nothing is more distant from my nature.—It is enough for me to testify my most earnest disapprobation, of the treatment you have experienced, and to express my unfeigned sorrow, that, a Scotch publication should have borne away the bell, in such manifest baseness of conduct.[2]—I am a Scotsman, and proud of my [3] country—and proud, too, of many parts of that magazine, which has always been the vehicle of much unjustifiable abuse, but some that are {c}onnected with it, know well, how much, by every means in my power, I have endeavoured to soften its illiberality—to make it more worthy of them and more useful to the world.—But these things are not the main object of this letter.—My design in writing you is to bear evidence of my real interest for your welfare, which I learn by [the] last Indicator,[4] is not what your friends would wish it to be.—I have watched over your dawning genius as warmly as if you had been my brother, and I hailed the appearance of your late interesting publication, with as much real gladness, as if it had freed me from all the sorrows which bad luck has hung about me.—I guessed that all was not well with you—and that I heard the parting beauty of the Swan's adieus in your numbers; but like every thing which gives us pain, I hoped that I was mistaken.—Would that it were in my power to yield you one real feeling of pleasure,—that aught within the reach of my influence could be welcome to you,—that I were a brother or a bosom friend to you, that by participation, any of your cares might be lessened.—But, alas, you will think that I am placed in a cold inhospitable clime where kind-hearts, and sunshine and loveliness and sympathy are equally rare— and how can I assure you that such is not the case. I may at-

---

[2] Lockhart in *Blackwood's Edinburgh Magazine,* III (1818), 519-524.
[3] *Written* of my of my.
[4] August 2 and 9, I, 337-352 (Hunt's review of the 1820 volume).

131

tempt to describe all the enjoyment which surrou{nd}s me, with partial language and which probably might have the effect of bringing you here—but how much would it mortify me if I had disappointed you.—But still I must endeavour to bring you to Scotland—although a land which you cannot love.—I must tell you that I am a young man; and [5] that a younger, amiable sister, is my housekeeper; and that within these islands there is not a spot better calculated to renovate a weakened frame.— Will you be persuaded to make the experiment?—I will meet you with open arms and with a kinder heart than beats between us; and if soothing affection, real sterling, Scottish kindness, and hospitality, can have any effect on your state of health you shall soon return happier and better if anything can make you so.—Nor shall your studies be interrupted.—My Library is select and extensive, and I can command numbers of others.—I have upwards of [a] thousand volumes—amon{g} which are the best productions of your cotemporaries—and many choice morceaux of the days that are gone.—Need I say more?—but more I cannot say than this that there is nothing selfish in my request.— It is prompted as much by the amiable qualities of your heart, which are so abundantly apparent in your productions as by the e{min}ence which you have attained—and may yet attain by your talents. In [6] short I love you—(as you <will> must of necessity do me)—for yourself alone.—I may add that if you wish it you can be unknown to any one, as an author—and my house is large enough to afford you any accommodation.—You can live as a hermit when you wish it—and something very different when your inclination desires it.—

Between London & Leith, there is now, p[r] the Smacks, such princely convenience, that you will feel yourself perfectly at home in one of them.—The expense is but triffling—and the

[5] *Written* and and.
[6] Slightly indented, perhaps for a new paragraph.

rapidity of their sailing is such that within three or four days after your leaving London you may count on feeling my warm shake of the hand in Dunbar.—There is the Mail too, and another excellent Coach, but during this excellent weather, by sea is by far the pleasantest.—If, by any of the Land conveyances, you pass through our ancient Town—and you will find me on the watch, as impatient to meet with you as if you were a young Lady.—I trust you will write me, and that your letter shall not, at least, state decisively that you will *not* come; as I have almost persuaded myself that you will in earnest visit me.—And now I am forced to conclude; assuring you that with real truth and sincerity I am

{Y}our real welwisher   J. Aitken

⇒⇒ 61 ⇐⇐

JOHN TAYLOR TO J. A. HESSEY [1]

31 August 1820

Morgan MS. Most of this letter (but none of the canceled words) was printed in *TLS*, April 16, 1914, p. 182 (by Colvin), by Colvin, pp. 475-477, and by Lowell, II, 449-451.[2]

London 31 August 1820

My dear Hessey,

I have had this Day a Call from Mr Blackwood We shook Hands & went into the Back Shop. After asking him what was new at Edinburgh, and talking about Clare, the *Magazine,*[3]

[1] A memorandum, or first draft, which was not mailed. A few of the canceled words cannot be read. For a briefer account of the conversation see Taylor's letter to his father, in Blunden, pp. 77f. See I, 42, for Bailey's similar remarks to Blackwood.

[2] Both *TLS* (*C*) and Lowell (*L*) are extremely inaccurate and non-literal. The chief verbal variants of each are listed in footnotes.

[3] *Blackwood's.*

Baldwin's,[4] Peter Corcoran,[5] & a few other Subjects, I observed
that we had published another Volume of Keats's Poems on
which his Editors would have another opportunity of <being
severe in their Remarks attacking the Author> being witty
at his Expense.—He said they were disposed to speak favorably
of M^r K this Time—and he expected that the article would
have appeared in this Month's Mag. "But can they be so in-
                <Can they now>
consistent? <as to say any thing in favor of the man they have so
<much abused>
strongly attacked?> It is <Ah [?] its> There is no Inconsistency
<to> in praising him if they think he deserves it— <I don't
know what you call it, but here is> After what has been said
<of his> of his Talents I should think it very inconsistent
<after what they have said against him to speak well of the
Man whom they had so much abused>.—Certainly they found
Fault with his former Poems, but that was because they thought
they deserved it— But why did they attack him personally?—
They did not do so.—<What> No? did not they speak of him
in ridicule as Johnny Keats, describe his <Dress> Appearance
while addressing <as they suppose> a Sonnet [6] Ailsa Crag,
and compare him as a Friesland [7] Hen to Shelley as a Bird of
Paradise; [8] <and> besides what can you say to that coldblooded

---

[4] Baldwin's *London Magazine. C has* Baldwin.

[5] See I, 116f.

[6] *C, L supply* to.

[7] *C* [?].

[8] In its December, 1819, issue *Blackwood's* (VI, 239) ridicules "Mister John
Keates standing on the sea-shore at Dunbar, without a neckcloth, accord-
ing to the custom of Cockaigne, and cross-questioning the Craig of Ailsa!"
It also remarks (p. 240) that "A bird of paradise and a Friezeland fowl
would not look more absurdly, on the same perch" than Shelley and
"Johnny Keates" in company.

Passage [9] <that> where [10] they say they will take Care he shall never get 50£ again for a Vol. of his Poems—what had he done to cause such Attacks as these?—Oh it was all a Joke, the writer meant nothing more than to be witty. He certainly thought there was much Affectation in his Poetry, and he expressed his Opinion only— It was done in the fair Spirit of Criticism.— It was done In the Spirit of <this [?]> the Devil, M[r] Blackwood So <because when> if a young Man is guilty of Affectation while he is walking the Streets, it is fair in another Person because he dislikes it to come and knock him down— No, says B. but a Poet challenge{s} public Opinion—<but> by printing his Book; but I suppose you would have them not criticized at all?— <I would not have them ill used merely because they fail in giving so but I asked why should they be> I certainly think they are punished enough by <the> Neglect, & by the Failure of their Hopes and to me it seems very cruel to abuse a Man merely because he cannot give us as much Pleasure as <they desire> he wishes. <to give. And besides but it was safer, I grant, you fall upon And is it esteemed— Why is it magnanimous on the other Side of the Tweed to fall upon a Man and beat> But you go even beyond this—[11] you strike a Man when he is down— <You let the> He gets a violent Blow from the Quarterly <is given first> & then you begin. I beg your Pardon says B. we were the first.—<But if you began first,> I think not but if you were the first you continued it after <wards>, for <I am sure that> that truly diabolical Threat about the 50£ <was published> appeared after the <Quarterly; and is it esteemed magnanimous beyond the Tweed M[r] B. to shew Valour in this Way?> critique in the Quarterly.—

[9] In Lockhart's fourth article on the Cockney School, August, 1818 (III, 524).
[10] *C* when.
[11] *C* beyond his [——?]; *L* beyond that.

You mistake that altogether s^d B. the writer does not like the cockney School, & so he went on joking M^r K about it.—Mr Blackwood,[12] Why should not the Manners of Gentlemen continue to regulate their Conduct <towards one another> when they are writing of each other as <well as> much as when they are in Conversation.—No man <dare> would insult Mr Keats in this Manner in his Company, and what is the Difference <which they there [13] is in the Cases,> between writing & speaking of a person [14] except that the written Attack is the more base from being made anonymously & therefore at no personal Risk.—I feel Regard for Mr Keats as a Man of real Genius a Gentleman, nay more as [15] one of *the gentlest of human Beings.* He does not resent these Things himself, he merely says of his Opponents "They don't know me." Now this Mildness makes those who are [16] his Friends feel <for him> the more warmly [17] <the Insults which are offered him at> when they see him <ill attacked> ill used. But this Feeling is not confined to them. I am happy to say that the public Interest is awakened to a Sense [18] of the Injustice which has been done him, and that the Attempts to ruin him will have in the End a contrary Effect.————Here I turned the Conversation to another Subject by asking B if he had read the Abbot,[19] and in about 10 Minutes more he made his Exit with a formal Bow & a good Morning—

The above is the Substance and as nearly as possible they are [20] the Words I made use of— His Replies were a little more

12 *C omits* Mr Blackwood.

13 Doubtful reading.

14 *L* poem.

15 *C omits.*

16 *C substitutes* [?] *for* makes those who are.

17 *C* severely.

18 So *C,* but the reading is not certain. It may be, as in *L,* Scorn.

19 Scott's novel, just published.

20 *C omits* they are.

copious than I have stated, but to the same Effect. I have written this Conversation down on the Day it took place because I
suspect some Allusion may hereafter be made to it in the Mag.[21]
and I fully expect that whatever Books we publish will be reviewed [22] with Reference to the Feeling it is calculated to excite
in the Bosoms of these <freebooting> Mosstroopers [23]

   In the [*word illegible*] [24] Conversation which preceded
our Discourse [25] on Keats I spoke most highly of the Review of
P Corcoran,[26] & as far as was necessary or just complimented
other articles [27] in the Mag.— B. said he knew Reynolds wrote
P C.—but I did not confirm it.—He also asked who wrote the
Lucubrations of a Gentm who had left his lodgings,[28]—evidently poaching about for facts for the *Mag*— But [29] I am
pretty [30] sure he <means> will never call on me again

*   *   *

[21] Keats, at any rate, was savagely attacked again in September, 1820, and
December, 1821 (VII, 665, 679; X, 696f., 699). Taylor, too, in August, 1824
(XVI, 179-183), was held up to scorn for his "cowardly spirit," "direct falsehood," "mean venom," "snivelling poltroonery" in connection with a review of Sir Walter Scott. When he replied in the *London Magazine*, October (X, 335f.), *Blackwood's* returned to the attack in its October number
(XVI, 438f.).
[22] *L* received.
[23] *C* freebooting [. . . ?].
[24] *C* first [?].
[25] *C* discussion.
[26] See I, 116.
[27] *C* artists.
[28] Lord John Russell's *Essays and Sketches of Life and Character. By a
Gentleman Who Has Left His Lodgings* (Longman, 1820), supposedly edited
by his unpaid landlord, Joseph Skillett (see Spencer Walpole, *The Life of
Lord John Russell*, I [1889], 94-96). It was announced as lately published
in the *London Magazine*, July, 1820 (II, 111). *Blackwood's* reviewed it in
August (VII, 528-534) with high praise, calling the anonymous author
"both a gentleman and a scholar."
[29] *C* omits He also . . . the *Mag*— But.
[30] *L* perfectly.

137

→≫ 62 ≪←

JOHN TAYLOR TO JOHN KEATS [1]

11 September 1820

Morgan MS. Printed by Lowell, II, 457f.

Fleet Street 11 Sept 1820

My dear Keats,

Before you go out of the Country I am desirous of explaining to you on what Terms we conceive ourselves to be acting as your Publishers.—In few Words we may state it thus.—Whatever we print we run the Risk of, and if it does not answer, the Loss is ours: whatever succeeds we deem the Profit wholly yours; but if one Work fails and leaves us a Loss which the Profit on another would make up, we should consider ourselves entitled to be reimbursed that Loss out of those Profits.—If all, or the Majority, do not repay the Expenses, then the Loss is wholly ours.—On these Terms we are willing to go on publishing if you choose to write; we shall charge no Commission for our Trouble, meaning to derive no Advantage; and we will render an Account of the Sales whenever you please, to shew you in what State your Finances are—

I have put it in this Light to make it plainer; but if we take the Matter in another point of View it will amount to the same Thing: consider then the Endymion ours, for the Copyright of which we gave 100£; and say that what we have already advanced to you in Cash since that Time, viz   £ is the Price of the Copyright of Lamia: now if we get anything beyond these Sums by either of the Books, so as to have in our Hands on the whole more than we have given you, we will transmit that Surplus to you; and so on with every future work.

[1] Taylor later endorsed this letter "Not sent."

I make this explicit Statement of what you would other-wise have discovered in due Time, to convince you that we have no selfish Ends to answer in encouraging you to write & publish; and also that you may correctly estimate the Means we have in our Hands of supplying you with Money while you are abroad.—At present we are out of pocket 135£ on Endymion, but that may be reduced by future sales if your other Works succeed— Lamia has not yet repaid the Expenses, there is there-fore the Advance on that to be added, making together with the Books mentioned in the inclosed Bill   £.—You shall have 50£ more to take you to Italy, and from thence you must draw for what you want, but I think you will not wish us to pay those Bills without placing some Money in our Hands for that pur-pose. If I were rich enough to do without the whole Sum that you might want I would gladly give it you, but if I wanted it I know nobody who would let me have it.—

You will do well to publish again as soon as you have the power to produce anything, and the Success you may rely upon it will in every Instance increase. I hope yet to see you as rich and as renowned as you deserve to be.—Meantime wishing you a pleasant Voyage, perfect Health, and all Happiness, I remain,
My dear Keats
Your faithful Friend
John Taylor

139

»» 63 ««

WILLIAM HASLAM TO JOHN TAYLOR

13 September 1820 [1]

Address: Taylor Esqre/ 93 Fleet Street— Printed in the Hampstead Keats, VI, lxxiv.

34 Leadenhall Street
Wednesday Morn^r—

Mr William Haslam presents his respectful Compts to Mr Taylor & begs by the bearer to be informed the name of the Vessel & of the Agents to the Vessel in which Mr Keats' Passage is taken.—

Mr Taylor will be happy to hear that the motive for this enquiry is to secure a second passage *for* Keats' Friend Severn.—

H—— slept at Hpstead last night Keats seems comfortable & well at ease.

---

[1] Keats wrote to Haslam on August 23 (the letter is printed by Hewlett, p. 425), telling of his impending trip to Italy and of asking Brown to accompany him. Brown did not reply. The present letter—delivered on Wednesday, September 13, by a special messenger who waited for Taylor's reply (see the next letter)—shows how narrowly Keats escaped the ill fortune of a solitary trip to Italy. Evidently Haslam talked to Keats "last night," September 12, about Severn, and then on the next morning secured the latter's consent to the voyage. Since the *Maria Crowther* sailed on Sunday, September 17, the fact emerges that Severn had at least five days in which to prepare for his journey—a fact unknown to Sharp, pp. 48f., Lowell, II, 460, and Colvin, pp. 487f. Hewlett, pp. 389f., remarks that Severn's "three days [of preparation] are generally accepted."

⋙ 64 ⋘

JOHN TAYLOR TO WILLIAM HASLAM [1]

13 September 1820 [2]

Address: Wᵐ Haslam Esqʳ/ 34 Leadenhall Sᵗ.

Fleet Street Wednesday

noon—

Dear Sir,

Your Letter has given me the greatest Pleasure, and to Keats it is most cheering. He has come here today to be ready to go by the Vessel, but we have just now learnt that it does not sail till Sunday Morning.—The Vessel is the Maria Crowther [3] lying off the Tower,—the Master, Thomas Walsh—Messrs. R. & H. Richardson are the Agents, Nº 3. Howford Buildings—

It will give me much Pleasure to see you here whenever you can make it convenient.—We dine at 5 today, & shall be happy to have your Company.

I am

Dear Sir

Very truly yours

John Taylor

[1] A reply by Haslam's messenger to the preceding letter.

[2] Lowell, II, 46of., says, "we must resign ourselves to ignorance of the day on which Keats left Wentworth Place" to stay "a day or two" in "Taylor's house, 91 New Bond Street" until the *Maria Crowther* sailed on Sunday, September 17. She finds no evidence to support Colvin, p. 488, who had said that Keats went to "Taylor in Fleet Street . . . on Wednesday September 13ᵗʰ." Colvin, of course, had seen the present letter. See I, cxxxix n. Fanny Brawne also vouches (Edgcumbe, pp. 4, 9n.) for Keats's leaving Wentworth Place on September 13.

[3] H. C. Shelley, *Literary By-Paths* (1906), pp. 261f., describes it as a "Brigantine rig," of 127 tons register, built in 1810, ordinarily on the Cardiff-Liverpool run, and finally wrecked near the Isle of Man on November 7, 1837. A colored drawing of the ship and another of "Moonlight at Sea" from its deck, both by Severn, were first published in the *John Keats Memorial Volume* (1921), facing p. 168.

⇒⇒ 65 ⇐⇐

JOHN KEATS: ASSIGNMENT OF COPYRIGHT [1]

16 September 1820

This Indenture made the sixteenth day of September in the year of our Lord One thousand Eight hundred and twenty—— **Between** *John Keats* of Hampstead in the County of Middlesex Esquire of the one part and *John Taylor* and *James Augustus Hessey* of Fleet Street in the City of London Booksellers and Copartners of the other part **Witnesseth** that for and in Consideration of the Sum of One hundred pounds of lawful Money of Great Britain to the said John Keats in hand well and truly paid by the said John Taylor and James Augustus Hessey before the Sealing and delivery of these presents (the receipt whereof he the said John Keats doth hereby acknowledge and of and from the same and Every part thereof acquit release and for ever discharge the said John Taylor and James Augustus Hessey and each of them and their respective Executors adm͞ors and assigns) He the said John Keats *Hath* Granted Bargained Sold assigned transferred and set over And by these presents *Doth* Grant Bargain Sell assign transfer transfer and set over unto the said John Taylor and James Augustus Hessey their Executors Administrators and assigns **All that** the Copy and Copyright of in and to and the sole liberty Licence

---

[1] Written apparently by a professional scribe who puts some words in imitation of italic and others of gothic (here printed as bold-face) type. He endorsed it on the back fold "16 Sep͏ʳ 1820./ John Keats Esqʳ/ to/ Messʳˢ Taylor & Hessey./ Assignment." Years later, beneath the foregoing endorsement, George William Childs (1829–1894), American publisher and philanthropist, wrote "Presented to/ Lord Houghton/ by his friend/ Geo. W. Childs/ Philadelphia U. S. A./ Nov. 6, 1875." Lowell, who had not seen this assignment, gives (II, 456f.) a confused account of Taylor and Hessey's financial dealings with Keats.

power and Authority of printing and publishing a certain literary Work or production already printed and published whereof the said John Keats is the Author and which is Entitled "Endymion a Poetic Romance by John Keats" or by whatsoever other name or Title the same Work or production is or hath been or shall be called known or designated *And Also* All and Singular the Manuscript and printed Copies thereof *And Also* all the Estate right title interest property benefit Claim and demand whatsoever present and contingent of him the said John Keats in to or out of the said Work production and other the premises hereby assigned or intended so to be And in particular all such Contingent Interest and Benefit as he the said John Keats is or shall be or otherwise might be entitled to under any Act or Acts of parliament in the Event of his being alive at the Expiration of Twenty Eight years from the time of the first publication of the said Work **To have hold** receive percieve take and enjoy the said Copyright of and in the said Work or production and all other the premises hereby assigned or intended so to be with their appurtenances unto and by them the said John Taylor and James Augustus Hessey their Executors admōrs and assigns absolutely to and for their own use and Benefit **And** the said John Keats doth hereby for himself his heirs Executors and Administrators Covenant and agree to and with the said John Taylor and James Augustus Hessey their Executors Administrators and assigns that he the said John Keats hath in himself good right full power and lawful and absolute authority to assign and set over the said Copyright and other the assigned premises unto the said John Taylor and James Augustus Hessey their Executors Admōrs and assigns in manner aforesaid and according to the true intent and meaning of these presents *And Also* that he the said John Keats his Executors and Admōrs and all persons claiming under him or them shall and will at all times hereafter at the request Costs

→» 66 «←

RICHARD WOODHOUSE TO JOHN KEATS˙

16 September 1820

Printed in *Letters,* p. 518, and by Lowell, II, 462.

My dear Keats,

Upon subjects like those in this letter, it is to me always more pleasant to write than to speak.—It gave me much pleasure to learn from Taylor that you are leaving us tolerably easy as to money matters:—the more so, as, from particular circumstances, my own finances have had, and for the next six months or so will have, considerable drains upon them; which would <render> make it not very convenient to me <to> *just now* to render you assistance in that way.—But when I am a little recruited, which will I hope be about the time I have above mentioned, <and before> if you should have any wants of that nature, it would give me the greatest satisfaction to answer your draft; & you would of course, to prevent any disappointments, give me as much previous notice as you could.—I am sure you would not needlessly call upon me:—and, with that conviction, I should be despicable in my own eyes, if, with the means, I wanted the will to assist you.—What is the value of Pelf after the supply of one's own wants?—Of none to me. And there is no one who would be more welcome than yourself to share my little Superfluities.—[1]

God bless you!—Take care of yourself,—if it be only for your friends' sake. Above all, keep your mind at ease. There are many who take more than a brotherly Interest in your welfare— There is certainly

[1] See I, 84.

145

————"one, whose hand will never scant
From his poor store of fruits all *thou* canst want."—[2]
And he is,
Yours very sincerely
& affectionately,
Rich[d] Woodhouse.
Kings Bench Walk Temple— Saty. Night. 16 Sep[r] 1820.—

—»» 67 ««‹-

JOSEPH SEVERN TO WILLIAM HASLAM [1]
19 September 1820

Tuesday Mor[g]
½ past 8

My dear Haslam

We are going on well—capitally well so far— Keats is
seeming and looking better—yesterday he was not so well—but
I think today he looks promising— I have the best possible
hopes.—

We are going on most delightfully—the second Lady [2] has
joined us—and it is a most singular coincidence—that she is
laboring under the very same complaint as Keats—the same
symtoms—and the same manner of cure One very good hope
is—we find sick people insisting and quarelling about being
worse than each other—nothing would make my poor Mother

[2] This is the concluding couplet of a sonnet "P. Fenbank," of Teignmouth,
sent Keats in November, 1818, along with a £25 note. Forman (in *Letters*, p.
258n.) agrees with Edmund Blunden that "Fenbank" was probably Woodhouse. That idea is, I think, negatived by Woodhouse's letter to Taylor,
November, 1818 (see I, 66).
[1] In No. 71 Haslam forwards this letter, which may not be incomplete, for
Taylor and Hessey to read.
[2] Miss Cotterell; see I, 165.

angry but for a sick person to insist on being worse than herself
in any denomination of sickness—now here we are better of—for
the Lady who is a very sweet girl about 18 but quite a martyr
to the complaint—she insists on [being] better than Keats—and
Keats feels she is certain[ly] worse than himself—here I must
stop for I begin to break down—we are now 13 miles from ³
Margate I am pumping away all the circumbendibusses ⁴ of my
craw are in motion my breakfast—is a matter just come to light
—from the Severn it has gone to some salmon—<for> Keats
I think looks very happy—for myself I would not change with
any one—the Ladies are the quintessence of good nature and
prettiness—I don't know which I like best this is written on the
side of the Ship

*   *   *

→»» 68 «««

TAYLOR AND HESSEY TO —— BROWN ¹

19 September 1820

Morgan MS. Printed by Lowell, II, 459.

Fleet Street
19 Sept 1820

<Gent> Sir

In Compliance with the Wish you expressed on Saturday
last we write to <assure you> inform you that we will <ac-

³ Above this word *Severn wrote* to.

⁴ Almost illegible word, meaning "twists" or "turns," for which *NED*
gives examples from 1681 to 1867.

¹ In Taylor's hand. A draft of the letter that was actually sent. Brown is not
listed as a banker in the *Post Office London Directory* for 1820 or the *Royal
Kalendar* for 1820. Possibly he was associated with the Poultry bankers Frys
and Chapman or the 25 Bucklersbury firm of Browne, Langhorne, and
Brailsford.

cept> honor the Bills <from> of Mr John Keats of Naples to the Amount of One Hundred and fifty Pounds; & you will much oblige us by <requesting> allowing & directing that those Bills should be negociated through the Medium of your House at Naples— Mr Keats sailed on Sunday last in the Maria Crowther—

We are [sin^{ly} y^{rs} [2]]

T & H

<Messrs> Brown Esqr Poultry

⇥≫ 69 ≪⇤

JOSEPH SEVERN TO WILLIAM HASLAM

21 September 1820

Address: Mr William Haslam/ 34 Leadenhall Street/ London. *Postmarks (part illegible):* NEW ROMNEY 92; D 25 SE 25. First printed in *TLS* (by Colvin), April 16, 1914, pp. 181f. Extracts given by Colvin, pp. 489-491.[1]

Dungee Ness—near the Down's

on Deck—Thursday [2] Mor^g

20th Sept^r

1820

My dear Haslam

It will be best to make a kind of journal in my letters to you—making a Quartett—for we are "hail fellow well met" [3]—

[2] Illegible.

[1] Colvin's reprints (*C*) are far indeed from literal. A transcript of the letter made by Hessey (*H*) is also in the Harvard collection. It does not follow Severn's spelling and punctuation exactly. Lowell, II, 465-470 (*L*), prints non-literal extracts, based, she says, on *TLS* (*C*) and *H*. In the footnotes I list the verbal variants of *H* and some of those of *C* and, occasionally, *L*. Words and figures written by Severn in the margin are printed between daggers.

[2] Thursday was September 21.

[3] Apperson, *English Proverbs* (1929), p. 277, gives examples dating from 1519.

148

the Ladies seem to wish communication to be made in London
and by including them in this—that object will be gained—
respecting Mʳˢ Pidgeon you will call on Mʳ Taylor—the half ☽
Gracechurch ⁴ Sᵗ—and for Miss Cotterell—apply to her father N°
9 Richmond Terrace Walworth————

† Sunday 17 Septʳ 1820 †
Keats thought I had neglected you— "Severn you should see
your friends ⁵ to the Ship-side"— I had seen my brother ⁶ off in
the Morᵍ and it was not a little painfull to me—at the same time
painfull to no purpose.—We were soon reconciled to every
thing about ⁶ᵃ from the Captain down to his Cat—is it not most
delightful that the less we have the less we want—this little
Cabin with 6 beds and at first sight every inconvenience—in
one hour was more endeared to us—and to our every purpose—
than the most stately Palace— Keats seem'd happy—seem'd to
have got at the thing he wanted he cracked his jokes at tea and
was quite the "special fellow" of olden time ⁷—the kind Mʳˢ
Pidgeon our Lady passenger did the honors of the tea table with
the most unaffected good nature—and we repaid her—most gallantly by falling into a ⁸ sound sleep—and serenading her with

---

⁴ *C reads* Half Moon Gracechurch.

⁵ According to a letter Taylor wrote to Fanny Keats (Adami, pp. 97f., 233,
282, and Hewlett, p. 392), the friends were Taylor himself, Haslam, and
Woodhouse (Blunden, p. 79, says that Taylor also took along his apprentice, William Smith Williams), who sailed with Keats to Gravesend, leaving
the ship at 4 P.M. Students of Keats, then, need to be warned that when in
his very last letter of November 30, 1820 (*Letters*, p. 527), Keats is represented as asking Brown to "tell Haslam I should not have left London without taking leave of him, but from being so low in body and mind," actually
the name "Haslam" was erroneously inserted by Milnes. Brown himself (see
II, 86) in copying the letter gave no name but merely four x's.

⁶ Tom Severn.

⁶ᵃ *H* about us.

⁷ *C* times.

⁸ Severn (but not *H* or *C*) *repeats* into a.

a snoring duett—for I have the vanity to think that Keats and myself would continue our harmony even in sleep— I awoke several times with the oddest notions—the first time in a Shoe makers shop—the next down in [a] [9] wine cellar pretty well half seas over—but we came [9a] to the last snore of our duett—rubbed our eyes and said—"we'll go to bed"—we slep[t] [10] most soundly— M[rs] P——— has [11] a side scene to retire to—

† 18 Sep[tr] Monday †
I arose soon and looked at Keats—he felt faint in his voice but in other respects well—our fair passenger came about 8—quite well{. We} [12] took breakfast and I can assure you enjoyd it— our Captain is a good fellow—if he makes us happy his object is gain'd— Keats took his breakfast well—<and has> I had proposed to go shore to [13] Gravesend—he thought this [14] a good opportunity to have some things from the Chymists [15]—which I got him—with ½ hundred Apples and 2 Dozen Biscuits—&c &c—the Captain and [16] was trying to buy a Goat for him—but was not successful—we all returned in a real full boat—to dinner —Keats was full of his waggery—looked well—ate well—and was well—at six came down my pasport—we were not surprised—for we made sure of it since our oak friend Haslam had the getting of it. The other Lady passenger arrived soon after a Miss Cotterell—very lady like—but a sad martyr to her illness—which is to a jot the same as Keats [17]—I told a fib just before—nothing

[9] No brackets in *H* and *C.*
[9a] *H* awoke.
[10] No brackets in *H* and *C.*
[11] *H* had.
[12] No brackets in *H* and *C.*
[13] *H* aShore at.
[14] *H* that.
[15] Including laudanum (see I, 203). *H reads* Chemists.
[16] *H omits. C reads* and the Captain.
[17] *H omits* which is . . . as Keats.

new with me) the pasport coming had unloosed all my prattle
—and in a short time <with> Keats backing me with his
golden jokes in support of my tinsel—† began to sail [18] † we
reco{verd} [19] Miss Cotterell—to laugh and be herself—my wit
would have dropt in a minute—but for Keats plying me—but
I was done up for all that—leaving him sole Master—but I
struck up again in my own language or Keats would have born
the Lady of in triumph—I began drawing my picture for my
dear Sister Maria—having received great supply in my cheek [20]
from the Captains beefs & tongues [21] This is it done to the
life [22]—fancy me with two things not knowing which to prefer—my eyes devouring both—after this I drew a Moonlight
scene from the Sea which took until 12 (middle watch)
<after> [23] "the house had gone to rest"— Keats was in a [24]
sound sleep———

† 19ᵗʰ Septr Tuesday off Dover Castle &c †
I arose at day break to see the glorious—eastern gate [25]—
Keats slept till 7— Miss C—— was rather ill this Morᵍ I prevailed on her to walk the deck with me at ½ past 6—she recovered much— Keats was still better this Morᵍ and Mʳˢ Pidgeon
looked and was the picture of health—but poor me! I began to
feel a waltzing on my stomach at breakfast when I wrote the
note [26] to you I was going it most soundly— Miss Cotterell

18 *C* omits.
19 *H* recovered, *C, L* made.
20 *H* cheeks.
21 *H, C* beef and tongue.
22 In the margin *H* writes "portrait," but the small piece of paper on which
it was drawn has been torn off.
23 Not deleted by *H.*
24 *C omits* a.
25 Compare *A Midsummer-Night's Dream,* III.ii.391, "The eastern gate,
all fiery-red," and *Paradise Lost,* IV.542, "the eastern gate of Paradise."
26 No. 67, preceding.

followed me—then Keats who did it in the most gentlemanly
manner—and then the saucy Mrs Pidgeon who had been laughing at us—four faces bequeathing to the mighty deep their
breakfasts—here I must change to a Minor Key— Miss C
fainted—we soon recoverd her— I was very ill—nothing but
laying [27] down would do for me— Keats ascended his bed—from
which he dictated surgically [28]—like Esculapius of old in baso-
relievo—through·him Miss C was recoverd—we had a cup of tea
each and no more went to bed and slept until it was time to
go to bed—we could [28a] not get up again—and slept in our cloths
all night— Keats the King—not even looking pale—————

† 19 Septr Wedsd [29]—off Brighton †
Beautiful Mor^g—we all breakfasted on deck and recovered
as we [30] were could enjoy it—about 10 Keats said a storm was
hatching—he was right—the rain cam[e] [31] on and we retired to
our Cabin—it abated and once more we came on deck—at 2
Storm came on furiously—we retired to our beds—the rolling of
the ship was death to us—towards 4 it increased and our situation was alarming—the trunks rolled across the Cabin—the
water poured in from the sky-light and we were tumbled from
one side to the other of our beds—my curiosity was raised to see
the storm—and my anxiety to see Keats for I could only speak
to him when in bed— I got up and fell down on the floor from
my weakness and the rolling of the ship— Keats was very calm—
the ladies were much frightened—and could [32] scarce speak—
when I got up to the deck I was astounded—the waves were in

[27] *H, C* lying.
[28] Severn began to write "professionally," and then wrote "surgically"
over it.
[28a] *H* would.
[29] Wednesday was September 20.
[30] *H omits.*
[31] No brackets in *H* and *C*.
[32] *C* would.

Mountains—and washed [33] the ship—the watry horizon was like a Mountainous Country—but the ship's motion was beautifully to the sea—falling from one wave to the other in a very lovely manner—the sea each time crossing the deck and one side of the ship being level with the water—this when I understood—gave me <great> perfect ease— I communicated below—and it did the same—but when the dusk came the sea began to rush in from the side of our Cabin from an opening in the planks— this make [34] us rather long [35] faced—for it came by pails-full [36]— again I got out—and said to Keats—"here's pretty music for you"—with the greatest calmess [37] he answerd me—[38] only "Water parted from the sea" [39]— I staggered up again and the storm was awfull—the Captain & Mate soon came down—for our things were squashing about in the dark—they struck a light and I succeeded in getting my desk of the ground—with cloth's— books—&c—the Captain finding it could not be stopped—tacked about from our voyage—and the sea ceased to dash against the Cabin for we were sailing against wind and tide—but the horrible agitation continued in the ship lengthways—here were the pumps working—the sailes squalling the confused voices of the sailors—the things rattling about in every direction—and us [40] poor devils pinn'd up in our beds like ghosts by day light—ex-

[33] *C, L* washed, *H* covered. (The word *looks* like "arched'" or "rocked.")
[34] *H, C* made.
[35] *H* wry.
[36] *H* pail fulls. *C, L* pail-fulls.
[37] *H, C, L* calmness.
[38] *H* me—"only; *C, L* me only by.
[39] Colvin, p. 490, explains: "A long-popular song from [T. A.] Arne's opera *Artaxerxes*" (1762). See Sharp, p. 72, for Haslam's comment on the quotation. Milnes, II, 75, following Severn's notes of October, 1845 (No. 182), has Keats to make this quotation during a "storm in the Bay of Biscay." Keats may have read in the *London Magazine*, June, 1820 (I, 690), a review, by Hazlitt, of a performance of *Artaxerxes*, which declares, "We believe that this is the most beautiful Opera in the world."
[40] *H* we.

cept Keats he was himself all the time—the ladies sufferd the most—but I was out of bed a dozen times to wait on them and tell them there *was* no danger—my sickness made me [get] [41] into bed very soon each time—but Keats this Morning brags of my sailorship—he says could I have kept on my legs in the water cabin— I should have been a standing Miracle— † 20th Sep^{tr} † I caught a sight of the moon about 3 oclock this Morning [42] —and ran down to tell the glad tidings—but the surly rolling of the sea was worse than the storm—the ship trembled to it—and the sea was scarcely calmed by daylight—so that we were kept from 2 oclock yesterday until 6 this Morning without anything—well it has done us good—we are like a Quartett of Fighting Cocks this Mor^g—the Mor^g is serene we now [43] back again some 20 Miles—waiting for a wind—but full of spirits— Keats is without even complaining and Miss Cotterell has a colour in her face—the sea has done his worst upon us— I am better that [44] I have been for years Farewell my dear fellow {Jos}^h Severn —show this to my family with my love to them.[45] When you read this you will excuse the manner— I am quite beside myself —and have written the whole this Morning Thursday on the deck after a sleepless night and with a head full of care—you shall have a better the [46] next time—

To William Haslam

[41] *H* made me into; *C, L* made me get into.
[42] Really September 21.
[43] *H* we were; *C, L* we are now.
[44] *H, C, L* than.
[45] *H* 'em.
[46] *H omits.*

⇒⇒ 70 ⇐⇐

J. H. REYNOLDS TO JOHN TAYLOR

21 September 1820

Address: John Taylor Esq/ 93 Fleet Street/ London. *Postmark:* B 23 SE 23 1820. Morgan MS. Printed in part by Lowell, II, 472f.

Exmouth
21 Sept[r] 1820

My Dear Taylor

I do not know when I have been more gratified at the receipt of a letter than now, for you give me the best of news, full to the brim, that Keats is positively off for a better Lungland.—There is no half-measure information of expected departure or promised amendment,—but smack you come down upon me with the *Ultimatum* Sir John. Your Alphabet commences at Z. Your Letter is in *finals* only. I could find in my heart to discuss the merits of an old wall, which is now stretching along before my eyes in all the stony incorrectness of antiquity,—(and very little of your speculative Ingenuity could wrench it into something Roman)— Or I could go into a slight inquiry, touching & concerning certain derivatives, which should carry us through all your thrice-column'd *tomes,* and all the Volumed Wealth of *Dick Woodhouse;*—if only to shew my sense of your kind & kindly-welcomed letter;—but that I dread the sorrow of your Family,—the decided tone of Hilton's reproof— The austere & chastened remonstrances of that Prelatical Worthy, whose scriptural & saintly visage [1] glooms over the fire place of your little back Oratory:—Indeed Hessey Hilton, Dewint— All would abhor me for touching on a subject which is potent in its mastery over your spirits and in its blanching of

[1] A portrait of Taylor's father: see I, 78.

the cheek. I resolved however to say something of your darling, dreary, torturing pursuit as a grateful return for your recollection of me—and <try> truly I opine that that one page, as incomprehensible & foggy as becomes the subject, is a full <retur> remuneration <for> to *you* for the time you have expended in my service.

Seriously, my dear Taylor, I am very, *very* much pleased at what you tell me,—and the more so, since Keats has departed so comfortably, so cheerfully, so sensibly. I cannot now but hold a hope of his refreshed health, which I confess his residence in England greatly discouraged, particularly as he was haunted by one or two heartless and *demented* people [2] whose opinions and conduct could not but silently influence the bearings of his Thoughts & hopes. Absence from the poor idle Thing of woman-kind, to whom he has so unaccountably attached himself, will not be an ill thing; And who would not be banished from the vain and heartless eternity of Mr Leigh Hunt's indecent discoursings. I quite pity you the three days visits of that feeble man,—not on account of the ill-conditioned power of his tongue (for I could not wish him a more wholesome medicine than your own good sense)—but for the irksome, wearing consciousness of a disgusting presence, than which I know of nothing more dispiriting. I wonder, I must say, at his asking himself to dinner at *your* Table!—But *dining out* is I conceive, the most rational plan of living for him;—and when he asks himself to another's Board, he does wisely to accept the invitation.—Keats then, by this, is at Sea fairly,—with England, and one or two sincere friends behind him,—and with a warm clime before his face! If ever I wished well to man, I wish well to *him!* I should indeed have liked to have seen him off with you,

[2] Possibly Brown and Haydon, as well as Fanny Brawne and Hunt.

Know all Men by these Presents, THAT WE,

John Jeffry & H. Needham

of the County of JEFFERSON, and Commonwealth of Kentucky, are held and firmly bound unto the said Commonwealth, in the full and just sum of FIFTY POUNDS, (equal to one hundred and sixty-six dollars and sixty-six and two-thirds cents,) current money; for the payment whereof, well and truly to be made to the said Commonwealth, we bind ourselves, our heirs, executors and administrators, jointly and severally, firmly by these presents, sealed with our seals, and dated this

day of *Janu* 184 *3*

The Condition of the above Obligation is Such, That, whereas there is a Marriage shortly to be had and solemnized between the above bound *John Jeffry & Georgiana A Keats Widow of Geo. Keats*

for which purpose a License has been this day issued by the Clerk of the County Court of Jefferson County, in the State of Kentucky: Now, therefore, in case there shall be no lawful cause to obstruct the said Marriage, then the above obligation shall be void, otherwise the same shall be and remain in full force and virtue.

TEST:

J. Cartmell Jr.

John Jeffry

H. Needham

[SEAL.]
[SEAL.]

To any Licensed Minister of the Gospel:

You are hereby permitted and authorized to join together, in the honorable estate of Matrimony, *John Jeffry* and *Georgiana A Keats* according to the usages and customs of your Church; the said *Georgiana A being Widow of Geo. Keats dec.*

and the said *John Jeffry* having given bond with security, according to law, in my office, as Clerk of the County Court of Jefferson County, in the State of Kentucky. In witness whereof, I do hereto set my hand, this *5* day of *January* 184 *3*

Curran Pope clk by J. Cartmell Jr.

I, a Minister of the Gospel of the *Unitarian* Church, licensed for the purpose by the County Court of *Jefferson* County, Kentucky, do certify, that I performed the Marriage Ceremony on this day, between the persons named in the above Marriage License, according to the usages and customs of the said Church.

Given under my hand, this *5th* day of *January* 184 *3*

John H. Heywood.

MARRIAGE BOND AND LICENSE OF GEORGIANA WYLIE KEATS
AND JOHN JEFFREY

THE GRAVE OF FRANCES BRAWNE LINDON

but Woodhouse & yourself [3] are a Host of friends in yourselves, and he is not unmindful of you, I warrant me, at this moment!

You scarcely tell me enough, I fancy, of the Brawnes, or whether Keats said anything of *them* before he left. They have been really attentive to him, which we should not forget. Severn will much like the voyage, & greatly pleasure Keats, if I mistake not: Though he is scarcely the resolute, intelligent or cheerful companion which a long voyage and a sickly frame so anxiously call for. I wish *you* yourself could have cast Fleet Street & Dull Care behind you, and have taken a trip with our ailing friend:—But we must not, as Sancho says,[4] look for better bread than's made of corn!

I am passing a quiet, happy, beneficial holyday at Exmouth, by the side of a very pleasant shore,—in the very eye of the wind, and under some of the finest evening skies that Novel-Readers could desire. Our clouds here are very rich and splendid,—and appear to have *left off* business *as* clouds and to have come to the Sea-side to cut a dash. They throw gold about the sky like dirt. At the same time, I should not forget our blues and our emeralds,—which are better than any colours in a Silk Mercer's or a Jeweller's. To the north of our Habitation, the River Exe stretches along in a noble manner,—and at Sunset, the brilliant and glossy lights, broken by the <the> a remarkably wide shore and relieved by old black boats and shattered vessells, are really of the most beautiful & varying kind. Dewint would qualify for a crown of straw, if he were here; and I have more than once wished for his art to fix imperfectly even on paper the fleeting splendours of the richest skies I ever looked

---

[3] Perhaps Taylor did not mention that Haslam (see I, 149n.) had also traveled on the boat to Gravesend.

[4] Peter Motteux's *Don Quixote* (1717), I.i.7. See Apperson's *English Proverbs* (1929), p. 42.

157

upon.—I could be pleased to smear down some of the "cloudy glories" about me on that rough paper, which I have admired in Dewint's portfolios.—Remember me to Hessey—cum Woodhouse. Is the latter flown?   Yours very faithfully

JHReynolds

⇻ 71 ⇷

WILLIAM HASLAM TO TAYLOR AND HESSEY

23 September 1820

Address: Messrs Taylor & Hessey/ 93 Fleet Street.

My dear Sirs

I have the enclosed [1] from Severn this morning—the thing is in itself so small that I have no heart to make extracts so send you the original—an original indeed you'll say.—

I called on Richardson's [2] this morning—& have made enquiry of our Agent at Lloyd's—
my conclusion is that they [3] sailed for Naples either Wednesday night or early on Thursday morning—

Yours my dear Sirs
very respectfully
W Haslam

34 LH.[4] Street
Saturday 23 Sept 1820

[1] No. 67.
[2] See I, 141.
[3] The *Maria Crowther* passengers.
[4] Leadenhall.

⇢⇢ 72 ⇠⇠

CHARLES BROWN TO WILLIAM HASLAM

30 September 1820

Address: To/ Mr Wm Haslam,/ Messrs Frampton & Sons,/ Leadenhall Street/London./ [*In lower left corner:*] Postpaid. *Postmark:* F 2 OC 2 1820.

Chichester. 30th Septr 1820.

Dear Haslam,

Pray direct this letter properly and forward it. If a letter from George [1] to me should come into your hands, I hereby duly & truly authorise you to open it with said hands, as it is possible the contents may be important, and I shall not be in my own house till 21st [2] Oct^r, whither you can forward it at that time.

I'll not trouble you with much chatter,—so present my respects to your wife's picture,[3]—that being all I have seen of her fair face,—& believe me,

Your's truly,
Chas Brown.

1 George Keats.
2 *Apparently* 21th.
3 See I, lxxxvii.

⋙ 73 ⋘

CHARLES BROWN TO JOHN TAYLOR

5 October 1820

Address: To/ Messrs Taylor & Hessey/ N° 93 Fleet Street/ London. *Readdressed:* Mr John Taylor/ Mesd^s Taylor & Hunt/ Leicester. *Postmarks:* OC 5 1820; F 6 OC 6 1820; OC A6 1820. Morgan MS. Printed by Lowell, II, 474f.

Chichester. 5th Septr 1820.[1]

Dear Taylor,

If neither Keats nor Severn has written from Portsmouth, and I believe neither of them has, I have some news gratifying to you & to our friends in London. They landed at Portsmouth after having been tossed about in the Channel for ten days. This was on Thursday 28th. Having a day to spare, they went to Bedhampton, a distance of 7 <days> miles, to visit M^r & Mrs Snook,[2] who were here yesterday afternoon & gave me the following particulars. His health was better than they expected from the accounts they had previously heard, and Severn talked cheeringly of him. On the following morning (Friday) his spirits were excellent. He abuses the Captain,[3] tho' he acknowledges him to be civil & accommodating. He likes one of the Ladies, and has an aversion for the other,[4] whom he ridiculed with all the bustling wit of a man in saucy health. He was so sick of the voyage, that a word might have sent him back to London. Unknown to Severn he put on a blister (on his chest) soon after he went on board, {conv}inced it would relieve him, and it appears he {belie}ves it has relieved him. Still however he is full

---

[1] Misdated: see the postmarks and the next letter.
[2] Mrs. John Snook was C. W. Dilke's sister. See I, lxxxiii, II, 222.
[3] See I, 149f., 167.
[4] Miss Cotterell and Mrs. Pidgeon.

160

of his old apprehensions. He knew I was here (within ten miles)
but did not dare to come, lest the wind should change;—how
strangely unlucky that we should *twice* have been so near a
meeting & yet not met! Had he known where I was at an earlier
hour on Thursday, I think he would have come no!—I am
mistaken,—he could not. I tell you every thing—trifles & all—
that you may form your opinion of him. Neither the boisterous
weather, nor his antipathies, nor his anger, will do him harm;—
on the contrary they will be of service,—they are good physic to
his mind, & will help to purge away his apprehensions. He
wrote to me in Scotland he was confident the indulgence of his
friends injured him,[5] & a letter from me to the same effect
crossed on the road. He sailed from Portsmouth on Friday afternoon, with a fair wind, which has continued ever since. Both
he & Severn said they should not write; I suppose they relied
on my doing so. I send this account to none but yourself, &
leave you to disseminate it as you please. Comp[ts] to M[r] Hessey.
I shall direct this to both of you, lest you should be out of
Town, & have too much postage to pay for my scrawl.

Your's most truly,

Cha[s] Brown.

➛➛ 74 ≪≪

J. A. HESSEY TO JOHN TAYLOR [6]

6 October 1820

Morgan MS.

Oct—6—1820.

D[r] John

I am uncertain where this is likely to find you but I shall
send it to Leicester at a Venture— M[r] Dilke called yesterday &

[5] See *Letters*, p. 493.
[6] Written at the end of the preceding letter.

gave me the same information in substance— I have no news at all here—we are all pretty well—

Yrs truly
J A H

⇶ 75 ⇜

J. A. HESSEY TO WILLIAM HASLAM

6, 21 October 1820

Address: Mr. Haslam/ 34 Leadenhall St. *Postmarks (part illegible)*: 7[?] o'Clock OC.21 1820 NT; T.P Ludgate Hill.

Fleet St. Oct. 6. 1820

Dear Sir

A letter,[1] of which the annexed is a Copy, from Mr Brown reached me this morning— I have forwarded the original to Mr Taylor, & have great pleasure in sending this for your Perusal & for {the} Information of the friends of Keats & Sev{ern.} When you have communicated the Intelligence you will oblige me by returning the letter that I may send it to Mr Woodhouse

Believe me
Yours very truly
J. A. Hessey

Oct. 21ˢᵗ

The above you will see has been written a long time and would have been sent before but I did not know your Number

I shall be glad to see Severns letter [2] again at your convenience

1 Probably No. 73.
2 Probably No. 69.

→» 76 «←

JOSEPH SEVERN TO WILLIAM HASLAM [1]

22 October 1820

Address: Mr William Haslam/ Messrs Frampton's/ 34 Leadenhall Street/ London. *Postmark:* F P O NO.11 1820.

Naples Octr 22 1820 [2]

My dear Haslam

Here we are thank God—but in quarentine—*therefore accordingly.*[3]—Close upon when I wrote you Keats began to droop—and the many privations coming in the want of fair winds—nice provisions—airing of beds—and———made him impatient—this brings on fever—and at times he has been very bad—but mind you I think from these things—for our passage has been most horribly rough—Keats has lived through it—but it is a wonder—no way could be worse for him—I had determined on returning with him to London from the conviction that he would die on the passage—and should—but from the English Channel (in which we were groaning for a fortnight) the difficulties seem'd to decrease—we skipp'd the rest in 3 Weeks—though quick yet not well—in the Straits of Gibralter I perceived great changes [4] in Keat[s] for the better—he seem'd recovering—at least looked like it—but in two days the blood came from his stomach. <and> with fever at night and violent perspiration all this had its cause in—but her[e] is our courier—this is only an opportunity—

Farewell Sincerely

Joseph Severn

Keats now is in a doubtfull state—I cannot guess what this climate will do—

[1] Badly discolored from fumigation. For Haslam's reply to this letter and the next see Sharp, pp. 72f.
[2] The ship had entered the Bay of Naples on the day before (Sharp, p. 58n.).
[3] These italicized words are doubly underlined.   [4] *Written* greats change.

→» 77 «←

JOSEPH SEVERN TO WILLIAM HASLAM

1, 2 November 1820

Address: Mr William Haslam/ Messrs Frampton & Co./ 34 Leadenhall Street/ London. *Postmark (part illegible):* 1820. Printed very inexactly in *TLS* (by Colvin), April 16, 1914, p. 182, and (except for the last sentence) by Colvin, pp. 498-500. Lowell, II, 481, 483, 490f., gives extracts via *TLS*.[1]

Naples—Novr 1. 1820

My dear Haslam

We are just released from the loathsome misery of Quarantine—foul weather and foul air for the whole 10 [2] days kept us to the small [3] Cabin—surrounded by about 2000 ships in a wretched Mole [4] not sufficient for half the number,—yet Keats is still living—may I not have hopes of him?—he has passed what I must have thought would kill myself.—Now that we are on shore and feel the fresh air—I am horror struck at his sufferings on this voyage,—all [5] that could be fatal to him in air and diet—with the want {of} [6] medicine—and conveniences he has weather'd {it} if [7] I may [8] call his poor shattered frame—and broken heart—weathering it.—For myself I have stood it

---

[1] A transcript made by Hessey is also in the Harvard collection, and its variants (*H*) in diction and in a few instances of punctuation are recorded in the footnotes. Some of the *TLS* verbal variants (*C*) are also added. For Haslam's reply to this and the preceding letter see Sharp, pp. 72f. On the circulation of the letter see Nos. 79, 82, 83, 88, 135.

[2] *H* 40.

[3] *H omits.*

[4] *C* hole.

[5] *H* voyage all.

[6] *C, H unbracketed.*

[7] *C* it, if. *H omits.*

[8] *H* may well.

firmly until this Mor^g when in a moment my spirits dropt—
at the sight of his suffering [9]—a plentiful shower of tears (which
he did not see) has relieved me somewhat—<but> what he has
passed still unnerves me.—But now we are breathing in a large
room—with Vesuvius in our view—Keats has become calm—and
thinks favorably of this place—for [10] we are meeting with much
kind treatment on every side—more particularly from an English Gentleman here (brother to Miss Cotterell [11] one of our
Lady passengers)—who has shown unusually humane treatment
to Keats—unasked—these—with very good accomodations [12] at
our Inn (Villa da Londra) have kept him up through dinner—
but on the other hand—Dr Milne is at Rome (wither [13] Keats is
proposing to go)—the weather is now cold [14]—wet and foggy—
and we find ourselves on the wrong side—for his hope for [15]
recovery,—(for the present I will talk to him—he is disposed to
it—I will talk him to sleep—for he has suffered much fatigue)———

Novr 2nd ———

Keats went to bed much recover'd— I took every means to re-

[9] *H* sufferings. For Fanny Brawne's comments on this letter and Severn's
"shower of tears" see Edgcumbe, pp. 13f.

[10] *C, H* place for.

[11] Writing to his sister Maria on February 20 (*London Mercury,* XXX
[1934], 344) Severn says that she "is now poor creature dying in the same
way as Keats." In the summer of 1825 he again saw Charles Cotterell in
Naples and learned that his sister had died there of consumption (Sharp,
pp. 148f.). Charles MacFarlane, *Reminiscences* (ed. J. F. Tattersall [1917],
p. 14), describes him as a former naval officer. If so, perhaps he was the
Charles Edward Cotterel who was appointed Purser in the Royal Navy
on July 31, 1812, serving on the *Thunder* till around March 24, 1814,
when he was transferred to the *Clio.* In the *Navy List* for December,
1815, and in many later issues his name appears unattached to any ship.

[12] *C* accommodation.

[13] *H, C* whither.

[14] *H* cold &.

[15] *H* hoped for. Severn wrote "hoped" and canceled the *d.*

move from him a heavy greif that may tend more than any thing to be fatal—he told me much—very much—and I dont know wether [16] it was more painful for me or himself—but it had the effect of much relieving him—he went very calm to bed [17]— Poor fellow!—he is still sleeping at [18] ½ past nine— if I can but cure [19] his mind I will bring him back to England— *well*—but <this> I fear it never can be done in this world—the grand scenery here effects him a little—but he is too infirm to enjoy it—his gloom deadens his sight to every thing—and but for intervals of something like ease he must soon end it—— You will like to know how I have managed in respect to self— I have had [20] a most severe task—full of contrarieties [21]—what I did one way—was undone another—the lady passenger though in the same state as Keats—yet differing in constitution required almost every thing the opposite to him—for instance if the cabin windows were not open she would faint and remain entirely insensible 5 or [22] 6 hours together—if the windows were open poor Keats would be taken with a cough (a violent one—caught from this cause) and sometimes spitting of blood—now I had this to manage continually for our other passenger is a most consummate brute—she would see Miss Cotterell [23] stiffened like a corpse <for> I have sometimes thought her dead—nor ever lend <her> the least aid—full a dozen times I have re- covered this Lady and put her to bed—sometimes she would faint 4 times in a day yet [24] at intervals would seem quite well— and was full of spirits—she is both young and lively—and but

[16] *H, C* whether.
[17] *H* calm—Poor fellow.
[18] *H omits.*
[19] *C* ease.
[20] Apparently followed by a colon.
[21] *H* contradictions.
[22] *Changed from* &.
[23] *C* Cottrell *here and earlier.*
[24] *H* but.

for her we should have had more heaviness—though much less trouble.—She has benefited by Keats advice—I used to act under him.—and reduced the fainting each time—she has recovered very much and gratefully ascribes it to us—her brother the same— The Captain has behaved with great kindness to us all— but more particularly [25] Keats—every thing that could be got or done—was at his service without asking—he is a good-natured man to his own injury—strange for a Captain—I wont say so much for his ship—it's a black hole—5 sleeping in one Cabin— the one you saw—the only one—during the voyage [26] I have been frequently sea-sick—sometimes severely—2 days together.— We have had only one real fright on the sea's—not to mention continued squalls—and a storm— "Alls well that ends well" and these ended well—our fright was from two Portugese Ships of War—they brought us too with a shot—which passed close under our stern—this was not pleasant for us [27] you will allow—nor was it decreased when they came up—for a more infernal set I never could imagine—after some trifling questions they allowed us to go on to our no small delight—our captain was afraid they would plunder the ship—this was in the Bay of Biscay—over which we were carried by a good wind. Keats has written to Brown—and in quarantine [28] another [29] to Mrs Brawn [30]—he requests you will tell Mrs Brawn what I think of him—for he is too bad to judge of himself—this Mor^g he is still very much better—we are in good spirits and I may say hopefull fellows—at least I may say as much for Keats—he made an Italian Pun today —the rain is coming down in torrents— When you write—direct Post Office Rome.[31]

[25] *H adds* to.
[26] *H punctuates:* only one during the voyage.
[27] *H* us as.
[28] Severn apparently omitted the first *n*.
[29] *H omits*.
[30] For these see *Letters*, pp. 522-525.
[31] *H omits this sentence*.

⇟ 78 ⇞

GEORGE KEATS TO JOHN KEATS [1]

8 November 1820

Printed somewhat inexactly by Forman *(F)*, IV, 393-395. Two sentences are quoted by Lowell, II, 388.

Louisville Nov 8ᵗʰ 1820

My dear John

Again, and Again I must send bad news. I cannot yet find a purchaser for the Boat, and have received no intelligence of the man who offered the price I accepted, it was only 500dollars more than the sum she cleared me last year. If I were to lower the price 500dollars it would be as difficult of Sale. I hope to be able to send you money soon untill I do I shall be fast approaching the blue devil temperament. Your inevitable distresses are subject of conversation to us almost every day, we wish you were here untill we could launch you into the world again with present means and future prospects. Had the Mill been finished within *a year* of the time agreed upon in my contract with the Builders you should not have wanted money now, it was not finished within 21 mos, such a dissappointment driving me to every shift to live, rent and servant hire unpaid, will weigh heavy upon me some time. The present is all I fear, by next Autumn I hope to live in a house and on ground of my own,[2] with returns at least three times my expenses, my gain

---

[1] This letter was opened in London by Brown, who (Sharp, p. 76) sent Severn a summary of it, adding that George "is a canting, selfish, heartless swindler, and shall have to answer for the death of his brother, if it must be so." Endorsed by Brown "George Keats."

[2] "The house which George expected to have was built for his residence 'by the concern in which' he was 'the acting partner and one third owner,' in the immediate vicinity of the saw-mills. . . . It was not till 1823 that he realized more than his expenses" *(F)*.

now is double my expenses, without receiving for my services which will be well paid as soon as my experience in the Business will justify my asking an allowance; our firm is 'Geo Keats & C⁰; my partners are the principal Iron founders in the western Country. I receive and pay all. They keep the engine in order, without expense to the Compʸ. Almost every day I am in the woods superintending the felling of Trees and cutting saw-logs, and the ground tinged [?] with leaves reminds me of your little prospect ³ of breathing a milder air this winter, such thoughts frequently render our fireside melancholy, if you fail us we lose the most material object ⁴ for which we now toil and save, in fact the goal to which we stretch is a future residence in England, and a communion once more with those who understand us and love us, you are the most prominent in our minds as one of those, your distress is ours. Here we are not understood if our conduct will bear two constructions, the worst is put upon it. Altho we have connections we have no genuine ⁵ exercise ⁶ of kindly feelings but between ourselves: we are happy in being most comfortable at home, where I arrive and am received with pleasure to every meal. We are not yet hacknied, careless man and Wife, we have no quarrels now altho' we had many before marriage, we are both major domo, and yet we are neither major domo, we live so quietly people hardly know what to make of us. All we want at ⁷ present is your health and happiness. Marriage might do you good, I will not offer any fusty remarks, but assure you that had I to chuse again I would marry and suffer as I have done, to common observers no marriage could have been more unpromising than ours. Give our love

³ *F* prospects.
⁴ *F* objects.
⁵ we . . . genuine *is repeated.*
⁶ *Written* excercise.
⁷ *Here* plea *is canceled.*

to Fanny,[8] Mrs Wylie, Henry, Charles,[9] we are su[r]prised we
have no news from them. Give our best rem^s to the Brawns
Reynolds, Dilk's, Brown, Rice & Haslam. Haslam does not
appear to have received the letter in which I informed him that
the articles Kent proposes to send are totally unsaleable here,
where almost every man is pressed for market money. If we
meet a safe opportunity for England we will send Miss Brawn
an india Crape dress or merino shawl or something scarce with
you, but cheap with us. she has our thanks for her kindness
during your illness. Our little live thing as George calls her is
in good health and offers bread and buttée and Apple-toottie [10]
to Uncle John every day. If Brooks,[11] Stationer, Oxford St. has
not started for this Country before your book [12] is out, we shall
expect it by him. I sent Reynolds Waverly, has he received it? [13]
To see your hand writing will be a great comfort to your Affectionate Brother & Sister.

　　　　　I am your Brother George.
　　　　　　　　　signed.　　　Georgiana Emily Keats.[14]

[8] Fanny Keats.

[9] His wife's mother and brothers.

[10] So apparently. *F has* wottie.

[11] John Brooks, 421 Oxford Street.

[12] See I, 279n.

[13] Evidently he had, for in *The Fancy* (London, 1820, p. 6) he wrote: "I
requested a friend to procure for me a copy of the small American edition of Waverley and Guy Mannering. . . . He purchased the books, and
left them . . . in his hut," finally sending them to London wrapped up
in the paper on which the play of "King Tims the First: An American
Tragedy" was written. West and Richardson published the first American edition of *Guy Mannering*, 2 vols., at Boston in 1815. No early
American copy of *Waverley* has been accessible.

[14] Georgiana Emily "signed" by having her hand guided by her father.

➤➤ 79 ««

J. A. HESSEY TO WILLIAM HASLAM

23 November 1820

Address: Mr Wm Haslam Junr/ 34 Leadenhall Street. *Postmark (part illegible):* 8 o'Clock NO 24 1820; T. P Ludgate Hi[ll].

Fleet St. Nov. 23. 1820

My dear Sir

I understand from Mr Reynolds that Intelligence has been received in Town of Keats's Arrival off Naples. when he wrote [1] he was performing Quarantine. He was not very well, I believe, but I have no particulars. I thought you would be pleased to know even the little that I could tell you

Yours very truly

J. A. Hessey

➤➤ 80 ««

DR. JAMES CLARK TO ? [1]

27 November 1820

All but the last sentence is printed by Lowell, II, 501f.

Extract of a letter from Dr Clarke—dated Rome Nov. 27. 1820

"Keats arrived here about a week ago & I have got him into comfortable lodgings. I can hardly yet give you a decided

[1] To Mrs. Brawne (see *Letters,* pp. 522f.) and to Brown (see *Letters,* pp. 523-525).

[1] A transcript by Hessey of part of a letter to an unknown person, whom Lowell tentatively identifies with Samuel E. Gray, author of a *Supplement to the Pharmacopoeia* (1818) and contributor to the *Medical Repository.* See I, 193, II, 437.

opinion of his case but will in my next. The chief part of his disease, as far as I can yet see seems seated in his Stomach. I have some suspicion of disease of the heart and it may be of the lungs, but of this say nothing to his friends as in my next I shall be able to give you something more satisfactory His mental exertions and application have I think been the sources of his complaints— If I can put his mind at ease I think he'll do well—get Mr Taylor or some of his friends to write him. I'm afraid the Idea of his expenses operates on his mind and some plan must be adopted to remove this if possible. The truth is, having come abroad for the purpose of restoring his health, every thing must be done to favor the ch{ange} of climate— I mean that he shall buy or hire {by the} month a horse to ride out whenever the w{eather perm}its & so forth— After all his expenses will {be very lit}tle, and he's too noble an animal to be allowed to sink without some sacrifice being made to save him. I wish I were rich enough his living here should cost him nothing. He has a friend with him who seems very attentive to him but between you & I is not the best suited for his companion, but I suppose poor fellow he had no choice. I fear much there is something operating on his mind—at least so it appears to me—he either feels that he is now living at the expense of some one else or something of that kind. If my opinion be correct we may throw medicine to the dogs.[1a] Let every thing be done to relieve his mind from any Idea of that kind as far as possible— I feel very much interested in him and believe me will do every thing in my power to be of serv{ice} to him. I am glad to find the Edinburgh Rev{iewe}rs have been just towards him.[2] He seems much pl{eased} with Rome and prefers it greatly to Na{ples. I w}as writing to some friends at Naples ab{out him a}t the moment he unexpectedly made h{is appear}ance here."

[1a] See *Macbeth*, V.iii.47, "Throw physic to the dogs; I'll none of it."

[2] A reference to Jeffrey's August review.

⇒⇒ 81 ⇐⇐

CHARLES BROWN TO WILLIAM HASLAM

1 December 1820

Address: To/ Mr Haslam,/ (Messrs Frampton & Co)/ Leadenhall Street/ London. *Postmarks (the second partly illegible):* Two Py Post Unpaid SOHampstead; 2[?] o'Clock DE. 2 1820.

Hampstead. 1ˢᵗ Decʳ 1820.

Dear Haslam,

This afternoon I had a letter [1] from Keats, dated Naples, first Wednesday in Novʳ, the day after their quarantine was over. It required an immediate answer, which I have complied with, & send it you to forward with all speed. He says—"write to *Rome,* (post restant)"—but I am afraid to give that address,—he is liable to strange errors of this sort,— Severn is the surer man, & I suppose you have heard from him giving reliable directions. Both to Mʳˢ Brawne [2] & to me he says "I refer you to Severn's letter to Haslam about my health,"—now, if you have recᵈ such letter,[3] pray send it us,—for this fortnight we have been impatiently expecting it,—do not fear it will be kept a day longer than you mention. I give you great trouble,—but in a matter relating to Keats I need scarce make an apology. I sent you a letter [4] from Chichester to be forwarded to him. With respects to Mʳˢ H,

& best wishes,

I am always your's

Chaˢ Brown.

[1] *Letters,* pp. 523-525 (which reproduces Milnes, II, 77-79), and see II, 83f.

[2] *Letters,* pp. 522f.

[3] See No. 77. It *was* sent: see No. 83 for Brown's letter of thanks.

[4] See No. 72.

≫≫ 82 ≪≪

J. A. HESSEY TO WILLIAM HASLAM

5 December 1820

Address: Mr W. Haslam/ 34 Leadenhall Street.

Fleet S^t 5 Dec. 1820

My dear Sir

I am very much obliged by your kindness in sending me Severns letter [1]— It is quite as favorable as could be expected under all the circumstances and its termination is satisfactory as it shews Keats & Severn too to be better after a Day & a nights rest on Shore. I have written a letter for him & will thank you to send it off with your own as you will know best how to direct to him. Reynolds promised to send me a letter to day to go by the same Mail but I have not yet received it—if it comes I will send it to you to be properly directed, or if you can let me know by the Bearer how you mean to address him I need not trouble you further. In g^t haste   Yours very sincerely

J. A. Hessey

≫≫ 83 ≪≪

CHARLES BROWN TO WILLIAM HASLAM

3 December 1820 [2]

Address: To/ Mr Haslam/ (Messrs Frampton & Co)/ Leadenhall Street/ London. *Postmarks:* Hampstead NO; 1[2] o'Clock [D]E 4 1820N^N.

Dear Haslam,

Thank you for the enclosed. I read it next door, skipping & adding, without the slightest suspicion on their [3] part. You

---

[1] See No. 77. Hessey made a transcript of it.
[2] This letter should precede No. 82, as the second postmark (tardily deciphered) makes certain. Sunday (see the end of the letter) was December 3.   [3] The Brawnes'.

call Severn's letter [4] a heavy narrative!—what would you say to Keats' letter [5] of despair to me? But I ascribe much of the dreary feelings of both to that damned quarantine. Yet the spitting of blood is a *fact,* that came upon me distressingly. In a few days we shall know the truth. I am glad he unburthened his mind to Severn,—that is good. I still have cheering hopes,—but I am afraid,—very afraid. Keats' letter to me *I must not show,*—I wish I might,—the showing it would even relieve me, for the thoughts of it quite weigh me down. What is to be done with George? Will he ever dare to come among his brother's friends?

Your's most truly,

Chas Brown.

Hampstead. Sunday

→»» 84 «««←

JOSEPH SEVERN TO CHARLES BROWN

14, 17 December 1820

A transcript made by Hessey.[1] It is printed in part by Lowell, II, 508-510.

Rome Dec. 14. 1820

My dear Brown

I fear our poor Keats is at his worst.—a most unlooked for relapse has confined him to his bed—with every chance

---

[4] No. 77.

[5] *Letters,* pp. 523-525 (which reproduces Milnes, II, 77-79), and see II, 83f.

[1] It is endorsed, "Copy of a Letter from Rome dated Dec. 14 & 17. 1820 from Mr Jo^s Severn to Mr Brown." The original letter, with the omission of a few sentences, is printed in Brown's life (see II, 87-89). The Hessey and Brown texts agree pretty closely, with the former probably being on the whole the more accurate. Another and a highly condensed version of the letter was printed by Milnes, II, 85-87, and thence by Sharp, pp. 69f. The former tells nothing about the person addressed,

against him: it has been so sudden upon what I almost thought convalescence—and without any seeming cause that I cannot calculate on the next change. I dread it, for his suffering is so great, so continued, and his fortitude so completely gone, that any further change must make him delirious. This is the fifth day and I see him get worse. but stop— I will tell you the manner of this relapse from the first.

Dec. 17 4 Morning

Not a moment can I be from him— I sit by his bed and read all day—and at night I humour him in all his wanderings. he has just fallen asleep—the first for 8 nights,[1a] and now from mere exhaustion. I hope he will not wake until I have written this, for I am anxious beyond measure to have you know this worse and worse state—yet I dare not let him see I think it dangerous.—I had seen him wake on the morning of this attack, and to all appearance he was going on merrily and had unusual good spirits—when in an instant a Cough seized him, and he vomited near two Cup-fuls of blood.—In a moment I got Dr Clarke, who saw the manner of it, and immediately took away about 8 ounces of blood from the Arm—it was black and thick in the extreme. Keats was much alarmed and dejected— O what an awful day I had with him!—he rush'd out of bed and said "this day shall be my last"—and but for me most certainly it would. At the risk of losing his confidence I took every destroying mean from his reach, nor let him be from my sight one minute. The blood broke forth again in like quantity the next morning—and the doctor thought it expedient to take away the

---

whereas the latter says it was written "to Mrs. Brawne," and begins his text, "My dear Madam." But the references to Mrs. Brawne in the third and fifth paragraphs prove clearly that the letter copied by Hessey and given by Brown could not possibly have been addressed to her. Bodurtha, pp. 118-121, enumerates most of the extremely numerous variants in the Brown, Milnes, Sharp, and Lowell printed texts.

[1a] See also "9th day" in the next paragraph. Severn's date of December 17 is probably an error for December 18.

like quantity of blood—this was in the same dismal state, and must have been from the horrible state of despair he was in—but I was so fortunate as to talk him into a little calmness, and with some English newspapers he became quite patient under the necessary arrangements

This is the 9ᵗʰ day, and no change for the better—five times the blood has come up in coughing, in large quantities generally in the morning—and nearly the whole time his saliva has been mixed with it—but this is the lesser evil when compared with his Stomach—not a single thing will digest—the torture he suffers all and every night—and best part of the day— is dreadful in the extreme—the distended stomach keeps him in perpetual hunger or craving—and this is augmented by the little nourishment he takes to keep down the blood— Then his mind is worse than all—despair in every shape—his imagination and memory present every image in horror, so strong that morning and night I tremble for his Intellect. The recollection of England—of his "good friend Brown"—and his happy few weeks in Mʳˢ Brawn's Care—his Sister and brother— O he will mourn over every circumstance to me whilst I cool his burning forehead—until I tremble through every vein in concealing my tears from his staring glassy eyes.—How he can be Keats again from all this I have little hope—but I may see it too gloomy since each coming night I sit up adds its dismal contents to my mind.

Dʳ Clarke will not say so much—although there is no bounds to his attention, yet with little success—"can he administer to a mind diseased" [2]—yet all that can be done most kindly he does—whilst his Lady, like himself in refined feeling, prepares and cooks all that poor Keats takes—for in this wilderness of a place (for an Invalid) there was no alternative. Yesterday Dʳ Clarke went all over Rome for a certain kind of fish, and got it— but just as I received it from Mʳˢ C delicately prepared, Keats

[2] See II, 88, 126, and *Macbeth*, V.iii.40.

was taken by the spitting of blood and is now gone back all the 9 days.—this was occasioned by disobeying the Doctors commands.—Keats is required to be kept as low as possible to check the blood—so that he is weak and gloomy.—Every day he raves that he will die from hunger—and I was obliged to give him more than allowed— You cannot think how dreadful this is for me—the Doctor on the one hand tells me I shall kill him to give him more than he allows—and Keats raves for more till I am in complete tremble for him. But I have talked him over now.—We have the best opinion of D^r C's skill—he seems to understand the case, and comes over 4 & 5 times a day—he left word at 12 this morning to call any time in case of danger

I heard Keats say how he should like Mrs Brawn and Mrs Dilk to visit his sister at Walthamstow—will you say this for me—and to Mr Taylor that Keats was about to write favorably on the very time of his relapse— For myself I am keeping up beyond my most sanguine expectations— 8 nights I have been up, and in the days never a moment away from my patient but to run over to the Doctor—but I will confess my spirits have been sometimes quite pulled down—for these wretched Romans have no Idea of comfort—here I am obliged to wash up—cook— & read to Keats all day—added to this I have had no letters yet from my family—this is a damp to me for I never knew how dear they were to me— I think of my Mother & I think of Keats for they are something the same in this tormenting Indigestion— But if Keats recovers—and then letters bring good news—why I shall take upon myself to be myself again. I wrote last to my good friend Haslam—it will tell you all the events up to the relapse of Keats— I had put the letters in post on the same morning—it was my custom to walk until Keats awoke—we did breakfast about 9 o'Clock— My head begins to sally round so much that I cannot recollect— I will write to Mr Taylor [3] on

[3] See No. 85.

the next change in my friend, and to the Kind Mʳˢ Brawn when I have any good news.[4] Will you remember me to this lady— little did I dream on THIS when I saw her last in London. Will you, my dear Brown, write to me—for a letter to Keats now would almost kill him—give Haslam this sad news.—I am quite exhausted—farewell— I wish you were here my dear Brown

Sincerely   Joseph Severn
(Signed)

To C. Brown Esq—direct Post Office. Rome

I have just looked at him—this will be a good night.

⇢⇢⇢ 85 ⇠⇠⇠

JOSEPH SEVERN TO JOHN TAYLOR

24 December 1820

Address: John Taylor Esqʳ/ Messʳˢ Taylor & Hessey/ Booksellers/ Fleet Street— London/ England. *Postmarks:* FPO JA.20 1821; ROMA. A first draft of a small part of the opening paragraph is printed by Sharp, pp. 80f., who also gives a facsimile of it.[1]

Rome Decʳ 24 1820——
½ past 4—Morᵍ—

My dear Sir

Keats has changed somewhat for the worse—at least his mind has much—very very much—and this leaves his state much the same—and quite as hopeless—yet the blood has ceased to come—his digestion is better—and but for a cough he must be improving—that is as far as respects his body.—but the fatal

---

[4] See No. 89.

[1] He describes it as "an unfinished letter . . . probably intended for Mr. Taylor." The draft is also printed by Rennell Rodd and H. N. Gay, Keats-Shelley Memorial *Bulletin,* No. 1 (1910), pp. 41f., and is quoted by Colvin, p. 506. The letter here printed is badly torn and extremely difficult to decipher.

179

prospect of Consumption hangs before his "minds eye [2]—and turns every thing to despair and wretchedne{ss—he} will not bear the idea of living much less strive {to live—} I se{em to} lose his confidence by trying to give him this hope {—he} will not he{a}r that his future prospects are favorable—he says {tha}t the continued stretch of his imagination has killed him—and were he to recover he could not write another line—then his {go}od fr{ie}nds in England—he only cherishes the idea of what they have {done} and this he turns to a load of care for the future—the {hig}h hopes of him—his certain success—his experience [3] h{e shakes his} head at it <all> and bids it fare-well.—The rememberance {of} his brothers death— I cannot kept from him—all his own symtoms he re[c]ollects in him [4] and this with every cough and pain—the many troubles—perse-cutions—and I may say cruelties he has borne now weigh heavy on him—if he dies I am witness that he dies of a broken heart and spirit.—would that his enemies could see this martyrdom of the most noble-feeling and brightest genius to be found in existence— I only wish this for their punishment.—he is now only a wreck of his former self—the knawing weight upon his mind—with the intire loss of bodily strength and appearence;—push him to malevolence—suspicion—and impatience—yet every one is struck with him and interested about him— I am as-tonisted and delighted at the respect paid him—but even this—I mean the general utmost endeavour he receives—his dreadful state of mind turns to {per}secuti{on and some}times even murder—he is now under the {. . .} [5] was administered to him by an individual in London—. All that fortitude and as it were—brav{ery} of mind against bodily suffering are away

[2] *Hamlet*, I.ii.185. See I, 239n.
[3] *Originally followed by* ne.
[4] *Originally* his brother.
[5] Four or five words missing or unreadable.

from him—and the want of some kind hope to feed his voracious imagination leaves him to the wreck of ideas without purpose—imagination without philosophy—yet this night he said to
me "I think a malignant being must have power over us—over
whom the Almighty has little or no influence—yet you know
Severn I cannot believe in your book—the Bible—but I feel the
horrible want of some faith—some hope—something to rest on
now—their must be such a book—and I know that is it—but I
can't believe it— I am destined to every tor{ment i}n this world
—even to this little comfort on my death bed {. . .}" [5a]—O! my
dear Sir you cannot imagine what {I} sometimes feel— I have
read to him incessantly—until no more book{s} could be had—
for they must be new to him—and above a{ll} the book he has
set his mind upon all through this last {week?} is no{t} to be
had—the works of Jeremy Taylor—his des{ire to ha}ve these
read to him is very great—and yet not to be {had—is not} this
hard—the other books he wished me write down are not in
Rome—they were Madam Dacier's Plato [6] and the Pilgrims
Progress— I have read to him Don Quixote at his request and
some of Miss Edgeworths Novels—but there are no Books in
Rome—we sometimes get some English papers

Now observe my dear Sir I dont for a moment push my
little but honest Religious faith upon poor Keats—except as far
as my feelings go—but these I try to keep from him— I fall into
his views sometimes to quiet him and tincture them with a
somewhat of mine—but his many changes <and> both body
and mind render my charge most affecting and even dangerous
—for I cannot leave him without some one with him that he
likes *— This is the third week—and I have not left him more

---

* He does not like any one—he says—a strange {face
makes} him misera{ble.}

[5a] About two words missing.

[6] Anne Lefèvre Dacier, *The Works of Plato Abridg'd* (London, 1749).

than two hours—he has not been out of bed the whole time—he says this alone is enough to kill him was he in health—and then seeing no face but min{e . . .} [7] him he {. . .} [8] say it makes him worse to think how I should be occupied and how I am <I do> sometimes I succeed in persuading him that he will recover and go back with me to England.—I do lament a thousand times that he ever left England—not from the want of medical aid or even friends—for nothing can be superior to the kindness of Dr Clark &c—but the journey of 2000 Miles was too much for his state—even when he left England—and now he has most surely broken down under it— I have thought he would die before he reached this place—journies too and about Jatatu [?] are not for an Invalid.

Dr Clark gives very little hope of him—he says he may {rec}over from {th}is by some change in his mind—but he will {m}ost certainly die (at some not distant period) of Consumption—{n}o disorganisation exists at present—but a total derangement {of} the digestive powers—they have nearly lost their functions {and} it is this cause that produces the blood from the heads of {. . .} [9] on the chest.——it does not come at present—

For myself my dear Sir—I still keep up nearly as we{ll} as I did—altho' I have not got any person to relieve me— {Keats} makes me carefull of myself—he is my doctor—a change {of sc}ence might make me better—but I can do without it.—It is 6 oclock in the Mor^g I have been writing all night—this is my 5th Letter— Keats has just awoken— I must leave of and boil my kettle—he hears me writing and inquires— "Tell Taylor I shall soon be in a second Edition—in sheets—and cold press"—he desired me tell you some time since—that he would

---

[7] About two words missing.
[8] One word missing.
[9] Two words missing.

have written you—but felt he could not say anything—it gave
him pain— We have received 5 Letters—3 to Keats—<2 to my-
self>—he read one from Mr Hessy and another Mr Brown—but
the third he could not read and was effected most bitterly—he
says—"no more letters for him—even good news will not lift him
up—he is too far gone"—but he does not I think this—nor does
he know D^r Cs opinion—but his own knowledge of Anatomy is
unfortunate—farewell my dear Sir— Jos^h Severn

Tell my f^d Haslam I will write him by next post.—and
the first good news shall be for the kind Mrs Brawn <for> I
still hope to have Keats better—he has waked very calm— I have
got leave to have him up today—he will not take any food—
I have been afraid that he would refuse to take food—and the
like of medicine—the Doctor seem'd to think this yesterday—he
is much changed this Mor^g in appearance for the worse—but he
remains (9 oclock) very calm and goodnatured (4 oclock) dozing
between wiles—he has eat a small pudding and taken his milk—
he is still composed—but low— I am rather alarmed about
money—at Naples I expended nearly all my stock <and> here
I can get more by my Minature Painting—perhaps quite as
much as we could want should Keats's fail—but now I am kept
from it—no one to relieve me with Keats—<but> I dare say I
shall manage well—for here are above a dozen to sit to me[—]
I am quite concerned at the expences here for an invalid—Italy
is only for persons in health—for had I fallen into Keats's view's
and these cursed Italians imposition—all his money must have
been gone—but the kindness of D^r C—— has saved much expence— Horses—and Coaches have been the greatest charge—
proper lodging is dear—and as for proper food it cannot be got
for money—that is it cannot be got— Dr Clark went all over
Rome for a fish proper for Keats—if I get a proper thing one
day I can't get it the next—they cannot make 2 pudding
thr{ee?}—the price of a Horse per Month in English Money—

6£—lodging £4.16—and {a} dinner 4sh—the money remaining at the Bankers 260 scudi—about £52—with here £70—

4 oclock [10] This moment the doctor sends {me wor}d that my Landlady has reported to the Police that Keats is dying of a Consumption—now this has [made] me vent some curses against her—the words dying and Consumption has rather dampt my spirits—the laws are very severe—I do not know the extent of them—should poor Keats die—everything in his room is condemned to be burned even to paper on the walls the Italians are so alarmed at Consumption <that> the expences are enormous after a death—for examinations—and precautions to contagion— Fools. I can hardly contain myself— O! I will be revenged on this old Cat—for putting the notion in my head of my friends dying—and of Consumption—but stop I know the Doctor half thinks so—but will not say it—he has brought an Italian Physician here who thinks Keats has a malformed chest —should he die the law will demand him to be opened.——I have got some books—Scots Monastery and some travels—he seems inclined to hear me read all this evening—— Keats has just said <that> it is his last request that no mention be made of him in any manner publically—in Reviews Magazines or Newspapers—that no Engraving be taken from any Picture of him— Once more—farewell————

10 This paragraph is written vertically across the writing on page 3.

⋙ 86 ⋘

RICHARD WOODHOUSE TO JOHN TAYLOR

1820 (?) [1]

Address: Mr Jno Taylor. Morgan MS.

Dear John,

I have just had a note from a friend, whose Introduction to the Law Society, I had charged myself with today, to say that he is prevented from accompanying me thither.

This will leave me at liberty to chuse between the legal & the Poetical quill-drivers—Hyperion to a Satyr.[2]—I shall have much pleasure in availing myself of your Invitation. But say, p[er] bearer, vivâ voce the *last* Moment you can allow me *"till"* and depend upon punctuality—

Yrs truly

R^dWoodhouse.

⋙ 87 ⋘

DR. JAMES CLARK TO ? [3]

3 January 1821

Printed by Lowell, II, 511.

Extract of a Letter from Dr Clarke. Rome Jan. 3. 1821

"In my last I said a few words about poor Keats. Since that date he has had another attack of bleeding from the lungs

---

[1] This date is a pure guess.

[2] *Hamlet*, I.ii.140.

[3] A transcript by Hessey of part of a letter possibly addressed to "Gray," for whom see I, 193, 206n. Brown in a letter to Severn, vaguely referred by Sharp, p. 76, to a date around January 29, says: "Three days since we heard, by a letter from Dr. Clark to one of his friends, that there was no hope and no fear of a lingering illness." Fanny Brawne was told of this letter on January 31 (Edgcumbe, p. 19).

which has weakened him greatly, and he is now in a most deplorable state— His stomach is ruined and the state of his mind is the worst possible for one in his condition, and will undoubtedly hurry on an event that I fear is not far distant and even in the best frame of mind would not probably be long protracted. His digestive organs are sadly deranged and his lungs are also diseased—either of these would be a great evil, but to have both under the state of mind which he unfortunately is in must soon kill him. I fear he has long been governed by his imagination & feelings {&} now has little power & less inclination to ende{avou}r to keep them under. I feel much interested i{n the} poor fellow indeed—it is most distressing to {see a} mind like his (what it might have been) in th{e de}plorable state in which it is. His friend Mr. Sev{ern is} most attentive to him. Were Christianity of no us{e b}ut to give tranquillity to the sick bed it were the greatest blessing on earth. I am sorry indeed, and much disappointed in having to communicate such sad accounts of poor K. When I first saw him I thought something might <have been> be done, but now I fear the prospect is a hopeless one"—

>>> 88 <<<

CHARLES BROWN TO WILLIAM HASLAM

5 January 1821

Address: Mr William Haslam/ Messrs Frampton & Sons/ No 34 Leadenhall Street./ London. *Postmarks (the second in part illegible):* HampsteadNO; JA 6 1821.

My dear Haslam,

Severn's letter [1] is more satisfactory than any Keats would deign to write,—it enters into those particulars which friends

[1] No. 77.

are always anxious about. I carried it next door [2] with your Comp[ts]. When I *travelled* into the City, to Frampton & Sons, it was merely to show you how much better Keats appeared to be, and, provokingly, you were away. You have heard, or may hear, of my letter to George.—I read a copy of it to Taylor;—should you hear news of that *money brother* pray let me know,—as for remittances from him,—we must dream about them.— Wait a month, and if George remains still silent, give him such a sting as he has had from me,—it will pierce deeper from you than from me.[3] The return of this letter has been delayed a day,—I'll be a good boy & do so no more.

Your's sincerely,
Cha[s] Brown.
Hampstead. 5th Jan[y] 1821.

[For a letter of George Keats to Fanny Keats,
January 6, 1821, see Letter 50.]

→» 89 «←

JOSEPH SEVERN TO MRS. SAMUEL BRAWNE [1]

11 January 1821

Rome Jan. 11. 1821.
1 o'Clock morning

My dear Madam

I said that "the first good news I had should be for the kind M[rs] Brawn." [2] I am thankful & delighted to make good

---

[2] To the Brawnes'.

[3] For George's references to such "stings" see I, 222n., 329.

[1] A transcript by Hessey, printed in part by Lowell, II, 511-514. The chief variations from the original, which is printed by Forman (*F*), IV, 203-208, and by Sharp, pp. 77-79, are given in footnotes.

[2] See I, 179.

my promise—to be at all able to do it—for among [3] all the horrors hovering over poor Keats this was the most dreadful that I could see no possible way and but a fallacious hope for his recovery. But now thank God I have a real one. I most certainly think I shall bring him back to England—at least my anxiety for his recovery and comfort make me think this—for half the cause of his danger has arisen from [4] the loss of England—from the dread of never seeing it more. O this hung upon him like a torture—never may I behold the like again even in my direst enemy— Little did I think what a task of affliction & danger I had undertaken—for I only thought of the beautiful mind of Keats, my attachment to him—and his convalescence.

But I will tell you dear Madam the singular reason [5] I have for hoping his recovery— In the first fortnight of this attack his memory presented to him every thing that was dear & delightful—even to the minutiæ [6]—and with it all the persecution & I may say villainy practised upon him—his exquisite sensibility for every one save his poor self—all his own means & comfort expended upon [7] others—almost in vain— These he would contrast with his present suffering—and say that all was brought on by them—and he was right. Now he has changed to calmness & quietude, as singular as productive of good, for his mind was [8] certainly killing him. He has now given up all thoughts hopes or even wish for recovery—his mind is in a state of peace from the final leave he has taken of this world and all its future hopes. this has been an immense weight for him

[3] *F* amid.
[4] *F* for.
[5] *F* reasons.
[6] *F* minutia.
[7] *F* on.
[8] *F* was most.

to rise from   He remains quiet & submissive under his heavy fate

Now if any thing will recover him it is this absence of himself. I have perceived for the last 3 days symptoms of recovery— Dr Clarke even thinks so— Nature again revives in him— I mean where art was used before— Yesterday he permitted me to carry him from his bed room to our sitting room —to put him clean things on, and to talk about my Painting to him— This is my good news— Don't think it otherwise my dear Madam, for I have been in such a state of anxiety & discomfiture in this barbarous place that the least hope of my friends recovery is a heaven to me

For Three weeks I have never left him— I have sat [9] up at night— I have read to him nearly all day & even in the night— I light the fire, make his breakfast & sometimes am obliged to cook—make his bed and even sweep the room. I can have these things done, but never at the time when they ought & must be done—so that you will see my alternative— What enrages me most is making a fire I blow—blow—for an hour—the smoke comes fuming out—my kettle falls over on the burning sticks— no stove—Keats calling me to be with him—the fire catching my hands & the door bell ringing—all these to one quite unused and not [10] all capable—with the want of every [11] proper material come not a little galling—

But to my great surprise I am not ill, or even restless nor have I been all the time—there is nothing but what I will do for him—there is no alternative but what I think and provide myself against—except his death—not the loss of him—I am not [12] prepared to bear that—but the inhumanity the bar-

[9] *F* set.
[10] *F* not [at?]
[11] *F* ever.
[12] *F* omits.

barism of these Italians. So far I have kept every thing from poor Keats, but if he did know but part of what I suffer for [13] them and their cursed laws it would kill him—just to instance one thing among many. News was brought me the other day that our gentle landlady had reported to the Police that my friend was dying of [14] consumption— Now their law is that every individual thing in each room the patient has been in shall without reserve even to the paper on the walls be destroyed by fire [15]— This startled me not a little, for in our sitting room where I wanted to bring him there is property worth about 150£ besides all our own books &c invaluable—now my difficulty was to shift him to this room and let no one know it—this was a heavy task from the unfortunate manner of the place—our landladys apartments are on the same floor with ours—her servant waits on me when it pleases her and enters from an adjoining room— I was determined on removing Keats let what would be the consequence—the change was {most} [16] essential to his health & spirits—and the following morning I {set ab}out [17] accomplishing it. In the first place I blocked up the door so that they could not enter—then made up a bed on the Sofa & removed my friend to it. the greatest difficulty was in keeping all from him— I succeeded in this too by making his bed and sweeping the room where it is—and going dinnerless with all the pretensions of dining—persuading him that the [18] Servant had made his bed, & I had been dining—he half suspected

[13] *F* from.

[14] *F* of a. (The landlady's name seems to have been Anna Angeletti; see the Keats-Shelley Memorial *Bulletin*, No. 2 [1913], p. 96.)

[15] *In F this sentence runs:* now their Law is—that every individual thing even to the paper on the walls in each room the patient has been in— shall without reserve be destroyed by fire—the loss to be made better than good by his friends——.

[16] No brackets in *F*.

[17] No brackets in *F*.

[18] *F* their.

this but as he could not tell the why & the wherefore there it ended. I got him back in the after[noon] [19] & no one save D[r] Clark knew of it.

D[r] C.[20] still attends him with his usual kindness, and shews his good heart in every thing he does—the like of his lady— I cannot tell which shews us the most kindness— *I* am even a mark of their care—mince pies and numberless nice things come over to keep me alive—and but for their kindness I am afraid we should go on very gloomily. Now my dear Madam I must leave off—my eyes are beginning to be unruly, and I must write a most important letter to our President Sir Tho[s] Lawrence before I suffer myself to [21] sleep

Will you be so <good> kind as to [22] write Mr Taylor that it was at Mess.[rs] Torlonias Advice Mr Keats drew a Bill for the whole Sum £120 this was to save the trouble & expence of many small bills—he now draws in small sums. I have the whole of affairs under charge and am trying the nearest possible way. Mr Taylor will hear from Dr C [23] about the bill— it will be well arranged—present my respectful Compts to Miss B. who [24] I hope & trust is quite well—now that I think of her my mind is carried to your happy Wentworth Place—[25] O I would my unfortunate friend had never left it—[26] for the hopeless disadvantage [27] of this comfortless Italy—he has many many times talked over the few happy days at your House the only time when his mind was at ease. I hope still to see him with you again

[19] No brackets in *F*.
[20] *F* Clark.
[21] *F* to go to.
[22] *F* omits.
[23] *F* Clark. (For the letter see No. 91.)
[24] *F* Brawn[e] whom.
[25] *F* place—where all that peacefull English comfort seems to exist—.
[26] *F* left your Wentworth Place.
[27] *F* advantages.

farewell my dear Madam— One more thing I must say—poor Keats cannot see any letters—at least he will not—they affect him so much and increase his danger— The two last I repented giving—he made me put them into his box unread. more of these when I write again—meanwhile any matter of moment had better come to me—I will be very happy to receive advice & remembra{nce} [28] from you— Once more farewell

(Signed) Jo^s Severn [29]

I have just looked at hi{m—he} [30] is in a beautiful sleep—in look he is very much more him{self—} [31] I have the greatest hopes of him—

→» 90 «←

TAYLOR AND HESSEY TO WILLIAM HASLAM [1]

12 January 1821

Address: Mr W. Haslam/ Leadenhall Street/ [*In lower left corner*] 34.

Fleet St. Jan. 12. 1821

Dear Sir

We are much obliged by your sending us the Letter respecting poor Keats—it is indeed melancholy Intelligence, and the more distressing from being so little expected— We have never seen the letter you allude to—the last we saw was that written [2] the day after they arrived at Naples

Yours very truly
Taylor & Hessey

28 No brackets in *F.*
29 *F* Your obed^t and affectionate [?] Servt/ Joseph Severn/ 3 o'clock mor^g.
30 No brackets in *F.*
31 No brackets in *F.*
1 In Hessey's hand.
2 See No. 76.

→» 91 «←

DR. JAMES CLARK TO GRAY [1]

13 January 1821

One page, badly torn; printed (except for the last sentence) somewhat
inexactly by Lowell, II, 515f.

Rome January 13th 1821

I have not lost a Post, My dear Gray, in replying to your
letter relative to p{oor Kea}ts as I am anxious to prevent any
{fur}ther misunderstanding as {to} the Bill affair; I say misunderstanding becaus{e} it appears to me that there has been
something of this kind either on Keats part or that of his
friend Mr Severn. The truth I am sorry to inform you, is that
Keats is at present so ill that he must know nothing of the
matter, and therefore his particular motives for deviating from
Mr Taylors instructions, or whether he quite understood these,
cannot now be unde{r}stood, and perhaps it matters not much
as things stand relative to the Bill. His friend informs m{e that}
it was proposed by the Banker that instead of dra{wing} the
stipulated sum in small Bills it should be {drawn all} at once,
as incurring less expence, & the money {draw}n from him according as it was required. {This} plan as you know was adopted
& about half the su{m} & rather more has already been drawn
fro{m the Ba}nker & the greater part of this sum spent. {This
bei}ng the case the Banker (Torlonia) to who{m} I explained
the whole matter advises, as the plan {in}curring the least

---

[1] In an earlier letter (see No. 89) Severn remarked, "Mr Taylor will hear
from Dr C about the bill." The present letter is mentioned and quoted
by Hessey (see No. 96) in such a way as to suggest that Gray (see I, 185, 206)
was an employee of Taylor and Hessey. In his files Milnes also preserved
(and Harvard now has) an engraved visiting card ("Sir James Clark./
22 B. Brook Street."), on which the latter wrote (1848), "With many
thanks for the Keats."

expence, that t{he} Bill sho{uld} be paid when due and that he will {reta}in {the} money now in his hands as the proper{ty of Mr.} Taylor &c till he receiv{es} information authori{zing him} to pay it to Mr Keats. This appears to me also {the best} plan to arrange the matter; do you then ex{plain th}is to Mr Taylor or Mr Cowie and write me or {the Ban}ker here without delay as until he receives inf{ormation} directly or thro' me he will let Mr Keats have {no more mon}ey. Keats howe{v}er in his present state {. . .}t ² wh {. . .} ³ nor must he know any thing of the matter, as it could answer no good purpose & might add greatl{y} to his present sufferings to know that he ha{d done any} thing to displease gentlemen that had treated {him} so kindly. Write me therefore as soon as you have explained this matter to Mr Taylor and in {t}he meantime I will take {ca}re, if Keats is in want of any thing, that it shall be supplied.—Poor fellow he is now so ill as to be constantly confined to bed, his stomach is still in a very bad state, the affection of his lungs is increasing and the state of his mind is the most deplorable possible—under such melancholly circumstances amendment I fear is scarcely to be looked for, recovery almost out of the question. His friend Mr Severn is most {atten}tive to him indeed scarcely {ever leaves} him. {His l}odgings are pretty comfortable & I do not beli{eve that he} would have a better chance of recovery any{where} else unless it were among friends who had the power {of} calming his mind— He has no religion—he has been {ro}bbed of that— & philosophy I fear is seldom su{fficient} to produce tranquillity of mind under suc{h sad circum}stances as he is placed —his certainly is not suffic{ient}.—Pray when you write tell me if it was c{ons}umption his brother died of.

I have now my {d}e{ar Gr}ay explained to you the

---

² Three or four words missing.

³ Perhaps two words missing, *followed by* pa{ }.

whole of th{is sad} affair & the melancholly situati{on of poor} Keats who in my opinion will ne{ver leav}e Rome. I must now attempt to fill {up this} sheet tho' tis past {. . .} [4] my head is a

*   *   *

→≫ 92 ≪←

JOSEPH SEVERN TO WILLIAM HASLAM

15 January 1821 [1]

Address: Mr William Haslam/ Messrs Frampton & Co./ 34 Leadenhall Street/ London/ Inghilterra. *Postmarks:* ROMA; F P O FE. 3 1821. Printed in part by Colvin, pp. 508f.[2]

Rome—Jany 15th 1821
Sunday Night ½ past 11—

My dear Haslam

Poor Keats has just fallen asleep— I have watched him and read to him—to his very last wink—he has been saying to me "Severn I can see under your quiet look—immense twisting and contending—you dont know what you [3] are reading—you are induring for me more than I'd [4] have you— O! that my last hour was come—what is it puzzels [5] you now—what is it

[4] Six or seven words missing or illegible.
[1] Severn began this letter on Sunday the fourteenth shortly before midnight.
[2] Verbal variants in a transcript made by Hessey (*H*), also in the Harvard Keats Collection, are given in the footnotes. Part of Hessey's transcript is quoted by Lowell, II, 519-521. Milnes, II, 87-89, evidently had the original letter, but he greatly condenses it, omitting words and sentences and running unrelated sentences together, all without notice. His version is reproduced by Sharp, pp. 90f., who, however, guessed it to be "one of Severn's February letters to Brown."
[3] *Written* your.
[4] *H* I'll.
[5] *H* that puzzles.

happens"— I tell him that "nothing happens—nothing worries me beyond [6] his seeing—that it has been the dull day."—getting from myself to his recovery—and then my painting—and then England.—and then—but they are all lies—my heart almost leaps to deny them—for I have the veriest load of care—that ever came upon these shoulders of mine— For Keats is sinking daily—he is dying of a consumption—of a confirmed consumption—perhaps another three weeks may lose me him for ever— this alone would brake down the most gallant spirit— I had made sure of his recovry when I set out— I was selfish and thought of his value to me—and made a point of my future success depend on his candor to me—this is not all— I have prepared myself to bear this now—now that I must and should have seen it before—but Tolonia's [7]—the bankers—have [8] refused any more money—[9] the bill is returned unaccepted—"no effects"—and I tomorrow must—aye *must*—pay the last solitary Crowns [10] for this cursed lodging place—yet [11] more—should our unfortunate friend dye—all the furniture will be burnt—beds— sheets—curtains and even the walls must be scraped—and these devils will come upon me for 100£ or 150£—the making good —but above all—this noble fellow lying on the bed—is dying in horror—no kind hope smoothing down his suffering—no philosophy—no religion to support him—yet with all the most knawing [12] desire for it—yet without the possibility of receiving it.— It is not from any religious principles I feel this—but from the individual sufferings [13] of his mind in this point— I would not

6 *Written* beyong.
7 *For* Torlonia's. *H* Torlonia.
8 *H* banker has.
9 *Here* the last solitary *is canceled.*
10 *H* Crown.
11 *One word* (here's?) *canceled.*
12 *H* gnawing.
13 *H* suffering.

196

care from what source—so he could understand his misfortunes
—and glide into his lot— O! my dear Haslam this is my greatest care—a care that I pray to God may soon end—for he says
in words that tear my very heartstrings—"miserable wretch I
am—this last cheap comfort—which every rogue and fool have [14]
—is deny'd me in my last moments—why [15] is this— O! I have
serv'd every one with my utmost good—yet why is this—I cannot [16] understand this"——and then his chattering teeth—if I
do break down it will be under this—but I pray that some
kind of comfort may come to his lot.—that some angel of goodness will lead him through this dark wilderness.—— ——

Now Haslam what do you think of my situation—for I
know not what may come with tomorrow— I am hedg'd in
every way that you can look at me—if I could leave Keats for
a while every day I could soon raise money by my face painting—but he will not let me out of his sight—he cannot bear
the face of a stranger—he has made me go out—twice and leave
him solus— I'd rather cut my tongue out than tell him—that
money I must get—that would kill him at a word— I will not
do any thing that may add to his misery—for I have tryed on
every point to leave [17] for a few hours in the day—but he wont
unless he is left alone—this wont do—nor shall not for another
minute whilst [18] he is John Keats——————

Yet will I not bend down under these— I will not give
myself a jot of credit—unless I stand firm—and will too—you'd
be rejoiced to see how I am kept up—not a flinch yet— I read
—cook—make the beds—and do all the menial offices—for no
soul comes near Keats exc[e]pt [19] the Doctor and myself—yet

[14] *H* has.
[15] *H* yet why.
[16] *H* can't.
[17] *H* leave him.
[18] *H* while.
[19] *H* *unbracketed.*

I do all this with a chearfull heart—for I thank God my little but honest religion—stays me up all through these tryals— Ill pray to God tonight that he may look down with mercy on my poor friend and myself.—I feel no dread of what more I am to bear but look to it with confidence————————————————

You see my hopes of being kept by the Royal Academy —will be cut off—unless I send a picture—by the Spring— I have written Sir T Lawrence some bold things that I have been feasting my mind on in this confinement—no less than a project—by which to copy (same size) Rapheles grand pictures in the Vatican—the Sanctum Sanctorum of Painting—8 in number.—I think this will save me at all events————————

I have got a volume of Jeremy Taylors Works—which Keats—has heard me read to night—this is a treasure—and came when I thought {it} [20] hopeless—{why} [21] may not other good things come?—a{nd} [22] even money— I will still keep myself up with the best hope

D[r] Clark is still the same altho' he has received notice about this bill— I have said to him—that if Keats is wanting in any possible thing now—that would give him ease—but would be out of his agreement—or at least fears the payment for— I will be answerable [23] in any way he may think fit—but no he does his every thing— I lament a thousand times that M[r] Taylor did not tell me about this money—that it was to be drawn in small bills [24]—I could have stopt this—as it is I dont know what to do—unless money is coming [25] through your means—altho' I know you cannot—but farewell—pray my dear fellow dont [26]

[20] *H unbracketed.*
[21] Unreadable because of the seal; *H* and.
[22] *H unbracketed.*
[23] *H. adds* for it.
[24] See I, 191, 207.
[25] *Another* is coming *is here canceled.*
[26] *H* do not.

ask me for journals ²⁷—every days ²⁸ would have been more or less like this Not a word at my Fathers

Sincerly—ever ²⁹—

Joseph Severn

This letter is for thine own eye and own heart—or as you see fit I wrote by last post to Mʳˢ Brawn ³⁰—I think she should know these—but it will be a severe blow—see Brown too—though I do you injustice to tell you—on Wednesday I write to Mʳ *Hunt*

The proofs state ³¹ of Keats's present state—are expectoration continually—of a fawn colour—sometimes streaked with blood—his still wasting away—altho he takes as much food as myself—a dry cough—night sweats—with great uneasiness in his chest Dʳ C ³² is afraid the next change will be to diarrhoea— Keats sees all this—his knowledge of anatomy makes it tenfold worse at every change—every way he is unfortunate— I cannot see him ³³ any way without something to "dash the cup from his lip"—yet every one offers me aid on his account—but he cannot bear it— I must not leave him night or day— I am quite well—thank God—once more good bye—only one letter from you yet— I am in doubt wether ³⁴ you shall have harrowing

²⁷ On December 4 Haslam wrote to Severn (Sharp, p. 72): "Why have you not kept your diary? I ask you solemnly, for no one thing on earth can give such satisfaction at home as such minute detail as you set out with. If you have discontinued it, in God's name resume it, and send it regularly to me, only that, however, I may see fit to circulate it. I will zealously preserve each section (number each, or letter it, that I may do this unerringly, and write on *bank post paper*), so that you may possess the entire diary whenever you call upon me for it."

²⁸ *H* day.

²⁹ *H* yours.

³⁰ See No. 89.

³¹ *H omits.* Severn apparently tried to blur the word out with his finger.

³² *H* Clarke.

³³ *Written* him him. *H apparently has* him turn.

³⁴ *H* whether.

things [35] like this—poor Keats cannot read any letters—he has made me put 2 by unopened—they tear him to pieces—he dare [not] [36] look upon the outside of any more—make this known —and should any communication be required to make let it come to me— I will frame it to his ear—he places the greatest confidence in me

⇶ 93 ⇷

CHARLES BROWN TO JOSEPH SEVERN

15 January 1821

A transcript in an unidentified hand, addressed at the end. The original as printed by Sharp, pp. 75f. (*S*), differs in various details, some of which are given in the footnotes.

Hampstead 15th Jan. 1821

My dear Severn

Your letter [1] of 17th Dec[r] arrived here last Thursday the 9th I cannot dwell on the subject of it Either I am shortly to receive more favorable accounts or to suffer the bitterest news. I feel—and I cannot help it—all your attentions to my unhappy Keats as if they were shown to myself,—yet how difficult I have found it to return you thanks—until this morning it has been utterly out of my power to write on so melancholy a story. He is present to me every where and at all times—he now seems sitting by my side and looking hard in my face,—though I have taken the opportunity of writing this in company,—for I scarcely believe I could do it alone. So much as I have loved him I never knew how closely he was wound about my heart. M[rs] Brawne was greatly agitated when I told her of—and her daughter—I don't know how,—for I was not present,—yet she bears it with great firmness,—mournfully but without affectation,—

[35] *H* letters.
[36] *H unbracketed.*
[1] See No. 84.

I understand she says to her Mother, I believe he must soon die, when you hear of his death, tell me immediately,—I am not a fool! Poor girl! she does not know how desolate her heart will be when she learns there is no hope, and how writched she will feel,—without being a² fool. The only hope I have rests on Dr Clarke not considering the case in so gloomy a light as you do,—for his kindness ask him to receive a stranger's thanks. But you and I well know poor Keat's desease is in the mind,—he is dying broken hearted. You know much of his grief, but do you know how George has treated him? I sit planning schemes of vengeance upon his head. Should his brother die exposure and infamy shall consign him to perpetual exile. I will have no mercy,—the world will cry aloud for the cause of their Keat's untimely death, and I will give it. O Severn nothing on my part could stop that cruel brother's hand.³ I have already written to him. Not a penny remitted yet?⁴—I authorise you to open my letters to Keats,—if he is still alive, you may perhaps cull out something to cheer him,—if not it is no matter,—but take care you do not open a letter with *my* hand writing on the address which *contains another* hand writing,— there *is* such a letter, and you can avoid opening it by peeping inside. I hear your family are well but I suppose you are by this time satisfied on that score. Tak{e} care of your own health. While attending a sick lad,⁵ I know, by experience we can bear up for a long long [time],⁶—but in the end we feel it severely

God bless you	Joseph Severn Esqr
Yours sincerely	Poste Restante
Chas Brown	Rome ⁷

² *Written* a a.
³ S hand—indeed I knew not, till after he quitted us the second time for America, how cruel he had been.
⁴ S yet! not a word in excuse for not remitting!
⁵ S sick-bed.
⁶ Unbracketed in S.
⁷ S omits the name and address.

⇛ 94 ⇚

JOSEPH SEVERN TO JOHN TAYLOR [1]

25, 26 January 1821

Address: John Taylor Esqr/ Mess^s Taylor & Hessy/ Booksellers/ Fleet Street/ London/ Inghilterra/ [*In lower left corner*] da Roma. *Postmark:* F P O FE. 17 1821. Part printed by Lowell (*L*), II, 522-524.

Rome Jany 25th 1821—

My dear Sir

Another week and less and less hope— I have still greater cause to fear—that poor Keats is now upon his death bed—he has shewn still worse symptoms every day—clay-like expectoration—in large quantities—night sweats—a ghastly wasting-away of his body and extremities—with the approaches to a diarrhoea by laxity and griping of the bowels—his food passing through him very quick and but little digested.—Yet from all this he <could> might get up if he could bear over that intense feeling—and those unfortunate combinations and passions of mind —from which no medicine in the world can relieve him—nor any other means—for they are a part of his nature— It now quite astonishes me that he has lived so long without the almost essence of human-life— I mean that sometimes calm of mind to keep the machinery of the body going—this I am certain poor Keats never possesed or even felt—he has described to me many parts of his life—of various changes—but all moving to this restless ferment—no doubts all the <sensations> emotions of his mind even to his happiest sensations—have brought him to this dreary point—from which I pray God speedily to lift him up—his suffering now is beyond description—and it in-

---

[1] This letter was sent for Haslam's perusal on February 17 (No. 101). For Taylor's comments on it in a letter to his father see Blunden, p. 81.

creases with increasing acuteness of his memory and imagination—his nerves will not bear the only [. . .] [2] comfort from things that "smell of mortality" [3]—and to any other source he has still greater horror—he cannot bear any books—the fact is he cannot bear any thing—his state is so irritable—is so every way unfortunate—that I begin to sink under the very seeing him—without the labor—without the want of rest and occupation— I shall be ill from this cause alone.—The hardest point between us is that cursed [4] bottle of Opium [5]—he had determined [6] on taking this the instant his recovery should stop—he says to save him the extended misery of a long illness—in his own mind he saw this fatal prospect—the dismal nights—the impossibility of receiving any sort of comfort—and above all the wasting of his body and helplessness—these he had determined on escaping—and but for me—he would have swallowed this draught 3 Months since—in the ship—he says 3 wretched months I have kept him alive—and for it—no name—no treatment—no privations can be too bad for me— I cannot reason him out of this even on his own ground—but now I fall into his views on every point—before I made every sacrifice for his personal comfort in his own way—trying every manner to satisfy him—now I must do the same mentally— I even say he should have this bottle—but I have given it to Dr Clarke—the fact is I dare not trust myself with it—so anxious I was to satisfy him in every thing————

Poor fellow! he could not read your letter when it came—altho he opened it— I did not regret it for not a syllable had I let

[2] A word (certainly not "illusory," as *L* has it; possibly "druary" for "dreary") illegible.
[3] *King Lear,* IV.vi.136.
[4] *L* cursed unused.
[5] See I, 150.
[6] *Written* dertimened.

him know about the Bill [7]—it would have killed him— I trembled when he looked at your name—but he wept most bitterly
—and gave the letter to me— D[r] Clark has rec[d] yours respecting
the Bill—it is now quite right—you will have received my ex-
planations about it—and I am once more at rest about it————

I have been taken ill in this last week—in 6 weeks I have
not had 6 hours fresh air—and sometimes sitting up 3 nights together—now I cannot sleep although I may—and the consequence is a heaviness of mind—no power of thinking—but at my
altered appearance today Keats is much alarmed—he has talked
it over—and proposing having a nurse for no one has come near
him but the Doctor and myself— I hope this will soon bring me
round—but my anxiety would alone make me ill—without the
bodily fatigue I am under—every one is astonished that I have
kept up so long——

The Doctor has <done> most certainly done all that
could be done—but he says Keats should never have left England—the disorder had made too great a progress to receive
benefit from this Climate—he says nothing in [the] world could
<ever> cure him even when he left England—by this journey
his life has been shortened—and rendered more painful—yet it
will be a satisfaction to you as it is to me—that for delicate
climate nothing could exceed this in mildness—the fruit trees
have been long in blossom—perhaps every thing that could be
done for Keats has been—you will have seen my f[d] Haslam—
I have been in great trouble about a most painfull letter [8] I
wrote him— Say to him that I was in a dreadfull state of mind—
but could not wait sending—the post goes once <per> a week—
Yours very truly

Joseph Severn

[7] See I, 198, 207, and "Keats's Last Bank Account" (November 15–April
16, 1821), Keats-Shelley Memorial *Bulletin,* No. 2 (1913), pp. 94f.
[8] See No. 92.

If I can get a nurse—I shall not leave Keats for more than an hour in the day—merely to keep up my health—[9]

26th

The nurse has just been—but I am afraid she wont do—there are so many little things that no one can do but myself—that I think I will not leave poor Keats at all— I feel something better this Mor^g—and have determined to keep on—without any more going out—Keats is wanting to say something or have something done every minute in the day—no one to do these—he may become irritated—for I can assure [you] his mind is bordering on the insane—

11 oclock— The doctor has just been—nature cannot hold out another fortnight—he says—the mucus is collecting in such quantities <and> the body & the extremity receive no nourishment—and above all poor Keatss mind is determined on being worse and worse—nearer and nearer his death—that he cannot possibly last but a short time— Keats is desiring his death with <with> dreadfull earnestness—the idea of death seems his only comfort—the only prospect of ease—he talks of it with delight—it sooths his present torture— The strangeness of his mind every day surprisses us [10]—no one feeling or one notion like any other being——

[9] The remainder of the letter is written vertically across the writing on p. 3.
[10] Or *perhaps* me.

→》》 95 《《←

J. A. HESSEY TO WILLIAM HASLAM

29 January 1821

Address: Mr Haslam/ 34 Leadenhall Street.

Fleet St Jan 29. 1821

Dear Sir

Enclosed is an extract [1] from a letter which we have just seen—it is the latest intelligence we have rec^d— We have rec^d one from Severn dated a few days earlier—it is not at this moment in our possession or we would send it with this—you shall see it in a day or two when we receive it again—it is of the same hopeless tenor as the enclosed— Have the goodness to let us have this extract again when you have perused it.

Yours very sincerely

J. A. Hessey

→》》 96 《《←

J. A. HESSEY TO WILLIAM HASLAM [2]

31 January 1821

Address: Mr Haslam/ 34 Leadenhall Street. *Postmarks:* 7 o'Clock JA. 31 1821 [N]T; T. P Ludgate Hill.

Fleet St. Jan. 31. 1821

Dear Sir

Enclosed is Severns Letter to Mr. Taylor— We have received a short note from Dr Clarke dated 13th Jany explaining

[1] Perhaps No. 87.

[2] Hessey encloses No. 85, and mentions and quotes Dr. Clark's letter of January 13 (No. 91) in such a way as to suggest that Gray, to whom Clark explained "the Money Business," was an employee or agent of Hessey and Taylor.

the Money Business satisfactorily—it was as we supposed—the Banker advised him to draw for the whole as the least expensive way. D[r] C. gives the same Acct. of poor K. "under such melancholy circumstances amendment I fear is scarcely to be looked for, recovery almost out of the Question."

Yours very truly

J. A. Hessey

Brown has just rec[d] a canting, cold, unsatisfactory letter from George Keats but no Remittance.

➤➤➤ 97 ◄◄◄

EARL FITZWILLIAM [1] TO JOHN TAYLOR

3 February [2] 1821

Address: M[r] Taylor/ 93 Fleet st.

Lord F. desires M[r] Taylor to apply the amount of the above Bill to the use [of] Keats.

[1] Charles William Wentworth Fitzwilliam, third Earl Fitzwilliam (1786–1857). His draft for £50 (see I, 215, 219, 234) was written on this note, and was detached from the top of page 1 to be presented for payment. [2] Taylor wrote his father on February 3 (Olive M. Taylor, *London Mercury*, XII [1925], 259), "To-day I received from Lord Fitzwilliam 50£ for the use of poor Keats, whose Situation at Rome is very deplorable. . . . Another friend here [Woodhouse?] has sent him 50£—and five others have clubbed the like sum to which Lord F.'s added makes up a little fortune again. Another Friend [Haslam or Reynolds?] has sent a Letter of Credit on a Banker at Florence for 50£ if he should get well enough to find his way there in the Summer."

-»» 98 «««-

TAYLOR AND HESSEY TO WILLIAM HASLAM [1]

10 February 1821

Address: Mr Haslam.

Dear Sir

We have no further Accounts of poor Keats since those contained in your Letter which we return enclosed with thanks It is certainly a melancholy Account—but we fear we shall have no better

Yours very truly

Taylor & Hessey

Fleet St. Feb. 10. 1821

The Cast [2] shall be left for you the first time our Man passes your House—or you may have it any time if you can send for it—

-»» 99 «««-

BENJAMIN BAILEY TO JOHN TAYLOR

12 February 1821

Address: John Taylor Esqrᵉ/ 93 Fleet Street/ London. *Postmarks (partly illegible):* [N]ORTHAM[PTON] 12 FE 12 1821. Morgan MS. A few sentences are quoted by Blunden, p. 87.

Dallington, Northampton.

Febʸ 12. 1821.

My dear Sir

It is long since I have written you, or have had the pleasure of hearing from you. Your last friendly letter now lies be-

[1] In Hessey's hand, enclosing No. 92, which had reached the London Foreign Post Office on February 3. Severn's letter to Taylor (No. 94), written ten days later, reached the F.P.O. on February 17.

[2] Probably of the life mask made by Haydon in 1816. For its history see Williamson, pp. 98f.

fore me, and bears, I am ashamed to confess, so early a date as the 14ᵗʰ August. But I have been troubled by domestic affliction and indisposition since that date, and have been indisposed to write more letters than necessity called for. I lost a child in the Autumn, just when it had lived long enough to wind itself around one's affections. And I have myself been very unwell, with small intermission, almost ever since. But I have at last applied to a Physician, and am daily gaining strength. What afflicts me most is that I may not read so closely as I desire.

I hope poor Keats's health is recovered. If he be in London, or if he be on the Continent, when you write him, give him my kindest remembrances, and assure him of my constant Regard. I shall be very happy to hear from him at any time. What you say of the progress of his mind affords me sincere pleasure. I confess that there are traces of it in his last volume. Much, however, requires to be yet done. The Hyperion I think, the best in the volume; but this appears not to be the opinion of the Reviewers. It having been reviewed in the Edinburgh is, I trust, an earnest of its success. I hope you have sold more copies than you expected.

I wish you could give me some information, or obtain it for me, respecting the new Series of the New Monthly Magazine. I hear that Campbell [1] is the Editor. I wish some <occasion> work of the sort with which I may be so connected as occasionally to contribute—more to give me a little interest in the literary world, which dies away a good deal in retirement. If I sent them an article occasionally, such as they might approve, would they send me the Magazine; and if my articles were worth aught I would take it in books as readily as in money. I shall feel obliged to you if you could obtain for me these particulars—the terms of remuneration to the contributors, and the principles of the book; because if they espouse any freethinking notions I have done with them.

[1] The poet Thomas Campbell (1777–1844).

I perceive you have published a new edition of Cary's Dante in 8ᵛᵒ ² Send me a copy neatly bound, with ribbons. At the same time you can possibly inform me respecting the New Monthly. I shall be obliged to you likewise, if yo{u} would obtain for me the pr{o}spectus of a new & complete edition of Cudworth's works, by the Subdean of Lincoln.³

I write in great haste to save post. I am, my dear Sir,

Yours very sincerely

B Bailey

→≫ 100 ≪←

BENJAMIN BAILEY TO JOHN TAYLOR

16 February 1821

Address: John Taylor Esqʳᵉ/ 93 Fleet Street/ London. *Postmarks:* NORTHAMP[TON] 16 FE 16 1821; A 17 FE 17 1821. Morgan MS. A few sentences are quoted by Blunden, pp. 87f.

Dallington. Febʸ 16. 1821.

My dear Sir

I have this morning received your Packet. I am very much pleased with the Dante; ¹ and I cannot but add, in justice to you as a bookseller, that it does you great honour to bring out such an excellent book in so becoming a form. Your handsome octavo will attract many a Reader who would pass the other despicable edition ² with the contempt which was due to the exterior alone.

I am deeply affected with your communication respecting

² See I, 80.

³ Henry Vincent Bayley, later archdeacon of Stowe. *Blackwood's*, December, 1820 (VIII, 340), however, announced that the edition was being prepared by the archdeacon of Lincoln, who was Charles Goddard. No edition of Ralph Cudworth by either of these men is listed in the British Museum catalog.

¹ See I, 80.

² Boyd's (see I, 80).

poor Keats. "The flower in ripened bloom unmatched, must fall the earliest prey." [2a] Still there is this consolation, in the dispensation of a kind Providence—that his sanguine temper would have been rendered miserable by the excitements produced by successive disappointments. And I fear he is not possessed with philosophic nor religious Resignation enough to have borne the slow ascent up the ladder of literary Fame. Poor fellow, my heart bleeds for him; but human sorrow is very unavailing. Pray be so good as apprize me of any material change in him.

I owe you many apologies for asking you to make an enquiry which I ought to have supposed that professional delicacy would have made disagreeable. You will, I am sure, believe it was done in Ignorance—or at least inconsideration. If I write any thing, I will send it in some way agreeable to your advice. I certainly will not trouble you.

I wrote in such haste the other day that I neglected one or two subjects of some importance. Has the new edition of Jer: Taylor's works complete yet appeared? [3] I am curious to know how it is executed. I suspect it is not done with that care it required and deserved. I have not abandoned, though I have suspended, my search after the M.S.S. volume of Sermons. [4] I think I told you that the agent of Lord Camden [5] had been applied to; but by some neglect of the gentleman who made the application the answer was not forwarded to me at St Andrews until after his Lordship had left Scotland. If you are as desirous to print it as you appeared to be at our first conversation, and could procure me his Lordship's address in London, or in any part of England, I think I could find some one whose applica-

---

[2a] Byron, "And thou art dead," lines 27f.

[3] Reginald Heber's edition was announced as in preparation by the *Gentleman's Magazine*, December, 1820 (XC, 540). It appeared in 15 vols., 1822.   [4] See I, 11.

[5] John Jeffreys Pratt (1759–1840), second Earl and first Marquis of Camden.

tion would be of sufficient weight to ascertain the certainty of the existence, or non-existence of the manuscript. If you are earnest in this, I will do what I can to arrive at some certainty one way or other. With one Scotch nobleman, Lord Kellie,[6] I am on very friendly footing—his family having been very intimate with some ancestors of my wife's, and being himself a very fast friend of the Episcopal church. But I would not apply to him until other applications through Bishop Gleig &c had failed. I think this an excellent time to bring out such a Publication; & I would give much to have such writings, as they must be if genuine, in my possession. I am besides at more leisure now than I have been a long time.—It has occurred to me that it may be the M.S.S. of the volume published in his Life time.— At all events let me hear from you on this, and whether you can procure Lord Camden's address.

I have one more Boon to ask at your hands. There is a publication at Edinbro' in which I am interested as the Son in law of the Primus of the Scottish Episcopal Church in which I shall most probably end my career; & which publication I am told has not yet reached London. It is a quarterly publication which has hitherto been known by the title of the *"Literary & Statistical Magazine for Scotland,"* [7] and henceforth to be denominated the *"Scottish Episcopal Review & Magazine."* [8] It is conducted by Episcopal clergymen in Edin & its neighbourhood. The editor, an intimate friend of mine, is a man who writes in most of the Publications of the day. Bishop Gleig occasionally writes in it.[9] I have not yet contributed,[10] but I shall occasionally

6 Thomas Erskine (1745?–1828), ninth Earl of Kellie.
7 Fourteen vols., 1817–1820.
8 Three vols., 1820–1822.
9 As in December, 1821 (II, 506-517, 542-547), March, 1822 (III, 22-29, 58-60), June, 1822 (III, 192-202, 266-268).
10 Perhaps he was the "B." who wrote a review-letter about Heber's Jeremy Taylor in June, 1821 (II, 311-313).

in future. It is published by *Macredie & Co* [11] *Princes St Edin.* There are Prospectuses of the new Series & Title; but it has been conducted by our clergy for the last twelvemonth. It is published quarterly, and is only 3/6 a number. I wish you would order a few numbers, & do what you can for it. I have but space to add how truly I am, my dear Sir, your sincere friend Write soon.

B Bailey

→≫ 101 ≪←

TAYLOR AND HESSEY TO WILLIAM HASLAM [12]

17 February 1821

Address: Mr Haslam/ 34 Leadenhall Street. *Postmarks:* T. P. Ludgate Hill; [o'] Clock **FE.** 17 1821 **EV.**

Dear Sir

We have just received the enclosed and we send it for your Perusal— Severn mentions your Name & is anxious you should hear soon, so we lose no time in forwarding it— Yours truly

Taylor & Hessey

Feb. 17. 1821

[11] Macredie, Skelly and Company, 34 Princes Street.
[12] In Hessey's hand, enclosing Severn's letter, No. 94, which reached the Foreign Post Office on February 17.

→≫ 102 ≪←

TAYLOR AND HESSEY TO GEORGE KEATS [1]

17 February 1821

Address: Mr George Keats/ Louisville/ Kentucky/ N. America. Summarized and discussed by Lowell, II, 517f.

London Feb: 17th 1821

Dear Sir

You have no doubt heard of your Brothers Journey to Italy. He left England in September last, & arrived, after a tedious passage, at Naples from whence in a few days after he went to Rome. He is there under the care of a very eminent English Physician to whom providentially we were able personally to recommend him and all that human aid can do for him will be done, but we are sorry to say that we have very unfavorable Accounts of the state of his health, and it appears too probable that he will never return to England

Before he left this country he had no money left in his possession as you know.—he therefore applied to us for the loan of a sum sufficient to carry him through his Journey, and he directed that whatever remittances were received from you should be paid over to us in liquidation of the debt, adding that if they exceeded the amount advanced they should be as a fund on which he might draw in future It was inconvenient to us to spare the money, but we knew that the only chance for his life according to the opinion of his physician Dr Darling consisted in his immediate departure from this Country, and therefore we did not hesitate to give him a letter of credit to some

---

[1] In the hand of Hessey, who had just read No. 94. Another copy of this letter (compare the next two documents), also in Hessey's hand (*H*), is in the Harvard Keats Collection. It was apparently the text quoted by Blunden, pp. 82f.

Bankers at Naples to whom we were known, authorizing them to discount his Bills on us to the extent of £150.—Sterling—supposing that before it was all drawn we should be in the receipt of Cash from you. The first Bill for 30£ was paid on the 10th of January last—the next for £120.—was paid this day. And [2] as it is inconvenient to us at the present time to spare this money, and it is uncertain when remittances may arrive, we have drawn on you in the usual manner for the Amount of the two Bills, viz £150—in favour of Mr James Tallant.

As this sum before now is expended, and your brother must not be allowed to perish for want we have obtained from a few friends the promise of 50£ if needful, and from Lord Fitzwilliam a further sum of 50£ of which sums being at his disposal we have advised your Brother, desiring him to draw on us as usual, not letting him know how they were obtained, knowing that his generous nature could not bear the sense of such an obligation. We shall be happy if you empower us to return these Sums to those who have so generously contributed them.

We were glad to hear such favorable Accounts of your health and [3] Comfort and Domestic Happiness from a letter of our friend Mrs Tallant. Wishing you a Continuance of every blessing we remain

Dear Sir

Yours very truly

Taylor & Hessey

We [4] are sorry to tell you that the Poems do not sell so well as to produce any return of Profit. We are still minus £110 by "Endymion," and about 100£ by the last Poem "Lamia."

Mr George Keats.

> [2] *H omits.*
> [3] *H omits.*
> [4] *H P. S. We.*

215

⇛ 103 ⇚

TAYLOR AND HESSEY: DRAFT ON GEORGE KEATS [1]

17 February 1821

London the 17th *February 1821 For* £150. Sterling *At* Sixty Days sight *Pay this first of Exchange to the Order of* Mr James Tallant, the Sum of One hundred and fifty pounds Sterling————

Value received————*which place to Account* as advised

    To Mr George Keats

Merchant *In* Louisville,   Taylor & Hessey

1[st 2]   Kentucky. N. America [3]

[1] This unpaid draft, which George Keats declined to honor, was enclosed in the letter to Drury next following, and Hessey's "Copy of Bill on M[r] Geo. Keats" (*H*) is also in the Harvard Keats Collection. The draft is on a partially printed form, and I have indicated the printed words by italics.

Before April 10, 1824 (see No. 133), or, indeed, as soon as he heard of his brother's death, George had promised to pay the bill. In spite of what he considered a shady trick on the part of Taylor and Hessey (see I, 287), he did pay it through Abbey in London, and on August 17, 1828 (No. 144), Charles Wylie wrote to Taylor, asking him for an order on "M[r] Tallant of Cincinnatti to give up the Bill or Bills" Taylor and Hessey had drawn against George. Evidently Tallant refused. Indeed, he must have sent the draft back to Taylor, who gave it or loaned it to Charles Brown. The latter in turn sent it, no doubt as evidence of George's duplicity, to Woodhouse in a cover addressed, "For,/ Rich[d] Woodhouse Esq[r]/," to which another hand added "11 King's Bench Walks/ Temple."

[2] *H omits.*

[3] *H adds:* Second of Exchange same Tenour & Date.

⋙ 104 ⋘

JOHN TAYLOR TO MICHAEL DRURY [1]

19 February 1821

Address: Mʳ Michael Drury/ Merchant/ Philadelphia/ N. America/ [*At top:*] In case of Absence, to be forwarded to/ Mʳ *James Tallant, Cincinnati./* who is requested to open it. *Postmark:* NEW-YORK MAY 15; SHIP. *Endorsed:* Taylor/ London/ with Bill Exᵍᵉ. Summarized by Lowell, II, 517.

London 19 Febry 1821

My dear Friend,

Will you allow me to trouble you with the inclosed Bill,[2] to get it accepted & if possible paid— I am in some Doubts whether Mʳ George Keats will consider himself bound to pay this Sum to us, and he may possibly deny that he is; in that case will you have the goodness to make such further appeal to him as the following Circumstances will suggest to you—it may save the Time of another Application from us.—By this post I have advised Mʳ G. K. of the Bill being drawn, & for your Government will inclose a copy of that Letter.—

The Circumstances which induce us to apply to Mʳ G. K. are briefly these.—He was in England in the early part of last Year, and then as I understand in want of Money, John Keats, the Poet, was at that Time possessed of about 800£ according to the best Estimate his Friends can make but some suppose it to have been rather more.—George borrowed so much of this from John as to leave him 70£ only. The following Day John gave this Sum which he said was all his Brother had left him, to

1 A copy of the letter in Hessey's hand (*H*) is also in the Harvard Keats Collection, and apparently it was the source of the quotations in Blunden, pp. 84-86.

2 *H adds* (1ˢᵗ & 2ᵈ Exch. for 150£ on Geo Keats). For the bill, or draft, see No. 103.

a Friend in whose House he was living, desiring him at the same Time ³ to pay several Bills with that Money which Bills he handed to him. These amounted to 80£, so that John was then 10£ in debt,—besides owing us upwards of 70£ which was not taken into the Account.—John was taken ill soon after, and his Physician having expressed an opinion that his Health could not be re-established without passing a Winter in Italy, George was written to by one of John's Friends to send 200£ for the purpose of enabling his Brother to undertake the Journey— He replied that he could not then spare the Money but that it should be sent as soon as possible.—In the meantime John's health received another Shock, and as it was then Autumn time his Medical Friends represanted the Necessity of his going to Rome as so very urgent, that in fact they said it afforded the *only* chance for his surviving the Winter.—To save his Life was an Argument too strong for those who knew him, to resist; & we accordingly advanced him the requisite Sum. Thirty Pounds was ⁴ added to the former 70£ making 100£ for which he assigned us ⁵ the Copyright of his last published Poem *Lamia*, as formerly we had given the same Sum for *Endymion*. Without the remotest Prospect of gaining any thing by this Speculation (for we had lost at that time 130£ by publishing Endymion) we gave the Money as an Inducemᵗ to him to hope for better Things & to go on writing.—Beyond this we gave him a Letter of Credit for 150£ Sterling which Sum he has drawn since he went to Italy, & as we are inconvenienced by remaining dispossessed of it we have thought the best way was to apply for it by a Bill on George Keats in <your> Mr James Tallant's favour.⁶ —We know that George ⁷ has not remitted anything; for John

³ *H omits.*
⁴ *H* were.
⁵ *H* to us.
⁶ *H* in favor of Mr James Tallant.
⁷ *H* Mr George Keats.

left Instructions that if any Remittances were received they were to be placed in our hands as a Set-off.—Unfortunately this Sum will not suffice, and as we could spare no more I have been compelled to beg from a few Friends [8] 10£ each, making 50£ & from the Earl Fitzwilliam the further Sum of 50£ which will be drawn for ere this, as John has been advised of this further Advance being ready, tho' not of the way in which it has been raised, for that would destroy him at once—.—I can hardly suppose George Keats will hesitate an Instant about paying our Bill, nor will his Pride I should think allow his Brother to remain dependent on the Bounty of Strangers: he will probably commission us to disc{h}arge this Debt to Earl F & the others.— But if he h{as a} greater Regard for Money than for his own Reputation, let {him} be made acquainted with the Consequences—his Brother is on his Deathbed; his Life is a Subject of public Interest, and it will be written. These Facts will be therein stated; & in my Opinion the Effect of such a Statement coupled with Georges Refusal to spare anything for the Relief of such a Brother will be—what I want words to express, & hope Language will not be necessary to make known.—

If George Keats should say he has not received our Letter, put a Wafer in the inclosed & give it him. And if he talks of writing to us, please to urge our Claim with such Arguments & Statements drawn from the above Particulars as may render such a Proceeding on his part unnecessary.—

If Mr Michael Drury has left America I shall consider myself greatly obliged if Mr James Tallant will take his Place in regard to this Transaction— To my Cousin Mary I beg to be most affectionately remembered.—I hope, dear Mich^l I am not giving you an uncomfortable Office in thus requesting your Assistance— Please to deduct Commission & all Expenses when

[8] See I, 235.

you remit the Amount.—All Friends are well.—I am, my dear **Friend,**

Yours very sincerely

John Taylor

It may be proper to inform you that we are still 200£ out of Pocket on the *Poems.*

→» 105 «←

JOSEPH SEVERN TO WILLIAM HASLAM

22 February 1821

> *Address:* Mr William Haslam/ Messrs Frampton & Co/ 34 Leadenhall Street/ London./ Inghilterra. *Postmarks:* ROMA; F P O MR. 15 1821. Printed by Milnes, II, 92f., in a greatly condensed and inaccurate version, which Sharp, pp. 92f., reprinted.[1]

Rome Feby 22nd 1821

My dear Haslam

O! how anxious I am to hear from you—none of yours has come—but in answer to mine from Naples [2]— I have nothing to break this dreadful solitude—but Letters—day after day—night after night—here I am by our poor dying friend—my spirits—my intelects and my health are breaking down— I can get no one to change me—no one will relieve me—they all run away—and even if they did not poor Keats could not do without me— I prepare every thing he eats—

Last night I thought he was going— I could hear the Phlegm in his throat—he bade me lift him up in the bed—or he would die with pain— I watched him all night—at every cough

---

[1] Sharp calls it "one of the most pathetic of all Severn's letters," as, in the original version here first printed, indeed it is—a striking contrast to the gay, gossipy letter Severn wrote to his sister Maria on February 20 (*London Mercury*, XXX [1934], 343f.).

[2] Nos. 76, 77.

I expected he would suffocate—death is very fast approaching
for this Mor by the pale daylight the change in him frightened
me—he has sunk in the last three days to a most ghast[l]y look—
I have these three nights set up with him from the apprehension
of his dying— Dr Clark has prepared me for it—but I shall be
but little able to bear it—even this my horrible situation I cannot bear to cease by the loss of him— As regards Money my
dear Haslam you will have known that the kindness of Mr Taylor sets me quite easy—

    I have at times written a favorable letter to my sister—
you will see this is best—for I hope that staying by my poor
friend to close his eyes in death—will not add to my other unlucky hits—for I am still quite prevented from painting—and
what the consequence may be— Poor Keats keeps me by him—
and shadows out the form of one solitary friend—he opens his
eyes in great horror and doubt—but when they fall upon me—
they close gently and open and close until he falls into another
sleep— The very thought of this keep[s] me by him until he
dies—and why did I say I was loosing my time—the advantages
I have gained by knowing John Keats—would to gain any other
way have doubled and trebled the time—they could not have
gain'd— I wont try to write any more—the want of sleep has
almost taken away the power— The Post is going so I would try—
Think of me my dear Haslam as doing well and happy—as far
as——will allow—

                Farewell— God bless you
                           Sincerly
                             J Severn

I will write by next post to Bro{wn}—a 2nd letter has just come
from him—

→≫ 106 ≪←

GEORGE KEATS TO CHARLES BROWN

3 March 1821

Printed in *Letters*, pp. 527f.[1]

Louisville March 3rd 1821

Sir

I am obliged for your's of the Decr 21st informing me that my Brother is in Rome, and that he is better. The coldness of your letter explains itself; I hope John is not impressed with the same sentiments, it may be an amiable resentment on your part and you are at liberty to cherish it; whatever errors you may fall into thro' kindness for my Brother however injurious to me, are easily forgiven. I might have reasonably hoped a longer seige of doubts would be necessary to destroy your good opinion of me. In many letters of distant and late dates to John, to you and to Haslam unanswered, I have explained my prospects, my situation, I have a firm faith that John has every dependance on my honour and affection, and altho' the chances have gone against me, my disappointments having been just as numerous as my risques, I am still above water and hope soon to be able to releive him.

I once more thank you most fervently for your kindness to John, and am Sir

Your obt Hbl Serv.

George Keats.

[1] Where it is said to be "a reply to one from Severn." More likely, it was addressed to Brown. George considered Brown and Haslam his chief traducers (see I, 279), who "taunted" him with "goading letters" (I, 329). In naming them to Dilke on April 10, 1824 (I, 279), he asks "if Severn was with John when he died." If the (lost?) letter of December 21, 1820, to which George is here replying, had been from Severn, he would have known Severn's Rome address and would not have been in April, 1824, "entirely ignorant" of his brother's last days. Furthermore, the letter is endorsed "George Keats." in Brown's hand.

→≫ 107 ≪←

JOSEPH SEVERN TO JOHN TAYLOR

6 March 1821

Address: John Taylor Esqʳ/ Messʳˢ Taylor & Hessy/ Booksellers/ Fleet
Street/ London/ Inghilterra. *Postmarks:* ROMA; F P O AP.3 1821.
Lowell, II, 527f., quotes the second and third paragraphs.[1]

Rome March 6ᵗʰ 1820 [2]

My dear Sir

I have tried many times to write you—but no— I could
not it has been too much for me to think on it— I have been ill
from the fatigue and pain I have suffered—the recollection of
poor Keats hangs dreadfully upon me— I see him at every
glance— I cannot be alone now—my nerves are so shattered.—
These brutal Italians have nearly finished their monstrous business—they have burned all the furniture—and are now scraping
the walls—making new windows—new door's—and even a new
floor [3]— You will see all the miseries [?] attendant on these

[1] A copy of the second, third, and part of the fourth paragraphs, made
from this letter by Fanny Brawne, who enclosed it in her letter of May
23 to Fanny Keats, is preserved in the Keats Museum. It is printed by
Edgcumbe, pp. 36f., under the date, apparently that on which Taylor
allowed it to be copied, of April 16. Sharp, pp. 95f., prints an "unsigned
and unfinished note" of March 3 in which Severn used some of the
phrases of the present letter. His text, as usual, is very inaccurate, as may
be seen by comparing it with that printed by Rennell Rodd and H. N.
Gay, Keats-Shelley Memorial *Bulletin*, No. 1 (1910), pp. 43f.

[2] An error for 1821: see the postmark. The letter reached Taylor on
April 3. For his reply of that date see Sharp, pp. 99f.

[3] Severn wrote his father on April 10, 1821 (*London Mercury*, XXX
[1934], 345), that everything had been burned, and "windows, doors,
wall, ceilings, floors, all new." The landlady had all this done "in the
most extravagant way thinking that I must pay for all. But no! I have
been protected by a Roman who has made [paid?] them just one sixth
their demand."

laws— I verily think I have suffered more from their cursed cruelties—than from all I did for Keats— These wretches have taken the moments when I was suffering in mind and body— they have inraged me day after day—until I trembled at the sound of every voice— I will try now once more to write you on our poor Keats—you will have but little for I can hardly dare to think on it—but I will write at intervals—and pray you to take it as my utmost endeavour—when I am stronger I will send you every word—the remembrance of this scene of horror will be fresh upon my mind to the end of my days——

Four days previous to his death—the change in him was so great that I passed each moment in dread—not knowing what the next would have—he was calm and firm at its approaches— to a most astonishing degree—he told [me] not to tremble for he did not think that he should be convulsed—he said—"did you ever see any one die" no—"well then I pity you poor Severn— what trouble and danger you have got into for me—now you must be firm for it will not last long— I shall soon be laid in the quiet grave—thank God for the quiet grave— O! I can feel the cold earth upon me—the daisies growing over me— O for this quiet—it will be my first"—when the morning light came and still found him alive— O how bitterly he grieved— I cannot bear his cries—

Each day he would look up in the doctors face to discover how long he should live—he would say—"how long will this posthumous life of mine last"—that look was more than we could ever bear—the extreme brightness of his eyes—with his poor pallid face—were not earthly— <These fo>

These four nights I watch him—each night expecting his death—on the fifth day the doctor prepared me for it—23ʳᵈ at 4 oclock afternoon— The poor fellow bade me lift him up in bed —he breathed with great difficulty—and seemd to lose the power of coughing up the phlegm—an [4] immense sweat came over him so that my breath felt cold to him—"dont breath on me—it comes like Ice"—he clasped my hand very fast as I held him in my arms—the mucus was boiling within him—it gurgled in his throat—this increased—but yet he seem'd without pain—his eyes look'd upon me with extreme sensibility but without pain—at 11 he died in my arms— The English Nurse had been with me all this da{y—} this was something to me—but I was very bad— n{o} sleep that night— The next day the doctor had me over to his house— I was still the same.—these kind people did every thing to comfort me— I must have sunk under it all—but for them— On the following day a cast was taken—and his death made known to the brutes here—yet we kept a strong hand over them—we put them off untill the poor fellow was laid in his grave— On Sunday the second day Dr Clark and Dr Luby with an Italian Surgeon—opened the body—they thought it the worst possible Consumption—the lungs were intirely destroyed—the cells were quite gone—but Doctor Clark will write you on this head— This was another night without sleep to me— I felt worse and worse— On the third day Monday 26th the funeral beasts came [5]—many English requested to follow him—those who did

[4] *Originally* and.

[5] Just as the exact date of Keats's birth cannot be definitely established, so there is an extraordinary mix-up about the dates of his death and burial. In 1828 Leigh Hunt (*Lord Byron and Some of His Contemporaries*, p. 268) asserted that he died on December 27, 1820, whereas in 1859 Severn (Williamson, facing p. 94) gave the date February 20, 1820. Eyre, in *The Old Stones of Rome*, a lecture delivered at Rome on February 1, 1875, has the date (p. 8) as February 21, 1821, and Sir B. W. Richardson, *Disciples of Aesculapius*, I (1900), 20, as February 3, 1821. Others, Sharp (*Century Magazine*, February, 1906 [LXXI, 543f.]) observes, give February 27 or 28. Some of the confusion is caused by the fact that in the register of the Protestant Cemetery the entry runs (H. N. Gay, Keats-Shelley Memorial *Bulletin*, No. 2 [1913], p. 44): "Died the 24th, of February 1821. Buried the 25th, ditto, in the morning at 15 [i.e. 9] o'clock. Aged 26." (The actual entry, the fifty-first, p. 10, in the

burial register, 1765–1841, runs: "Giovanni Keats Poeta Inglese Mori li 24 Febraro 1821. Sepolto li 25 do. di Mattina ad ore 15 d'anni 26.")

A recent student, J. H. Pershing, discussing these matters (*PMLA*, LV [1940], 805-814), concluded that Keats actually died after midnight—on February 24. He quotes Severn's letter, dated February 27, to Brown (see II, 94), "I lifted him up in my arms [at 4 P.M., February 23]. The phlegm seemed boiling in his throat, and increased until 11, when he gradually sunk into death," etc., as meaning, "the boiling phlegm increased until eleven, and then, not *immediately* but *gradually* and quietly, Keats *sank* into death." Pershing is adequately refuted by H. E. Briggs (*PMLA*, LVI [1941], 594-596), who points out that in his unfinished draft-letter of March 3 (see note 1, above) Severn says, "I kept holding him until 11 o'clock, when he died in my arms." The present letter, unknown to Briggs, categorically asserts, "at 11 he died in my arms." (Incidentally, it is remarkable that no one has commented on Severn's statement here and in the March 3 draft, that the English nurse was at the death-bed.) According to the Roman method of reckoning time, whereby one day ended and another began at 6 P.M., Keats did die on February 24 at 5 o'clock, so that the date given in the cemetery register, as well as later on the gravestone and the Keats House in Rome, is correct.

As to the day of the burial, the register, as has been said, gives February 25, which M. B. Forman (*Letters*, p. xxxii; Hampstead Keats, I, lxi) and Hewlett, p. 422, accept. On the other hand, Forman, IV, 216, Colvin, p. 512, Lowell, II, 528, and Evans (*Keats* [1934], p. 135) give February 26; while the *Encyclopaedia Britannica*, 11th ed. (1911), and Ernest de Sélincourt (*Poems of John Keats*, 5th ed. [1926], p. 594) give February 27. The entry in the cemetery register is clearly a mistake: Keats was not buried on February 25 nor was he twenty-six years of age. The register has obvious mistakes in other entries; different hands appear in it; and frequently (as the present director of the cemetery, Signor Piermattei, remarks) the dates of burials were not recorded immediately after they occurred. According to Gay (*Bulletin* [1913], pp. 38f.), "non-catholics [in Rome] were obliged to bury their dead at night," though permission was sometimes granted for morning funerals, as to Sir Walter Synnot (January, 1821) to bury his daughter. He also remarks: "The regulation requiring a night funeral was suspended in his [Keats's] case, perhaps out of consideration for Severn's state of exhaustion; there is no record as to how the favour was obtained from the authorities." Since the register makes no mention of this "favour," obviously it may be unreliable in other details.

Poynter (see note 6) specifically says, "We started [for the cemetery] so were Dr Clark & Dr Luby Messrs Ewing—Westmacott—Henderson—Pointer—and the Revd Mr Wolf [6] who read the funeral service—he was buried very near to the monument of Caius Cest[i]us—a few yards from Dr Bell and an infant of M^r

---

before daylight, a necessary precaution on a Protestant demonstration, . . . and arrived just at daybreak." Since there was actual or supposed danger of an anti-Protestant demonstration, it seems unlikely that Severn would have arranged for a Sunday (February 25) morning burial, although the register *does* record the interment of Anna Elizabeth Ballimoier, aged 13, on January 7, 1821, at 9 A.M. (entry 48, p. 9, with no reference about a day instead of a night funeral), and of Frederick Gundlach Mechlenburg, aged 50, on August 26, 1821, at 6 A.M. (entry 56, p. 11), each date a Sunday.

But apart from all these details, Severn several times refers to the three days elapsing between death and burial, and at least twice specifically names Monday as the day of the latter. It is impossible that, writing less than two weeks after Keats's death, he could have manufactured the details of the present letter: "On the following day," "On Sunday the second day," "On the third day Monday 26th." Earlier, in a pardonably confused letter to Brown (see II, 94), dated or misdated February 27 (Tuesday), Severn wrote of "four nights' watching," apparently gave the date of the autopsy as February 24, but said that he followed Keats's body "to the grave on Monday," February 26. A preliminary unfinished draft of this letter, which is printed by Sharp, p. 94, runs: "On Saturday a gentleman came to cast the face, hand, and foot. On Sunday his body was opened. . . ." There seems, then, no doubt that Keats was buried on February 26.

6 For William Ewing, artist, and Richard Westmacott, Jr. (1799–1872), sculptor, see I, 240, 249. No facts about Henderson are available. Ambrose Poynter (1796–1886) was a well-known architect, and Wolff the English chaplain at Rome. Severn's list of the mourners is probably accurate so far as it goes. Sharp, pp. 96, 105, names them as Severn, Clark, Ewing, Kirkup, and "several English visitors"; Lowell, II, 528, as Severn, Clark, Luby, "and four more"; Hewlett, p. 422, as Severn, Clark, Luby, Wolff, Ewing, Kirkup, Henry Parke (1792?–1835), architect, and Poynter. Around 1850 the last (see Hewlett, p. 426) recalled only Severn, Parke, Wolff, and himself as having been in the funeral party; while on April 4, 1868 (*Atlantic Monthly*, December, 1891 [LXVIII, 748]), Kirkup reminded Severn that "We were together at his [Shelley's] funeral. I should have attended Keats's, but I was in bed with the fever."

Shelly's.[7]— The good hearted Doctor made the men put turfs of daisies upon the grave—he said—"this would be poor Keats's wish—could he know it"— I will write again by next post but I am still but in a poor state—farewell

Jos[h] Severn

—The expence I fear will be great—perhaps 50£— I owe [?] still on the Doctor— I have not received the 50£ you mention at least Tolonias have had no notice of it— The Doctor pays everything for me and would let me have any money I

⇉ 108 ⇇

CHARLES BROWN TO TAYLOR AND HESSEY

7 March 1821

Address: To/ Mess[rs] Taylor & Hessey/ 93 Fleet Street/ London. *Postmarks:* 7 o'Clock MR. 7 1821 N. T.; HampsteadNO.

Dear Sirs,

I found a letter from Severn [1] on my return home last night. Poor Keats was yet alive & calm. I tell you this before you begin the letter, that you may read on without fear. Tho' I talked so much about wishing his sufferings at an end, I confess I blundered thro' the letter in a horror lest my wishes should

[7] John Bell (1763–1820) died at Rome on April 15. Shelley's son William was buried there on June 8, 1819.
[1] Presumably Severn's letter of February 8 (see II, 90-94). Taylor passed Brown's news on to Clare in a letter of March 9 (Blunden, *Shelley and Keats* [1925], p. 79).

have been realised. Comp^ts to Mr Haslam when you see him,—
you can send the enclosed to him,²—for I do not want it before
Saturday.

Your's sincerely,
Cha⁸ Brown
Hampstead.
Wednesday Morn^g

On Saturday I shall want it, as Mr Richards ³ will be here.

→》 109 《←

TAYLOR AND HESSEY TO WILLIAM HASLAM ⁴

9 March 1821

Address: Mr. Haslam/ 34 Leadenhall S^t.

Dear Sir

You will see by the enclosed Note from Brown that he
wishes to have Severn's Letter again on Saturday (i. e. tomorrow)— Have the goodness when you have read it to put it into
the twopenny Post for him

Yours truly
Taylor & Hessey

Fleet St. Mar. 9. 1821

² See the next letter.
³ Thomas Richards, a close friend of Keats's.
⁴ In Hessey's hand, enclosing the preceding note and Severn's letter to
Brown.

229

→≫ 110 ≪←

CHARLES BROWN TO JOHN TAYLOR

18 March 1821

Address: To/ Mr Taylor,/ N° 93 Fleet Street,/ London. Morgan MS.

Dear Taylor,

Read the enclosed [1]—it is all over. I leave to you the care of inserting his death in the papers,[2]—word it as *you* please,—you will do it better than I can,—in fact I can't do it.

I have sent this sad news to Rice & Dilke & to Mr Abbey.—not to Haslam, for you can send him the <note> letter. On second thoughts I will destroy the note to Mr Abbey, & write to Haslam to call & inform him of it.

Your's most truly,

Chas Brown.

Hampstead. Sunday. 18 March.

[1] See II, 94f.

[2] None are available, but the death was noticed in the *Gentleman's Magazine*, March, 1821 (XCI, 282); the *Examiner*, March 25, 1821, p. 184; the *London Magazine*, April, 1821 (III, 426); *Blackwood's*, May, 1821 (IX, 245, with the date of March 23); and many other periodicals. "Y." (probably C. C. Clarke) began his tribute to Keats in the *Morning Chronicle*, July 27 (Blunden, *Shelley and Keats* [1925], pp. 69-71), "I find by the Daily Papers that the young Poet, John Keats is dead." *The Annual Biography and Obituary, For the Year 1822* (VI, vi) remarks: "Several memoirs, and, among others, those of Sir John Macpherson, . . . Mr. John Scott, Mr. Keats, Admiral Hunter, Mr. Perry, . . . and Mrs. John Hunter, have been prepared, but are also unavoidably delayed." In the next volume Macpherson, Hunter, James Perry but not the others are memorialized. In his biography of Shelley, 1847 (ed. Forman [1913], p. 302), Thomas Medwin tells that he arrived in Rome before February 23, sent to Keats's address "a large packet of letters or MSS." from Shelley, and heard of his death long after it occurred. At Pisa Mary Shelley wrote on April 5, "Keats they say is dying at Rome," and learned that he was dead about April 17 (F. L. Jones, *Letters of Mary W. Shelley* [1944], pp. 138f.).

⇨≫ III ≪⇦

CHARLES BROWN TO WILLIAM HASLAM
18 March 1821

Address: To/ Mr Haslam/ Messrs Frampton & Sons/ Leadenhall Street)
London.

Hampstead.
Sunday. 18 March.

Dear Haslam,

It is all over,— I had a letter from Severn last night, telling me poor Keats died on 23^d Feb^y,—the letter is forwarded to Taylor.[1] I was about to write to Mr Abbey, to inform him of this sad news, but request you will without delay call on him for that purpose,— I say *without delay,*—lest Miss Keats should hear of it by the papers or thro' some other means. Taylor will show you the letter.[2] I can't write more.

Your's most truly
Chas Brown.

[1] For Severn's letter, February 27, see II, 94f., and Milnes, II, 93f.; part of its first paragraph is quoted by Sharp, p. 94, from an unfinished draft once among Severn's papers.

[2] Taylor also talked about it to Barry Cornwall, who thereupon wrote a very kind obituary notice of Keats that appeared in the *London Magazine,* April (III, 426; see Olive M. Taylor in the *London Mercury,* XII [1925], 260). Taylor's own letter from Severn (No. 107) reached him on April 3.

BENJAMIN BAILEY TO JOHN TAYLOR

26 March 1821

Address: John Taylor Esq.ʳᵉ/ 93 Fleet Street/ London. *Postmarks:* NORTHAMPTON 26 MR 26 1821; A 27 MR 27 1821. Morgan MS. A few sentences are quoted by Blunden, p. 90.

Dallington. March 26. 1821.

My dear Sir

I was very much shocked at seeing poor Keats's death in the newspaper. He had so endeared himself to all who were acquainted with him that the stroke will be severely & generally felt among his friends. It is, however, but what has been long expected: and if we consider his anxious & excited character, we cannot but arrive at the conclusion that this, like other visitations from Providence, is a merciful severity. Yet with human hearts and affections, we cannot but feel a painful sensation that one so young, so amiable, & so promising, should have been so early cut off. His early death has indeed fulfilled the patriarchal picture of human life—its <shortness> fleetness, brevity, & sorrow. For our poor Friend was emphatically "of few days, & full of trouble. He came forth like a flower, & was cut down." [1]— But it is vain & useless to indulge in unavailing sorrow. We must leave his spirit in the <hands> keeping of his merciful God, where the weary and heavy-laden with sorrow & affliction are at rest.

Reynolds told me, when I was last in London, that poor Keats attributed his approaching end to the poisonous pen of Lockhart.[2] If it be so, here is one more victim of that "insatiable

[1] Job 14:1, 2.
[2] Keats himself once said to Brown (Finney, II, 746), "If I die you must ruin Lockhart."

archer" [3] of the envenomed arrows of unfeeling satire and unjust criticism. A friend writes me from Edin that he felt Scott's death acutely; and if he knows how far he has contributed to the melancholy & untimely fate of poor Keats, his feelings must be such as are not to [be] desired. I perceive that a subscription is set on foot for the widow;—and I am very glad of it. I hear that Christie [4] is yet on the Continent, but intends to surrender himself at the Trial. I feel for him. He is a different character from Lockhart.

Do you know who has the custody of poor Keats's papers. I have occasionally written him letters freely & confidentially. Such letters one would not wish to fall into indifferent hands. I should feel much obliged to you, if you have any opportunity of doing it, to request that my letters may be destroyed, or returned me. I think it not unlikely that, before he went abroad, poor Keats took the precaution of burning his letters.

I shall be glad to hear from you at your leisure.

I am, my dear Sir,

Yours very truly

B Bailey

P S.

I forgot to mention, when I saw you, the Scottish Episcopal Review & Magazine, & request you to let a number constantly lie on your counter. It is published by Underwoods & Rivingtons [5] in London. It is conducted by clergymen, and is

---

[3] Young, *Night Thoughts,* Night 1 (*Poetical Works,* Aldine ed., I, 7).

[4] John Scott, editor of the *London Magazine,* was mortally wounded in a duel, February 16, 1821, by Jonathan Henry Christie, friend and defender of Lockhart. He died on February 27. See Jacob Zeitlin, "The Editor of the *London Magazine,*" *JEGP,* XX (1921), 328-354.

[5] Thomas and George Underwood, booksellers, 32 Fleet Street; F. C. and J. Rivington, booksellers, 3 Waterloo Place and 62 St. Paul's Churchyard.

the only work of the kind in Scotland, and very necessary to support our Church there. The first Number[6] is expected shortly, and perhaps may already be published.

I beg my best Compts to Mr Hessie.

⇝⋙ 113 ⋘⇜

JOHN TAYLOR TO RICHARD WOODHOUSE

March 1821 (?)[1]

Address: Richd Woodhouse Esqr/ Temple. Morgan MS.

Waterloo Place
Wednesday

Dear Richard

It is the Wish of my Mother that I should sell a sufficient N° of the Regent Canal Shares to produce me the 1000£ I want. Will you let me know whether they are vendible just now & at what Price?—

Did you ever write to Walton[2] about Keats's Death being sufficiently notorious to satisfy the Law? I should like to touch the 150£. I have found the Letters which authenticate the Advance or Loan or Gift of 50£ to him from Lord Fitzwilliam[3]— And it is true that previously to that 5 friends had

---

[6] See I, 212f.

[1] Presumably written after George Keats had refused to honor Taylor and Hessey's draft of February 17, and before Abbey's letter of April 18 (No. 114). On the back of the first page Woodhouse has figured thus:

53 | 1000 | 20
—————————————————
        106

The Regent's Canal Company had offices at 108 Great Russell Street. The *London Magazine* quotes its shares (compare Blunden, p. 39) at £27 in April (III, 471).

[2] Probably a member of Walton and Gliddon, attorneys, 39 Basinghall Street.   [3] See I, 207, 219.

advanced 10£ each (Bonsor, Percival,[4] Rice, Hilton & Dewint) which we paid over to Keats. Their Gift deserves to be mentioned to Abby, who may do what he pleases about it.

I remain

Dear Rich^d

Your sincere Friend

John Taylor

→» 114 «←

RICHARD ABBEY TO JOHN TAYLOR [5]

18 April 1821

Address: John Taylor Esqr/ Fleet S^t/ [*In lower left corner*] 93. Morgan MS.

Pancrass Lane April 18. 1821

Sir

I beg pardon for not replying to your favor of the 30th Ult respecting the late M^r Jn° Keats—

I am obliged by your note but he having withdrawn himself from my controll and acted contrary to my advice, I cannot interfere with his affairs—

I am Sir

Your Mo Hble St

Richd Abbey

To John Taylor Esqr

[4] Reverend John Percival (1788–*ca*.1837), Fellow of Wadham College and a long-time friend of Taylor's. Lowell, II, 517, listing the donors, misdescribes Bonsor (see II, 395) in her index as "painter."

[5] There is a copy of this letter in Woodhouse's Book of Transcripts of Keats's Letters (Harvard), p. 106.

235

⇢⇢ 115 ⇠⇠

BENJAMIN BAILEY TO JOHN TAYLOR

28 April 1821

Address: J. Taylor Esqʳᵉ/ Bookseller/ 93 Fleet Street. *Postmarks (the second partly illegible):* 10 o'Clock 1.MY 1821 1.Nⁿ.; TwoPyPo Unpaid. Morgan MS. Three sentences are quoted by Finney, II, 434, and one sentence by Blunden, pp. 9of.

Dallington. April 28. 1821.

My dear Sir

I wrote you a letter some time since, to which, I own, I have long ere now expected an answer. It was indeed upon a very melancholy and a very delicate subject; but I trust I stand higher in your opinion than that you would think it possible I could, in my own bosom, or in that of others, violate feelings I have ever respected. I suppose, therefore, that your many business and other engagements, or your inability to arrive at the information I desired, have been the only cause of your silence.

I happen to have an opportunity of sending you a letter by a private hand, which will tax you with a twopenny postage only. I therefore write you a few lines to request you will not forget the subject of my last. I have observed with pleasure in the papers that you intend to publish the Literary Remains of our poor young friend, with an account of his Life. I hope it will come out as soon as, with a careful selection of all the interesting particulars as so short a Life, it can appear. If it be not intended to be kept secret, I am naturally curious who will write it. Will Reynolds? I could select passages from letters I possess of poor Keats's which will tell honorably to his feelings and his talents. Never by nature was there a more amiable character. I think his unhappy life might be a means of exposing the

236

nefarious spirit of that most odious publication of Blackwood's. I wish I were in London at this time. Were such an exposure intended I can have no objection that the conversation I have related to you between Lockhart & myself [1] should be stated *anonymously,* but so as that *I* shall be referred to by L—— or any other person who, on his behalf, may desire it. In which case, I should state it to the Biographer in my own Language; so that he might state the fact, as it was, either in my language, or not, as it suited his Biography.—Of course you will send me the work as soon as it is published.

I am most happy that Christie is acquitted. He is as fine & honorable a man as I ever was acquainted with; & my first intimate knowledge of him resulted from circumstances which put his character to the strongest test. And it stood that test. I dislike Lockhart as much as I like Christie: so that my feelings have a strange *antithesis* (if I may so express myself) on this melancholy subject. What becomes of Patmore? [2]

I hope shortly to hear from you. I have been very unwell of late, and am now supported in my chair by pillows, not having been out of bed until 4 or 5 oclock for the last three days. With compts to Mr Hesse[y], I ever am,

My dear Sir,

Yours faithfully

B Bailey

[1] See I, 34, 245-247.
[2] See I, 233n. Peter George Patmore (father of Coventry, the poet) was Scott's second in the duel with Christie. Christie and his second, James Traill, were tried for wilful murder on April 13 and found not guilty. Christie lived till April 15, 1876.

⇶ 116 ⇷

JOSEPH SEVERN TO WILLIAM HASLAM

5 May 1821

Address: Mr William Haslam/ Messrs Framptons/ Leadenhall hall [*sic*]
S^t/ London/ Inghilterra. *Postmarks:* F P O MY.28 1821; ROMA. A few
sentences are quoted by Milnes, II, 98.[1]

Rome May 5th 1821

Pardon me my dear Haslam—that for a moment I should
think you had forgotten me— I was worn down with night-
watchings—deprivation from my pursuits—and above all the
prospect of poor Keats's death—the prospect of a scene which I
trembled to think on—the Letters at this time were a great comfort to me—yet none came from my good friend Haslam—this
was hard upon me—when I felt to want your advice—but
nomore on this— I have said this much—in excuse for myself—
Your 2 letters of the 22nd March and 2nd April gave me very
great pain— I knew how deeply you would feel these awful
things—and I knew that the distance we were from you would
increase these feelings—but now thank God it is all quit and
over—poor Keats has his wish—a humble wish indeed—he is at
peace in the quiet grave— I walkd there a few days ago and
found the daisies had grown all over it—it is in one of the most
lovely retired spots in Rome—the Pyramid of Caius Cest[i]us
and the Roman Walls are in the same place—the grave of
Surgeon Bell [2] is next to our poor friend—and many other English are lying in the same romantic spot—you cannot have any

[1] He says Severn wrote ten weeks after Keats's death, and his quotations
are based only on the first paragraph, with words and phrases changed,
omitted, or jumbled together quite inexplicably. Sharp, p. 97, reproduced Milnes's version, dating it "in the early summer."
[2] See I, 228n.

such place in England— I visit the place with a most delicious melancholy—which on many occasions has relieved my low spirits—when I recollect that Keats in his life had never one day without ferment or torture of mind and body—and that now he lies at rest in a grave—with the flowers he so much desired upon him—and in a place such as he must have form'd to his minds eye [3]—with no other sound than a few simple sheep and goats with their tinkling bells—this is what I feel grateful for— it was what I pray'd might be— I did pray most earnestly that his sufferings might end there was not one grain more of comfort for him in this world—

I will not as I intended say to you more on Keats's death now it must still be at a future time— I am now ill and low in spirits and these very recollections will break me down—yet I have had one month [4] in capital health and spirits—and it is only in the changes of weather—or the difficulties of my Painting that my spirits are low—then comes Keats—Keats—to my mind I can see his poor face—and his poor still hands and I am no longer master of myself.—It has been fortunate for me that my Painting required such a revolution in my ideas—or I might have been laid up with a fever.—But why am I writing all this low spirited state to you— I should not be so—for I am certainly most fortunate— I have received the most polite attention here although we came strangers— You are right in your conjecture in my having friends—but you cannot imagine to what extent— I have received so many presents—and so many introductions—that I am astonished when I reflect on them—one good fellow [5]—sent me [a] splendid paint box with every thing—another lends me

[3] See I, 18on.
[4] *Written* months.
[5] Seymour Kirkup (1788–1880), so-called Baron Kirkup, Knight of the Orders of SS. Maurice and Lazarus and of the Corona d'Italia, friend of Haydon, Landor, the Brownings, and Trelawny. See the next paragraph.

the finest Study in Rome [6]—a third [7] brings a party of English Noblemen to see me— But more than all—and what I know will glad my dear friend Haslam is that I have above half finished an Historical Picture of 8 figures [8]—this is for the Council of the R. A.—for my pension—so far it is much liked— I think I have gained very much by coming here—this place is a heaven for an Artist— Raphels pictures I had so long wished to see and I knew them all so well from the prints in London—that they have given me a most expanded notion of art——

There are here a number of English Artists but none of highest ability—except the Sculptors—we have here M͏r Westmacott—a son of the celebrated Sculptor in London [9]—they are all kind and good fellows—so far I am astonished at their generosity—you will be thankful and say Providence is over me upon me when I tell you that the Gentleman who has shown me the greatest respect and who gave me the paint box is in almost every point like poor Keats.—his noble mind—his learning—his taste—and his good heart remind me of Keats—every one here seem[s] to love him—and have something good to say of him— his name is Kirckupp—he has a small fortune and is studying Historical painting—he is a fine Musician—this good little fellow—(for he is just the same size as Keats) has done me most essential service—f{earing} that I may lose the pension from the R. A.—he {has} explained my case to all the higher classes of English her{e}—he has shown to them that I must paint my Miniatures for support should I fail— I have already got 40 Guineas and through him could have had a 150 Guineas in a short time—but my picture must be done—so he has prepared

[6] Thomas Campbell (1790–1858), the sculptor, installed him in the study of Sir Charles Lock Eastlake (1793–1865), artist (Sharp, pp. 103f.).

[7] See Crawford, two paragraphs below.

[8] "The Death of Alcibiades."

[9] The son (see I, 227n.) of Sir Richard Westmacott (1775–1856).

my way for the next season—he talks to me and advises me with great honesty—I see him every day—this I can assure [you] is my greatest consolation for the loss of Keats— I should tell he has even purchased a Piano Forte for my playing on—he accompanys me on the Violin or Guittern———

Last night I had the honor to receive an Invitation with Lord Colchester & Riven—and the Ladies Westmorland and Riven [10]—with many others of the English gentry here— Ah and I am quite at home with them—they look up to has [11] an English Painting— This invitaition [12] came from a Mr Crawford—a most splendid man here—this Gen[t]leman has invited me to dine with him every day for a long time past [13]—which I do not receive [14]— Upon the whole this place is everything for me— I look forward with great hope and delight— I have the most glowing prospect before me—a noble profession—a prospect of capital health—in the finest situation in the World— I have youth and above all I have a very contented mind—any thing sati[s]fies me— I can live on very little— So my dear fellow it will be a long time before you see me back— Thanks thanks—to the end of my days for making me come to Rome—farewell— remember me to your lovely partner—and to all my friends tell them I am happy and success[f]ul—farewell

ever yours

Joseph Severn

[10] Charles Abbot (1757–1829), first Baron Colchester; James Ruthven (1777–1853), seventh Baron Ruthven of Freeland, who married Mary Hamilton Campbell (died 1885); Jane Huck-Saunders (died 1857), second wife of John Fane (1759–1841), sixteenth Earl of Westmorland.

[11] *Sic.*

[12] *Sic.*

[13] Mr. Crauford is first mentioned by Sharp, p. 137 (see also pp. 144, 186), in May, 1823, when he commissioned Severn to copy a painting of Raphael's.

[14] *Sic.*

Tell the good Mr Taylor—that I will do all he requests me—but not now [15]— I will write to him when I am in better spirits—he of course has my letter—with notice of a bill for 50£—April 25th—this I think will cover all expences—they have not finished the Rooms yet— I dont know the price

they think my present picture is a great improvement on my last picture—particularly the Composition and Invention—in less than 3 Months you will have it in England please God— write me a good many particulars—tell me about my family— but dont write at 2 in [the] Morning—this shocks me—tell me how you get on————

<speak to Brown about the grave>

A [16] number of English Artists here have offered their services to make a grave stone— I have not heard from Mr Brown about this— I want very much to hear— I have proposed to introduce a Greek Lyre—very simple [17]—with four of the strings broken—this was Keats's idea a long time back in England— Brown will find a drawing of mine in his Copy of Endymion— done at Keatss request— Tell Brown to write me the Inscription————

[15] Taylor (see I, 247n., and Sharp, pp. 108-110) had asked for Keats's papers and books and for Severn's assistance in writing Keats's biography.

[16] What follows is written vertically across the writing on page 1.

[17] *Written* simble.

→»» 117 «←

J. A. HESSEY TO WILLIAM HASLAM [1]

5 May 1821

Address: Mr. Haslam/ Leadenhall St/ [*In lower left corner*] 34. Postmarks *(part illegible):* 2 o'Clock MY.5 1821 A. Nⁿ.; T. P. Ludgate Hill.

Dear Sir

Enclosed is Severn's Letter which I named to you— You will see he mentions you in it.

Yours truly

J. A. Hessey

Fleet St

May 5. 1821

retᵈ by Holmes

13ᵗʰ.

→»» 118 «←

BENJAMIN BAILEY TO JOHN TAYLOR [2]

8 May 1821

Address: J. Taylor Esqʳᵉ. Morgan MS. The first paragraph is quoted by Blunden, p. 91.

Dallington. May 8. 1821.

My dear Sir

Herewith you receive such of Keats's letters as I conceive can be of use to you as his Biographer. I have made occasional observations on the outsides which may serve as memoranda.

---

[1] Enclosing a letter of Severn's, perhaps No. 94, which mentions Haslam, and which apparently was sent to and returned by Edward Holmes (see No. 201).

[2] Enclosing the long Note next following.

There are two [3] which I have tied up separately that relate to Hunt and may fully exculpate him with the public from the imputation of Hunt overlooking or correcting his Poem of Endymion. You are aware that he wrote the third book of that Poem when he was on a visit to me at Oxford. If you notice his visit to Oxford I should wish it to be done anonymously—that he visited a friend who was graduating at Oxford and who staid there during the long vacation. My memory often reverts with melancholy pleasure to the time he spent with me. I have never known a young man more worthy the attention of his friends than poor Keats.

I have drawn up as shortly as I have been able the account of that conversation with Lockhart previous to that first scandalous attack upon Keats. You will make what use of it you see right. I have not supposed that Z is Lockhart after his declaration that he should not write the article. If he be, the reproof is sharper than an open attack on his veracity. And it is enough for him to answer the suspicion which necessarily attaches to him of being the person, like the filthy Jackall, who provided materials to the writer. Of course I do not wish to be brought forward more than I can help—especially as the conversation took place at the table of my father in law, Bishop Gleig. I have therefore written it cautiously; and you may notice it in your own words or in mine as you please, or not at all, if you think it not of sufficient consequence. Upon this you will decide. I have sent the no. of the Mag: which I happened to have by me among some odd ones. It breaks no set and is of no value to me. The passages I have marked to save the irksome trouble of copying in my vile hand.

I would have sent them sooner; but in addition to my indisposition, it has pleased God to visit me with a heavy family

[3] See *Letters*, pp. 52f.

affliction. This is the first thing I have seriously sat down to for many weeks.

I hope to hear a better account of your health in a longer letter than your last. Let me hear from you in acknowledgment of the accompanying as soon as you can find time to write me more at full than your last.

I should wish the letters returned when you have done with them. Many thanks for your promise to get me my own letters if you can get access to them.

I hope you are upon the Life. You will not forget the circumstance mentioned p[ag]e 17 of Southey's Life of K. White respecting the Monthly Review.⁴ Something may be <may be> made of it, if you intend to speak at any length concerning poor Keats's usage by Blackwood's.

Give my kind regards to Reynolds when you see him. And believe me in great haste

My dear Sir,

Yours very faithfully

B Bailey

→≫ 119 ≪←

BENJAMIN BAILEY: NOTES ON HIS CONVERSATION
WITH LOCKHART ¹

8 May 1821

Morgan MS. Printed in part by Lowell, II, 77, and Finney, II, 434f.

In the Month of July, 1818, a friend of poor Keats met with one of the supposed Editors of Blackwood's Edin—— Magazine in Scotland. It was not doubted at that time that he was a principal conductor of this Miscellany. He may have since

⁴ In Southey's *Remains of Henry Kirke White,* I (1810), 17-24.
¹ Enclosed in the preceding letter to Taylor. For Bailey's other accounts of the conversation see I, 34, and II, 298-300.

relinquished this office, as the public disavowal of it on a late unhappy occasion must force us to conclude.

Keats's Endymion had just been published. It was acrimoniously criticized by the writer in Blackwood's, & as warmly defended by the friend of the unhappy Poet, who was classed among those authors which were designated by the writer Z in Blackwood's Mag: the "Cockney School of Poetry." He was in short supposed by this gentleman to be under the *Patronage* of Leigh Hunt.

The friend of Keats deprecated [?] the idea that because the young Poet had been in the first instance introduced to public notice by Leigh Hunt, he was to be considered as under the *patronage* of that gentleman, & to have borrowed from him his Style of Poetry. Mr Hunt, he knew, had not seen, much less corrected Endymion prior to its publication.

He moreover explained that Keats was of a <good> respectable family; & though he & his brothers & sister were orphans, they were left with a small but independent Patrimony. He had been brought up to the profession of medicine which he had abandoned for the pursuit of Literature.

The critic in, if not the conductor, of Blackwood's Magazine, declared that *he* sh^d not attack Keats. It cannot be supposed therefore that he did make that violent, cruel, and ungentlemanly attack <which> contained in the article no iv of the "Cockney School of Poetry," signed Z, which appeared in the August following. This was the first direct attack on this amiable and unhappy young man. After the above avowal the gentleman alluded to could not so forfeit his title to veracity as to be the writer of this article. Nor is it for an instant supposed that he was. But some particulars of that article must nevertheless lay him under suspicion that he furnished materials to one of his coadjutors with a view to the nefarious purpose of making that shameless attack, so full of contempt & scorn, that no one who professes himself a Xtian can avow himself the author of it without subjecting himself to the aversion of all good men. And until this suspicion is removed, he must appear an accessory to the perversion of facts, which were in themselves honorable to Keats, to the wicked purpose of sinking a respectable, unoffending, & amiable man into the lowest contempt. Witness the following passages:—

(See them marked with ink in the accompanying no: of the Mag:) [2] Beginning—

"His friends, we understand, destined him for medicine &c &c "This precocious adulation (of Leigh Hunt in the Exam[r]) confirmed &c—

and the insolent & contemptuous concluding Paragraph—

"And now good morrow &c—

❯❯❯ 120 ❮❮❮

JOSEPH SEVERN TO JOHN TAYLOR [1]

16 May 1821

Address: John Taylor Esq[r]/ Mess[rs] Taylor & Hesseys/ Booksellers &c/ Fleet Street/ London/ Inghilterra. *Postmarks:* ROMA; F P O JU.2 1821.

Rome May 16th 1821

My dear Sir

I find myself obliged after all to draw for the remaining 50£—30£ I have to pay to D[r] Clark, for the money he so kindly

[2] For the quotations see *Blackwood's,* August, 1818 (III, 519, 524).
[1] Here Severn promises to assist Taylor in writing his proposed life of Keats, but before July 17 he had sent Keats's papers to Brown, who had no doubt of Taylor's unfitness for the work. See Sharp, pp. 106-112, for the correspondence of Brown and Severn on this subject. It was not until the end of August that Brown sent the first version of the inscription on Keats's tombstone (Sharp, p. 112), and even on that matter he and Taylor could not agree.

advanced me—and the only remainᵍ debt then will be the
funeral— I will go about it today—for here the English are
looked upon as so great and honest—that they are very rarely
applied too for money.—After I have paid it I will wait your
instructions about the over-plus—I mean more particularly
what I am indebted to you—for my money was nearly all gone
when I came to Rome—and as I was debarred from painting my
Miniatures—I was obliged to share in your kind supply to my
poor Friend— I have kept an account and will make a point
next Winter of returning to you one third of our expences—
this was my agreament with Keats.—at the present I cannot for
altho' I am in posses[s]ion of 40£ from my painting faces and
am likely to have some little more—yet the dread of the summer is before my eyes— I am still unwell— I fear my nerves are
much weakend—yet thank God I find great spirits and power to
go on with my Painting—and I think myself very fortunate in
this occupation after the scenes I have passed— I cannot yet
speak with certainty about my health—certainly I must and will
leave Rome in the summer—so many people have had the
Malaria— I think of going to Florence—where I can pursue my
studies most delightfully without the fear of bad air.—I am
much obliged by the interest you take in my affairs—it sur-
prises me that the Academy should defer the consideration of
my case until after the next prize [2] is gained—it will make it
nearly a year after the usual manner—be it as it may I am not
risking any fault or blame now—my picture will soon be finished
—if I have health— I can hope for the same protection from
God—that I have had all through <this> these dreadfull
scenes.—I prayed to God for strength and fortitude—and had it—
I prayed that no harm might come to me for the sake of my
dear Fammily—no harm—rather blessings beyond my most sanguine wishes have come to me.—for certain brutal people here—

[2] *Written* pize.

told me I was blind and foolish—and perhaps bringing on my
ruin by staying with the poor suffering fellow at the risk of my
health and fortune— I never could think so—and now that poor
Keats is dead and gone—it is the greatest consolation I have—
you would have [been] astonished at [the] brutality of some
Misanthropists here————

I am very happy at what you tell me about your intended
memoir of Keats—his bea[u]tiful character will astonish people—
for very few knew it.—I will make every communication to you
—but not yet— I cannot stand it—only writing this has made me
like a child.—I have begun a small whole length of him—from
last seeing him at Hampstead [3]—this I will finish and send to
you— I have likewise a drawing taken in middle of night with
the cold sweat on his face—about 3 Weeks before his death [4]—
The casts [5] I must send another time—because I shall require
them to finish the picture from{—} His papers I will have
packed this week to yo{u}— You will think it hard that I do
not write you more particulars— I know it is—but I cannot yet—
You will [see] a Gentleman in London soon—a Mr Ewing [6] who
has been very kind to me here—he knew more of Keats than

[3] This oil portrait, finished in 1823, is now in the National Portrait
Gallery. See for details and a reproduction Williamson, p. 105.
[4] The original (Williamson, pp. 102f.) is in the Keats-Shelley Memorial,
Rome. It is reproduced by Sharp, facing p. 84.
[5] See I, 225, 227.
[6] Severn's letter introducing Ewing (see I, 227) to Brown is printed by
Sharp, p. 103n. It says that Ewing "gave us all the attention of an old
friend, and that of the most valuable kind. . . . I had no other soul to
help me. Except Dr. Clark and myself, he saw more of Keats than any
one. . . . You will find this gentleman to possess extraordinary skill as a
Sculptor—his works in ivory are to me the most beautiful things of the
kind I ever saw." In England Ewing met Taylor, called on Brown and
twice dined with him (Sharp, pp. 108f., 112f.), and talked for a few
minutes to Fanny Brawne (Edgcumbe, p. 47) but "seemed so flustered
and confused" that she "could make nothing of him." What Fanny
Keats thought, after she talked to him, is not known.

249

any other person here—he will give you much information—
this is a great pleasure to me—he is a very good fellow— I hope
my dear Sir your health is restored—you do not tell me this.—
and I have not received yours and Brown's advice about poor
Keats grave stone—the inscription particularly————

        farewell my dear Sir
                your obliged friend
                        Joseph Severn

→≫ 121 ≪←

JOSEPH SEVERN TO WILLIAM HASLAM

12 July 1821

Address: Mr William Haslam/ Messrs Framptons &c.[1]/ 34 Leadenhall
Street/ London/ Inghilterra/ July 12 [*At the bottom is written*] turn-
over [*Readdressed in another hand on the back of the folded letter*]
Mr Wm Haslam,/ Mrs Dockers/ Greenwich/ Kent. *Postmarks:* F P O JY.
28 1821; *(twice impressed)* 4 o'Clock JY. 28 1821 EV.

                            Rome 12 July 1821

My dear Haslam

    The Picture I have been some time painting for the pen-
sion from the Royal Academy—is now on its way to England [2]—
it left here last night and is to meet the Kings Messenger at
Ancona—after which I have every reason to hope it will [be] in
London by the 1st August— The Case is directed to "The Under
Secretary of State London." [3]—with "J Severn from Rome."—
Will you my dear Friend go there for it—at your first oppor-

[1] *Or possibly* Frampton & Co.

[2] On the journey of Severn's "Death of Alcibiades" and on his pension
from the Royal Academy see Hessey's letter of August 7 (No. 124) and
Sharp, pp. 104, 106-108, 112f.

[3] William Richard Hamilton (1777–1859), Undersecretary for Foreign
Affairs.

tunity—and order it to be sent to 6 Goswell St Road—opposite Spencer S^t— Should the Messenger require payment for duties &c—say that Mr Parke [4] the British Consul in Rome (who has mos{t kindl}y and politely undertaken to send th{e Pict}ure) will be answerable for the paym{ent an}d at the same time he will also mak{e the} Messenger a present—over the price of duty &c— Should you see Mr Hamilton the Under Secretary— present my Comp^ts and thanks to him—he will recollect me when you say that I am the Student in Painting from the R. A.— Say if you please that the urgency of my case induced Mr Parke to send the Picture by the Messenger————

Respecting this affair as yet in hope—poor Keats made me promise—that should I have lost any part of my hopes <been injured> by my attentions to him—or that Illness should prevent me from compleating my picture to my or to the satisfaction of the Council—that I would earnestly {reques}t Mr Taylor to speak to W Hilton Esqr {about} my unfortunate case— and that he was {sure M^r Hi}lton for his sake would do every thing {. . .} [5]—in his power Keats said this but a few days before his death for he had in view what a many unseen [?] things might come against me— Yet I think myself fortunate in my health and spirits permitting me to proceed as I have with my Picture————

Will you my dear Haslam write on the back of the Picture— "The assassination of Alcibiades" Robertsons [6] Greece Book 3—Chap 1—"for the i{n}spection of the Council of the R. A."

At this time I am not in good health—nor good spirits—

[4] John Parke (see the *Royal Kalendar* [1821], p. 142).
[5] One word missing.
[6] William Robertson's *History of Ancient Greece* (Edinburgh, 1768), translated from the French of P. A. Alletz.

I am waiting with great anxiety answers from three Letters—
Yourself—Brown [7]—and Mr Taylor [8]—did you receive mine of
10th May [9]— I have feared that the hot & dangerous weather
would come on and oblidge [10] me to go away without placing a
Grave Stone upon poor Keats's Grave— I wait the inscription
more {par}ticularly— The English Sculptors here have {of}fered
me their services to make something w{or}thy his memory———
but the weather continues mild and wholesome here—so that I
shall not go away—poor Keatss grave is still covered with daisies
—and if I do not have answers with the inscription by the next
Post—why I will proceed with the Stone—the design I have made
is this— A delicate Greek Lyre with half the strings broken—
signifying his Classical <Genius and> Genius—left unfinished
by his early death— Mr Gibson [11] the finest English {artist} here
will execute it in Marble— The Stone in form {will} be like a
Greek Altar— Now pray write me—remem{ber} I am here in
Solitude

ever your {true} friend
Joseph Severn

Remember me to your lovely Partner—and to all inquiring
friends— I have a long Letter preparing for you & B [12]

[7] Possibly the letter which Sharp, pp. 106f., vaguely dates "before the
end of July."
[8] Probably No. 120.
[9] Perhaps he meant No. 116 of May 5.
[10] *Apparently* obildge.
[11] John Gibson (1790–1866), sculptor.
[12] Brown.

→» 122 «←

CHARLES BROWN: LIST OF KEATS'S BOOKS

July (?) 1821 [1]

Morgan MS. Endorsed in another hand "Keats's Books." [2]

List of Mr John Keats' Books

Wordsworth's Poems [3] . . . . 8vo —2 vol:
Fairfax's Tasso [4] . . . . "   —1 -"- (bound)
Petrarch's Sonnets & Odes [5] . . . . "   —1 -"-

[1] The date is a guess, but the list was certainly made before Brown wrote his letter of July 24 (No. 123) to Hessey, forwarding him the ten volumes commented on in notes 51 and 54. Colvin (who is followed by *Letters*, pp. 137n., 334n.) mistakenly says that the list was made by Woodhouse.

[2] The Morgan MS. also contains another "List of Mr John Keat's Books" copied by an unidentified hand (not, I think, Woodhouse's) from Brown's. That it *is* a copy is proved by the following facts. It omits the three titles canceled (one in ink, two in pencil) by Brown. It omits also Lamb's name, canceled in pencil in the list of names, and inserts that of Mrs. Jones, which is added, apparently by Brown, in pencil. It gives the second, third, and fourth in the list of names as "Browne." After Brown's second title (Tasso) the figure 5 is penciled in and a few other titles have penciled numbers added: in the second list the 5 is in ink, and the other figures appear in ink or pencil. Where Brown wrote "Italien Franç," the copyist put "Italien Franz." The copy has only a few other minor variants (all accidental), but since Colvin, pp. 558-560, printed it, not Brown's original list, he reads "Ariosto da Boschino" (the copy seems to me to have "Boschina") and "Levy's Roman History" instead of "Boschini" and "Livy's." Colvin also omits the marginal letters "m" and "w" which appear to be in Woodhouse's writing in the copied list, and the meaning of which I have not determined. (An obvious guess would be "mine" and "Woodhouse.")

[3] Probably *Poems in Two Volumes*, London, 1807. (I have attempted no identification of books when, as in the case of Burns's *Poems* or Bacon's *Essays*, there are numerous possibilities.)

[4] Fourth ed., with a glossary, London, 1749.

[5] John Nott's *Petrarch Translated in a Selection of His Sonnets and Odes*, etc., London, 1808.

Hazlitt's Principles of Human
  Action [6] .... " —1 -"-
Drayton's Poems (Ed^n Jno
  Smethwick) [7] .... " —1 -"-
m/ Chaucer's Poems [8] ....12mo—7 -"-
Hunt's Descent of Liberty [9] ...... 8vo —1 -"-
m/ Dante's Inferno, by Carey [10]....... " —2 -"- (bound)
Herrick's Poems [11] .... " —1 -"-
m/w/ Burton's Anat. of Melancholy [12]... " —2 -"- (bound)
Aikin's History of the Year [13]......12mo—1 -"- (bound)
<m/w/ Shelley's Cenci> [14] .... 8vo —1 -"-
Potter's Grecian Antiq^s [15].......... 8vo —2 -"-
Adam's Roman d^o [16].............. " —1 -"-
m/ Davies' Celtic Researches [17]........ " —1 -"-

[6] *Essay on the Principles*, etc., London, 1805.
[7] Smethwick published various 8° editions during 1610–1631.
[8] This copy, Edinburgh, 1782 (14 vols. bound as 7), is now in the British Museum (Finney, II, 766).
[9] London, 1815.
[10] Cary's Taylor and Hessey edition, 3 vols., 1814, which Keats gave to Fanny Brawne, and which evidently was not in the chest of books, now belongs to M. B. Forman. Another copy said to have been owned by the poet and later in the possession of George Keats and his daughter Mrs. Philip Speed is mentioned in the New York *World*, June 25, 1877, p. 3.
[11] *Select Poems*, Bristol, 1810 or 1816.
[12] Eleventh ed., London, 1813. The second volume only is in the Keats Museum (see its *Guide* [1939], p. 20).
[13] John Aikin, *The Natural History of the Year*, probably the 4th ed., London, 1815.
[14] Shelley sent Keats a copy: see No. 57 and *Letters*, p. 507.
[15] For Keats's use of John Potter's *Archaeologia Graeca*, 1697, 1699 (probably in the London, 1804, or Edinburgh, 1813 or 1814 edition) see Douglas Bush, *PMLA*, L (1935), 785-806.
[16] Alexander Adam, *Roman Antiquities*, 6th and 7th eds., London, 1807, 1814.
[17] By Edward Davies, London, 1804.

254

Spelman's Xenophon [18] . . . .   " —1 -"- (bound)

Vertot's Roman Revolutions (F) [19] . .   " —3 -"- (bound)

Lady Russell's letters [20] . . . . 12mo—2 -"-

Bacon's Essays . . . .   " —1 -"-

Boyle's Reflections [21] . . . .   " —1 -"-

m/   Cowley's Essays [22] . . . .   " —1 -"-

Locke's Conduct [23] . . . .   " —1 -"-

Clarendon's Essays [24] . . . .   " —1 -"-

Bacon's Essays . . . . 8vo—1 -"- (bound)

French Prayer book . . . . 18mo—1 -"- (bound)

Erasmus' Moriæ Encomium [25] . . . . . . 36mo—1 -"- (bound)

French Rabelais . . . . 12mo—1 -"- (bound)

Ovid's Metamorphoses [26] . . . . 18mo—1 -"-

m/w   Ariosto, da Boschini [27] . . . .   " —6 -"-

[18] Edward Spelman, *The Expedition of Cyrus*, 1742 (probably the London 1811 or 1813 edition).

[19] Presumably "F" means "French." Probably the book was René Aubert de Vertot d'Aubeuf's *Histoire des révolutions arrivées dans le gouvernement de la république romaine*, 3 vols., 6th or 7th ed., Paris, 1778, 1786.

[20] Rachel Wriothesley Russell, Baroness Russell, *Letters*, etc., ed. Thomas Sellwood, 2 vols., London, 1819.

[21] Robert Boyle's *Occasional Reflections*, perhaps the London, 1808, 8o, edition.

[22] London, 1819.

[23] John Locke's *Some Thoughts on the Conduct of the Understanding*, etc., London, 1762 and 1813.

[24] Edward Hyde, first Earl of Clarendon, *Essays Moral and Entertaining*, etc., ed. J. S. Clarke, 2 vols., London, 1815 (the only 12o edition in the British Museum catalog).

[25] Perhaps the Amsterdam, 32o, 1629 edition.

[26] Probably an English translation, like Thomas Orger's, London, 1811 (see note 41).

[27] G. B. Boschini was a well-known translator and editor but I find no work of his on Ariosto.

m/ Coleridge [28] Lamb & Lloyd........ 8vo —1 -"- (bound)
    Prayer Book................... folio—1 -"- (bound)
    Southwell's Bible [29]............. " —1 -"- (bound)
    Chaucer (black letter) [30].......... " —1 -"-
    Livy's Roman History (1686) [31].... " —1 -"- (bound)
    <Selden's Titles of Honour [32]>... " —1 -"- (bound)
    Auctores Mythographi Latini [33].... 4to —1 -"- (bound)
    Siecle de Louis XIV (Voltaire)..... 12mo—5 -"-
    Raleigh's Hist of the World...... folio—1 -"- (bound)
    Guzman d'Alfarache [34] .... " —1 -"- (bound)
    Les Ouvres d'Ambroise [35]........ " —1 -"- (bound)
    Ciceronis Orationes.............. 8vo —1 -"- (bound)
/w/ Lempriere's Class. Dict [36].......... " —1 -"-
    An Atlas...................... " —1 -"- (bound)

[28] *Originally* Coleridges. The second edition of his *Poems on Various Subjects. . . . To Which Are Now Added Poems by Charles Lamb and Charles Lloyd*, Bristol, 1797.

[29] Henry Southwell (or rather Robert Sanders), *The Universal Family Bible*, London, 1773.

[30] Possibly Thomas Speght's 1602 or 1687 or Timothy and William Thomas' 1721 folio edition.

[31] London, 1686, now in the Keats Museum (*Guide* [1939], p. 19).

[32] Canceled in pencil. Keats's copy (London, 1672) is now at Harvard (Lowell, II, 604f.).

[33] Leyden, 1742. This copy was given to Bailey (see II, 280, and note 67, below).

[34] This book (London, 1634) is now at Harvard (Lowell, II, 578-587, and No. 298). Given by R. H. Stoddard to the Authors Club of New York, it was at some date after 1925 disposed of so casually that Jerome P. Drennan, of Brooklyn, bought it at a New York second-hand bookshop on November 11, 1937, for fifty cents. He sold it on May 31, 1938, for an undisclosed sum to Dr. A. S. W. Rosenbach, from whom it passed into the possession of Mr. A. A. Houghton, Jr.

[35] An unidentifiable edition of Saint Ambrose, Bishop of Milan.

[36] A copy (6th ed., London, 1806) supposed to be Keats's is in the Keats Museum (*Guide* [1939], p. 19).

m/w/ Ben Jonson & Beaumont &
  Fletcher [37] .... 8ᵛᵒ —4 vol:

  Rime di Petrarca................12ᵐᵒ—1 -"- (bound)

  Ainsworth's Dict: [38]............. 8ᵛᵒ —1 -"- (bound)

  Z. Jackson's Illusˢ of Shakespear [39].. " —1 -"-

  Carew, Suckling, Prior, Congreve,)
  Blackmore, Fenton, Granville, and)
  Yalden [40] ....) 8ᵛᵒ —1 -"- (bound)

w/ Ovidii Metamorphoseon [41]........ 8ᵛᵒ—1 -"- (bound)

  Bailey's Dictionary [42]............. " —1 -"- (bound)

  Hunt's Juvenilia [43]............... " —1 -"- (bound)

  Fencing familiarized [44]............ " —1 -"- (bound)

  <Dudley's Memoirs> [45] .... " —1 -"- (bound)

[37] This title begins page 2 of the List. Three volumes (II-IV) of this edition of the *Dramatic Works* of Jonson, Beaumont, and Fletcher (London, 1811), presented to Keats by his brother George, are in the Keats Museum (*Guide* [1939], p. 19).

[38] Probably, if an 8ᵒ, Thomas Morell's abridgment of Robert Ainsworth's *Thesaurus linguae Latinae compendiarius*, Edinburgh, 1812. See I, 65, note 4.

[39] This book (London, 1819) is now at Harvard (Lowell, II, 590-592).

[40] Colvin has "Malden." The name is that of Thomas Yalden (1670–1736). Keats's book seems to have been made up from the works of Carew and Suckling which were printed with separate title pages in 1793 before making up (with Drayton) volume III of Robert Anderson's *The Works of the British Poets* (London and Edinburgh, 1792–1794) and from most of volume VII, which contained with separate title pages (1794) the poems of Parnell, Garth, Rowe, Addison, Hughes, Sheffield, and (in the order Brown follows) the six other authors from Prior to Yalden.

[41] London, 1806. Now in the Keats Museum (*Guide* [1939], p. 19).

[42] Nathan Bailey, *The New Universal English Dictionary*, 7th ed., London, 1776 (compare *Letters*, pp. lxv-lxix).

[43] London, 1801 (3d ed., 1802).

[44] By J. Olivier, London, 1771, 1780.

[45] Canceled in pencil. Presumably *Memoirs of the Life of Joshua Dudley*, London, 1772.

Aminta di Tasso [46] . . . . 12mo—1 -''- (bound)

Burton (abridged) [47] . . . . 8vo—1 -''-

Poetæ minores Græci [48] . . . . '' —1 -''- (bound)

Greek Grammar [49] . . . . '' —1 -''- (bound)

Terentii Comœdiæ . . . . '' —1 -''- (bound)

Bishop Beveridge's Works [50] . . . . '' —1 -''- (bound)

Old Plays (5th vol. with Reynolds) [51] . '' —6 -''-

Bible . . . . 12mo—1 -''- (bound)

Conducteur à Paris [52] . . . . '' —1 -''-

Horatii Opera . . . . '' —1 -''- (bound)

Burns' Poems . . . . 18mo—1 -''- (bound)

Mickle's Lusiad [53] . . . . '' —1 -''- (bound)

Palmerin of England [54] . . . . 8vo—4 -''- (bound)

Vocabulaire Italien-Franç . . . . '' —1 -''- (bound)

Baldwin's Pantheon [55] . . . . '' —1 -''- (bound)

Ouvres de Moliere [56] . . . . 12mo—6 -''-

Dict: Phil: de Voltaire [57] . . . . '' —14 -''-

[46] "Corrette da E. M. Tourner," Edinburgh, 1796.

[47] The earliest abridged edition of *The Anatomy of Melancholy* I have seen was printed at London in 1801. The second volume of a complete Burton (London, 1813) owned by the poet is in the Keats Museum (*Guide* [1939], p. 20).

[48] By Ralph Winterton, Cambridge, 1635. Many other editions.

[49] Possibly Richard Valpy's *Elements of Greek Grammar*, London, 1805, or later.

[50] William Beveridge's *Works* was published at Oxford in *six* volumes, 8º, 1817, 1818.

[51] Presumably Dilke's *Old English Plays*, London, 1814–1815. See I, lxxx, 261, 264.

[52] No doubt a guide-book. I have seen one of 1823 with a title similar to this.

[53] Probably the 24º edition, London, 1809.

[54] Robert Southey's translation (London, 1817), owned by Lucius Wilmerding, of New York (Lowell, II, 592-604).

[55] By "Edward Baldwin" (William Godwin), London, 1806, 1809, 1810, 1814.

[56] Perhaps the Paris edition, 1818, 6 vols., 12º.

[57] Paris, 1816.

Essai sur les Moeurs de d⁰ [58] . . . .   " —8 -"-

Nouv. Heloïse (Rousseau) [59] . . . .   " —4 -"-

Emile [60] . . . . .d⁰. . . . .   " —3 -"-

Description des Antiques [61] . . . .   8ᵛᵒ —1 -"-

Spectator—(1ˢᵗ lost) [62] . . . .   8ᵛᵒ —7 vol: (bound)

m/ Shakespear (6ᵗʰ lost) [63] . . . . .12ᵐᵒ—7 -"-

Marmontel's Incas (3ᵈ lost) [64] . . . .   " —2 -"- (bound)

Hist. of K. Arthur (2ᵈ lost) [65] . . . . . .18ᵐᵒ—1 -"-

Odd vol. of Spencer,—damaged [66]

1—Mʳ B. Bailey [67]		6— " Dilke
2—Mʳˢ Brawne		7— " Haslam
3—Mʳ S. Brawne		8— " Hessey
4— " Brown		9— " Hunt
5— " Clarke		10—Miss Keats

[58] Voltaire's, Paris, 1804, 1805.

[59] Paris, 1792.

[60] *Colvin adds* (Rousseau). Perhaps the Edinburgh translation, 3 vols., 12⁰, 1763.

[61] Possibly *Description abrégée des antiquités de la ville de Nismes*, by Mr. B., 2d ed., Nimes, 1786.

[62] Such 8⁰ editions appeared in London in 1765, 1793–1794, 1803, 1819.

[63] On this edition (7 vols., Chiswick, 1814), then owned by George Armour, of Princeton, Caroline F. E. Spurgeon based her *Keats's Shakespeare* (1928). The sixth volume is not "lost," and the complete set is now at Harvard.

[64] Marmontel's *Les Incas* (see II, 164) appeared at Paris in *two* volumes, 12⁰, 1777 and 1778 (so also at Frankfurt-am-Main and Leipzig, 1809).

[65] Probably the version of Malory, London, 1816, 2 vols., 12⁰, called *The History of the Renowned Prince Arthur, King of Britain*.

[66] This odd volume, the first of a six-volume edition (London, 1715) is now at Harvard (Lowell, II, 545-574).

[67] All these names are on page 3 with no heading. Without explanation or warrant Colvin inserted the heading, "Names of friends to whom Keats had either given or lent certain works." Colvin forgot that Taylor and Hessey often and others, like Woodhouse and Haydon, occasionally loaned the poet books which he returned tardily, if at all. See *Letters*, pp. 109, 511, and Nos. 13 and 123. Blunden, p. 96 (who is followed by Garrod, p. xxxiv n.), also misdescribes the document as "the list of those who had borrowed books from Keats."

11—<Mʳ Lamb>—Mʳˢ Jones [68]   15— " Richards

12— " Mancur [69]   16— " Severn

13— " Reynolds   17— " Taylor

14— " Rice   18— " Woodhouse

In his letter of August 14, 1820, to Taylor (*Letters*, pp. 511f.) Keats had enclosed an informal will, the last sentence of which runs, "My Chest of Books divide among my friends." M. B. Forman (*Letters*, p. 512n.) says, "Whether . . . [Keats's] wish was carried out I do not know; but . . . it seems likely that it was." That it *was* carried out is certain. Bailey (see II, 280) wrote in the flyleaf of the *Auctores mythographi:* "This book formed part of the collection of the late John Keats. . . . He desired that his books should be distributed among his friends: & . . . this volume, with a print of Shakspeare, was sent me by Charles Browne Esqʳᵉ—July 1823." Again, *The Rogue* (see note 34, above) has the following note by Rice (Lowell, II, 579): "Purchased by me A.D. 1819—and given to John Keats and upon his death 1821—returned to me. Rice." See further I, 261. On April 10, 1824, George Keats inquired of Dilke (I, 280), "what became of Johns books." Evidently Dilke replied that they had all been given away, since on April 20, 1825, George wrote (see I, 286f.): "Not a single volume, Picture, bust, Cast—is reserved for me. . . . More *should* have fallen to your share." Lowell (II, 156) seems to be correct in saying that Brown "divided Keats's books among his friends in a rough and ready fashion, allotting to each friend such volumes as each had given the poet, returning lent copies to their rightful owners, and as to the rest, giving some away and keeping the remainder himself"; and Finney (II, 753) is certainly right in describing the present document as "a list of the persons to whom Keats's books were given by Charles Brown after Keats's death." It will be observed that the only notable omissions Brown made were George Keats and Haydon. Perhaps he had the approval of Taylor, who told Severn on April 3, 1821 (Sharp, p. 99), that "in a little *will* . . . which . . . constitutes me a kind of executor, he [Keats] desired me to divide his books among his friends." In a letter to Milnes, however (see II, 49), Brown calls himself "Keats's literary executor."

68 Lamb's name is canceled and Mrs. Jones's added in pencil, apparently by Brown. Lowell, II, 154, denied the existence of Mrs. Isabella Jones, but see II, 469, and Blunden, pp. 96-98.

69 Mancur, a friend of Brown's, is twice mentioned in Keats's letters, the second time as having been at the claret feast of April, 1819, at which all present "got a little tipsy" (*Letters*, pp. 266, 325). His name occurs frequently in M. B. Forman's *Some Letters*.

→≫ 123 ≪←

CHARLES BROWN TO J. A. HESSEY

24 July 1821

Address: To/ Mʳ Hessey/ Fleet Street. Morgan MS. Lowell, II, 592, quotes a brief extract.

Hampstead. 24ᵗʰ July 1821.

Dear Sir,

I return with many thanks the two vols of Letters from Scotland,[1] which you had the kindness to lend me. They would not have been detained so long, as I told you two months since, had I known what books belonged to your house in Mʳ Keats' trunk, as I wished to send them all together. The Ancient Drama and Palmerin of England [2] I understand are your property, and therefore I can add those to the parcel.

Mʳ Taylor promised me some time ago to let me speedily have the four MS books in my hand writing [3] of Mʳ Keats' poems. I suppose they are copied by this time. It will be a great gratification both to myself and {to} my friends to have them returned as soon as convenient;—pray ask Mʳ Taylor to have the goodness to forward them by the coach.

Your's truly,
Chaˢ Brown.

[1] Perhaps *Letters from an Officer in the North of Scotland to His Friend in London,* 2 vols. (1815).
[2] See I, 258, notes 51, 54, and I, 264, note 2.
[3] See I, 264.

→» 124 «←

J. A. HESSEY TO WILLIAM HASLAM

7 August 1821

Address. Wᵐ Haslam Esq/ Post Office/ Ramsgate. *Postmark:* AU. B7 [1]821.[1]

London Aug. 7. 1821

My dear Sir

I am ashamed and concerned & vexed beyond measure to find that I have caused you so much uneasiness by not answering your Letters till today   In fact I did not think the first required any immediate reply, and as I was going yesterday to see Hilton I deferred writing till my return, and then forgot it till after post-time. Every thing had been done before you sent Severnes Letter, by his Sister who had heard from him and had spoken to Mr Bond [2]—but the Picture is not yet arrived.[3] the Messenger having left Ancona before the Picture reached it. There is yet a chance that it may have been sent off by some conveyance & may yet arrive, but it is, I believe, a mere chance. I have requested Hilton to do what he can, but unless a council should be called before the day of Election, of which there is not any immediate prospect, he says he can do nothing: but he has advised Severnes Father to write to the Council & give a Statement of the Case, as the most likely mode to succeed. I hope poor Severne will be enabled to take his place as a Candi-

---

[1] The date here, as on Nos. 126 and 308, seems intentionally to have omitted the first digit.

[2] William Bond, the engraver to whom Severn had once been apprenticed (Sharp, pp. 6-9, 106).

[3] The picture (see I, 266) turned up at the Royal Academy late in October, and in November the Council awarded Severn a pension of £130 annually for three years (Sharp, p. 113).

date at least—the result of the contest must depend on his Merits as exhibited in his Picture— Nothing that we can do shall be left undone, but I fear there is nothing for us but to hope which I do most sincerely

Yours very truly

J. A. Hessey

→» 125 «←

CHARLES BROWN TO JOHN TAYLOR

12 August 1821

Address: To/ Mʳ Taylor/ 93 Fleet Street/ London. Morgan MS.

Wentworth Place.

12ᵗʰ Augᵗ Sunday.

Dear Sir,

Yesterday evening I received a letter from Mʳ Severn. It is dated Rome 17ᵗʰ July. Among other matters he menti{on}s his great anxiety about his Picture.[1] He says you had been so kind as to consult with your friend Mʳ Hilton respecting the time of its arrival for the inspection of the Council, and that he understood *September,* and then adds—"when a week since my Sister Maria wrote that she had seen a notice in the Hall of the R A requiring the Picture by the 10ᵗʰ of August." Fearful of a mistake in your letter,—and, at all events, resolved if possible to be on the safe side,—he intrusted it without delay to the King's Messenger. The worst is that in his hurry he has sent it in an unfinished state. He seems much worried at the idea of its not arriving in time;—and in the midst of his perplexities he is not in a good state of health. I shall write to him by Tuesday's post, and if you have any thing to say on this subject

---

[1] See I, 262, and, for another account, Brown to Thomas Richards, August 15 (M. B. Forman, *Some Letters,* pp. 4f.).

I shall be happy to send it. He desires me to present his <Compliments to you> remembrance<s> to you and to request {you} will have the goodness to answer his last letter, the subject of which he talks of as another source of anxiety. He {i}ntends to remain at Rome during the bad season, not deeming it prudent with his means to travel elsewhere, tho' he fears he may yet suffer more in his health.

About three weeks ago (I think) I sent to Mr Hessey the books he had the kindness to lend me, together with the Old Drama and Palmerin of England which you mentioned as some of those books which belonged to you.[2] Have they arrived safe?

I have again to request that the Mss in my hand writing of Keats' poetry may at your earliest convenience be returned. They would prove, especially at this time, most gratifying to me, and to one more, otherwise I would not urge the Copyist [3] to finish them.

Your's truly,
Cha' Brown.

→»» 126 «←

J. A. HESSEY TO WILLIAM HASLAM

18 August 1821

Address: Mr Haslam/ N⁰ 2 Neptune Place/ Ramsgate. *Postmark:* AU A18 [1]821.[1]

London Aug. 18, 1821

Dear Sir

I understand from Mr Hilton that the day fixed for the Election is gone by and I cannot learn that Severns Picture is

[2] See I, 261.
[3] Woodhouse.
[1] See the note on the postmark of No. 124.

arrived. I hear however that no other Picture has been sent in, so that no Election has taken place, and therefore I presume Severn has his chance still, if any one has, but of that I am by no means certain.[2]

Your London Magazine was sent to Shadwell where I suppose it now lies unless you have rec^d it since you wrote.

Yours truly
J. A. Hessey

→→→ 127 ←←←

CHARLOTTE (?) REYNOLDS [1] TO RICHARD WOODHOUSE

1821 (?) [2]

Morgan MS. Printed by Finney, I, 346.

Miss Reynolds' Compliments to Mr Woodhouse—she will feel obliged if he will send by the bearer her Album which he took away from Little Britain in August last with the kind intention of writing in— Miss R—— is sorry to trouble M^r W—— but she has a friend who is anxious to gratify her by contributing some lines to it

If quite convenient Miss R—— will thank M^r W—— to let her have poor Keats's letter [3] at the same time as it is of course now very valuable to her—

Thursday Morn^g

[2] See the preceding letter and I, 262.
[1] Finney attributes this letter to Jane, Lowell, I, 114, to Charlotte, Reynolds. The handwriting bears no resemblance to that of Jane twenty-three years later (No. 348).
[2] The date is a pure guess.
[3] Possibly that of September 5, 1817 (*Letters*, pp. 35-37), now known only because Woodhouse transcribed it.

⇛ 128 ⇚

JOSEPH SEVERN TO JOHN TAYLOR

5 January 1822

Address: John Taylor Esqr/ Mess^s Taylor & Hesseys/ Fleet Street/ London/ Inghilterra/ [*In lower left corner*] from S— Rome. *Postmarks:* F P O JA.22 1822; ROMA.

Rome Jany 5th 1822

My dear Sir

Your kindness in speaking to Mr Hilton about me—had great effect— I understand he said many things to better my unfortunate cause.—He [1] must have done much to my final success [2]—So that I have to be more in your debt than before.— Will you [3] please to present my thanks to Mr Hilton—and offer my services to him— I have been terribly dash'd in my spirits and had not withal to write to you.—The undertermined [4] pension was present to take all my comfort.—it prey'd about my health—for I could not tell what was to be my fate.—this doubtfull state was horrible—and has prey'd my spare flesh of my bones—but now I thank God the cause is removed.—I did hope when I left England that for the purpose I set out upon I should not suffer—and so it has turned out.—for I bless the day on <that> which I came to Rome.—it was marked out by God for my Good.—not only that I should serve my poor friend—but that I should be advancing onward to my purpose.—I reckon that the experience I gained in the advice of Keats has advanced me much— I can feel and recollect the things he said to be true and real.—How goes the Memoir my dear Sir?—though I should

[1] *So apparently, written over* and.
[2] See I, 262n.
[3] *Written* your.
[4] *Sic.*

be the last to inquire [5] since I have given you so little help.—
but I crave your pardon.—for I cannot write.—I cannot put my
thinking to paper.—Did you know it was Keats intention to
make a long Poem upon the Story of Sabrina.[6]—he mentioned
this many times to me.—it would have been a most beautiful
subject for him.—he intended Sabrina to be modelled on Spen-
cers Una.—or its principal to have been moral Beauty— It was
wonderfull how deeply Keats felt beauty.—I even think much
of this gave him such pain on his death bed—it was not at all the
fear of dying—but the leaving this World of Beauty so soon.—
before he had experience in it—or knew the purpose of his life.—
One Morning early in February. (before his death) I was delighted to find the Spring had commenced here—and when the
poor fellow awoke I told him of it—I told him I had seen some
trees in blossom.—this had a most dreadful effect on him— I had
mistaken the point—he shed tears most bitterly.—and said—
"The spring was always enchantment to me—I could get away
from suffering.—in watching the growth of a little flower.—it
was real delight to me—it was part of my very soul—perhaps the
only happiness I have had in the world—has been the silent
growth of Flowers— Ah! why did you let me know this.—why
show me that this comfort is gone.—that I shall never see the
Spring again.—I hoped to die before the spring came— O I
would to God—that I were in my grave—*quiet and insensible to
these ghastly hands—these knobbed knees*— The grave—with
flowers on its top.—send me to it now"——— On another occasion
I remember it.—In the Ship when we were performing Quarantine.—it was proposed that the Sailors should sing us some songs
to kill the time—2 or 3 sung—coarsely & brutally enough—but I
was astonished at the effect on Keats—he started up.—and said—
"O! God! I doubt the immortality of my Soul—this grossness

[5] *Or perhaps* enquire.
[6] See Lowell, II, 483, 504; Hewlett, p. 412.

takes away my belief— I fall into a brute even to hear it.—why do I live if these are my fellow creatures."?—[7]

The picture [8] is not yet compleated—I cannot finish it to please me.—without the Mask [9] I have seen at your [10] House.— Will you be so kind as [to] procure me one.—and I shall hope to make the picture worthy your acceptance.—at present the face is too like him in the last half year of his life—but it reminds me of him much—it is a whole length figure.—painted as near as possible to the last recollection I had of him at Hampstead —I have directed my Sister to purchase for me your Dante by Carey.[11]—and to send for the Mask of Keats.—they are preparing a small packing Case and these are on the list.—Think my dear Sir—if you know of any Copy of Stothards work on Costume.[12] —I shall be much in want of it soon.—for all my painting prospects are made up of Romance & Gothic History.—I think all the copys are sold—but there may be one to resell—if there should be pray let my Sister know—that I may have it.—Mr Horace Smith [13] has not yet come—there are at present here about 1000 English.—many Noblemen— I shall now be able my dear Sir—to return you the money you were so very kind as lend me.—it has been a great comfort to me.—I shall soon draw for the 1ˢᵗ half year of my pension—when I shall be most happy to pay this back.—At present I am going on cheerily.—an English Nobleman here seems to have an inclination to my large picture of Alexander [14]—now going on.—I shall finish it before the sum-

[7] See Hewlett, p. 402.
[8] See I, 249.
[9] See I, 208n., II, 343.
[10] *Apparently* yours.
[11] *Or perhaps (correctly)* Cary. See I, 80.
[12] Charles Alfred Stothard (1786–1821), *Monumental Effigies of Great Britain*, 12 parts, 1811–1832.
[13] Joint author (1779–1849) of *Rejected Addresses* (1812).
[14] "Alexander the Great Reading Homer."

mer—after that I finish the picture I brought with me—and then for a large composition————

Pray how is your Health?—if you will please write me soon I shall consider it a great favor.—present my respects to M[r] Hessey—and to M[r] Reynolds—whom I should be most happy to hear of————

Your most Obliged Friend

Joseph Severn

43 Via di S. Isidoro—2[d] piano—

poor Keats works are here much read and much admired— I cannot but think they *will* be popular.—many who condemned now admire them—he is much talked of—and I think the great respect shown me here—is still owing to his Memory and works. —you would be astonished at the interest the Nobility here have taken in my affairs.—but I know it is as the Friend of Keats————

→≫ 129 ≪←

FREDERICK SALMON [1] TO RICHARD WOODHOUSE

15 February 1822

Address: Paid/ Richard Woodhouse Esq[r]/ lot/ Kings Bench Walks/ 11/ Temple. *Postmarks:* RAMSGATE 75; F PAID 16 FE 16 1822. Morgan MS.

My dear Richard

I find myself so much *bettered* by the trivial stay I have had in this place, that it is not my Intention to return to London till Wednesday next. If you see your brother say as much to

---

[1] Surgeon (1796–1868) and author of several treatises dealing with rectal diseases. In 1823–1824 (Pigot's *Commercial Directory*) he lived at 31 Bucklersbury; in 1855 (Watkins' *Directory*) his residence was at 18 Lower Berkeley Street, Portman Square, his office at 12 Old Broad Street. See I, 274.

him, and that I wish his servant to continue her present plan
of treatment till I see her on Wednesday next. Keats Father was
Head Ostler at the Swan & hoop Pavement—Moorfields—married—Jennings the proprietors daughter— Keats had two
Brothers and one Sister—the younger brother is dead. he was
educated entirely with Mr Clark at Enfield Middlesex—served
his apprenticeship to an Apothecary Hammond at Edmonton—
went to St. Thomas hospital—and after that period <he>
Charles Clarke supposes you know all about him. your very
sincere friend

Fred^k Salmon

Bell Vue house
   Ramsgate—Friday Feby 15. 1822.

≫≫ 130 ≪≪

JOSEPH SEVERN TO WILLIAM HASLAM

1 June 1823

> *Address:* To William Haslam Esqr/ per favor of/ Messrs Unwin/ 144
> Leadenhall Street/ London/ Inghilterra/ [*In upper right corner:*] from
> J. S. Rome [*On outside back fold:*] J S/ Roma—/ 10th June 1823.—
> *Postmarks:* F P O JU.19 1823; ROMA.

Rome June 1st 1823.

My dear Haslam

   Your letter fills me with melancholly—more as it shows
me the greivous cause [1] of your long silence—<how> I long to
see you and be with you—more than ever—how strange that the
Heart more craves to sympathize in scenes of misery—than revel
in prosperity and luxury—so I feel it now—I feel a pang at the
least—(even natural change) of scenes dear to me in England—
I am yet untamed by the laws of Nature—nay by my absence

[1] The death of his "lovely partner" in October. See I, lxxxviii f.

am become more savage— A pretty little garden at my Fathers
has been built upon a place in itself quite unworthy notice—
but it <is> was where I tossed my Ball and fired my Cannon
—dear dear to me as long as I am mortal— When I think that I
shall never see it again—it brings the tears in my eyes

But the breaking up of the dear home of my Friend—
whose happiness will ever be one of my comforts—is like the
approaches of Old Age in the shape of Human misery I bear
these things poorly— I cannot be reconciled to them wether it
is that my pursuit is a false thing—turning to me *only* Natures
beautiful look and perfection—and leaving me less prepared
for its misery and deformity.—How I should like to see you and
have you set me right in these points—your letter tells me of
horror to the very brink—but yet it carries its own Balm with
it.—I am perhaps thankful that I did not have your former letter
on this account— I am wretch^y broken down by cares and
troubles and the separation from all that is dear to me—it seem's
like 30 years upon my head— I am hasting on to Florence to
see my dear friend Brown whose will be the first English face
for my longing sight since I left England— Ah how jealous and
avaricious I am of bating one jot of my dear England— I cannot
bear to think of your loss—you must write to me and set me
better in these things— I know you are capable—

I have been miserably ill—to a much greater extent than
I liked to tell my family—because I love them better than myself—because I live for them—but away with misery—it knaws
enough when it exists—my good friend Dr Clark assures [me]
that my illness has been my own fault—and by little attention to
my Stomach I shall be well and strong—so far it is true for now
I am well—in some spirits—my pictures going on well nay all
well—save these things from England— I seem to think that I
shall in the end be found dead in my painting room—and they
will lay me by poor Keats— Yet I wont complain—I am thank-

271

full to God for my success in all the things I came for—except poor Keats life— I have made a decent progress in my darling Paint—and now cut some figure in "the Eternal City.—I have just compleated a picture [2] of 6 figures—the subject is—Greek Shepherds rescuing a Lamb from a Vulture—the scene is on a Mountain looking down to the Sea—it seems to be very much liked for its originality and colouring— I have intended to send it for the Inspection of the R. A. agreable to their Laws.—Another and large picture is done of Alexander studying Homer at night.[3]— it is to show the effect of Homer on the mind of Alexander—the size is 11 feet by 9— I have near[y] compleated 12 Compositions from the Tempest of Shake[s]peare—which are after your heart —and I have cover{ed} 2 large Rooms with Copies and studies of my {own} hand—in these things I hope to come home fat

I should be very happy to have you here with me— I can give you rooms <here>— There is a most delightful Society of all kinds of English—and I cannot but think it would have a great effect on your mind.—if it can be managed [4] come by all means—you will find me surrounded by the most superior and amiable people—perhaps the kindness and respect I have received in Rome is the most happy point of my Life

For our money affair—my dear Haslam I fear it will at present be quite out of my power—unless I chance to sell one of my pictures—of this I have hope— You see my studies are now very expensive—my Income is not equal to them every farthing is sacrificed to the accomplishment of my object—since now I am sure of success—what I have now began— I must find money to

[2] "Greek Hill-Shepherds Rescuing a Lamb from an Eagle," begun in the autumn of 1821. It was suggested by a passage in *Endymion* (Sharp, pp. 126, 134), and is now in the Keats Museum.
[3] See Sharp, p. 126, and I, 268.
[4] *Written* mangaed.

get through with but my pension will not be enough—next winter I shall turn in something from the sale of my Pictures. I have been going on a most rigorous course of Study—so now I can paint and draw with facility—such as I scarce hoped to attain— Yet the living here is very cheap—if you are with me I will ensure your expences at so little as 3 Shillings per day—and yet <yet> not lacking anything— I have just put up the Tomb to poor Keats—it has cost me 16£—but Brown insists on paying half [5] Farewell— I will write again from Florence in about 3 Weeks— I will pray that God may lift up and support you—and that I may see you here Farewell

ever ever yours   Joseph Severn [6]

Our Keats Tomb is simply this—a Greek Lyre in Basso relievo— with only half the Strings.—to show his Classical Genius cut off by death before its maturity.—the Inscription is this "This Grave contains all that was Mortal of a Young English Poet— who on his death-bed—in the bitterness of his heart—at the malicious power of his enemies—desired [7] these words to be engraven on his Tomb Stone"

  "Here lies one whose name was writ in Water" [8]

The picture [9] I have now began is very large 12 feet by 18—it

[5] Severn wrote to Brown (Forman, IV, 371), January 21, 1823, saying that he hoped the tomb would be finished "this week." According to Sir Charles W. Dilke (*Papers*, I, 17), Severn paid all the expense, taking no money from Brown.

[6] The words from "Farewell—I" to the signature are written on one of the outer folds of the letter, below the seal.

[7] Brown's first draft read (Sharp, p. 112), "death-bed, in bitter anguish at the neglect of his countrymen, desired."

[8] The sentences from "Our Keats" to "Water'" are written upside down in the top margin of pages 2 and 3.

[9] "Lorenzo de' Medici Rescued from Assassination by His Friends" (Sharp, pp. 137f.).

will [contain] upwards of 30 figures the size of Life—but more anon [10]

direct me Poste Restante—Firenze—[11]

⇒⇒ 131 ⇐⇐

RICHARD WOODHOUSE: NOTES ON KEATS'S LIFE
21 August 1823

Morgan MS. Part printed by Finney, I, 8.

21 Aug[t] 1823.—
I dined at F. Salmon's [1] with C. C. Clarke from whom I learned that JK's father was ostler at the Swan & Hoop on the Pavement in Moorfields— He was a short thickset man like K. <but> in height but stout— The name of the person who kept the Inn was Jennings, <he> K's father married the Daughter— He was a man much above his sphere in life. The Ch[n] were sent to C. C. C.'s Father's School at Edmonton—where the Father often went to see them— The father died—afterw[d] the Mother of a Consumption—& the grandmother was very kind to them— John was her favorite.

———

One of the earliest things JK wrote was a *Sonnet to the Moon* [2] wh: he gave to C. C. C.— He wrote a Sonnet also on the Bells which disturbed him in his lodg[gs] at N°   Cheapside, where he lodged after he left (or while he was at) S[t] Thomas's hospital— Also a Sonnet respect[g] Nebuchadnezzar.[3]

———

[10] These two sentences are written upside down in the bottom margin of pages 2 and 3.
[11] This sentence is written upside down in the top margin of page 4.
[1] See No. 129.
[2] Not known today.
[3] See I, 3n., II, 154.

C. C. C. was to lend me 2 Sonnets in the literary Pocket Book N⁰ 1.⁴

————

→» 132 «←

CHARLES COWDEN CLARKE TO RICHARD WOODHOUSE

29 December 1823

Address: —— Woodhouse Esqʳ/ 1. King's Bench Walk/ Temple. Morgan MS.

Office of works
Guildhall 29ᵗʰ Decʳ 23.

Dear Sir

I have had the enclosed ¹ for, and to return you ever since my last interview. It has so happened however, that every Sunday for many weeks past I have been engaged; <for> and it is the only day I now have to bestow upon my friends. Will you do me the favour to send me those lines of Keats's upon the mystery of the Maidenhead.² I think them very beautiful.

Many pleasant returns of the Season to you, and believe me

Your's very truly
C. C. Clarke

⁴ See II, 155. Attached to these notes is a slip on which Woodhouse wrote (compare No. 24, note 6):
"he can conceive a billiard Ball to be soothed <by a sense of its own smoothness> & feel pleasure from a consciousness of its <own> own smoothness—& the rapidʸ. of its Motion.
"I wodᵈ endeavour to forget the expression, & retain only the wi[s]dom of the <Sentiment>. observⁿ."
¹ Perhaps the sonnets mentioned in the preceding letter.
² Perhaps "O blush not so!"

⇢⇢⇢ 133 ⇠⇠⇠

GEORGE KEATS TO C. W. DILKE

10 April 1824

Address: Cha⁵ Dilke Esqʳᵉ/ Navy pay Office/ Somerset House/ London./ or Great Smith Street/ Westminster. A long extract is printed by Forman, IV, 396-399, and a short one by Lowell,[1] I, 171f.

Louisville April 10ᵗʰ 1824
Kentucky

My dear Sir

I cannot let pass an opportunity of sending letters by a sure hand without addressing one to you, as the man numbered among the Friends of my Brother John the least likely to be influenced by those reports so injurious to my honor— Brotherly affection—common honesty—which have so cruelly estranged others whose good opinion of me I had hoped would have required stronger testimony to have removed. Entertaining as I do the utmost certainty of your Friendliness [2] I will not make any excuses for troubling you with the proof that I not only did not wrong my Brother in money concerns, but that I owed him little or nothing, and if I did that it was impossible to remit, being without the means. Thro' a relation [3] of Mʳ Taylor's now living at Cincinnati I heard that he had been informed that I had brought away 700 £ of John's money: to show that it was impossible that he could be in possession of that sum clears me

---

[1] Who tries, I, 47f., II, 381f., to summarize George's financial statements, which Forman omitted. These statements convinced Dilke, who on July 31 (the letter is now in the Keats Museum) forwarded a summary of them to Brown. The latter's unfavorable reactions are set forth in a letter to Severn (Sharp, p. 147). A few of Forman's variants *(F)* are given in footnotes.

[2] *F* Friendship.

[3] James Tallant (see Nos. 43 and 104).

to that large amount, leaving it possible that I may have taken
all he had, and if I show that all he had was probably owing to
me, as far as common transactions go I am cleared altogether.
John and I left school at the same time he immediately paid
200 Guineas and expences to be bound to a Surgeon [4] and during his apprenticeship spent more than the interest of his
money. I was with my Guardian at no expense: between the
time of John's leaving the Surgeon and his coming of age, he
and Tom (who had been with Mr Abbey and left him) spent 3
times their income, to make up a considerable part of which
I borrowed and pd when I became of age, besides the various
sums John had to pay for dressership and Fees, books and instruments which Mr A. advanced for him: thus you see my
Brothers' property rapidly dimi[ni]shing and mine stationary.
The first material reduction of mine was paying debts con-
tracted on their account principally Tom's, whose expenses
were cons[i]derably encreased by his sickness, and his income
comparatively trifling. Now [5] sum this up presuming 1500£ was

$£200$

the amount each of us possessed. Suppose with the *premium*

$£30$ $£50$

to Mr Hammond and *apprenticeship* fees, *dressership* and

50£ $£20$ 20

other *hospital* fees, *books* and surgical *instruments,* and the
£160 per an. Tom being with him.

current expenses between the time of [6] getting his indentures
untill he was of age, nearly 4 years, he spent £1000, a most
moderate calculation, he had but 500£ left to lend 175£ which
he informed me he did and spend at least 200£ per annum
untill I started to America, almost 2 years, when I left him with

---

[4] Thomas Hammond.
[5] *F* omits the long passage "Now sum this . . . sum to my Credit."
[6] *Written* of of.

nearly 300£. Up to that time then I am probably £375 in advance.—I left England three mos after I was of age with £1100; the price of stocks advancing, the sale of mine produced 1600£, leaving 500£ and a present Mr Abbey made me the amount of which I do not remember suppose 75 or 100£ to discharge about 100£ of debts and leave some means to my Brothers. So far I certainly have considerable demands on my Bros, but we were so intimately connected that we never contemplated making future demands on each other, and kept no accounts; we had every thing in common.—The present slander—however—has no connection with these facts, if I may judge from the amount specified £700, the exact amount I brought from England the last time I left, accruing from Tom's estate; after paying his debts about 1100£ was left to be divided, to 100£ of which my Sister had an extra right; before my arrival John had drawn £100 and had remitted 100£ to me leaving 800£ to be divided, viz 540£ for our share of which John had £100, leaving me 440£ which with the £100 before mentioned, what my Guardian advanced in consideration of what I had done for Tom, and a further sum from himself made up the 700£. How then could I have taken from him 700£ when that was more than [7] the amt due to both of us. According to this latter calculation about 200£ will appear to my debit, but in the former there is a larger sum to my Credit. John himself was ignorant of the real state of his funds, it was so painful a subject and in our private communications he was so extremely melancholy that I always had to shew him the pleasing side of things; when I left London I had not courage to say that the 700£ I had obtained was not all ours by right; he therefore imagined it was,[8] but he never thought and never could have informed any one of his Friends that the whole was his. I never considered it necessary

[7] *Written* that.
[8] *F omits* he therefore . . . was.

to let him know the rights of it, since I did not intend to limit my remittances but by my means: suppose [9] however I had taken from him £7000 to do myself a great benefit with a view to advantage him, and had been wrecked, should I have been considered dishonest, I am no more to blame now than I should have been under those circumstances, my inability to remit has been occasioned by the faults of others not by any extravagance or carelessness of my own, I could no more help myself than in a storm at sea. Altho' in justice I do not owe my Bro estate a shilling I will do my utmost to liquidate his debts, it was always my intention to keep him under the idea that I was in his debt, in the case of Taylor and Hessey I promised payment and have given my notes. It is possible this explanation may not make any alteration in the opinion entertained of my integrity; if it do not I must submit to let my character remain black untill I can whiten it by paying Johns debts.—I wrote an explanation to this effect about 2 years since but upon a reconsideration I would not send it to the party to whom it was addressed, Haslam or Brown should have had it long ago if I could have <offered> submitted to offer palliatives to men who domineered as they did.

You will oblige me much by writing what is the impression concerning this matter, please to mention if Severn was with John when he died & [10] where a letter will find him, and what you know interesting about John for the last year of his life, about which I am entirely ignorant, his last letters to me were so melancholy that I feared it would terminate with our Family Complaint. I have not even the last book that he published,[11] and should be highly gratified with your opinion of its

[9] *F omits* suppose however . . . circumstances.
[10] Doubtful reading, but not (as in *F*) a comma.
[11] Fanny Keats sent him a copy of the *Lamia* volume before February 7, 1825 (Forman, IV, 402).

merits, if it sustained or injured his poetical reputation. Did you hear what became of Johns books [12] &c there were some miniatures which can be of no value to any body but me, it is likely Mr Brown or Severn knows what became of them.— Blackwood's magazine has fallen into my hands, I could have walked 100 miles to have dirked him a l'Americaine, for his cruelly associating John in the cockney school, and other black-guardisms, {su}ch paltry ridicule will have wounded deeper than the severe[st] criticism particularly as he regarded what is termed the Cockn{eyism} of the coterie with so much disgust. He either knew John well and touched him in the tenderest place purposely, or knew nothing of him and supposed he went all lengths with the set in their festering opinions and cockney affectations. I do not know that my feelings against Blackwood on John's account mislead me, but I cannot help feeling sur-prised that such persevering cruelty could have been borne by the public, or passed by by [13] the parties ridiculed [14] with <im-punity> out revenge. I have read plenty of unfair criticism, but this seems an exterminating blackguardism of Persons not of writings, that required other answer than the "paper bullets of the brain." [15] That there was a cockney school that deserved ridicule [16] I do not doubt, and probably John at the age of 14 and 15 was a little infected, but I do not see that either *he* or *John Reynolds* as *I knew him* should have been embodied with it.[17] Fanny writes me John Reynolds is married I suppose to Miss Drew, wish him joy for me.—What's become of your Brother.[18] Fanny says that Charley [19] still goes [to] Westminster

[12] See No. 122.
[13] *Sic.*
[14] *F* rediculed [*sic*].
[15] *Much Ado about Nothing*, II.iii.249.
[16] *F* redicule.
[17] *F ends here.*
[18] See I, lxxxiii, 286.
[19] See I, lxxx-lxxxii, lxxxiv, 289.

School.—Mr Abbey writes that a Mr Brown informed him that I was 70£ in his debt, I really don't know any thing about it, not remembering to have had any money transactions with him besides the purchase of a peice of linen for shirts, the money for which I gave to John at our last separation at Brown's desire: suppose he has some claim on John. I have written so much that I may reasonably doubt if you have patience enough to peruse it thus far, if indeed I have decoyed you, I will strain your patience no longer but inform you "right away" that I am

Your sincere Friend
G^eo Keats.

P. S. I will ask Mr Briggs [20] (an old schoolfellow) to let you know when he returns, that you may send a letter by him, he is an intelligent man and will be able to give you what information you desire concerning "these woods." G K.

→» 134 «←

BENJAMIN BAILEY TO JOHN TAYLOR

10 May 1824

Address: Mr Taylor/ Bookseller/ 13 Waterloo Place. Printed in part by Blunden, p. 99.

Burton on Trent. May 10.
1824.

My dear Sir—

I have been expecting a parcel from you of one of Coleridge's new works,[1] and Rose's new volume of the Orlando

[20] Charles Briggs, of New Orleans (see I, 3, 283, 319f.). Keats writes to Fanny, May 3, 1819 (*Letters*, pp. 342f.), that George and his wife "had the good chance to meet at Louisville with a Schoolfellow of ours." He mentions Briggs by name in January, 1820 (the same, p. 451).

[1] *Aids to Reflection*, which Taylor and Hessey, after negotiations begun in 1823, published in May of the following year. See II, 310.

Furioso.[2] The latter might be sent me, tho' the former is not out, by the conveyance formerly pointed out.

I have sent up a tale in verse—between 7 and 800 lines—to Andrews,[3] not to publish himself, for he declines being a publisher, but to dispose of for me if he can. You would not, I apprehend, have any objection to peruse the M.S, and if tolerable, to publish it for me—as it will be no great risque, and may take. He will very probably send it you.

I have often thought of inquiring whether you had prosecuted your determination of writing a life of poor John Keats, and whether you had made use of the papers I sent you. If you had not, and as time has gone on since his death, I think I had much rather that my facts, relative to Lockhart,[4] were not made use of. I will tell you why. It is not unlikely that I may go to Scotland again, and may live there, and it might involve me in an unpleasant state of literary hostility for no adequate end. Indeed it is doubtful whether much good will be done by reviving the matter so long after poor Keats's death. But this is for your consideration. My opinion of the treatment of this poor young man, and my dislike of that publication, have never varied. Let me however hear whether you have proceeded far in this work, and whether it is in the press, and what use you have made of my facts. I would not put you to inconvenience & expence, and of course can retract nothing; but if without inconvenience you can cancel my statement as directly applying to me, I shall be better pleased. Of the letters you are of course welcome to make what use you please.

Let me hear from you soon in the parcel.

Yours truly

B Bailey

[2] William Stewart Rose's translation, with notes, was published by John Murray in eight volumes, 1823–1831.
[3] Bookseller, 167 New Bond Street. For the fate of the poem see Nos. 340 and 342.
[4] See No. 119.

→» 135 «←

J. H. REYNOLDS TO J. A. HESSEY

About 1825 (?) [1]

Great Marlbro St
Thursday

Dear Hessey

I know not how you came to conclude that I had Severn's letter giving an account of Keats' Death.—The fact is I never even read it or saw it. Taylor lent me one of Severn's letters to Haslam, written on the arrival of himself & Severn—& that letter I have now— But the particular one you want I can give you no account of.   Yours ever

JHReynolds

→» 136 «←

GEORGE KEATS TO C. W. DILKE

20 April 1825

Address: Mr Chas Dilke,/ Navy Pay Office/ Sommerset House/ London/ [*In upper left corner:*] To the care of Chas Briggs Esqre/ at Messrs Gordon & Forstaled's [1]/ New Orleans./ [*In lower left corner:*] Harmony. *Postmarks:* C 5 AU 5 1825; SHIP LETTER LIVERPOOL; STEAM. Extracts are quoted by Milnes, II, 42-45, Lowell, I, 13f., 23, II, 84, and Forman, IV, 402-407.[2]

Louisville April 20th 1825

Mr Chas Dilke
Navy Pay Office, Sommersethouse

My dear Sir.

I have lost all the time between the receiving of your's per Briggs, and the date of this in endeavouring to arrange a

[1] The paper is watermarked 1824, but the date of 1825 is a mere guess. Perhaps Reynolds refers to Nos. 107 and 77.

[1] Paxton's *Supplement to the New-Orleans Directory* (1824) lists Gordon and Forstall, merchants, négociants, at 105 Royal. The 1827 directory locates them and Briggs, merchant, négociant, at 23 Toulouse. All three appear in the 1830 directory, but Briggs is not in that of 1835.

[2] A few of Forman's variations (F) are given in footnotes.

sure channel to convey letters, and am obliged at last to adopt a somewhat precarious mode of conveyance.

Your letter has in some measure releived my mind of a load that has sorely pressed for years. I felt innocent of the unfeeling, mean conduct imputed to me by some of my Brother's Friends, and Knew that the Knowledge of the facts would soon set that to rights, but I could not rest while under the impression that he really suffered thro' my not forwarding him money, at the time when I promised, but had not the power. Your saying "that he knew nothing of want either of Friends or money" and giving proofs of the truth of it, made me breath freely—enabled me to cherish his memory without the feeling of having caused him misery however unavoidably while a living Friend, and Brother. I do not doubt but that he complained of me, altho' he was the noblest fellow whose soul was ever open to my inspection, his nervous morbid temperament at times led him to misconstrue the motives of his best Friends, I have been instrumental times innumerable in correcting erroneous impressions so formed of those very persons who have been most ready to beleive the stories lately circulated against me, and I almost beleive that if I had remained his companion, and had had the means, as I had the wish to have devoted my life to his fame, and happiness, he might have been living at this hour; his temper did not unfold itself to you his Friend untill the vigour of his mind was somewhat impaired and he no longer possessed the power to resist that pettishness he formerly considered he had no [3] right to trouble his Friends with. From the time we were Boys at school where we loved, jangled, and fought alternately untill we separated in 1818 I in a great measure releived him by continual sympathy, explanation, and inexhaustible spirits, and good humour, from many a bitter fit of hypochondriasm, he avoided teazing any one with his miseries

[3] *Originally* not.

but Tom and myself and often asked our forgiveness; venting, and discussing them gave him releif.—I do not mean to say that he did not receive the most indulgent attention from his many devoted Friends, on the contrary I shall ever look with admiration on the exertions made for his comfort and happiness by his numerous Friends; no one in England understood his character perfectly but poor Tom and he had not the power to divert his frequent melancholy, and eventually encreased his desease most fearfully by the horrors of his own lingering death. If I did not feel fully persuaded that my motive was to acquire an independence to support us all in case of necessity, I never should forgive myself for leaving him, some extraordinary exertion was necessary to retrieve our affairs from the gradual decline they were suffering—that exertion I made whether wisely, or not, future events had to decide. After all Blackwood and the Qua[r]terly associated with our family desease Consumption were ministers of death sufficiently venemous, cruel and deadly to have consigned one of less sensibility to a premature grave, I have consumed many many [4] hours in devising means to punish those literary gladiators, but am always brought to the vexing conclusion that they are invulnerable to one of my prowess. Has much been said in John's defence against those libellers both of his character and writings? His writings were fair game, and liable to be assailed by a sneaking poacher, but his character as represent'd by Blackwood was not, a good cudgelling should have been his reward if he had been within my reach; John was the very soul of courage and manliness, and as much like the *holy Ghost* as *Johnny Keats*. I am much indebted for the interest you have taken in my vindication, and will observe further, for your satisfaction, that Mr Abbey who had the management of our money concerns in a letter lately received expressed himself "satisfied that my statement of the

[4] *F omits.*

I neglected to tell him to recover the Copyright if it should appear that I had a right to it—you who understand the business will oblige me very much by calling on him (4 Pancrass Lane) and acqua[i]nting him with the probable state of the case; at the end of this I will write an introduction to him, that will render it easy for you to open the business, it is possible you could do it without troubling him, as you please.—Writing is so easy to you that it is not tasking you too much to write me all about John and his works that will appear to you interesting to me <to know>, of what his Posthumous works consist I have not the slightest knowledge. I think you are right as to what should be the nature of his life and I regret very much that I cannot come to England to consult and give all the information I am in possession of to elucidate his character. My Father was killed by a fall from his Horse and I remember nothing of him but that he had dark hair, I have heard him praised as a man of good sense and very much liked, My mother I distinctly remember, she resembled John very much in the Face was extremely fond of him and humoured him in every whim, of which he had not a few, she was a most excellent and affectionate parent and as I thought a woman of uncommon talents, she was confined to her bed many years before her death by a rheumatism and at last died of a consumption, she would have sent us to harrow school as I often heard her say, if she could have afforded. I am not competent to write a life and shall be very happy to communicate any materials I am in possession of to any person to whom I have no positive objection as the author of John's life. Reynolds and yourself are I think <are> every way Competent to execute it with truth, feeling, and good taste. Give [11] Mrs Dilke my warmest thanks for her kindness to Fanny and tell her I have not forgotten the Country dance we named after her: altho here "I dance not, tread no

[11] *F omits* Give . . . frequent correspondent.

measures" [12] I hope before sorrow saddens, or age withers me, to lead her down a merry English country dance, Charley must be almost a man, I cannot fancy what he is like—my four Girls, to wit—Georgiana, 6 years old dark eyes and hair very much like John, Rosalind lighter complection but dark eyes, 4½ years old —Emma Frances 2½ years old very much like Georgiana, and Isabel 8 weeks—all famous beauties, well formed, and as fatiguing and troublesome as heart could wish. M^rs K enjoys pretty good health and is considering our few acquaintance, cheerful and contented, we seem liked as man and woman, but distrusted I may say disliked, as English People, we are still thoroughly English, and have not learnt with most foreigners the art of flattering the *egregious, excessive* vanity of the Americans at the expence of all other Countries in the world, we are therefore kept a little out of society, which however from its extreme dryness, and insipidity, is no great deprivation; we are looked upon as proud, and treated with consideration, and respect, but not with kindness or familiarity, all as it should be, if we had but a few Friends to enliven life's dull stream. I sincerely hope before our Girls are old enough to be irreclaimable, to be able to move them out of this vortex of petty mean[n]esses and low vices, I would much rather risque them in the giddiest circles of London, the reputed hot bed of vice, I should not feel satisfied to remain here if I had boys instead of Girls. If you wish to learn the state of society and manners here from a Resident not unfriendly to America tell me, and I will endeavour to give you my ideas of them, you formerly took considerable interest in those subjects and have thought a great deal of this Western Country, I now know it pretty well, and have attended enough to Politics to be able to see the bearings of our lax governments upon the morals of a People already sufficiently corrupt. I have now the prospect of being more completely occupied in business

[12] Compare *Endymion*, III.338.

than hitherto, being far advanced in erecting a Grist Mill (in addition to the Saw Mill) that will grind 75 Barrels of Flour every 24 hours, Of these establishments, when combined the most extensive in this country, I am the entire manager, viz, cheif engineer, cashier, clerk, without the interference or controul of the other owners except that I am bound to make a settlement of the Books once a year. I own 1/3ʳᵈ of the establishment, and receive 20 per Cent of the profits for my services, which of itself when the Grist Mill will be in operation will be sufficient to support my Family. The neat convenient little House in which I live, prettily situated at the head of the Falls close to the Mills, was built by the concern and releives me of Rent, a very considerable item of expence in this Country. The Grist Mill was of my projecting and planning and my time is fully occupied in superintending its building and my ordinary business, so that occupation is no farfetched excuse when advanced as a reason for not being a frequent correspondent. I hope to visit England before trading has worn out my love of letters, and old Friends, and to express personally my gratitude and thanks to that Generous Fellow Rice, and those kind Friends Reynolds, Severn, Brown and particularly yourself and Lady for all your delicate, persevering, untired attention to my needful Brother, who should by right have received those duties from me. Other Friends may not be mentioned who are deserving of my thanks from my ignorance of their kindness, to Mʳˢ Brawn and her lovely daughter I did intend to have written but on considering the trouble and difficulty of looking after letters I will be contented for the present with conveying to them thro' you, my best respects and wishes for their happiness, for their welfare,¹³ in which Mʳˢ Keats most cordially joins. <for her affection for John> I wrote to Fanny a few weeks since {and} have only to send my love, and hopes to hear from her

¹³ *F ends here.*

soon. {And pray} say what is thought of Shelly it appears he becam in {. . .} [14] he wrote an elegy on his death which I have requested {Fanny to send} me a copy of.[15] How is Severn getting on in his art, and {tell me if} he be within the reach of a letter.—Haydon seems doomed to poverty and disappointment, is the public opinion of his genius changed, for I cannot doubt but that he had genius, or has he worn out his eyes, or his enthusiasm, I have heard that he is married, and been in prison, that his pictures were sold for a mere nothing at auction, information so melancholy that [16] it cannot be worse and what you have to communicate must necessarily take something from the horrors of the picture. There are several works published in America that regularly extract the most interesting articles from the English periodicals and I have not unfrequently met with trains of thought and reasoning that were evidently the growth <and reasoning> of our old circle, if you will name some of those articles you think the best, both of your's and Reynolds' I shall take pleasure in looking back and read them again with the encreased zest of knowing them to be your's. You must be leading an agreeable life with your authorship, and ready communication with all sorts of books, and authors, after all <it is> these things are perhaps so entirely within your reach that you wish for something *beyond them* as ardently as I long for *them.* We have a Philosophical Society here, not altogether uninformed, or unphilosophical, but certainly unpoetical, I am a lately elected member and in preference to many influential men who were at the same time refused. To night it [17] will meet at my House and discuss "whether the ancients or moderns are

14 About three words missing.
15 On June 5, 1825 (Forman, IV, 407), George repeated the request. See I, 297n.
16 *Written* that that.
17 *Changed from* they.

the greater" We had the question of Phrenology warmly con-
tested, what is thought of it now in England, I think well of it.
Write full sheets to your

old and obliged Friend

Geo Keats.

I have no idea of the cost of postage please to inform me that I
may regulate my letters accordingly, we pay here A Quarter
dollar for a *single* letter from any Port in the United States.

G. K.

→≫ 137 ≪←

WILLIAM HOWITT TO WILLIAM HONE [1]

16 February 1826

Address: Wᵐ Hone Esqʳ.

Nottingham 2ⁿᵈ mo 16ᵗʰ 1826.

Dear Friend

I should have replied to thy friendly letter much earlier,
but I wished to forward David Love's papers [2] at the same time;
and, partly that I have been much occupied by trade affairs, and
partly that I did not happen to see David, but have had to ex-
plore the way to his dwelling through allies and other obscure
regions, till now, unknown to me, it has occasioned some delay.

---

[1] Howitt (1792–1879) was a miscellaneous writer, many of whose productions were the result of collaboration with his wife Mary (see No. 225).
In his letters Keats several times refers to Hone (1780–1842), writer and
bookseller, who in 1817 had been prosecuted for publishing satires
against the government and acquitted.

[2] There are two articles on David Love, the walking stationer of Nottingham, in Hone's *Every-Day Book* (referred to in the postscript), II (1827),
cols. 225-230, 1575f. Love, who had published his autobiography in
twenty-four penny issues, died on June 12, 1827, aged seventy-seven. See
the sketch in *DNB*.

I send the life adorned by the pictures of himself and his paragon of a spouse, with all the *"Sybilline Leaves"* come-at-able, for David does not always hesitate to sell the last copy, and some of these sent must have been preserved by miracle. As to paying for them, I shall hold myself repaid, with large interest, if they contribute, in any way to thy amusement. To most men I should say—pray dont be disappointed. But I know that thou hast such a relish for every curiosity in character that I shall not be surprised if these papers afford thee some gratification, nor, with thy genuine humour, if thou shouldst shape something out of them, which may tickle the public fancy.

To my great surprise, I learned the other day from David that Miss Love of Covent-garden is *his daughter!* It seems from his account that she was, at one time, the mistress of a gentleman who left her an annuity of £50. <per annum> on condition of her continuing single. During this period she was very kind to her father, but losing her annuity by marriage with Mortimer the actor,[3] she has not since favoured him by any tokens of her remembrance. Since her husband's death she has assumed her *maiden name,* and, if she is able, it would not be amiss if she were to assume her *maiden memory.* David however, still remembers & thinks of her with true parental [4] solicitude, and when I told him the book was for a gentleman in town, he was very inquisitive, and expressed much solicitude that no use might be made of it to the injury of his daughter—

If my communication gave thee pleasure, it certainly was

---

[3] See Lillian A. Hall, *Catalogue of Dramatic Portraits,* III (1932), 104-106, for portraits of Emma Sarah Love and, p. 232, of one Mortimer. Many of Miss Love's roles are enumerated by Genest, *Some Account of the English Stage,* IX (1832), 298f., 303, 307ff., and so on. Mrs. C. B. Wilson, *Our Actresses,* I (1844), 267-275, tells of her lover, "a noble Lord," of her marriage to Lieutenant Granby Calcroft, but nothing of David Love or Mortimer.

[4] *Written* patrental.

equally gratifying to me to know that, and I shall congratulate myself upon it if it lead to a further correspondence & knowledge of each other. Our little book [5] is not exactly what we should think of publishing now—yet we have received so much benefit in the way of friendship from it that we do not repent of putting it forth. In case of a second edition, of which we do not dispair, we should make considerable alterations in it, yet so as to preserve its character of *rurality*. We have a vol: in M.S. [6] now, in the hands of our friend Wiffen the translator of Tasso, [7] of which he says "There is no question that it is very much superior to your former work, and whenever it is published will greatly increase your reputation." We have delayed its appearance this season owing to the bad state of the book-market but hope to get it out early in the next.

As to the mention of Hunt, Keats &c [8]—we got soundly abused for that in the Literary Gazette,[9] the editor of which set us down "on the same form" (no dishonour we thought)— forged bad rhymes [10] to abuse us by, and, in short, was so flippant and ridiculous about it, that though it would undoubtedly quash the sale of it amongst many of his readers, yet it excited the disgust of some of the authorly part of them, and procured

[5] *The Forest Minstrel, and Other Poems* (1823).

[6] *The Desolation of Eyam and Other Poems* (1827).

[7] Jeremiah Holmes Wiffen (1792–1836). His Tasso was published in 1821, 1824, 1825. See S. R. Pattison, *The Brothers Wiffen* (1880).

[8] In *The Forest Minstrel*, p. x, the Howitts express a preference for "those exquisite touches . . . of things animate and inanimate, which all have seen and felt, but few have thought of describing; which form one of the chief charms in our beautiful old bards; of which Keats and Hunt have given us some delightful instances; but which abound in all the freshness, the vigour, and the very essence of real existence, in every page of Wordsworth and Crabbe."

[9] September 27, 1823, p. 611. The editor was William Jerdan (1782–1869).

[10] *Written* ryhmes.

us several friendships, for which, <we> tho' we do not thank him, we are nevertheless indebted. I am however, one of those stubborn fellows that neither form their oppinions by editorial authority, nor care a great deal for their fulminations, and <in an> I have again committed the sin of taking a motto from Keats, in an introductory poem [11] for 'Time's Telescope' for this year,[12] a work to which he always contributes his "peppercorn of praise," [13] yet whose editor [14] was induced to notice the book, though a perfect stranger to us, through Jerdan's critique.

I read thy account of thy last interview with poor Keats with real pity.[15] In him we undoubtedly lost one of the most promising geniuses of modern times. The display of imaginative power in his "Hyperion" is such as to forbid us to calculate at all what would have been the scope of his spirit in its maturity; and the sweetness originality & graphic beauty of all his compositions will never cease to be admired by the truly poetical.

We do not *indeed* exclude Coleridge from our list of great poets, yet we cannot say that we place his [16] poetical "throne higher than the thrones of the other kings" in our poetical Babylon. Think of Wordsworth &, as Don Quixote says, "there is "much may be said on both sides" [17] Indeed such has been the out-pouring of poetical inspiration in our times that it would be difficult to convince people of good, & yet of different, tastes which, out of 3 or 4 names which might be men-

[11] "The Influence of Nature and Poetry on National Spirit," with the motto " '*The poetry of Earth is never dead.*' Keats."

[12] On Keats and *Time's Telescope* see Rollins, *JEGP*, April, 1946 (XLV, 220).

[13] Cowper, *The Task*, line 110.

[14] John Millard, assistant librarian of the Surrey Institute.

[15] Compare the account in Hone's *Table Book*, I (1827), col. 810.

[16] *Originally* him on the.

[17] Also in Henry Fielding's *Covent Garden Tragedy*, I.viii, and Addison's *Spectator*, No. 122.

tioned, stood the highest. It is no easy thing, poet[r]y is so much a matter of taste, to decide upon the claims of writers of different schools. I am no bigot in literature,—I never desire to look, at poet[r]y especially, through political spectacles, & therefore I can, and do, find subjects of admiration in all literary sects. Wordsworth, Coleridge, Southy, Campbell, Rogers &c—let others decide their exact standing— I am content <with> to enjoy them—but perhaps I should be inclined to place them as I have now done, yet with some doubts whether Rogers should not precede Campbell.

I am sorry to hear thee expressing a sense of social solitude in the great literary city—yet I am not surprised at it—such is too commonly the case with those who think *for* rather than *with* the multitude—they <are> cannot sympathise with many —& the few with who they could, do not always come in contact with them. However, whilst thou enjoyest the society of such men as Charles Lamb I cannot pity thee overmuch. My "gudewife" desires me to communicate her kind regard, and hoping to hear from thee again I subscribe myself very truly & respectfuly thy friend

W Howitt

P. S. As I get my "E—d. B." in parts I do not yet know whether David has appeared, but I have ordered a "no." or 2.

→≫ 138 ≪←

FANNY KEATS LLANOS AND VALENTIN LLANOS TO
GEORGE KEATS [1]

31 May 1826

Address: Mr George Keats/ Louisville/ Kentucky/ United States/ Amer-ica. *Postmark:* PAID 10 JU 10 1826. Printed by Rollins, *PMLA*, LIX (1944), 204-207.

May 31st 1826

My dear George

I hear Mr Dilke received a letter from you a week, or two ago, as also Mr Rice, and even that consummate villain Abbey, and yet not one line for your sister, does this proceed from indifference, neglect, or revenge for my not having written to you, if you wished to punish me I can assure you your silence has produced the desired effect, and now a truce to penance if you please and allow me to justify myself, and oblige you if I can to pronounce a verdict of not guilty. In your last you men-tioned a Mr Sunderland, by whom I hoped to have sent letters; but as you must be aware [I] have never either seen or heard from him, had you not expressed a wish for Shelley's monody I should have written immediately by post but being unwilling to send a letter without the wished-for article I deferred writing from month to month always hoping that some opportunity would offer itself of forwarding it to you, for the future how-ever I shall depend upon the post as my best and only friend.

[1] One side of the page is almost covered with Fanny's transcript of stanzas from Shelley's *Adonais* (see I, 328), part of her own words being written between the columns of stanzas at right angles. On the other side, *Adonais* is continued, leaving room for the rest of her letter and Valentin's note. Fanny silently omitted stanzas 19-24 (probably because she was following the *Literary Chronicle*, December 1, 1822, pp. 751-754) and reproduced Shelley's text rather inexactly.

I must now communicate a piece of intelligence which I think will surprise you a little. I am married to a Spaniard of good family, and consequently well educated, he is an intimate friend of Mrs Brawne and is highly respected and esteemed by the Dilke's as indeed he is by the whole circle of his acquaintance, he was also known to our dear John. You will very naturally wish to know what kind of a monster he is and as I have so little room I must endeavour to give you an idea of his tout ensemble in as few words as possible. He is handsome, elegant and graceful in his manners and [2] deportment, accomplished and possessed of considerable talent as may be seen by two works of which he is the author, called Don Estaban, and Sandoval, and believe me you have as great reason to be proud of your brother as I have of my sister. I can safely say with what feelings you may imagine that under the canopy of heaven there does not exist a nobler minded or purer hearted being. My encomiums may perhaps be thought exagerated; but when Mr Dilke writes he will probably mention Valentine when you will perceive that my picture is not <overcoloured.> too highly coloured. We are doing every thing in our power to oblige Abbey to refund the money; but I fear we shall not be successful. I thought you knew he was not an honest man from principle, but merely because he had no occasion to rob being at the time you were in England possessed of considerable property. I find he has deceived you most shamefully respecting the sum of money you were to receive out of the Court of Chancery, would to God you had sent the power of Attorney [3] to Mr Dilke or Rice. There is some property of yours in the Bank standing in my name, being your share of Tom's and John's property out of Chancery, after paying all debts. I cannot say the exact amount; but as Mr Rice intends sending you a statement I shall refer you to him. When you write to Mr Dilke I must beg of you to thank him

[2] *Written* and and.
[3] See I, 300f.

most warmly for his great kindness to me, and also Mr Rice who has interested himself very much for me. I believe you sent a power of Attorney to Mr Rice, it has not yet arrived.

You mentioned having a miniature of Tom's, I should be delighted if you would get it copied for me or send it to England for that purpose the first opportunity, my husband is at present copying John's, and he talks of employing a young artist [4] of some merit to make a bust, one has already been made by some one of the name of Smith; [5] but I am told it is not good, though it certainly bears a very strong resemblance. I should very much like to have your miniature, given to me by John; but now in the possession of M^r H Wylie, it was lent to him to copy. I would call upon him, but am not acquainted with his place of residence as Miss Brawne informs me he has left the Hampstead Road, perhaps you will be kind enough to mention my wish to him. [6]

A short time since I accidently met with Charles Clark of Enfield, he is now a partner of Hunt's the editor of the Examiner. Old Clark [7] is dead and his wife is living at a small village near Bath, one of the Miss C's married very well and the other resides with her mother. [8] Hodgkinson [9] and Johnson are pros-

[4] Probably Patrick MacDowell, R.A., whose bust of Keats, made according to Williamson, p. 110, on September 9, 1828, under the supervision of Fanny Keats and Fanny Brawne, is in the Keats Museum.

[5] Frederick William Smith's "Bust of the late John Keates" was exhibited at the Royal Academy in 1822. Its whereabouts were unknown to a writer in the *Athenaeum*, November 16, 1895, p. 687, and according to Williamson, p. 105, it "has been entirely lost sight of."

[6] See Edgcumbe, p. 55.

[7] John Clarke died in December, 1820 (C. C. Clarke and Mary C. Clarke, *Recollections of Writers* [1878], p. 29).

[8] Mary C. Clarke (*My Long Life* [1896], p. 49) says that Mrs. Clarke lived "at Frome, in Somersetshire, with her unmarried youngest daughter [Eliza]. . . . Her married daughter, Mrs. Towers, resided at some miles distant from her, at Standerwick." On Mrs. Towers, author of *The Children's Fireside* (1828), see also II, 206n., and No. 345.

[9] See I, xl.

perous I believe: the latter is not yet married—Frith is married and keeps a grocers shop in Bishopsgate St Beilby is married or ought to be to Sarah [10] who lived at Pancrass Lane when you were there, he has two or three children. Wilkinson [11] is dead— This is poor news but I have none more interesting to communicate if our friends will not marry, and die, and thus afford me the employment of being the reporter for America it is no fault of mine. With best love to my sister and little neices, and earnestly requesting you to answer this soon I remain my dear Geo

Your most affec Sister

F. M. Llanos

My dear Sir and brother.

The indissoluble engagemints I have lately entered into with our dear Fanny render excusable the liberty I now take of writing to you, to assure you that though we are both strangers to each other, I shall feel a great pleasure in cultivating your friendship and in subscribing myself your affect. brother and servant.

V. Llanos.

⇢⟫ 139 ⟪⇠

GEORGE KEATS TO C. W. DILKE

18 October 1826

Extracts are printed by Rollins, *PMLA*, LIX (1944), 207.

Louisville October 18th 1826

My dear Sir

The Power of Attorney [1] sent by Turner will I fear prove

10 Can this be a reference to the Sarah Butler mentioned by Keats (*Letters*, p. 139)?

11 Perhaps a lawyer in whose office George had worked: see Lowell, I, 298, and Naomi J. Kirk in the Hampstead Keats, I, lxxxi.

1 See I, 298. For the financial details behind this letter see Adami, pp. 117-119.

useless, the Lawyer who drew it out having ommitted the Christian names of R & R [2] and the words jointly and severally. The one sent to Abbey was on a printed form sent by him to me to fill up and execute. I have not yet made up my mind if I shall forward another, or wait to hear from Rice if the one forwarded will or will not answer the purpose, I am rather inclined to the latter course considering that some mistake may be made in any other we may manufacture here, the necessity of sending a Form cannot fail to occur to him as it did to Abbey. Letters in answer to some sent by Turner have arrived here so that it cannot be long before I shall learn from Rice if another will be required. I cannot but think that the immense distance I am from London and the consequent difficulty of correcting a trifling informallity will operate in causing the Power to be received as sufficient. Accept my warmest thanks for the trouble you have taken in my concerns and be assured that the obligation thus conferred shall never be forgotten— I am fully aware what it is to have one's hands full of business and to be at the same time teazed with the complicated affairs of another, that you have been successfull and of so much service to Fanny and myself I know will be most gratifying to you, and be considered by you sufficient reward, she begs me to express her gratitude. Expecting to receive from Rice an exact statement of all accounts I will make no observations on that you have sent— To reallize such sums would place me in a most commanding situation, in this Country where money is so scarce. I shall not write to Rice in less than a month unless I hear from him.—Abbey is entitled to a considerable allowance on account of advances for Tom who spent at all times more than double the Interest of his money, he advanced some when Tom went to Lyons [3] and subsequently to John & myself on account of the assistance we gave him, what would be a fair charge I don't know. As you

2 Rice and Reynolds.
3 See Lowell, I, 172.

301

direct I have drawn on you for two Hundred and twenty five
Pounds Sterling at 35 days sight in favour of S. H. Cook Esqre—
I preferred drawing on you to Rice having your signature grant-
ing permission to draw, altho' you ought to be troubled as little
as possible, remember to pay yourself out of my funds for all
postages and expences past and present. In future when any
money can be reallized for me I would have a Bank Post Bill
bo^t at 60 days sight made payable to me (accepted) and forwarded to me. It would be adviseable to get first, second, and
third of exchange or any other plan that is customary with B.
Post Bills to insure against misscarriage &c.

Wishing to forward this immediately and having to prepare for a week or fortnights journey on Horseback (starting
early tomorrow) and withall not being well must excuse more
from me at present.—Best wishes to Mrs D. & Charley and love
to Mrs Llanos.[4] I am

My dear Sir
Your obliged Friend
Geo Keats.

➤➤➤ 140 ⬅⬅⬅

JOHN TAYLOR TO RICHARD WOODHOUSE:
MEMORANDA ON THE KEATS FAMILY

20, 23 April 1827

Address: Richd Woodhouse Esq/ King's Bench Walk/ Temple. *Postmarks:* TP Coventry St; 12.NOON.12 24. AP 1827. Lowell calls these
memoranda the Abbey Memoir, and quotes extracts at I, 8-12, 15,
44, 184f. Finney (F) has printed the entire letter at I, 11-13, 15, 139, with
some verbal misreadings, most of them here indicated in the footnotes.

Waterloo Place 20 April
1827

John Keats was born in the Parish of St   [1] His

[4] Who had gone to France in August (Adami, pp. 124f.).
[1] Taylor left the blank space thus.

Mother was a singular Character & from her he may be supposed to derive whatever was <of a> peculiar in his Mind & Disposition.—She was the Daughter of —— Jennings, a Livery stable Keeper, in Moorfields who [2] lived next door to the Moorgate Coffee House on the Pavement, <Moorfields>.—His Temper appears to have influenced that of his Daughter.—He was excessively fond of the pleasures of the Table, and for 4 Days in the Week his Wife & Family [3] were occupied in preparing for the Sunday's Dinner He was a complete Gourmand:—His Daughter in this respect somewhat resembled him, but she was more remarkably the Slave of other [4] Appetites, attributable probably to this for their exciting Cause.—At an [5] early Age she told my Informant, Mr Abby, that she must & would have a Husband; and her passions were so ardent, he said, that it was dangerous to be alone with her.—She was a handsome, <but not a tall> little woman— Her Features were <of a Superior> good & regular, with the Exception of her Mouth which was unusually wide. A little Circumstance was mentioned to me as indicative of her Character— She used to go to a Grocers in Bishopsgate Street, opposite the Church, probably out of some Liking for the Owner of the Shop,—but [6] the Man remarked to Mr Abby that Miss Jennings always came in dirty Weather, & when she went away, she held up her Clothes very high in [7] crossing the Street, & to be sure, says the Grocer, she has uncommonly handsome Legs.[8]—He was not however fatally wounded by Cupid the Parthian—

But it was not long before she found a Husband, nor did

[2] *Apparently* who *is written over* He. *F reads* where [*canceled*] He.
[3] *F* Maid.
[4] *F* these.
[5] *Originally* any.
[6] *F* and.
[7] *Or perhaps* on (*F*).
[8] *F italicizes.*

she go far for him—a Helper in her Father's Stables appeared
sufficiently desirable in her Eyes to make her forget the Dis-
parity of their Circumstances, & <she> it was not long before
John [9] Keats had the Honor to be united to his Master's Daughter.—He did not possess [10] or display any great Accomplishments.
—Elevated perhaps in his Notions [11] by the sudden Rise of his
Fortunes he thought it became him to act somewhat more the
Man of Consequence than he had been accustomed to do—but
it was still in the Way of his Profession— He kept a remarkably
fine Horse for his own Riding, & on Sundays would go out with
others who prided themselves in the like Distinction, to High-
gate, Highbury, or some other places of public Entertainment
for Man & Horse.—At length one Sunday Night he was returning with some of his jolly Companions from a Carouse at one
of these Places, riding very fast, & most probably very much in
Liquor, when his Horse leaped upon the Pavement opposite the
<Wesleyan> Methodist Chapel in the City Road, & falling
with him against the Iron Railings so dreadfully crushed him
that he died as they were carrying him Home. <or immediately
after>

I think it was not much more than 8 Months [12] after this
Event that Mrs Keats again being determined to have a Husband, married Mr Rawlins, a Clerk in Smith Payne & [13] Co's—
I know [14] very little of him, further than that he would have
had a Salary of 700£ a year eventually had he continued in his

[9] *Sic for* Thomas.
[10] *F* present.
[11] *F* habits.
[12] Actually two months, for Thomas Keats was buried on April 23, 1804,
and his widow married William Rawlings on June 27 (Pope, *TLS*, December 22, 1932, p. 977).
[13] *F* Smith Payson. The *Royal Kalendar*, 1804 and 1827, shows that
Smith, Payne, and Smiths (now the National Provincial Bank) were
bankers in George Street, Mansion House Place.
[14] *F* knew.

Situation.—I suppose therefore that he quitted it on becoming the Proprietor of the Livery Stables by his Marriage with Mrs Keats, but how long the Concern was carried on, or at what period Mr Jennings died, or relinquished it, I did not [15] learn— It is perhaps sufficient to know that Rawlins also died after some little Time, and that his Widow was afterwards living *as* the Wife of a Jew at Enfield, named Abraham [16]

Mrs Jennings the Grandmother of John Keats the Poet, was living after the Death of her Husband—at Edmonton, & here she took care of the Children <of> Her unhappy Daughter, <who> after the Death of her first Husband, <took> [17] be- came addicted to drinking and in the love [18] of the Brandy Bottle found a temporary Gratification to those inordinate Appetites which seem to have been in one Stage or other con- stantly soliciting her.—The Growth of this degrading Propensity to liquor may account perhaps for the strange Irregularities— or rather Immorality of her after-Life— I should imagine that her Children seldom saw her, and would hope that they knew not all her Conduct.—The Grandmother was a very different kind of Woman, & when left to herself appears to have acted the part of a discreet Parent to the Children.—One of Keats's most beautiful Sonnets [19] is addressed to his Grandmother. It might be thought that he was speaking of a young and beautiful Woman, so entirely [20] had her <Affection> Goodness & Affec-

[15] *F* didn't.

[16] *Apparently* Abrahams *with the* s *canceled.* Hewlett, p. 19, says that Rawlings was alive in 1825.

[17] *F* drank.

[18] So *F* but the word must be guessed at.

[19] "As from the darkening gloom a silver dove." Mrs. Jennings was buried on December 19, 1814. The sonnet was written about December 24, according to Garrod, p. 529, whereas Finney, I, xi, 98, dates it Febru- ary, 1816.

[20] *F* actively.

tion filled him with pure & fervent [21] Love for her—

She was a Native of Yorkshire, born in the Village of Colne at the Foot of Pendle Hill.—From the same Village came Mr Abby, who was the Guardian of these Children, and my Informant in these Particulars. He appears to have had a real Friendship for Mrs Jennings & to have been a sincere well-wisher to the Family, but his Views & those of the young Men as they grew up were not at all accordant. His Care of the Grand Children of his Townswoman was not a solitary Instance of his Desire to serve those who had the Claim of a common Country & Birthplace to plead as a Passport to his Favor. One Day Mrs Jennings was visited by <the> a young Woman who came from Colne, but was then in Service as a Lady's Maid— This young Person subsequently married, & lived near Mrs Jennings, who exercised [22] the usual offices of a friendly Neighbour [23] <to her>, but greater Calls were soon after made upon her. This young Woman, who was a delicate sensible Creature was murdered by her Husband.—He laid her dead at his Feet by a Blow of his Fist,—and when Mrs Jennings who was sent for arrived, she saw a little Girl 2 years old playing about the Room quite naked, unconscious of course of its Mother's Fate, and a Boy not more than 2 or 3 Months old in the [24] Cradle—.—She sent for Mr Abby and said that if he would take Charge of the Girl till the Parents of their late Mother should come to take them, she would provide in the meantime for the Boy.—Abby chearfully consented & brought the little creature home to his Wife. At the End of a Month the old Grandmother arrived in London to take the Children, and the Boy was given up to her, but the little Girl was requested to be left till an Opportunity which

[21] *F* finest.
[22] *F* exceeded.
[23] *Here apparently* to her (*F* when) *is canceled.*
[24] *F* his.

would soon occur afforded them the Means of sending her safely to Colne in the Care of another Friend.—When that Time came however Mrs Abby was grown so fond of the Child that she could not bear to part with her.—The old Grandmother was easily persuaded to let her stay and she is at this Moment with Mr Abby having been brought up by him as a Daughter.—She was the playmate of the young Family of the Keats's and seemed always chearful & happy till of late when she has drooped & pined. They are afraid she is going into a Decline, but Mr Abby suspects that she has become acquainted with the unhappy Story of her real Parents, & that secret Grief is consuming her Health & Spirits.

With so kind hearted a Man as Abby some Children would have been very happy, but he was not the Man for these, especially for John Keats who seems to have given him nearly the same kind of unavailing anxiety which the Ducklings caused the old Hen who hatched them.—John was apprenticed to a Surgeon at Edmonton, who did not however conduct himself as Mr A. conceived he ought to have done to his young Pupil, & partly to punish him by the Opposition,—partly because Mrs Jennings was known & respected in the Neighbourhood, on which Acc^t her Grandson had a better Introduction there than elsewhere, it was Mr Abby's Advice that John should commence Business at Tottenham as a Surgeon. He communicated his Plans to his Ward but his Surprise was not moderate, to hear in Reply, that he did not intend to be a Surgeon— Not intend to be a Surgeon! why what do you mean to be? I mean to rely upon my Abilities [25] as a Poet— John, <are you Mad or Silly> you are either Mad or a Fool, to talk in so absurd a Manner. My Mind is made up, said the youngster very quietly. I know that I possess Abilities greater than most Men, and therefore I am determined to gain my Living by exercising them.—Seeing

[25] *F* Ability.

nothing could be done Abby called him a Silly Boy, & proph-
esied a speedy Termination to his inconsiderate Enterprise.—
He brought me not long after, says this worthy Man, a little
Book which he had got printed— I took it & said I would look
at it because it was his writing, otherwise I should not have
troubled my Head with any such Thing— When we next met I
said, Well John I have read your Book, & it reminds me of the
Quaker's Horse which was hard to catch, & good for nothing
when he was caught— So your Book is hard to understand &
good for nothing when it is understood. Do you know says the
old Man, I don't think he ever forgave me for uttering this
Opinion, which however was the Truth.

   Abby is a large <fat> stout good natured looking Man
with a great Piece of Benevolence standing out on the Top of
his Forehead.—As he spoke of the Danger of being alone with
Miss Jennings I looked to see if I [could] discern any of the
Lineaments of the young Poet in his Features, but if I had heard
the whole of his Story I should have banished the Thought
more speedily than it was conceived.—Never were there two
people more opposite than the Poet & this good Man.—He
appeared at the Girdler's [26] Dinner yesterday introduced by
Mr Macauley,[27] who when he <first> saw him enter the Room
scarcely knew him. The Reason was this, he had that Day put
on Trousers for the first Time, having worn till then white
Cotton Stockings & Breeches & half Boots.—<But> When
<he said> for a long Time there had been no other Man on
the Exchange in that Dress, <exc> & he was become so con-

----

[26] *Apparently not* Girdlers' (*F*). Taylor himself was a member of the
Girdlers' Company by 1811 (Olive M. Taylor, *London Mercury*, XII
[1925], 165).

[27] So apparently, but no Macauley is mentioned in W. Dumville-Smythe's
An Historical Account of the Worshipful Company of Girdlers, London
(1905).

spicuous for it as to <find him> be an Object of attention in
the Streets, he had at last <had> resolved to <be in the>
come into the Fashion.

This is the whole of what he told me respecting John
Keats, excepting such particulars as I was better acquainted
with perhaps than he himself— He added that George was working like a Turk in America & that Miss K was just married to
a Spaniard (I have since heard that his Name is Llanos.

My dear Rich^d

These are not Materials for a Life of our poor Friend
which it will do to communicate to the World—they are too
wretched to be "told by a Cavern Wind unto a Forest old" [28]—
How strange it seems [29] that such a Creature of the Element as
he should have sprung from such gross Realities.—But how he
refined upon the Sensualities [30] of his Parents!—Yours
My dear Fellow
Very truly
John Taylor

April 23 1827

[28] *Endymion*, II.830f.
[29] *F* was.
[30] *F* Immoralities.

->>> 141 <<<-

GEORGE KEATS TO C. W. DILKE [1]

25 March 1828

Address: Chas Dilke Esqre/ Navy Pay Office/ Sommerset House/ London/ England/ [*In upper left corner*] via New York. March 27th 1828. *Postmarks:* LOUISE^E K^Y MAR. 27; G 14 MY 14 1828; LIVERPOOL *SHIP LETTER;* PAID.

Louisville March 25th 1828.

Mr Chas Dilke
Navy Pay Office

My dear Sir

I write to you in tribulation caused by the return of a dft I drew on Mr Ja^s Rice for £350 at 90 days sight which appears to have been accepted by him on the 5th October 1827 and protested for non payment on the 7th of Jany 1828. He wrote on the 5th April 1827 requesting powers to authorize yourself and consols him to receive £129.4.0 and £56.4.2 money and informing me that my Sister was indebted to me £7.18.7 money and £341.11.9 stock, and desiring me to point out the mode in which said sums were to be remitted, thereby to a considerable extent justifying me in drawing on him for £350 which you will observe is considerably within the amount specified. The present inconvenience caused by this drft's coming back is that I must either impair my credit, or dispose of part of my Mill at a sacrifice and be encumbered with a partner, added to which the damages on it are 20 per cent besides expences. I fear moreover that those claims which you have been so mainly instrumental

---

[1] The financial details herein mentioned are more or less cleared up in the letters that follow. They are also briefly touched on by Adami, p. 134, and Rollins, *PMLA,* LIX (1944), pp. 207f., n.

310

in almost reallizing are again jeopardized, if not lost— I am mistaken in signs of failure, of bankrup[t]cy, if the non payment of an accepted bill coupled with a removal of residence do not smell of it. I sincerely hope for the sake of Rice & Reynolds as well as for myself that it is not so, such however is the impression of the holder of the bill, and I cannot but think that the grounds for the beleif are plausible, I have not received a line of explanation. These are my fears and under these impressions I write, if I am wrong the fault rests with Rice for not writing and not with me for surmising. It is too bad to trouble you any more with this matter, but I am constrained, I have no other staff on which to lean, you are associated with Rice in all powers delegated to him, you comprehend the business, you fostered the child and will naturally take some pride in raising it to maturity. Since the bill was accepted on the 5th of October it is fair to presume that my letter arrived about [the] same time enclosing powers, in it I entreated an immediate answer, no such answer arrived, you don't write, my Sister is silent, I am in the dark and may be forgiven if in groping I strike on some strange ideas. I shall write by this same post to Mr H^y Wylie requesting him to call on you and to take as much trouble off your hands as possible, please to explain the business to him and employ him— You will much oblige me by writing immediately on the receipt of this, indeed I write to H^y. Wylie principally to multiply chances of getting information, which has hitherto only arrived once a year. I shall send M^{rs} K to London If I can possibly manage it in a very short time, she had my promise to visit her Mother in 1829 if I could afford it, she shall now go in my distress and at the same time that she performs her long promised visit, she may perhaps be the means of settling my affairs— in doing which I am persuaded she will have every assistance in your power to render.—

It is still possible that all is going on well, that inatten-

311

tion caused the protest &c. I hope so. I am not in spirits to write about any thing else. Give my best wishes to Mrs D. and Charley and your Brother.

I am

Your most obliged Friend

George Keats.

➤➤➤ 142 ◄◄◄

GEORGE KEATS TO C. W. DILKE

16 April, 12 May 1828

Address: Charles Dilke Esqre/ Navy Pay Office/ Sommerset House. A few sentences are quoted by Lowell, I, 9, 13. Forman (IV, 407-409) prints a long extract from the May 12 letter.[1]

April 16th 1828 Louisville

My dear Sir

In consequence of not receiving information I am driven to conjecture a thousand possible causes of the non payment of my draft on Rice. Influenced by the general Opinion here I thought it was the inability of Rice to pay it, on further consideration however I have given up that opinion and shall think of so unsatisfactory a business as little as possible, untill I hear something explanatory from some one who can put me in possession of Facts. Mrs Keats' object in visiting England is twofold, to see her Mother and Brothers from whom I robbed her in 1818, and to settle my business; I had intended to put off her visit untill 1829 when my returned bill without a line of explanation seemed to require my presence in London. I could not possibly come and Mrs Keats had nought to detain [her] but our regret to be so long separated, so we have considered it better that she should make the journey immediately. I am

---

[1] He begins with the second paragraph and ends with "to write his life."

312

fully persuaded she will have your advice and assistance which
in case of difficulty is my main dependance. Give my best respects to Mrs Dilke, your Son & Brother and beleive me

dear Dilke

Your most obliged Friend

George Keats.

New York May 12th 1828

My dear Dilke

    I made up my letters at Louisville not intending to ac-
company Mrs Keats further than Cincinnati, I however could
not trust her to the world's politeness, and have continued with
her thus far; within two Stages of the end of her journey.

    Meeting with Hunt's Lord Byron and his contempora-
ries [2] has raised in my mind a crowd of old associations, it
reminds me that you had some idea of writing a life of John,
and of the materials that I am able and willing to furnish for
that purpose to you or any one who is competent to do it well—
Hunt's sketch is not altogether a failure but I should be extremely sorry that poor John's name should go down to posterity
associated with the littlenesses of L. H., an association of which
he was so impatient in his Lifetime. He speaks [3] of him patron-
izingly, that he would have defended him against the Reviewers
if he had known his nervous irritation at their abuse of him,
and says that on that point only he was reserved to him; the
fact was he more dreaded Hunt's defence than their abuse—
You know all this as well as I do— In conferring upon John
what he may consider the loftiest praise, namely, that between
them "there was no such thing as obligation, except the pleasure
of it." He then tells you that he lived with him, that he lived
with Brown, that it was a pleasure to his friends to have him

[2] London, 1828.
[3] Pages 256f.

at their Houses &c.[4] Now no Man who ever lived was more
impatient at being under an obligation than John, as long as I
knew him, and he misled me himself if he did not divide with
Brown the expences of House Keeping at Hampstead.[5] I have
no doubt of Hunt's Friendliness and Hospitallity and it is probable that John accepted an invitation to reside in his House a
few weeks and it may have extended to months,[6] Such a case
is common with other than gifted Men, but it is not the thing
to hand down to posterity that John was [x] *born in wretched-
ness* [7] and lived with spiritless carelessness on Mess[rs] Hunt and
Brown— John was noble and manly, he was more magnanimous
in conferring than in receiving a benefit, he felt *too* impatient
of obligations. If you wish I will enlarge on these topics, if not
I suppose that all I know of John will die with me, for I have
not capacity or authorship enough in me to write his life.
<myself.> It may appear strange to you who are living in the

[x] My Grandfather was very well off as his will shews, and but
that he was extremely generous and gullable would have been
affluent, I have heard my Grandmother speak with enthusiasm
of his excellencies, and M[r] Abbey used to say that he never saw
a woman of the talents and sense of my Grandmother, except
my Mother. I do not remember much of my mother but her
prodigallity, and doting fondness for her children, particularly
John, who resembled her in the face.

[4] Pages 257f.
[5] "When Brown rendered a statement of his running account with Keats
he made it clear that the poet's share was duly acquitted up to the end
of 1819, that Keats paid him £40 in February 1820, and was behind hand
again in May 1820 when they parted, owing to the expenses of the illness, and a loan of £50. George Keats paid the whole balance of the
account" (Forman's note).
[6] "It extended from the 23rd of June to the 12th of August 1820"
(Forman's note).
[7] Page 247.

bustle of a busy world in a crowd o{f} Friends, that *I* the thought of whom probably occurs to you about once in a year should look upon y{ou} as the best Friend I have in the world; yet so it is and {I feel} no little mortification at receiving so little attention from you but such as my pecuniary interests require—once more good bye.

Your Friend
Geo Keats.

→≫ 143 ≪←

GEORGE KEATS TO C. W. DILKE

12 July 1828

Address: Chas W. Dilke Esqre/ Navy Pay Office/ Sommerset House/ London. One sentence is quoted by Forman, IV, 409.

Louisville July 12th 1828

My dear Sir

Your promptness in arranging my disagreeable affairs once more exacts from me expressions of enduring gratitude. I can clearly see the feeling with which you received the news of my distress, and the energy with which you acted to releive me from it; withdrawing me from a sea of troubles [1] and anxieties. By the help of a good credit I have been able to get along through the accomodation afforded me by the United States Bank, but not being a scheming financier, and not liking to ask my acquaintances to endorse for me, I was fretting terribly under my new burthen. The writing to you is evidence that I expected as much, but allow me to observe that the fresh assurance which this unfortunate affair has given birth to of your enduring friendliness for me, is to me matter of considerable

[1] *Hamlet,* III.i.59.

gratification. Notwithstanding our long separation you are the man of all others to whom I am most closely allied in feeling, you have had confidence in my integrity when others have condemned me unheard, and I beleive, for the most part unregretted, you have proved my friend when (perhaps) *all others* have deserted me, and *taken some trouble* to spread accounts of my unworthiness: Haslam for instance did his best to make Charles Wylie think me a scoundrel, I suspect Brown of the like proceedings where I was open to a still more sensible hurt. Mr Bull [2] the bearer of this will convey to Mrs Keats evidences of the amount I paid in liquidation of the returned bill and damages— I leave the affair to the consideration of R & R. [3] Write to me at your leisure what changes have taken place in the looks, manners and language of Mrs Keats. Time has been impartial with us, and has left on our persons and faces about equal marks of his progress: your flesh is too well filled out to show so distinctly the evidences that we endure only for a season "Grass and Hay." [4] I am now very busy, both mind and body, the new crop of wheat has commenced pouring in, M^rs K can tell you what sort of work it is. Give my kindest regards to Mrs Dilke. My sister writes that Charles is a fine young man reasonably endowed with amiabilities; he ought to be so to repay your great anxieties and nevertiring cares: I do not know the man who has so conscienciously and so sedulously acted the part of Father as you have done. Remember me to him and your Brother most kindly. Both the remittances arrived by the same post say £450.—Fanny says that I have been unjust to you in imputing to you carelessness of my interests: in what words and to whom I made the imputation I don't know; I certainly never

---

[2] Perhaps John P. Bull of Bull, Rankin, and Leight, merchants. He lived at Walnut and Third Streets.
[3] Rice and Reynolds.
[4] Isaiah 40:6; Psalms 103:15.

willed it— She *has* painted your exertions to shame me. You
have penetration enough to see how this business operated on
my mind without my being at the expence of explanation.

I am

dear Dilke

Your very grateful Friend

George Keats.

⇢»» 144 «« ⇠

CHARLES G. WYLIE [1] TO JOHN TAYLOR

17 August 1828

Address: M͏ʳ Taylor/ N 30 Upper Gower Street/ Bedford Square. *Postmarks:* 8.MORN.8 AU.20 1828; T.P LombardSt. Morgan MS. Printed
by Blunden, p. 95.

Mʳ Taylor

Sir

I am Requested by Mʳˢ G. Keats to state that having been
refered to you by Mʳ Hessey, begs the favour of your giving her
an order on Mʳ Tallant of Cincinnatti to give up the Bill **or**
Bills now in his possession drawn by Messʳˢ Taylor & Hessey
upon Mʳ George Keats of Louisville (Kentucky), the amount
having been paid by Mʳ Abbey— Mʳ Tallant refusing to give
them up without an order from you

I am Sir

for Mʳˢ Keats

Your Obᵗ Serᵗ

C G Wylie

14 Godliman Sᵗ

Doctors Commons

Augᵗ 17ᵗʰ [2] 1828

[1] See I, xcvi, and No. 104.
[2] 17 *originally* 18.

317

→»» 145 «««

GEORGE KEATS TO MRS. C. W. DILKE

19 March 1829 [1]

Address: Mrs Dilke/ No 9 Lower Grosvener Place/ Pimlico/ London.
Postmarks: 8.MORN.8 MR. 27 1830; T.P Newgate St.

Louisville March 19th 1829.

My dear Mrs Dilke

I recd your letter with great pleasure, which with your occasional notes to Mrs K, preserved by her for my inspection, have brought to my mind with vivid distinctness all old associations. You are still the same lively, chatty being, you were in 1818, pray remain so untill I can come and talk with you, and laugh with you, and dance with you. I beg likewise you will not endeavour to improve your Husband, I am satisfied with him as he was, even to the taking of snuff, I can see him now in the very act—and the sight, the so palpable sight is as gratifying to me, as the gentlemanly scent is grateful to him.

I am sorry he did not write by Mrs K. the circumstance of his being out of Town has proved to me a misfortune: I have not heard from him since I left England on any other subject than my pecuniary affairs. I will one day write to him a page of questions about books and authors, John's Fame &c &c and insist upon an answer on pain of a duplicate every month by the post untill I receive an answer. I have not any correspondent in England who understands me, or the things that interest me, Assured by his repeated kindnesses, I look to Mr Dilke as my

---

[1] This date is evidently correct, in spite of the fact that the letter was postmarked in London over a year later. Georgiana Keats's return from her trip to England (see No. 142, May 12, 1828) was still fresh in George's mind, and noticeably he does not mention his sixth child, Clarence, who was three months old in May, 1830.

anchor in my native sod, and so long as my cable of love of Country, and kindly feeling lasts, I shall cherish a hope that I shall one day haul my vessel to his hearth. I wrote to him a few lines by Briggs,[2] and promised more by the bearer of this, but I fear I shall hardly have time to dispatch my first letter to you and the Reynolds. Mr Hartford [3] passed thro' this place yesterday on his way to Cin[1] where he will remain two or three days only, and to which place I am to send this. Present to M^r D my warmest wishes for his welfare, and thanks for his many favours: I hope it will prove consistent with the plans of the ministry to keep him in his office untill he is tired of it. So little Charley (to whom present my kind remembrances) is Mr Wentworth Dilke, and resembles both you and his Father, what he *was* I distinctly remember, what he *is* I cannot imagine. M^{rs} K says that M^r W^m is very thin; convey to him my regards, and hopes that I shall shake hands with him before very very long, I have not forgotten his willingness to have penetrated to my western dwelling had he known where to find me.[4] M^{rs} K was much pleased with the Reynolds and Mr Hood—they behaved to her with great kindness, M^{rs} R and Marianne wrote very gratifying letters to me— I shall write to them by this opportunity. *It seems "odd,"* as you *English* say, that Jane should have captivated so facetious a genius as Hood, I have long enjoyed his admirable fooling, and shall be pleased to make his acquaintance. I always had a particular liking for Marianne, and greive that her health is so indifferent, I think her worthy of almost any man, and sincerely hope that her lover's fortunes may enable him to pluck her from her solitary virgin stalk and engraft her on an enduring stem of never failing *Green.*[5] M^{rs} R's letter denotes that she has still the

[2] See I, 281.

[3] Of Bristol (see I, 332).

[4] See I, 286.

[5] She married H. G. Green. See I, cxxv.

same enthusiasm as of old, it must be gratifying to her to witness the s{uc}cess of John, whose start in life was by no means so promising. M^rs K has received much benefit from her journey which may operate to hasten my visit to my native Isle. Georgiana is well and was improved in looks and manners [6] by her sojourn with M^rs K's sister, little John improves and gives me great hopes that he will be an honour to my name, he is much more spritely than the other children were and has decoyed me into the common parental vanity that I have been free from untill now. beleive me My dear Mrs Dilke

Yours very truly and sincerely.

Geo. Keats.

M^rs K desires to be kindly rem^d.

⇻⟫ 146 ⟪⇷

GEORGE KEATS TO C. W. DILKE

14 November 1829

Address: Chas Dilke Esqre/ Navy Pay Office/ Somerset House/ London/ England/ via New York. *Postmarks (one illegible):* LOUISE K^Y NOV. 17; *SHIP LETTER* LIVERPOOL; PAID. One sentence is quoted by Adami, pp. 135f.

Louisville Nov 14th 1829.

My dear Sir

　　Your letter by Mr Briggs [1] is now before me. The anger you have so long cherished towards me arises from a supposition that I have not taken any notice of a certain letter sent to me when Mrs K. was in England: for authorising an application to you for a settlement of accounts between us and the rough

---

[6] Dilke notes in his copy of Milnes (Morgan Library) that Mrs. George Keats visited his home, "& brought with her a daughter as wild as a red Indian."

[1] See I, 281.

manner in which Cha⁺ Wylie applied for it: and for abstracting
a certain sum for the a/c of R & R ² and charging you with it
when I supposed they might possibly be insolvent. In the first
place I never received the letter you speak of, your remittances
are the last communications I have received from you. Cha⁺
Wylie promised me thro' Mʳˢ K. that he would send me a statement of what was doing, and led Mʳˢ K to expect that the letter
was partly written and should be dispatch'd immediately, but I
never recᵈ it, nor have I heard positively that it was sent, I have
not to this moment seen his hand writing of a later date than
two years since, altho' he ought to have written on business
several times. In the second place: in five pages of instructions I
wrote for Mʳˢ K's guidance are contained these passages "Dilke's
a/c with me stands thus—he had in his name for my benefit
£333.9/6 *stock,* I drew on him for £225 *money,* he will have to
be credited with the postage of <several> many letters addressed to his care and other expences" and again in summing
up the various affairs she had to attend to, at the top of the list
is "Dilke's small a/c either in my favour or otherwise" On these
memorandum's Charles acted, Mʳˢ K. tells me roughly and in-
judiciously, they were founded on your letter of July 26. 1828—
it contains this passage "I have the very great pleasure of adding
that I was present yesterday when the balᶜᵉ admitted to be due
          £ s d
to you of 333.9.6 stock was transferred into my name and Rice's
and which I need not add we shall be happy most happy to
remit or pay agreeably to your order and direction.—Should
you draw on me it will be well not to draw for more than about
£225: as our funds are only 76, and may fall lower, but if you
direct us to remit, and tell us how, I will forward the exact sum
&c"— I drew for £225 (I think) and made up my mind that it
was nearly a balᶜᵉ, on this only was founded my directions to

² Rice and Reynolds.

Mrs K., not from any ac/ of R & R which I never saw untill the return of M^{rs} K to America, nor does that acc contain the sum mentioned; it contains a credit of *money* rec^d of Mr Llanos of
     s d
£289.6.3 and a debit of £220, being a bill drawn on Messrs Dilke
     £
& Rice (which I think ought to [be] 225 on Chas Dilke Esqre) All the statements I had formerly rec^d from R & R merely amounted to my original claims on the estate, no account current with themselves. Chas must have been very obtuse to make you my "debtor £100 and more" and you cannot have examined R & R's account or you could not have come to the conclusion that I had abstracted an amount for R & R account and charged it against you, when no such am^t is to be found in their acc. Not having rec^d any acc. from R & R I did not know that the sum you wrote about was to be embodied in their acc altho' I now see clearly that it is right it should be so. *I now state* that the passage quoted above from your letter, is the only ground I have of any accs between us, excepting the claim you have on me for expences. You enlarge on the impossibility of my being uninformed in every particular and evidently remain convinced of my carelessness mean[n]ess and I know not what. I can only repeat that thro' your persevering kindness and Rice's clear exposée I knew all that was due to me, but untill M^{rs} K arrived with R & R's acc current I was necessarily ignorant of the true situation of my affairs with you, Mr Llanos, and them. The only intimation of your disatisfaction was from M^{rs} K who at the conclusion of the letter in which she informed me of it said that you were satisfied that I was not to blame; when I rec^d R & R's acc I saw all clear enough and did not dream of the necessity of writing any explanation to you who must have been informed of the real state of the accs. If you are willing to beleive that I never rec^d your letter, or the one Charles Wylie did or did not send and find that R & R did not supply any acc current before

the one you were kind enough to procure from them for M^rs K you must necessarily acquit me of being the guilty cause of the mortification you have met with. In looking over your letters to find the passage mentioned above, I found so much evidence of your great kindness to me, that you had performed so much disagreeable labour on my acc, that you waded thro so many calculations and figures for my benefit, of a nature so disagreeable to your particular frame of mind, that I could not for an instant cherish any of those sp[l]enetic feelings your supposing me capable of abstracting an item from the acc of a supposed bankrupt and placing it to yours, was calculated to raise.—I now most earnestly beg that you will assure yourself of my endless gratitude for the services you have rend^d me, and more[o]ver my most particular partiallity for you independantly of any gratitude for benefits confered, which would alone have protected you from any wrong on my part, did not my good principles protect every man. "What fools these mortals are" [3] While I have been turning over in my mind the possibility of visiting England you being incorporated with every vision welcoming me and smiling me on, you have been harbouring suspicions of my worthiness, nay beleiving me guilty of fraud. I am most anxious to hear from you and entreat that you will at your earliest convenience bestow enough words upon me to inform me of your estimate of this explanation. M^rs K is full of regrets at what has happened, she remembers with so much satisfaction your and M^rs D kindness to her. She sends her kindest rem^s to both of you and hopes for an improvement in the health of Mrs D. M^rs K has been a good deal unwell the summer past and promises to encrease the family in three mos. My Sister talks of residing in Valladolid, I fear Mr Llanos speculation [4] has failed and doubt if the author of Estaban and Sandoval can expect a quiet life in the kingdom of the beloved Ferdinand if the bigot

[3] Compare I, 327n.
[4] See I, 330.

monarch is what he is described in those works. I should like to
see Fanny before she goes, and may possibly have that pleasure
since if I can spare the time my circumstances have so improved
in these two last years that the cost of the journey would not
prevent. I am however all in doubt.

Hoping this explanation will reinstate me in your and
your good Ladie's good opinion I subscribe myself

Your true and obliged Friend
Geo Keats.

Louisville Nov 14th 1829.

Having seen Messrs Rice & Reynolds acc. current it is evident to me that the account presented to Cha⁸ Dilke Esqre Navy
Pay Office by Mr Cha⁸ Wylie on my part and in my favour, is
founded in error and proceeded from my ignorance of the real
situation of my accounts: and I hereby declare that to the best
of my knowledge I have not any claim whatever on the said
Cha⁸ Dilke up to this 14 Nov. 1829

George Keats.   seal [5]

→⟫ 147 ⟪←

GEORGE KEATS TO C. W. DILKE

7 May 1830

Address: (Single letter)/ Cha⁸ Dilke Esqre/ Navy Pay Office/ Sommerset-
house/ London/ England/ via New York. *Postmarks:* LOUIS^E K^Y MAY
10; C 30 JU 30 1830; *SHIP LETTER* LIVERPOOL. Forman (*F*),
IV, 410-415, prints the long opening paragraph (ending "strike a light"),
and brief extracts are quoted by Lowell, I, 23, and Adami, p. 135.

Louisville May 7th 1830

My dear Sir

Your welcome and unwelcome letter of the 7 February
arrived this morning, 3 months on the way, we have in the

---

[5] The word is written and surrounded by an inked outline representing
a seal.

papers London dates of the 7th Apl. The assurance that my exposee of affairs between us is satisfactory, is most welcome, for I have looked upon you as my best friend one half of my life. The threatened life of poor John by Brown, involving the sacrifice of my good name is most unwelcome. The very nature of Brown's mind is such that however much he may intend to honor his memory, he will hurt him as much by false painting as he will me from obstinacy, and misinformation— He has no impulsive instantaneous love of goodness or beauty, his judgement says this is vice, and that is virtue, good taste directs abhorrence of the one and admiration of the other, the detecting and demonstrating the enormity and vileness of the one, gives him as much pleasure, as the acknowledging the excellence of the other. He is nothing if he is not critical. It would give him dissatisfaction to find me blameless, and I doubt if he would confess it, altho John admitted he had good points, he would not much relish his general opinion of him. If he gives up the plan of handling the reviewers roughly, sacrificing the opportunity of picturing a virtuous indignation, he will give up the idea of writing the life, he cannot reach a sufficiently lofty key without such an inspiring accessory. He is the antipodes of John, he is close, painstaking and calculating, John was open, prodigal, and had no power of calculation whatever. John's eyes moistened, and his lip quivered at the relation of any tale of generosity of benevolence or noble daring, or at sights of loveliness or distress—he had no fears of self thro interference in the quarrels of others, he would at all hazzards, without calculating his power to defend, or his reward for the deed, defend the oppressed and distressed with heart and soul with hand and purse. You will remember the tale of his fight with a scoundrel in Livery in a blind Alley at hampstead about cruelty to a cat [1]—

[1] "I suppose this is the butcher of Hunt's and Clarke's recollection" (*F*). See II, 152.

How much of this is like Brown, did not Brown rather laugh at these qualities, and chuckle at the foolery of their exhibition, than love and respect the possessor of them for their sake. He doubtless duly appreciates John's kindness of heart, his generosity of character and general disinterestedness, but it is his genius and notoriety that mainly attract[2] him, <but> the situations in which the possessor of these noble qualities in their widest sense will be placed, would lead such as Brown into the notion that they were extravagantly indulged in without judgement and prudent caution. Brown has unquestionably good qualities, for God made him and he has kept some good company, and I feel grateful to him for his attentions to John whatever were his *motives, which* never would have been questioned by me if I had not read Hunt's mistakes. I cannot swear that John paid half the expences of housekeeping with Brown throughout, but I can that it was understood between them that he should, and that a certain sum was due when I was in England, and that John had the money to pay it,[3] and that I beleive he did pay up to the time of my departure in 1820, and afterwards I directed Mr Abbey to pay a demand of Brown's against John of £70 or £80 which I beleive was likewise paid, and John having been six months in Rome before his death only leaves about 4 mos of his existence in which he to my knowledge could have lived upon the bounty of either Brown or Leigh Hunt "without any such thing as obligation" He having died in December 1820.[4] Hunt entirely mistook his character altho' there are passages in his notice of him that are characteristic and worth preserving, he would accept hospitallity with pleasure but he was not so <fall> faultless in the particular that

[2] *F* attracts.
[3] See *F*'s note to the preceding letter.
[4] George took this date (December 27) from Hunt's *Lord Byron and Some of His Contemporaries* (1828), p. 268. Keats sailed from Portsmouth on September 29.

Hunt insists on as not to be most impatient under obligations of the sort he mentions. Brown knows this, and if Hunt has not told exactly the truth in saying—"Mr Keats and I were friends of the old stamp, between whom there was no such thing as obligation, except the pleasure of it. He enjoyed the usual priviledge of greatness with all whom he knew, rendering it delightful to be obliged by him and an equal, but not a greater delight, to oblige." It was a pleasure to his Friends to have him in their houses, and he did not grudge it. When Endymion was published he was living at hampstead with his Friend Cha^ Brown &c" [5]— Brown ought to contradict it.—So that Mr Cha^ Brown and Mr L. Hunt were the munificent patrons of Jno Keats. Altho he was often at Hunt's after Brown went from home in 1820, I presume you know he did not live, reside there, and I firmly beleive that he did not live with Brown one week without a debtor and creditor account being kept of it— If he did, and it is to be bruited to the world, I know John's imperfections well enough to be sure that he would be most anxious to liquidate the debt. Endymion was published before my marriage, and not when John was living with Brown.—I would fain have all expences paid, for Brown's kindness and attention he can only be paid by the gratitude of [the] world, poor me included, and the satisfaction with which virtue rewards its votaries. What fools we mortals are,[6] how we are straining for ever so small a niche in the temple of Fame, I claim being the affectionat{e} Friend and Brother of John Keats I loved him from boyhood even when he wronged me, for the goodness of his heart and the nobleness of his spirit, before we left school we quarrelled often and fought feircely, and I can safely say and my school fellows will bear witness that John's

[5] Quoted a bit inexactly from Hunt, pp. 257f. The quotation marks after "oblige" should be omitted.
[6] *A Midsummer-Night's Dream*, III.ii.115. See I, 323n.

temper was the cause of all, still we were more attached than Brothers ever are— After we left school we never passed an opposing word, he was allways melancholy and complaining, devoted and affectionate, and I shall never beleive but that it was the want of my ear as a safety valve to let his sorrows escape, that he after *I left england* allowed so many things to prey upon his mind and his health, *therein* was my fault— When I returned in 1820 he was not the same being, altho' his reception of me was as warm as heart could wish, he did not speak with his former openness and unreserve, he had lost the reviving custom of venting his greifs. Brown however will kick me out of this niche, and step into it himself by representing John to have impaired his fortune by liberallity to an unfeeling Brother placing him in a situation to receive obligations from Cha' Brown. There is a passage [7] in Shelly's Adonais (preface) that is gall and wormwood to me, and seeing from Hunt's work that Brown and Shelly were acquainted I cannot but infer that he received from him the false impression, and fear that for the sake of consistency he will repeat the wrong. Where did John get the fortune that he lavished upon me. I certainly promised to remit and should have done so had he owed me £10.000, and was justified by my prospects in thinking I should be able, it turned out that I was not able, on the contrary I was more miserably distressed than John, being as pennyless or more so and having a wife and child to partake of my miseries. I could at the time have exhibited a picture of distress that would have

[7] In the Galignani *Poetical Works of Coleridge, Shelley, and Keats* (Paris, 1829), it runs (p. 159): "I am given to understand that the wound which his sensitive spirit had received from the criticism of Endymion, was exasperated by the bitter sense of unrequited benefits; the poor fellow seems to have been hooted from the stage of life, no less by those on whom he had wasted the promise of his genius, than those on whom he had lavished his fortune and his care." Someone must have copied the preface in England and sent it to George, for it was November or December (see the next letter) before he saw the Galignani volume.

brought tears and forgiveness from John, the reasons why I did
not are manifest, he had troubles enough and this would have
capped them all. M^rs K can bear witness, how much I suffered
from my inability to remit, taunted as I was by the goading
letters of Haslam and Brown. *Knowing* you are persuaded that
I did not willingly add one pang to the sorrows of poor John,
I hope that Rice & Reynolds are of the same opinion, and that
the three may influence Brown to blot out from his tablets if
not from his mind [8] the obnoxious passage relating to my unworthiness I do not see how a life of John can be written without noticing the effect that severe reviews and abominable
personal reflections had upon his sensitive mind, it ought to be
done temperately not for the purpose of cutting at those
worthies and exciting their spleen, but as circumstances that
surrounded and operated upon the mind and body of the Poet—
I am perfectly willing to put you in possession of my recollections of John's early life, of his inward mind and his letters to
me which are very long and numerous, and think with you, that
Reynolds and not Brown is the man to write it. If {it} were not
for the claims my family have upon my time and industry I
would come to England as it {is} I cannot without making great
sacrifices, pray let me hear from you soon, and through some
more speedy channel which can be discovered by enquiring of
some american merchant in what way to send letters—in the
mean time I will commit to paper <what> my recollections, and
take the first safe opportunity to send them, and the letters, to
do with them as to you may seem good. I do not however see
that if the publication you mention progresses with the ordinary
speed of modern times, that there is any probability of my fur-
nishing any matter in time, even if either yourself or Reynolds
were to undertake the life. It seems to me *now*, that I have a
great deal to communicate altho' it is more than likely, that

[8] Compare *Hamlet*, I.v.98.

when I sit down, to put it on paper, I shall be as a Flint, that requires a Steel, yourself or Reynolds, to come in contact with me to strike a light—

When I heard from my Sister that Mʳ Llanos was going to Spain, it appeared to me probable, that all the visions of wealth that was to result from the bridle bit patent,⁹ had flown, what you say only confirms my suspicions. You say my small interest in the Walthamstow property shall be attended to, for which I thank [you], I however desire that my Sister may first get from it *all* her demands upon it, and if when she has been fully paid there is any left, I shall be well pleased to receive it, I have written as much to Reynolds & Simmons. My circumstances are now such, that I have no fears about being able to support m{y} family, and educate my children respectably, and if I live 5 {years} longer of placing my means in such a situation as to insure {com}petence, and comfort to my family in case of my death. I have {en}joyed better health for the two last years, than the three preceeding, and may say I am well and hearty, but not robust English well and hearty— Mʳˢ Keats is pretty well as are the five children, to wit, your friend Georgiana, Emma, Isabel,¹⁰ John, and Clarence, the last 3 mos old. I feel most anxious to see you all again, but have no hopes of being able to spare time for 5 years having entered into a partnership in an extensive timber concern ¹¹ for that period commencing Janʸ 1ˢᵗ 1830.—Do you never feel anxious to visit the rising west, if your mind runs in the same channel it used to do I should

---

⁹ See I, 323, II, 5, 9f.; Adami, p. 134; Bennet Woodcroft's *Alphabetical Index of Patentees of Inventions, From March 2, 1617 . . . to October 1, 1852* (1854), p. 342. Among "Patents Lately Granted" the *New Monthly Magazine*, February, 1829 (XXVII, 74), includes, "V. Llanos, of Hampstead, for an improvement or improvements on bits. Communicated by a foreigner. December 15, 1828."

¹⁰ Changed from "Rosa[lind]." See I, xcvii f.

¹¹ Smith and Keats.

have some hopes of seeing you on this side of the Atlantic, and promise if you do come to devote a month to you to travel where you please. In Louisville I can make you comfortable, if a hearty welcome and good quarters can produce that effect. Perhaps a long voyage might benefit Mrs Dilke   we should be most happy to see the trio Father, Mother and son— You might calculate on a month at sea both ways altho all the last passages were short from 14 to 20 days: 7 days from New York to Louisville and all other travelling at the same rate, and not expensive, from New York to Louisville about 50 dollars each person. Give my best wishes to Mrs Dilke and Charles and respects to all Friends and beleive me very truly your Friend

Geo Keats.

→» 148 «←

GEORGE KEATS TO C. W. DILKE

22 November 1830

Forman (*F*), IV, 415, quotes the opening sentences from "I would" to "Keats poems."

Louisville Nov. 22nd 1830.

My dear Dilke

I would not allow M^r [1] Cuthbertson to leave this for London without conveying to you my best wishes and kindest regards, I have not time to dwell upon any subject whatever, and am [2] sorry to confess that I have left undone the sketch of my Brother's life that I fully intended to send to you—my poor excuse is that soon after I wrote, I understood that the publication that was to contain a Life was already in the press and that therefore I must necessarily be too late— I now hear that

1 *F* Mrs.
2 *F* I am.

the work is for sale in the eastern Cities and have sent for a copy: the volume advertised contains "Shelly, Colridge and Keats poems." [3] I am sorry I cannot come and see you, I am now so linked in Business that requires my constant attention that I cannot hope to be able to come for four or five years. It will be gratifying to you to hear that my success is equal to my most sanguine expectations, I am looked upon as a rising man which in this country is half the battle, all are willing to help such a man. I look forward to the time when I can visit England without having cause to fear the amount of my expences or the loss of my time, and more especially I look to the great pleasure I shall have in once more shaking you by the hand and sitting by your fireside with yourself, and merry Mrs D.—Remember me most kindly to her and the Reynolds tell them that the letters sent by them per M^rs K are carefully laid by and occasionally reperused, and that another parcel by the return of Mr Cuthbertson will be received with honour and read with delight— I answered them all by a Mr Hartford of Bristol, but have not received any intimation of the safe arrival of my letters. In haste

Your Friend and well wisher
Geo. Keats.

[3] *The Poetical Works of Coleridge, Shelley, and Keats. Complete in One Volume*, A. and W. Galignani, Paris, 1829. George thought it contained Brown's life of Keats. See I, 325.